JACQUES LACAN BETWEEN PSYCHOANALYSIS AND POLITICS

A charismatic and controversial figure, Lacan is one of the most important thinkers of the 20th century and his work has revolutionized a range of fields. The volume aims to introduce Lacan's vast opus to the field of international politics in a coherent and approachable manner.

The volume is split into three distinct sections:

- **Political significance of psychoanalysis**: this section will frame the discussion by providing general background of Lacan's engagement with politics and the political.
- **Lacanian psychoanalysis and the political**: each chapter will focus on different key ideas and concepts in Lacan's thought including ethics, justice, discourse, object *a*, symptom, *jouissance*.
- **Psychoanalysis and political encounters**: seeks to represent different ways of engaging with Lacanian thought and ways of adopting it to explain and comment on global political phenomena.

Bringing together internationally recognized scholars in the field, this volume will be an invaluable resource to students and scholars in areas including critical theory, international relations, political theory and political philosophy.

Samo Tomšič works as researcher in the interdisciplinary laboratory 'Image Knowledge Gestaltung' at the Humboldt University in Berlin, Germany.

Andreja Zevnik is a Lecturer in International Politics at the University of Manchester, UK.

INTERVENTIONS

Edited by:
Jenny Edkins, Aberystwyth University and Nick Vaughan-Williams, University of Warwick

The series provides a forum for innovative and interdisciplinary work that engages with alternative critical, post-structural, feminist, postcolonial, psychoanalytic and cultural approaches to international relations and global politics. In our first 5 years we have published 60 volumes.

We aim to advance understanding of the key areas in which scholars working within broad critical post-structural traditions have chosen to make their interventions, and to present innovative analyses of important topics. Titles in the series engage with critical thinkers in philosophy, sociology, politics and other disciplines and provide situated historical, empirical and textual studies in international politics.

We are very happy to discuss your ideas at any stage of the project: just contact us for advice or proposal guidelines. Proposals should be submitted directly to the Series Editors:

Jenny Edkins (jennyedkins@hotmail.com) and
Nick Vaughan-Williams (N.Vaughan-Williams@Warwick.ac.uk)

> As Michel Foucault has famously stated, 'knowledge is not made for understanding; it is made for cutting'. In this spirit the Edkins–Vaughan-Williams Interventions series solicits cutting edge, critical works that challenge mainstream understandings in international relations. It is the best place to contribute post-disciplinary works that think rather than merely recognize and affirm the world recycled in IR's traditional geopolitical imaginary.

> Michael J. Shapiro, University of Hawai'i at Mānoa, USA

The series aims to advance understanding of the key areas in which scholars working within broad critical post-structural and post-colonial traditions have chosen to make their interventions, and to present innovative analyses of important topics.

Titles in the series engage with critical thinkers in philosophy, sociology, politics and other disciplines, and provide situated historical, empirical and textual studies in international politics.

Critical Theorists and International Relations
Edited by Jenny Edkins and Nick Vaughan-Williams

Ethics as Foreign Policy
Britain, the EU and the other
Dan Bulley

Universality, Ethics and International Relations
A grammatical reading
Véronique Pin-Fat

The Time of the City
Politics, philosophy, and genre
Michael J. Shapiro

Governing Sustainable Development
Partnership, protest and power at the world summit
Carl Death

Insuring Security
Biopolitics, security and risk
Luis Lobo-Guerrero

Foucault and International Relations
New critical engagements
Edited by Nicholas J. Kiersey and Doug Stokes

International Relations and Non-Western Thought
Imperialism, colonialism and investigations of global modernity
Edited by Robbie Shilliam

Autobiographical International Relations
I, IR
Edited by Naeem Inayatullah

War and Rape
Law, memory and justice
Nicola Henry

Madness in International Relations
Psychology, security and the global governance of mental health
Alison Howell

Spatiality, Sovereignty and Carl Schmitt
Geographies of the nomos
Edited by Stephen Legg

Politics of Urbanism
Seeing like a city
Warren Magnusson

Beyond Biopolitics
Theory, violence and horror in world politics
François Debrix and Alexander D. Barder

The Politics of Speed
Capitalism, the state and war in an accelerating world
Simon Glezos

Politics and the Art of Commemoration
Memorials to struggle in Latin America and Spain
Katherine Hite

Indian Foreign Policy
The politics of postcolonial identity
Priya Chacko

Politics of the Event
Time, movement, becoming
Tom Lundborg

Theorising Post-Conflict Reconciliation
Agonism, restitution and repair
Edited by Alexander Keller Hirsch

Europe's Encounter with Islam
The secular and the postsecular
Luca Mavelli

**Re-thinking International
Relations Theory
via Deconstruction**
Badredine Arfi

The New Violent Cartography
Geo-analysis after the aesthetic turn
*Edited by Sam Okoth Opondo and
Michael J. Shapiro*

Insuring War
Sovereignty, security and risk
Luis Lobo-Guerrero

**International Relations, Meaning
and Mimesis**
Necati Polat

The Postcolonial Subject
Claiming politics/governing others in
late modernity
Vivienne Jabri

**Foucault and the Politics
of Hearing**
Lauri Siisiäinen

**Volunteer Tourism in the
Global South**
Giving back in neoliberal times
Wanda Vrasti

**Cosmopolitan Government
in Europe**
Citizens and entrepreneurs in
postnational politics
Owen Parker

**Studies in the Trans-disciplinary
Method**
After the aesthetic turn
Michael J. Shapiro

**Alternative Accountabilities in
Global Politics**
The scars of violence
Brent J. Steele

Celebrity Humanitarianism
The ideology of global charity
Ilan Kapoor

**Deconstructing International
Politics**
Michael Dillon

The Politics of Exile
Elizabeth Dauphinee

Democratic Futures
Revisioning democracy promotion
Milja Kurki

Postcolonial Theory
A critical introduction
Edited by Sanjay Seth

More than Just War
Narratives of the just war and
military life
Charles A. Jones

Deleuze & Fascism
Security: war: aesthetics
Edited by Brad Evans and Julian Reid

Feminist International Relations
'Exquisite corpse'
Marysia Zalewski

The Persistence of Nationalism
From imagined communities to
urban encounters
Angharad Closs Stephens

**Interpretive Approaches to Global
Climate Governance**
Reconstructing the greenhouse
*Edited by Chris Methmann, Delf Rothe
and Benjamin Stephan*

**Postcolonial Encounters in
International Relations**
The politics of transgression in
the Maghreb
Alina Sajed

**Post-tsunami Reconstruction
in Indonesia**
Negotiating normativity through
gender mainstreaming initiatives
in Aceh
Marjaana Jauhola

Leo Strauss and the Invasion of Iraq
Encountering the abyss
Aggie Hirst

**Production of Postcolonial India
and Pakistan**
Meanings of partition
Ted Svensson

War, Identity and the Liberal State
Everyday experiences of the
geopolitical in the armed forces
Victoria M. Basham

Writing Global Trade Governance
Discourse and the WTO
Michael Strange

Politics of Violence
Militancy, international politics, killing
in the name
Charlotte Heath-Kelly

Ontology and World Politics
Void universalism I
Sergei Prozorov

Theory of the Political Subject
Void universalism II
Sergei Prozorov

Visual Politics and North Korea
Seeing is believing
David Shim

**Globalization, Difference and
Human Security**
Edited by Mustapha Kamal Pasha

**International Politics
and Performance**
Critical aesthetics and creative practice
Edited by Jenny Edkins and Adrian Kear

**Memory and Trauma in
International Relations**
Theories, cases, and debates
*Edited by Erica Resende and
Dovile Budryte*

Critical Environmental Politics
Edited by Carl Death

Democracy Promotion
A critical introduction
Jeff Bridoux and Milja Kurki

**International Intervention in a
Secular Age**
Re-enchanting humanity?
Audra Mitchell

**The Politics of Haunting and
Memory in International Relations**
Jessica Auchter

**European-East Asian Borders
in Translation**
*Edited by Joyce C.H. Liu and
Nick Vaughan-Williams*

**Genre and the
(Post)Communist Woman**
Analyzing transformations of the
Central and Eastern European
female ideal
*Edited by Florentina C. Andreescu and
Michael Shapiro*

**Studying the Agency of
Being Governed**
*Edited by Stina Hansson, Sofie Hellberg
and Maria Stern*

Politics of Emotion
The song of Telangana
Himadeep Muppidi

Ruling the Margins
Colonial power and administrative rule
in the past and present
Prem Kumar Rajaram

**Race and Racism in
International Relations**
Confronting the global colour line
*Alexander Anievas, Nivi Manchanda and
Robbie Shilliam*

**The Grammar of Politics
and Performance**
Edited by Shirin M. Rai and Janelle Reinelt

**War, Police and Assemblages
of Intervention**
*Edited by Jan Bachman, Colleen Bell and
Caroline Holmqvist*

**Re-imagining North Korea in
International Politics**
Problems and alternatives
Shine Choi

On Schmitt and Space
Claudio Minca and Rory Rowan

Face Politics
Jenny Edkins

Empire Within
International hierarchy and its
imperial laboratories of governance
Alexander D. Barder

**Sexual Politics and
International Relations**
How LGBTQ claims shape
International Relations
*Edited by Manuela Lavinas Picq and
Markus Thiel*

Emotions, Politics and War
Edited by Linda Åhäll and Thomas Gregory

**Jacques Lacan between
psychoanalysis and politics**
Edited by Samo Tomšič and Andreja Zevnik

The Value of Resilience
Securing life in the 21st century
Chris Zebrowski

Political Aesthetics
Culture, critique and the everyday
Arundhati Virmani

Walzer, Just War and Iraq
Ethics as response
Ronan O'Callaghan

Politics and Suicide
The philosophy of political
self-destruction
Nicholas Michelsen

JACQUES LACAN BETWEEN PSYCHOANALYSIS AND POLITICS

Edited by Samo Tomšič and Andreja Zevnik

LONDON AND NEW YORK

First published 2016
by Routledge
2 Park Square, Milton Park, Abingdon, Oxon OX14 4RN

and by Routledge
711 Third Avenue, New York, NY 10017

Routledge is an imprint of the Taylor & Francis Group, an informa business

© 2016 selection and editorial material, Samo Tomšič and Andreja Zevnik; individual chapters, the contributors

The right of Samo Tomšič and Andreja Zevnik to be identified as authors of the editorial material, and of the individual authors as authors of their contributions, has been asserted by them in accordance with sections 77 and 78 of the Copyright, Designs and Patents Act 1988.

All rights reserved. No part of this book may be reprinted or reproduced or utilised in any form or by any electronic, mechanical, or other means, now known or hereafter invented, including photocopying and recording, or in any information storage or retrieval system, without permission in writing from the publishers.

Trademark notice: Product or corporate names may be trademarks or registered trademarks, and are used only for identification and explanation without intent to infringe.

British Library Cataloguing in Publication Data
A catalogue record for this book is available from the British Library

Library of Congress Cataloging in Publication Data
Jacques Lacan : between psychoanalysis and politics / edited by Samo Tomšič and Andreja Zevnik.
        pages cm
    1. Lacan, Jacques, 1901-1981–Political and social views. 2. Political science. 3. International relations I. Tomšič, Samo.
        JC261.L32J33 2015
        320–dc23

                        2015003521

ISBN: 978-0-415-72432-6 (hbk)
ISBN: 978-0-415-72433-3 (pbk)
ISBN: 978-1-315-85728-2 (ebk)

Typeset in Bembo
by Taylor & Francis Books

CONTENTS

List of figures	*xiv*
List of contributors	*xv*
Acknowledgements	*xx*

Introduction: Jacques Lacan between psychoanalysis and politics *Samo Tomšič and Andreja Zevnik*	1

PART 1
Political significance of psychoanalysis   **13**

1	Lacan's 'année érotique' (1968/1969) *Jean-Michel Rabaté*	15
2	Politics and psychoanalysis in the times of the inexistent Other *Jelica Šumič*	28

PART 2
Lacanian psychoanalysis and the political   **43**

2.1
Oedipus and the intricacy of language and sexuality **45**

3	'Freud's dream'?: Lacan and Oedipus *Philippe Van Haute and Tomas Geyskens*	47
4	Not even: The politics of Oedipus *Mladen Dolar*	62

xii Contents

5 Lacan's Imaginary: A practical guide 72
Juliet Flower MacCannell

6 Sexual is political? 86
Alenka Zupančič

7 Object *a* and politics 101
Dominiek Hoens

2.2
Politics and Lacan's theory of discourses 113

8 On the mastery in the four 'discourses' 115
Peter Klepec

9 Discourse and the Master's lining: A Lacanian critique of the
globalizing (bio)politics of the *Diagnostic and Statistical Manual* 131
Colin Wright

10 Psychoanalysis, capitalism, and critique of political economy:
Toward a Marxist Lacan 146
Samo Tomšič

11 Why should dreaming be a form of work?: On work, economy,
and enjoyment 164
Mai Wegener

PART 3
Psychoanalysis and political encounters 181

12 A stranger politics: Toward a theory of resistance in
psychoanalytic thought and practice 183
Juliet Brough Rogers

13 The truth of desire: Lack, law, and phallus 202
Ari Hirvonen

14 Kant *avec* Sade: Ethics entrapped in perversions of law
and politics 217
Andreja Zevnik

15 Political encounters: Feminism and Lacanian psychoanalysis 233
Kirsten Campbell

16 Divine ex-sistence: Theology between politics
and psychoanalysis 253
Slavoj Žižek

17 Metapsychology on the battlefield: Political praxis as critique of
the psychological essence of ideology   268
David Pavón-Cuéllar

18 Lacan avec Bataille avec Nietzsche: A politics of the impossible? 281
Panu Minkkinen

Index of names   *299*
Index of notions   *302*

LIST OF FIGURES

5.1	Identification	78
8.1	The four discourses	122
9.1	The Discourse of the Capitalist	143
10.1	The Master's Discourse	157
10.2	The University Discourse	158
10.3	The 'Fifth Discourse'	159
18.1	Léthier I	291
18.2	Léthier II	292

CONTRIBUTORS

Kirsten Campbell is a Reader in Sociology at Goldsmiths, University of London. She teaches and researches in the field of contemporary social theory with a particular focus on law and gender, international criminal law, and feminist methodologies. She is currently the principal investigator of the European Research Council-funded project, The Gender of Justice, previously she was a Director of the Research Unit in The Study for Global Justice at Goldsmiths. She published widely on international justice, gender, trauma, memory, and war including two monographs entitled *Jacques Lacan and Feminist Epistemology* (Routledge 2004) and *Lacan and Law* (Routledge forthcoming).

Mladen Dolar is Professor at the Department of Philosophy, Faculty of Arts, University of Ljubljana. His area of research stretches from German idealism to psychoanalysis and critical theory. He is the author of numerous papers and contributions to collective volumes. His publications include most notably *A Voice and Nothing More* (MIT Press 2006) and *Opera's Second Death* (with Slavoj Žižek, Routledge 2001).

Juliet Flower MacCannell is Professor Emerita of Comparative Literature and English at UC Irvine. She is currently co-chair of the California Psychoanalytic Circle, and co-editor of *The Journal of Culture and the Unconscious*. She is an Honorary Fellow of the Institute for Advanced Study, University of London. She is author of several books on psychoanalysis and philosophy in a social and political frame, including *Figuring Lacan: Criticism & the Cultural Unconscious* (Routledge 1986; reissued 2014), *The Regime of the Brother: After the Patriarchy* (Routledge 1991), *The Hysteric's Guide to the Future Female Subject* (University of Minnesota Press 2000), and over 90 articles. Her work has been translated into Spanish, German, Slovenian, and French. She is also an artist.

xvi List of contributors

Tomas Geyskens is a Doctor in Philosophy and a practising psychoanalyst (Belgian School for Psychoanalysis). He works in Zonnelied (Roosdaal, Belgium) with adults with an intellectual disability and severe emotional/behavioural disorders.

Philippe Van Haute is a Professor of Philosophical Anthropology at Radboud University (Nijmegen, The Netherlands). He is also a member of the Belgian School for Psychoanalysis. Recent books in English: *Against Adaptation* (Other Press 2002), *Confusion of Tongues: The Primacy of Sexuality in Freud, Ferenczi and Laplanche* (with T. Geyskens, Other Press 2004), *From Death Drive to Attachment Theory: The Primacy of the Child in Freud, Klein and Herman* (with T. Geyskens, Other Press 2007), *Towards an Non-Oedipal Psychoanalysis? Clinical Anthropology of Hysteria in Freud and Lacan* (with T. Geyskens, Louvain University Press 2012).

Ari Hirvonen is Adjunct Professor in Legal Philosophy at the Faculty of Law, University of Helsinki, Finland. He is the Vice-Dean of the faculty responsible for research and research training. He is a founding member of Helsinki Lacan Circle. He has written extensively on critical political and legal thinking, psychoanalysis, the concept of justice and tragedy. He was the director of the research project Law and Evil and the co-editor of *Law and Evil: Philosophy, Politics, Psychoanalysis* (Routledge 2010).

Dominiek Hoens teaches Philosophy of Art at RITCS (Brussels) and at Artevelde University College (Ghent). He has published on the intersections between philosophy, psychoanalysis, politics, and contemporary art. He is co-editor in chief of *Journal for Lacanian Ideology Critique*. Previously he was Advising Researcher at the Jan van Eyck Academie (Maastricht). Under the heading 'Capital Owes You Nothing' his most recent research interests include 17th-century theology, in particular the issue of human and divine will in Pascal and Fénelon.

Peter Klepec works as a Research Adviser at the Institute of Philosophy, Scientific Research Centre of Slovenian Academy of Sciences and Arts (Ljubljana, Slovenia). His main areas of research are contemporary French philosophy, German Idealism and Lacanian psychoanalysis.

Panu Minkkinen is Professor of Jurisprudence at the University of Helsinki, Finland. His numerous publications cover themes ranging from the critique of the neo-Kantian remnants of legal thinking to the legal dimensions of contemporary critical theory. He is co-founding member of the Cercle-Lacan Helsinki, an informal research collective that has been active for nearly 20 years.

David Pavón-Cuéllar holds a Ph.D. in Philosophy from the University of Rouen (France) and a Ph.D. in Psychology from the University of Santiago de Compostela (Spain). He is Professor of Social Psychology, Psychoanalysis and Marxism in the Faculties of Psychology and Philosophy at the State University of Michoacán

(Universidad Michoacana de San Nicolás de Hidalgo, Morelia, Mexico). He has taught psychoanalysis at the University of Paris VIII (France). His books include *Elementos políticos de marxismo lacaniano* (Paradiso 2014) and *From the Conscious Interior to an Exterior Unconscious: Lacan, Discourse Analysis and Social Psychology* (Karnac 2010). He co-edited, with Ian Parker, *Lacan, Discourse, Event: New Psychoanalytic Approaches to Textual Indeterminacy* (Routledge 2013). He belongs to the editorial boards of *Annual Review of Critical Psychology*, *Psychotherapy and Politics International*, *Teoría y Crítica de la Psicología*, and *Revista Marxismos: Educación, Política y Sociedad*.

Jean-Michel Rabaté, Professor of English and Comparative Literature at the University of Pennsylvania since 1992, is a curator of Slought Foundation, an editor of the *Journal of Modern Literature*, and a Fellow of the American Academy of Arts and Sciences. He has authored or edited more than 30 books and collections on modernism, psychoanalysis, and philosophy. His books include *Crimes of the Future* (Bloomsbury 2014), *The Cambridge Introduction to Literature and Psychoanalysis* (Cambridge University Press2014), *The Pathos of Distance* (Bloomsbury 2015) and the edited collection *1922: Literature, Culture,Politics* (Cambridge University Press 2015).

Juliet Brough Rogers is a Senior Lecturer in Criminology in the School of Political Sciences at the University of Melbourne, and Adjunct Professor at Griffith Law School, Queensland. She is currently an Australian Research Council DECRA Fellow undertaking an examination of the 'Quality of Remorse' after periods of political and military conflict and a Visiting Fellow at the University of Bologna, Italy. She is a member of the editorial boards of *Law, Text, Culture*, and *The Australian Feminist Law Journal*. She has published on questions of law, psychoanalysis, torture, remorse, and gender. Her recent publications include: *Flesh, Freedom and Human Rights: Female Circumcision, Torture and Sacred Flesh* (Routledge 2014).

Jelica Šumič is a researcher at the Institute of Philosophy, Scientific Research Centre of the Slovenian Academy of Science and Arts, and she also teaches at the Graduate School ZRC SAZU. She has written extensively on the relations between philosophy, psychoanalysis, and politics. She has published a number of philosophical works, including *Politik der Wahrheit* (with Alain Badiou, Jacques Rancière, and Rado Riha; Turia + Kant 1997), *Universel, singulier, sujet* (Editions Kimé 2000), *Mutations of Ethics* (Zalozba ZRC 2002) and *Eternity and Change: Philosophy in the Wordless Times* (Zalozba ZRC 2012).

Samo Tomšič works as a researcher in the interdisciplinary laboratory 'Image Knowledge Gestaltung' at the Humboldt University in Berlin (Germany). His research areas comprise psychoanalysis, structuralism, epistemology, and contemporary French philosophy. His forthcoming book is *The Capitalist Unconscious: Marx and Lacan* (Verso 2015).

xviii List of contributors

Mai Wegener (Ph.D.) lives and works as a psychoanalyst in Berlin and is co-organizer of the Psychoanalytic Salon Berlin which opened in 1998 (www.pasberlin.de). She is also an active scholar of Cultural Studies and the History of Science and lectures in Literature at the Technical University of Berlin. She has worked at the Max Planck Institute for the History of Science in Berlin (2009/10), as Guest Professor in Cologne at the Academy of Media Arts (2008), and for the Centre for Literature and Cultural Research, Berlin (2001–2005). In 2001 she obtained her Ph.D. under the supervision of Friedrich A. Kittler with the thesis *Neuronen und Neurosen. Der psychische Apparat bei Freud und Lacan. Ein historisch-theoretischer Versuch zu Freuds Entwurf von 1895*, which was published in 2004. Her recent English publication is: 'The Humming of Machines. To the End of History and Back' in *Media after Kittler*, ed. Eleni Ikoniadou and Scott Wilson (Rowman & Littlefield International 2015).

Colin Wright is Deputy-Director of the Centre for Critical Theory and Director of the MA in Critical Theory & Cultural Studies in the Department of Culture, Film and Media at the University of Nottingham, UK. His research interests are in continental philosophy generally and French critical theory particularly, with a focus on Lacanian psychoanalysis and political theory. He has published in international journals such as *Theory & Event, Subjectivity*, and *Culture, Theory and Critique*. His most recent monograph was *Badiou in Jamaica: The Politics of Conflict* (Re.Press 2013). He is also a practising Lacanian psychoanalyst, training at the Centre for Freudian Analysis and Research in London.

Andreja Zevnik is a Lecturer in International Politics at the University of Manchester. Her research interests include theories of subjectivity, political violence and resistance, aesthetic politics, law, and psychoanalysis. She is a convener of the Critical Global Politics research cluster and a member of the editorial board for the *Journal of Narrative Politics*. Her forthcoming book is entitled *Politics beyond Oedipus* (2016).

Slavoj Žižek is a Slovenian philosopher and cultural critic. He is a Professor at the European Graduate School, International Director of the Birkbeck Institute for the Humanities (Birkbeck College, University of London), and a Senior Researcher at the University of Ljubljana (Slovenia). He authored numerous books, including most recently *Absolute Recoil: Toward a New Foundation of Dialectical Materialism* (Verso 2014), *Event: A Philosophical Journey Through A Concept* (Melville House Publishing 2014), and *Trouble in Paradise: From the End of History to the End of Capitalism* (Allen Lane 2014).

Alenka Zupančič is a Research Adviser at the Institute of Philosophy of the Slovenian Academy of Science and Arts and Professor at the European Graduate School, Switzerland. She is the author of numerous articles and books on psychoanalysis and philosophy, including *The Odd One In: On Comedy* (MIT Press 2008),

Why Psychoanalysis: Three Interventions (Aarhus University Press 2008), *The Shortest Shadow: Nietzsche's Philosophy of the Two* (MIT Press 2003), and *Ethics of the Real: Kant and Lacan* (Verso 2000).

ACKNOWLEDGEMENTS

Too many scholars and students of politics and international politics attuned to critical theory and modern continental philosophy too often dismiss the French psychoanalyst and (anti-) philosopher Jacques Lacan as inaccessible or irrelevant to the study of the socio-political space.

Moreover, as with most philosophers, disputes over 'the right' interpretation of the original works dominate the Lacanian field. After a particular panel at the International Studies Association Conference of 2012 in San Diego, where the discussion somewhat obsessively revolved around providing an answer as to what 'Lacan actually meant', we were encouraged by Jenny Edkins to compile a volume on the thought of Jacques Lacan and the potentiality his theory holds for the study of politics (and international politics). This idea was well received and we soon put together a fantastic group of Lacanian scholars from different disciplines to reflect on Lacan's key concepts and their political capital. We have been privileged to work with this group of contributing authors who have all generously given their time to produce these chapters; their patience and enthusiasm through-out the production of this book is greatly appreciated. For the invaluable help and support we would also like to thank Interventions series editors Jenny Edkins and Nick Vaughan-Williams, and from the Publishers, Routledge, Nicola Parkin, Peter Harris and Lydia de Cruz.

Numerous individuals and academic environments have influenced this volume. We would like to thank our respective institutions, the Politics Discipline Area at the The University of Manchester and the interdisciplinary laboratory 'Image Knowledge Gestaltung' at Humboldt University in Berlin for their support and intellectual inspiration. In particular we are grateful to: Andrea Mura, Boštjan Nedoh, Jude Ornstein, Diane Rubenstein, Andrew Russell, Michael J. Shapiro, Davide Tarrizo, and the collectives at the Society for Theoretical Psychoanalysis (Ljubljana, Slovenia) and the Institute of Philosophy at the Scientific Research

Centre of Slovenian Academy of Sciences and Arts for their assistance in the peer-review process, discussion of ideas, support and always invaluable critique. Their massages, to paraphrase Lacan, always arrived at their destination please *keep them coming*.

This volume is more than just an exploration of the relevance of psychoanalysis for the study of politics, it is also a political intervention into the current state of Lacanian studies. The book is offered with this in mind.

INTRODUCTION

Jacques Lacan between psychoanalysis and politics

Samo Tomšič and Andreja Zevnik

Born in Paris in April 1901, Jacques Lacan is perhaps one of the most notorious, provocative, and divisive thinkers of the 20th century. With his 'opaque' discourse, as many of his readers like to point out, either favourably or in contempt, and a rather bohemian and at times peculiar lifestyle, Lacan made many intellectual and personal enemies.[1] However, nowadays it comes without a doubt that his teaching, which crossed the fields of philosophy and science, made a crucial intervention into the understanding of modern life. Without Lacan, the 20th century continental philosophy would probably look significantly different, while the Freudian theory of the unconscious would most likely have witnessed a less celebrated fate. Yet one should refrain from drawing hasty conclusions when engaging with Lacan's theory. For once, we are not dealing with philosophy in a classical sense, which would strive to theorize a quasi-metaphysical position of the common good or provide univocal solutions for the ongoing political struggles. Despite the philosophical legacy, influences, references, and finally the diverse audience that attended his seminars, Lacan claimed that his theory was above all a clinic and thus a practice that should continue to be actualized 'on the couch'. In addition to this, he saw himself more as someone who stirs his teaching towards the critical tradition. As with most of his work, one cannot take Lacan's words without stumbling upon ambiguities and paradoxes, which challenge thinking by confronting it with a deadlock where one would perhaps not expect it.

A brief overview of Freud's work permits the conclusion that psychoanalysis revolves around the relations between social institutions, the unconscious, and the subject. Contrary to common belief, its field is not so much the psychic apparatus, separated from every social context, but a grey zone, where the opposition between the subjective and the social, the intimate and the public, or the singular and the universal turns out short, inoperative, and oversimplified. Also, such a positioning makes psychoanalysis inevitably more theoretical than one would

2 Samo Tomšič and Andreja Zevnik

imagine and situates its relevance beyond therapeutic aims. Out of Freudian invention Lacanian psychoanalysis creates a particular form of thought, which for its rejection of instant solutions presents itself as a reinvention of the critical philosophical tradition. In this respect it is no coincidence that authors such as Hegel, Kant, or Marx accompany the various stages of Lacan's teaching. Lacan's psychoanalysis begins to voice critique of the social from the intersection of such a philosophical and clinical position. It exposes ways in which formal mechanisms supporting social reality are inscribed into the subject of the unconscious.

This volume interrogates the critical angle of Lacan's theoretical development and does so with reference to politics and political issues as they are picked up by Lacan himself. In this Introduction we first provide some necessary context of Lacan's engagement with political questions, outline the coordinates and the most immediate political implications of his teaching, before proposing a few guidelines as to how this volume should be read and introduce its key sections.

Lacan, politics and the 'return to Freud'

Before discussing Lacan's thought in a more theoretical manner, it is important to recall that his teaching is best known for its 'return to Freud', in which he combined psychoanalysis and linguistic structuralism. Such intervention placed Freud's discovery of the unconscious and everything it unveils about the nature of thinking, subjectivity, and social reality in an entirely new light. Instead of interpreting Freud in the light of neurobiology and discoveries in other positive sciences, Lacan positioned him alongside the Saussurean linguistic theory of signs. The mental operations such as condensation and displacement, the two central procedures, which according to Freud manipulate the content of thoughts and produce unconscious formations such as dreams, jokes, symptoms, etc., were translated into linguistic notions of the metaphor and metonymy. In this way the unconscious was detached from the scientific and phylogenetic context that the phenomena obtained in Freud's later metapsychological speculations. Instead, Lacan interprets Freud's unconscious as a fundamental and inevitable consequence of the linguistic apparatus which in turn constructed the subject of psychoanalysis as a speaking being (*parlêtre*, as Lacan later wrote), whose body is affected by language. This shift reveals that the unconscious, a particular feature of the human mental apparatus, is inscribed in the same symbolic networks as those that help ground social reality. Paired with this reinterpretation of the unconscious comes a new topology of political space, to which we shall return later on.

Lacan's focus on the relation between linguistic structures and social mechanisms did not come out of the blue. The traces of language and linguistic formations of the unconscious were already present in Freud's three groundbreaking works: *The Interpretation of Dreams, The Psychopathology of Everyday Life*, and *Jokes and Their Relation to the Unconscious*. Later in his work Freud became preoccupied with more general questions concerning culture, politics, and religion, as well as with concrete political events such as the First World War, the economic breakdown of 1929, and the rise of National Socialism. If his work began with the analysis of marginal and strictly private mental phenomena such as dreams, with the treatment of neuroses, which at first seemed far removed from the normativity and rationality of everyday political and social space, it progressively grew into a systematic exploration of social mechanisms and the role they have in the genesis of these apparently private illnesses. Neurosis did indeed become a *social symptom*. The most evident example in this context would be the undeniable traumatic impact of wars or economic crises, which intensify the 'production' of neurotic illnesses. For Freud social structures are endowed with the power of *causality*, and what they cause is what contemporary discourse unsuitably calls 'disorders' – a term that Lacanian psychoanalysis submits to harsh criticism, since it is embedded in normative discourses and ideologies of normalization and reintegration. From the Freudian point of view, the psychoanalytic engagement with social mechanisms is already more complex than the prevailing belief which dichotomizes and opposes the normal and the pathological or distinguishes between the norm and deviation.

The German Frankfurt School of critical theory was among the first philosophical and sociological currents which recognized the potential usefulness of Freudian concepts. For the contributors of the Frankfurt School those became important tools, with the help of which one could and should study social mechanisms. Their most visible representatives (Theodor W. Adorno, Max Horkheimer, and Herbert Marcuse) productively combined psychoanalysis with Marxist critique of ideology. Without restricting or rejecting their political understanding of psychoanalysis, Lacan's move towards linguistic structuralism (Saussure and Jakobson) proposed another possible contextualization of Freudian concepts for the study of socio-political mechanisms. In tying psychoanalysis to linguistics Lacan gave the nexus of psychoanalysis and politics a formalist and epistemologically inspired turn. Not only did he in a rigorous way reaffirm the rational character of the unconscious processes, but he also drew attention to the logical and topological intertwining of the subjective and social reality. The relation between the unconscious and social mechanisms was now approached through the idea of homology, which is possible only under the condition that language is taken in its double role: as the foundation of social link *and* as a privileged terrain of subjectivation. By claiming that the same logic drives both registers of reality, the subjective and the social, Lacan strived to move beyond oppositions such as inside–outside or private–public, without therefore risking psychologization of politics or collectivization of the unconscious.

The accent on logics remains in line with the general thesis traversing the various stages of Lacan's theoretical development: namely that the subject of the unconscious is neither psychological nor individual. These features bring the Lacanian subject closer to the Cartesian cogito, which is initially an abstract and evanescent point from which the methodological doubt arises, before being transformed into a positive thinking 'substance'. Lacan's definition of the signifier – 'the signifier is what represents a subject to another signifier' – adapts the Cartesian deduction of cogito by making the unconscious subject the flipside of the presumably autonomous consciousness. Politics is not to be exempt from this double level of subjectivity. Lacan's idea of the subject, that is the subject of the unconscious, reveals the repressed truth of various other ideas of the subject, which were elaborated throughout modernity in more or less explicit reference to the Cartesian model: notably the philosophical subject of cognition, the political-juridical *homo legalis*, and the political-economic *homo oeconomicus*. In a polemical response to these three fields, Lacan reconceptualized the subject as a decentred form without substance.

It did not take long before Lacan's 'return to Freud' antagonized the psychoanalytic community. Already in 1963 the International Psychoanalytic Association excluded Lacan from its organization. This event only intensified Lacan's interest in political questions. To his mind, the rejection of his thought has proven that the official psychoanalytic doctrines abolished the radical and critical significance of Freud's fundamental discoveries. The choice of the term with which Lacan described his exclusion – 'excommunication' – explicitly refers to the banning of Spinoza from the Jewish community and marks the institutional guardians of Freudian legacy as the fathers of a church. By founding the *École freudienne de Paris* in 1964, Lacan strived to establish a competing organization, where psychoanalysis would renew its critical edge and regain a subversive social role just as in Freud's time. We only need to be reminded of the scandal Freud's discovery of the unconscious and his sexual aetiology of neuroses caused in the scientific circles, pushing Freud into years of isolation. The excommunication of Lacan from the official psychoanalytic association had the opposite effect to that intended; it made the French public only more attentive to his work and to his new institution, which was, unlike the official psychoanalytic institutions, opened to analysts as well as to the non-analysts.

Another important factor in Lacan's progressive engagement with the political grammar of psychoanalysis comes as a response to the audience that began attending his seminar after 1963. Thanks to Louis Althusser, on whose invitation the seminar continued at the *École normale superieure*, Lacan could now present and develop his teaching in front of a broader audience composed not solely of psychoanalysts but also of students of humanities, artists, public intellectuals, and many others. The debates encouraged by the philosophical circle of *normaliens* and particularly the structuralist reading of Marx developed by Althusser's circle, progressively directed Lacan's interest towards the critique of political economy. Finally, with the political turbulences in France, which amounted to the nationwide protests of May 1968, Lacan began elaborating his theory of discourses, which undid the frames of classical structuralism and further addressed the problem of discursive production in the unconscious and in social reality. This shift in focus reframed the Freudian discussions of the libido as a social force and, contrary to the then predominant Freudo-Marxism of Reich and Marcuse, proposes a more complex reading of the relation between the social structures (institutions such as law, family, church, etc.), the subject of the unconscious, and the libidinal economy (the satisfaction of unconscious desires and drives). Lacan restrained from placing the libidinal forces such as desire or drive in simple opposition with the dominating social mechanisms, which in turn allowed capitalism to develop in other, more sophisticated directions, which also called for a fundamental rethinking of the relation between libidinal economy and social reality. In capitalist societies, enjoyment is no longer forbidden but imposed. The shift from prohibition to imposition contains important consequences for grasping the base of subjectivation and social production, where the power relations integrate the subject in the predominant social mode of production.

The link between the unconscious and language also bears consequences for a philosophical vision of politics. The focus on the structural mechanisms, which bring the subject into being, sheds new light on the Aristotelian definition of man as *zoon logikon* or an animal endowed with *logos* (speech, reason, rationality). Psychoanalysis explores the flipside of *logos*, where the subject is not so much speaking as it is *spoken*. In this way, Lacan provides his own contribution to the Hegelian-Marxist line, which detects in alienation the privileged operation, through which the constitution of social relations and the production of subjectivity should be approached. Consequently, thinking is no longer centralized around an ideal mental instance, the ego or the soul, and language is no simple tool or an organ (Aristotle's *organon*) of communication, which describes reality in an adequate way and allows humans to express their inner thoughts and affects. Instead, language is theorized as a mode of production, and what it produces is, on the one hand, decentred subjectivity and, on the other, an enjoyment endowed with a traumatic and disharmonious weight, which makes it foreign to the experience of pleasure.

The Lacanian subject is thus a particular product of the *logical autonomy* of language, where the discursive effects go beyond the grasp of conscious comprehension and control. The double Aristotelian definition of man, as *zoon logikon* and *zoon politikon*, already drew attention to the link between logic and politics, and thus between language and subjectivation. Language is undoubtedly a tool for expressing inner processes, and to exteriorize the interior; but moreover, as its logic is a necessary component of social links, language also interiorizes the exterior. With this double move Lacan proposes a topology of political space modelled on aspheric spaces, where the divide between the inside and the outside is relativized and undetermined. The concept of the discourse, which will be discussed in a series of essays later on, is the general name for this continuity.

At this point the Lacanian axiom 'the unconscious is structured like a language' unveils its full significance. First, it demystifies the Freudian unconscious and links it with the logic of linguistic mechanisms. Then, it thoroughly rejects the pragmatist theories of language, such as Aristotle's. Language is endowed with the power of causality, and the Freudian notion of the unconscious provides a case, a concrete demonstration of this causal relation. Finally, as there is no univocal border between the psychic inside and the social outside, the subject of the unconscious is necessarily a part of the political field, or as Lacan claimed in one of his still unpublished seminars, 'the unconscious is politics'. This intriguing statement specifies the meaning of the axiom 'the unconscious is structured like a language' and additionally places politics in the topological intersection of the inside and the outside. 'The unconscious is politics' can be translated as: the political space and consequently the political power relations are decentred in the same way as the subject. However, to avoid possible misunderstandings, Lacan does not suggest that psychoanalysis subscribes to the slogan 'the personal is political'. Instead he indicates a critique of every attempt to personalize or psychologize politics. Politics is not a reflection of personal neurosis (and thus of psychic conditions); a more appropriate guideline for the Lacanian intervention into politics would hence be: The *impersonal* is political. Differently put, what is most political in the discovery of the unconscious is the logic of its mechanisms and the impossibility of reducing the subject to conscious rationality, on which philosophy, and legal and political-economic theories grounded their respective representations and idealizations of subjectivity.

The discovery of the linguistic dependency of the unconscious reveals that language contains an autonomy, which escapes the control of the conscious ego and which seriously questions the centralized model of consciousness. This stands in direct continuity with Freud's famous passage where he points to political significance of psychoanalysis by claiming that its discoveries have insulted 'human narcissism', just as Copernicus' and Darwin's did before him. The insult coming from Copernicus' astronomy consisted of the progressive decentring of the universe. With the introduction of the heliocentric system and the new role of mathematics in modern astronomy the human observer no longer plays an important role in the progress of science. Alexandre Koyré, Lacan's main reference in discussions of the history of science, has famously claimed that modern mathematics does not 'sustain the phenomena' (i.e. take the way things appear to the human observer as the ultimate object of investigation), but grasps a real that violates and questions the human-centred regime of knowledge. Further, Darwinian evolutionary biology decentred the notion of life and abolished the hierarchical scale of being, which placed man at the pinnacle of creation. The biological and evolutionary claim that man is no longer the exception to the system presented the relationship between nature and culture as continuous, while it also deprived life of its presumed teleology, stability, and necessity. Finally, with the discovery of the laws of the unconscious (that the unconscious is not a blank chaotic space, instead it rigorously follows the rational laws of language), the ego turned out not to be the master in its own linguistic and social 'household'. For Aristotle, there is a master of *oikos*, the father, who holds the household together; and it is also him who accomplishes that same task as the political, juridical, and economic authority on the level of the state. Through 'the father' the political space is centralized and grounded in a stable symbolic relation and organized structure. Freud in contrast revealed that the symbolic authority is immanently split and anchored in an insurmountable conflict. It is thus exactly the opposite vision to the harmonious and stable character that political philosophy since Aristotle has repeated over and over again. Consequently, neither the mental nor the social 'household' know a stable and univocal centre (a firm foundation) although, from the point of view of consciousness, they always presuppose one.

The same decentring marks Freud's theory of sexuality, which problematizes predominantly normative models mostly concerned with anatomy. The very idea of the double beginning of sexual development, one in early infancy and the other in puberty, pictures sexuality as an unstable field without a transcendental and prefigured model. Instead of a linear and progressive sexual development, Freud's theory advocated its polymorphous scenario, which in the last instance breaks with the dichotomy of the normal and the pathological. Lacan condensed this lesson in the well-known statement 'There is no sexual relation', i.e. there is no regulative norm, and sexuality, despite its apparent anchoring in anatomy, is essentially metonymic. Anatomy is colonized and transformed with the interventions of the signifier, which makes it a privileged target of regulation or repression, but also of commodification.

From what has been said so far it becomes obvious that Lacan opened psychoanalysis to other disciplines and contextualized its fundamental concepts in a broader theoretical and political sphere. We thus conclude that the true question to ask is not 'Is psychoanalysis a science?' but rather 'What is a science that includes psychoanalysis?'.[2] This suggests once again that psychoanalysis extends the scope of the modern scientific revolution, something that Freud already insisted upon, but this extension does not leave the idea of scientificity unmarked. Following from this epistemological inquiry into science and psychoanalysis, the same path of questioning concerns the psychoanalytic relation to politics. Thus one should not ask whether psychoanalysis is political but what is politics that includes psychoanalysis; and how does psychoanalysis transform the field of the political and the scope of political intervention? If the mechanisms of the unconscious are determined by the same structures as those grounding the social mechanisms, then the proposed homology has an immediate impact on the very notion of politics. This is the place from which we intend to look at politics and how its relationship to psychoanalysis can be read as it appears in different political and psychoanalytic frames.

There is never an easy 'way in'

The above statement is Lacan's paraphrased utterance; he claimed that no initiation is easy, and thus wondered why he should make an entry into psychoanalytic practice and experience any easier. That is of course not to say that Lacanian theory is impenetrable, however, for its clinical yet at the same time 'interdisciplinary' references, it is by no means an easy approach to the study of society, socio-political life, laws, and logics that drive human institutions. This present volume is an attempt to provide a somewhat pedagogical entry into Lacan's theory but not at the expense of the argument or the importance of psychoanalytic intervention into the field of politics. The above-outlined relationship between politics and psychoanalysis makes this intervention particular in two ways. Unlike a number of the existing introductory texts, the one in front of you does not limit its intervention to the introductory elements of psychoanalysis, which often end up as explanations of clinical and theoretical foregrounds of the practice. While no doubt it is important to understand what psychoanalytic ideas and concepts stand for, a bare clinical explanation of their meaning often falls short in putting across its

8 Samo Tomšič and Andreja Zevnik

explanatory and thinking potential about socio-political life. Leaving the strict terminology aside (for its literal explanation is easily found elsewhere)[3] this volume focuses precisely on the connections offered by this rich theoretical and practical approach. Rather than seeking to understand every theorized concept or term, the presented contributions are exemplifications of how psychoanalysis can provide insight into the less evident mechanisms of politics. While the contributions strive to give a rather clear presentation and pedagogical engagement for a reader of this book, some background in political philosophy will be of additional help.

The work on this volume started from the observation that psychoanalysis as such is still rather marginal in the study of international politics. The references to the work of Slavoj Žižek, probably the best-known Lacanian author in the political field, have been present in critical accounts for a number of years now. A similar observation can be made about Judith Butler or other feminist theorists, who engage with psychoanalysis, such as Julia Kristeva, Juliet Mitchell, or Jacqueline Rose, whose work is a regular companion to political discussions. This volume thus aims to uncover some of the Lacanian foundations of thinkers otherwise more readily used in the study of politics and demonstrate a wider impact and the potentiality of psychoanalysis for political thinking, while also and in a more systematic way drawing out the cornerstones of psychoanalytic references for the domain of (international) politics. Instead of outlining the key ideas of psychoanalysis and demonstrating how they can be of relevance for political issues, the present contributions start from the assumption that psychoanalysis is already political both in its theory and in practice. Thus, to repeat, the question we are asking is what is politics that includes psychoanalysis, and what transformations of the knowledge of the political did psychoanalysis initiate?

It might be surprising that the contributors to this volume predominantly come from the field of humanities and critical cultural theory, rather than from psychoanalysis. This was a conscious decision. We are convinced that crucial theoretical and socially critical value of psychoanalysis derives from a similar move to that with which Lacan opened psychoanalysis to other disciplines; and we aim to do so (again in a similar vein to Lacan's) without drifting in an uncritical 'everything goes' notion of interdisciplinarity, where the speculative dimension of thinking is often rejected or pushed in the background as an unwanted bastard child of scientific research. Lacan's teaching shows that psychoanalysis is essentially what Althusser called *theoretical practice*. It is thus the labour of the concept that takes place in the analytic cabinet and that we are interested in here. Surely, psychoanalysis remains a practice rooted in clinical experience which never stops reinventing, verifying, and developing its fundamental concepts. Yet that is not all that psychoanalysis accomplishes. Lacan often enough insisted that psychoanalysis was not meant to be a closed field of self-sufficient expertise but a social link, which implies that its effects, already on the level of seemingly private and hermetic clinical experience, reach beyond the doorstep of an analytic cabinet. For Lacan clinical experience was not impenetrable but precisely something everyone was encouraged to *think* in an epistemological as well as political way. And more

Introduction **9**

importantly, the psychoanalytic clinic is also a laboratory for conceptual production, whose results significantly challenge the appearance and the established understandings of subjective and social reality. The present volume thus takes Lacan's claims concerning the transmission of psychoanalytic knowledge through the non-analysts seriously.

The present survey volume is divided into three sections and opens with the more general contextualization of the political significance of psychoanalysis. The contribution of Jean-Michel Rabaté discusses Lacan's teaching with reference to 1968, the year of student protests in France, which initiated Lacan's more systematic engagement with the critique of political economy. The intervention of Jelica Šumič, in contrast, offers a broader perspective on the philosophical and political potential of Lacan's teaching, and most notably of his idea of the 'inexistent Other' and the creation of the psychoanalytic school. The papers that follow, one could argue, touch upon this 'inexistent Other', which covers the inherent breaks and contradictions of the given social order.

In the following section 'Lacanian psychoanalysis and the political' the contributions examine concrete interventions of psychoanalysis in the field of political theories through the critical account of some of the fundamental concepts of Lacan's teaching. Philippe van Haute and Thomas Geyskens return to Lacan's re-reading of the Oedipus complex, which continues to provoke controversies concerning its epistemological and social-political signification. This line is pursued by Mladen Dolar, who returns to Lacan's reinterpretation of Oedipus through the lenses of the second part of Sophocles' tragedy. The contribution of Juliet Flower MacCannell further picks upon Lacan's notion of the Imaginary, which is often neglected in political discussions due to the prevailing reduction of Lacan's theories to its symbolic phase; while Alenka Zupančič returns to what remains the most radical political intervention of psychoanalysis, its theory of sexuality, and proposes a reading which exposes the ongoing relevance of Lacan's implicit differentiation between sexuality, anatomical sex, and symbolically constructed gender. Sexuality is irreducible both to anatomy and to symbolic performative, and precisely in this respect it assumes the status of a *real* discursive consequence. Finally, Dominiek Hoens engages with what Lacan himself claimed to be his most original invention, the object *a*, which remains one of the most complex Lacanian concepts and where the various aspects of Lacan's teaching, from the theory of sexuality to the logic of the signifier, come together.

In contrast to this series of concrete conceptual engagements, where the political significance requires more exhaustive reconstruction, stands the theory of discourses, with which Lacan responded to 1968 student protests and to critical voices, which saw in structuralism a rigid theory, incapable of thinking about political and historical events. Focusing on the problematic of mastery, Peter Klepec examines Lacan's take on the relations of domination and the different ways in which the subject, the social modes of production, enjoyment, and political authority are bound together. The interventions of Colin Wright and Samo Tomšič pursue this direction by exploring the links between the Lacanian notion of the discourse and the Foucauldian theory of biopolitics, on the one hand, and with the Marxist critique of capitalism, on the other. Finally the contribution of Mai Wegener returns to Freud's discussion of the function of work in the unconscious mechanisms, thereby pointing out the problem of discursive production that preoccupied Lacan after 1968.

The third section entitled 'Psychoanalysis and Political Encounters' reverses the narrative as it stands with an attempt to see how psychoanalytic theory is already a part of political imaginary. Some of the core political ideas and questions are taken on first. These contributions demonstrate what such psychoanalytic approach can reveal about the state of resistance or about the necessity of law and the ethical deadlocks. Juliet Rogers leans at the recent social movements and uprisings in Europe and across the Arab world in an attempt to extract a psychoanalytic theory of resistance and its social value. By contrast, Ari Hirvonen and Andreja Zevnik engage with questions of law and ethics, Hirvonen by further interrogating the relationship between desire and the imperative of authority as it appears in Hamlet, and Zevnik, by exposing the limits of ethics and the perversions of law as it is outlined in Lacan's text *Kant avec Sade*.

The concluding set of contributions continues with psychoanalytic political encounters by further looking at a few fields of study that bear political significance and that were already subjected to a significant encounter with psychoanalysis. Feminism produced two distinct engagements with Lacanian theory. One picks on Lacan's rather controversial statement on the non-existence of 'The Woman' and the 'phallocentrism' that at first glance perpetrates male domination. This is contrasted by a more constructive reading, which contextualizes Lacan's two logics of sexuation and the two different processes of subjectivation, which are independent from the biological sex. Kirsten Campbell's paper thus draws out the different feminist readings of Lacan's theory while advocating the possibility for new social links and feminine existence. Theology, in contrast, touches upon questions that have preoccupied the Freudian engagement with society and religion from the very offset. Lacan's work, too, is engaged in a permanent discussion with a range of theological thinkers and ideas. Slavoj Žižek's contribution here raises the question of the particular mode of existence that, according to Lacan, marks the divine. David Pavón-Cuéllar pursues a reading of psychoanalysis in connection to the Marxist critique of ideology in the field of psychology and psychological discourse. With a focus on the break with the Freudian metapsychology and Lacan's return to Freud, Pavón-Cuéllar explores the compromation of psychology with the governing ideology. And finally, as the discussions about the limits of politics or the 'way out' of what is perceived as a political deadlock are nowadays numerous, Panu Minkkinen's paper aims to show the conservative impasse in which psychoanalysis can find itself. Thus rather than a revolutionary potential, psychoanalysis can also end up advocating a particular type of conservatism and calls for some caution when in one breath speaking of revolution and psychoanalysis.

By no means are the presented accounts exhaustive of psychoanalytic potential for the study of politics. With their variety they offer possible entries into the political reading of Lacanian thought while also remaining faithful to its disciplinary origins. These interventions are also invitations to further reading and exploration of the political side of Lacan, that is, not Lacan's personal political engagements, but the political potential of his fundamental concepts, when read alongside other traditions and problematics of political theory.

Notes

1 For reasons of space and focus, this volume refrains from providing a more elaborate biographical presentation. For an extensive, up-to-date, and probably the best account of Lacan's life, see Elizabeth Roudinesco's biography of the personal and professional life of Jacques Lacan, entitled simply *Jacques Lacan* (New York: Columbia University Press, 1999), or a more recent shorter intervention *Lacan: In Spite of Everything* (New York: Verso, 2014).
2 Jacques Lacan, 'Report on the 1964 Seminar', *Hurly-Burly* 5 (2011): 18. See also Jacques Lacan, 'Science and Truth', in *Écrits*, ed. Bruce Fink (London and New York: W. W. Norton & Company, 2006), 728.
3 For example, see Dylan Evans, *An Introductory Dictionary of Lacanian Psychoanalysis* (New York: Routledge, 1996).

PART I
Political significance of psychoanalysis

1

LACAN'S 'ANNÉE ÉROTIQUE' (1968/1969)[1]

Jean-Michel Rabaté

UNIVERSITY OF PENNSYLVANIA

> Soixant'neuf, année érotique
> *Soixant'neuf, année érotique…*
> *Serge Gainsbourg and*
> *Jane Birkin*

In May 1973, as I was in charge of the 'ciné-club' of the École Normale Supérieure where I was a student, I decided to collect and screen documentary films about the May '68 'events'. It was just five years after the 'events' (as we still called them) had happened. We showed these amateur and professional documents in May 1973 to an avid crowd, still being in the same Parisian premises where so much had taken place, and to our surprise we felt as if we were watching images from another century. In five years, fashion had drastically changed, flower power had crossed the Channel, men had long hair, open shirts with garish colours, many sported ear-rings, finger rings, or weird leather hats and boots. We were astonished to see the white shirts and neat ties worn by Latin Quarter student leaders like Geismar or Sauvageot; only Daniel Cohn-Bendit's open collar was an exception, but he came from Germany … Our '68 activists had the looks of tired union workers after signing a resolution they had discussed all night, their demeanour evoked more William Burroughs' paranoid executive style than the funky orientalism of the Beatles whom we had started aping … *69 année érotique* indeed. Had it boiled down to this only – a revolution in fashion, accompanied by the belated discovery of a new libidinal body?

Historians like Tony Judt repeat Raymond Aron's diagnosis that May '68 was a French psychodrama acted by the children of the bourgeoisie who were foundering in ideological confusion and delusions. The root would have been the decision by students of Nanterre to allow females into male dorms – then a quite unthinkable transgression in the paternalist order of de Gaulle's hierarchical French society.

16 Jean-Michel Rabaté

While noting that the students' unrest in the 1960s had a strong sexual component, I would not want to reduce its impact to a sudden liberation of a young and privileged elite, a way for France and other European countries to catch up with international fashion marked by a Californian ethos of 'Make love not war' that was conquering the world of the baby-boom teenagers. This would mean in fact denying any political importance to the movement. Focusing on Lacan's layered responses to May '68, I will try to show that psychoanalytic discourse is best equipped to do justice to the libidinal (erotic) component involved even when political stakes are implied – to the point that the concept 'politics' has to be revised.

The French debate about the nefarious or positive influence of the heritage of May '68 has raged. In a talk-show aired by a French channel on 2 March 2008, Alain Finkielkraut dismissed May '68 because, allegedly, the movement triggered only disrespect for a traditional culture mistakenly identified with authority. Cohn-Bendit was more nuanced, arguing that right-wing President Sarkozy corresponded to the type of a 'soixante-huitard' who had succeeded because he applied to the letter the famous '68 slogan: 'Enjoy without fetters' (didn't he vacation on millionaires' yachts and marry a beautiful model and pop singer, Carla Bruni?). To sound a different note, I will follow the chronology of Lacan's responses to the students' unrest before generalizing from the models he elaborated.

The first perception of disruption appeared in *Seminar XV*. On 27 March 1968, Lacan noted that many 'seniors' and faithful auditors had not showed up. He blamed the diminished attendance on vacations, exams, and 'thousand other factors'. In fact, in the Latin Quarter Lacan knew unrest was brewing, people were plotting, chatting, preparing tracts and demonstrations. Lacan expressed both annoyance and relief because the small number allowed him to engage in conversations. So far, his seminar had been devoted to a definition of the psychoanalytic act and Lacan was moving toward a better formulation of the logic of sexuation. His displeasure at the disappearance of the 'old guard' of licensed analysts was compensated by a reassurance from the younger generation. He was relying on *Normaliens* like Nassif (named several times in that session) and Jacques-Alain Miller to help him formalize his logics of sexuality. March 1968 had seen the publication of the first issue of *Scilicet*, the notorious review in which Lacan alone was to sign his articles, the other contributors remaining anonymous. In the second half of this same seminar, Lacan surveys the ground covered that year.

He started from a clinical vignette: one of his male patients planned a romantic weekend in a chalet with a new girlfriend he was in love with, then found himself unable to have sex. A common occurrence, no doubt, which triggered disquisitions about the mother/whore paradigm. Lacan wondered why any 'naturalism' was expected in that situation: was it so 'natural' that the couple make love without any impediment? He went further:

> Why? Not at all to tell you things that are afterwards going to do the rounds
> of Paris, namely that what Lacan is teaching means that man and woman have

nothing to do together. I am not teaching it; it is true. Textually, they have nothing to do together. It is annoying that I cannot teach this without giving rise to scandal. So then I do not teach it, I withdraw it.

(Lacan 1967: 180)

Lacan describes a paradox that would be similar to the liar's paradox, yet is only a paradox if one takes for granted a naturalist frame of reference. Naturalism would be a norm as *doxa,* implying that men and woman 'go together', thus have sex without obstacle. What if the man who thinks he is in love with the girlfriend is in fact in love with his mother? The unconscious thought can trigger the effect of a castration. Meanwhile the woman has to struggle with the fact that is for him the object *a,* not herself. If an analyst interprets too fast, he risks reaching an untimely ending: the intervention will appear as a piece of shit to be promptly dumped.

Contrarily to what Dylan Evans (1996) writes in *Dictionary of Lacanian Psycho-analysis,* the first time that Lacan offered his formula of 'There is no sexual rapport' did not date to 1970 (1996: 181) but was stated in the 1967 seminar on the 'Logic of fantasy'. Lacan had said that there was a lack in the junction of sexual rapport with its subjective realization on 22 February 1967, adding then that there is no 'complementarity' between the male and the female side in sexuality (Lacan 1967). On 12 April 1967, he asserted explicitly that there was 'no sexual act': 'The great secret of psychoanalysis is that there is no sexual act'. He added: 'It is precisely because there is sexuality that there is no sexual act' (Lacan 1967: 12 April). Here lay the core of Lacan's new teaching, which might pass for revolutionary, even though the bad news would not help the student's rebellion.

When in 1968 Lacan mentioned the rumour going around Paris, he quoted the previous year's seminar ('I have formulated that "there is no sexual act" I believe that the news circulates in all the city, well, finally I didn't announce it as an absolute truth' (Lacan 1967: 19 April)); then Lacan offered a new 'truth' with Marxist-Leninist overtones; on 19 April 1967, he quotes Lenin's tag that 'Marx's theory will triumph because it is true'. Those terms define *jouisssance* in the social field as caught up in surplus in value. Such was the theoretical framework of the seminar from 1967–68, which deploys these striking formulations about sexuality.

The seminar of 8 May could not take place because of a general strike by the teachers' union, but Lacan chatted with those who were present. On the 9th, Lacan signed a manifesto supporting the protesting students, incited by his daughter and son-in-law, both involved in Maoist activities. Lacan then talked with students in psychiatry on strike; he was not impressed by their claim that they needed more dialogue with professors, as he questioned the very notion of dialogue. On 14 May, Lacan arranged a meeting with Cohn-Bendit and other leaders of the students' movement, praising on the next day Cohn-Bendit's witty retorts. Lacan did not hold his seminar but came prepared with notes. He began by insisting that he was speaking for psychoanalysts, then mentioned signing an open letter in reference to his own signature. Lacan praised the courage of those who stood up to the police:

... to be worthy of the events, I would say that even though psychoanalysts bear witness to their sympathy for those caught up in pretty hard encounters, for which one needs to have – this should be underlined – great courage, you should have received, as we analysts do, the testimony of what is experienced at these moments to measure better and at its true value what is represented by this courage. Because from the outside, like that, you can admire, of course, but you cannot always realize that the merit is no less great because these lads are really at certain moments carried away by the feeling of being absolutely bound to their comrades. They express it by saying that it is exalting to sing the International while being clubbed by police truncheons, but this is on the surface, since of course, the International may be a very fine song but I do not think that they would have this irrepressible feeling that they could not be anywhere other than where they are if they were not carried along by a feeling of absolute community ... something to be explored further.

(Lacan 1967/68: 189–90, modified)

Lacan mentioned an important commentator of the events, Raymond Aron, whom he presented as 'a comrade' and 'a friend'. Aron had just published an article in which he observed that there were students' demonstrations everywhere, alluding to American universities and to Poland. Praising the article's tone, Lacan added that it had missed a structural factor: the globalization of the phenomenon was crucial, but because of a new knot between knowledge and truth, a knot that only psychoanalysis could make sense of. Moreover, Aron's article argued that current teachings, including Lacan's, were rejected for not being dynamic enough. Indeed, Lacan knew from radical student leaders that Wilhelm Reich was often quoted by the Nanterre leftists, and stated his disagreement: 'Reich's ideas are not simply incomplete, they are demonstrably, fundamentally false' (Lacan 1967/68: 192). It was because psychoanalysts did not bear witness to their experience concerning sexes and sexuality that these misguided notions had spread.

As an interesting aftermath to this seminar, the last of that Spring, Lacan recognized that those who were missing were not students busy erecting barricades but the older analysts. The May events confirmed a split in his school, while opposing it to the psychoanalytic community. The disaffection of older psychoanalysts led to a schism in 1969. Jean-Paul Valabrega, Piera Aulagnier, and Francois Perrier left Lacan's school to found the *Organisation Psychanalytique de Langue Francaise*. Roudinesco has described the tension that mounted in 1968–69 between the old guard of clinicians and the new philosophers who were more radical in their politics. However, in a symptomatic gesture, Lacan borrowed de Gaulle's formula to express his disgust with traditional psychoanalysts:

It is rather curious that from the moment simply when some paving stones start flying, for at least a moment everyone has the feeling that the whole of society might be involved in it in the most direct way in its daily comfort and its future.

We have even seen psychoanalysts questioning the future of the trade. To my eyes, they were wrong to question it publicly. They would have done better to keep it to themselves, because all the same, people who saw them questioning themselves about it [...] found this a little funny. In any case one cannot say that the stock of psychoanalysis rose! // I have a crow to pluck with the General. He stole a word from me that for a long time I had – it was certainly not, of course, for the use that he made of it: psychoanalytic shit-in-bed (*la chienlit psychanalytique*). You cannot imagine for how long I wanted to give that as a title to my seminar. Now the chance has gone!

(Lacan 1967/68: 197–98, modified)

Even if Lacan assured his audience that he didn't use de Gaulle's phrase to accuse the students of 'shitting in their own beds', his attitude betrayed an identification with de Gaulle, the ageing founder of the Fifth Republic. Both had gone to Collège Stanislas, and shared a similar family background. De Gaulle, after he came back from Germany where he had considered a military action against the insurgents, launched the phrase: '*La réforme, oui, la chienlit, non!*' (Reform yes, shit-in-bed, no!) The June elections brought success for the Gaullists: the country, frightened by the spectre of civil war, rallied around the General. A second referendum failed in April 1969; this self-engineered political suicide led de Gaulle to resign from presidency on 28 April 1969. He retired and died in 1970. Lacan's continued identification with him extended beyond the immediate moment of the 'events'; he was pondering the implications of a political power ready to 'resign' in the session of the 19 March 1969. When no one, in spite of his request, asked a question, he said: 'Don't make me discouraged, for I, too, might well be tempted to resign' (Lacan 2006: 244).

If in May '68 de Gaulle coined the phrase of '*chienlit*' to imply that the leftist students had 'fouled their own nest', Lacan saw what was wrong not with the students but with official psychoanalysis: most psychoanalysts had fouled their nests when they had failed to remain true to the revolution in human subjectivity initiated by Freud. More hope came from the mixture of Marxism, Dadaism, surrealism, and anarchism combined in a strange brew by leftists. Lacan would not renounce that hope, all the while aware that the students were easily deluded. In the same June seminar, he made a typical aside about the logics of the excluded middle: '*Naturellement c'est bébé comme le mouvement du 22 mars*' (Lacan 1967/68: 318). He felt that he was grandparenting a movement that risked spinning out of control.

Consequently, the June 1968 seminar closed on a militant note. Lacan began with this declaration: '*Je ne suis pas un truqueur*' (Lacan 1967/68: 297; 'I am not a cheater') and ended about prophecy: 'At the level of the Other, there's nothing but prophecy. On the other hand, it is at the level of the Other that science is totalized, and thus for the subject, totally alienates itself. What matters now is to know whether there might still be for the subject something of the order of prophecy' (ibid.: 324). Also he deplored that he had to suspend his discourse on the psychoanalytic act because his main audience, the professional psychoanalysts, had vanished.

When the seminar resumed in November 1968 the first session offered no hint of changes triggered by the Spring. Lacan pursued the elaboration of new mathemes and formulas, alluding to Althusser and his disciples whose structuralist *Reading Capital* could be emulated. Marx had paved the way to a new understanding of the object *a* caught up in the economy of *jouissance;* one could revamp the concept of *Mehrlust* defined as homologous or parallel to *Mehrwert*. Lacan offered a framework in which capitalism played a key role. The May 'events', as a symptom of capitalism, testified to the clash between knowledge and truth, to the struggle between capitalistic accumulation of knowledge and the irruption of a truth linked with jouissance:

> I have been looking for the root of what has been ridiculously called the *events*. There hasn't been any event in this business but I'll explain this to you later. // The process by which science gets unified [...] reduces all knowledge to a single market. [...] What is it, then, that represents the discontent in civilization, as one says? It is a surplus jouissance (*plus-de-jouir*) brought about by a renunciation of jouissance, while the principle of the value of knowledge has been respected.
>
> *(Lacan 2006: 40)*[2]

Lacan presented May '68 as a gigantic strike of knowledge, whose truth had appeared only to be lost again. The perverse effect of the process was that it just modernized old-fashioned French institutions of learning to make them more competitive, machine-like, and bureaucratic:

> The way in which everyone suffers in his or her rapport to jouissance, in so far as we only connect to it by the function of surplus-jouissance, this is the symptom – it appears from this, that there only an average, abstract social truth. // This results from the fact that a knowledge is always paid at its price but below the use-value that truth generates, and always for others than those who are in truth. It is thus marked by surplus-enjoyment. And this *Mehrlust* laughs at us since we don't know where it's hidden. // This is where things are at, my dear children. That's why in May, all hell got loose.
>
> *(Lacan 2006: 41)*

Lacan qualified the uprising with more precision by alluding to Michel de Certeau's *La Prise de Parole: pour une nouvelle culture*. In that book, dated from 9 September 1968, de Certeau, not only a Jesuit and a historian of religious possession, but also a member of Lacan's school, compared the May uprising with the beginning of the French Revolution: '*En mai dernier, on a pris la parole comme on a pris la Bastille*' (de Certeau 1994: 40). Lacan comments humorously: 'This was a great *prise de parole*, as somebody who has in my field a non negligible place has stated. *Prise de parole?* I think that it would be a mistake to give this *prise* a homology with any *prise de la Bastille. Une prise de tabac ou de came, j'aimerais mieux*' (Lacan 2006: 41). Punning on '*prise*' used in 'taking the floor to speak', 'the storming of the Bastille', and 'a pinch of snuff', Lacan is sceptical facing de Certeau's positive book, which asserted that students and strikers attacked not real objects but symbolic structures. It was less the power that they 'contested' than an inability to be taken seriously in the Symbolic. The rejection of an older society questioned knowledge in the name of an Other that had been rejected at the margins (de Certeau 1994: 86). De Certeau concluded by quoting Marx who refused to be swayed by enthusiasm during the 1848 revolution – he would study political economy. The task was to continue thinking along the lines of this revolutionary event.

De Certeau pushed Lacan to assess the institutional stakes implied by the events. He quoted a book published by another psychoanalyst, Didier Anzieu. Anzieu's book on May '68 concluded that the events had proved that Sartre triumphed over Lacan. In *Ces idées qui ont ébranlé la France*, Epistémon, Anzieu's pen-name, claimed that the 'events' showed that Carl Rogers' group dynamics replaced Lacan's scholasticism, and that Sartre crushed the structuralists. De Certeau rejected this view (de Certeau 1994: 105), commenting on the nostalgia displayed by many May slogans: along with the practice of heaping up paving stones to make barricades, a hangover from insurrections in the 1830s, 1848, and 1871. Most of the posters were quotes, knowingly evoking slogans of Spanish anarchists, Dadaist jokes, or neo-romantic tags of the surrealists. Nevertheless, slogans also quoted Lacan: the word jouissance was displayed on Paris walls … De Certeau's book insisted that the time of '*parole in libertà*' had passed, that one needed to work theoretically and make sense of recent history, a task for which traditional psychoanalysis had proved inadequate.

In the Spring of 1969, Lacan mentioned with disdain a book on the '68 events written by two psychoanalysts from the Paris Psychoanalytic Society (IPA), Bela Grunberger and Janine Chasselet-Smirguel. Under the pseudonym of André Stéphane, they had published *L'Univers Contestationnaire*, alluding to '*univers concentrationnaire*', which implied that the leftists were totalitarian Stalinists. Lacan's review was scathing:

> Its title is such a disgrace that I won't quote it here. Under the explicit pretence of being two psychoanalysts, which they confess from the start, the book pretends to take stock of what they refer to as 'contestation'. After that, you know what to expect. Psychic regression, infirmity, sordid infantilism of all those who manifested themselves […] bring them back into a certain analytic framework. This never goes further.
>
> *(Lacan 2006: 266)*

Lacan was relieved to see that the authors did not belong to his school. The idea that '68 'revolutionaries' were caught up in an Oedipal revolt against the Father was too tempting for traditional psychoanalysts. These same IPA analysts

22 Jean-Michel Rabaté

denounced intellectual 'terrorism' coming from Lacan's school. Lacan added that this alleged terrorism was justified if it prevented this kind of lamentable drooling.

Lacan had appreciated de Certeau's idea that the students had quoted him: 'Even if it was at times bullshit, this was bullshit that sounded very much like Lacan's discourse. It even reproduced it textually at times. It was a coincidence, of course' (Lacan 2006: 4). However, he veers off into an attack facing 'a Communist priest' whom he nicknames 'Mudger Muddle' (ibid.: 42). Jacques-Alain Miller's notes (Miller in Lacan 2006: 415) identify him as Lucien Goldmann, the author of *The Hidden God*. This academic Marxist was a well-known patriarch of the Latin Quarter. Goldmann would always allude to Georg Lukacs, the worst sin was to ignore *History and class consciousness*. Lacan strikes:

> What is strange is the passionate interrogation that came from the soul of someone I'll call the communist priest (you recognize his silhouette) whose goodness had not limits in nature. One can trust him to be duly chided and moralized, these are things that come with old age. // I'll dub him forever *Mudger Muddle*, which is my coining. This is meant to call up a crocodile and the mud in which he wallows, and the fact that, with a delicate tear, he draws you into his well-meaning world. He told me that he was looking for a Marxist theory and was then inundated by so much ambient happiness. But it hadn't come into his thick head that happiness could be generated by truth when it is on strike.
>
> *(Lacan 2006: 42)*

Goldmann was one of the relentless debunkers of structuralism, as one perceives during the ferocious discussion that followed Michel Foucault's presentation on 'What is an author?' at the College de France, a lecture Lacan attended. Goldmann asked a question which covers four close-printed pages in the *Dits et Ecrits* volume. Goldmann attacks the 'negation of the subject' that he sees in Foucault, Lévi-Strauss, Barthes, Althusser, and of course Lacan, just to end his peroration with a quote from the May '68 slogans: 'Structures don't go down into the streets'.

Goldmann was wrong, as recent historians have shown. Frédérique Mattoni's 'Structuralism and Prophetism' demonstrates that a 'process of politization' (Jacques Lagroye's phrase) pervaded the groups of intellectuals who could be called 'structuralists', and that this process had begun just before May '68. Althusser and Foucault's attacks on a humanism still defended by Goldmann was instrumental in pushing an entire generation to the ultra-left, Mattoni (2008: 178–79) contends. This clinched the links between a 'scientific' discourse based on structural linguistics and the radical prophetism of younger intellectuals. Foucault had no difficulty in replying that, contrary to what Goldmann assumed, he did not believe in the 'death of the author' – against Roland Barthes, because he needed that notion to produce an archaeology of knowledge. The same was true of the notion of 'man': alluding to Nietzsche who prophesied the end of 'man', Foucault analysed the historical rules governing the appearance and function of the concept of 'man'.

Echoing without knowing it Lacan's remarks on crocodile tears, Foucault (2001: 845) concluded snappishly: 'I have done the same for the author-function. Let us thus hold back our tears'.

Let's jump ahead to the new year, duly saluted by Lacan: 'I wish you a happy new year. 69 is a good number' (Lacan 2006: 91). As he said, '69' was a better number than '68', which was contradicted when he saw an article penned by a professor of linguistics, George Mounin, who had published in the *Nouvelle Revue Française* a critical examination of Lacan's style (Mounin 1969). Mounin argued that Lacan had come late to structuralist linguistics, that he embraced it with the fervour of a neophyte who has not assimilated fully the concepts and methods. And Mounin deplored that Lacan's influence on young philosophers of the École Normale Supérieure had been encouraged by their institution. According to him, because of Lacan's prestige, 15 years of foundational research in linguistics had been wasted. Such a remark had repercussions, for indeed, at the end of the Spring of 1969, Lacan's seminar was cancelled. Flacelière, the new Director of the École Normale Supérieure, declared him *persona non grata*.

The 25 June 1969 seminar was devoted to scathing political remarks denouncing the Director's double game, which led to a chaotic sit-in in his office, a fitting emblem of Lacan's conflicted relations with official institutions. Here Lacan was following more in the steps of Chairman Mao, who repeatedly used the younger generations as a weapon against the old guard, than in those of de Gaulle, who had haughtily dismissed France as ungovernable. It was high time to start a psychoanalytically based cultural revolution.

Lacan surmised this when he reached the end of the academic year in the Summer of 1969 and revisited his interrupted seminar of May '68, seeing that there had been a link between the 'events' and the inability in which most psycho-analysts were to conceptualize the act (Lacan 2006: 341). A discussion of Pascal's gamble clarified the conditions needed for an act, defined as *en-je*, both 'stakes' (*enjeu*) and 'in-I' *(en-je)* (ibid.: 342). The psychoanalytic act has to be a provocation and an incitation to know, since it characterizes the link between the act, failure, and the logic of jouissance. Only by understanding how the act works, will one avoid acting-outs as when the students' rebellion petered out and generated random violence.

The psychoanalytic act, an incitation to know, a *scilicet*, underpins the funda-mental rule: analysands say whatever comes to mind, hoping they will be heard by a subject who knows; however, psychoanalysts only know how to produce knowledge, plus a few basic themes all hinging around the absence of sexual rap-port. Thus one acts in order to compensate for this lack – hence the sexual act, devoid of reciprocity or logical equality. Failure is inscribed in sexual rapport, it is called castration in psychoanalytic discourse. Psychoanalysis inverts the process of capitalism in that it leads to work that will let truth speak without being caught up in the dialectical twists of surplus-enjoyment. It inverts the usual link between truth and knowledge by pushing knowledge beyond its use in the 'exploitation' of men by men (Lacan 2006: 355).

24 Jean-Michel Rabaté

At the meeting of 11 June 1969 Lacan alluded to his son-in-law, Jacques-Alain Miller: like Paul on the way to Damascus, he had experienced a conversion to Maoism (Lacan 2006). Miller had told Lacan that the title of his seminar was too obvious (from one Other to the other). However, Lacan insisted that this trajectory allowed one to understand the genesis of surplus-enjoyment, and could not be found in Mao's little red book. Its proper site was Aristotelian logic. Lacan's revolution, waged in the name of Freud and of Marx, found its bearings in traditional logic. The synthesis of Marx and Freud returned to a classical logic in which the vagaries of sexual rapport and capitalistic exploitation found a common formalization. It was in 1969, in the aftermath of the May 1968 'events', that Lacan elaborated a system deploying his variety of Freudo-Marxism; it culminates in the theory of the four discourses developed in the fall of 1969 in *Seminar XVII*. This original theory combines Althusser's revision of the field of Marxism and Foucault's critical historicism he called 'genealogy'.

Lacan's elaboration was determined by further factors: first, he asserted that he considered himself as a structuralist even if the term was no longer fashionable; second, he needed to elaborate the concept of 'surplus jouissance' combining Freud's *Lust* with Marx's *Mehrwert*. If, as we saw, 'surplus-jouissance' was coined in 1967, in 1969, the term accounted for the social function of symptoms as well as for the libidinal energies invested in social labour. Meanwhile Lacan resisted what he saw as the institutionalization of his teachings via the university. The danger for him at that time was to be reduced to slogans. To counter the risk of deviation, the four discourses manifest the last efflorescence of structuralism in Lacan's thought. It was via his 'discourse' that he wanted to have an impact not only on enshrined academic culture but also on everyday social interactions.

Later, in 'Radiophonie', Lacan mentions a 'discourse of capital':

> For Marx, with the plus-value that his chisel detached so as to restitute it to the discourse of capital, paid the price one has to put to negate, as I do, that any discourse be pacified by a meta-language (of Hegelian formalism in that case); this price, he paid it by forcing himself to follow the naive discourse of ascendant capitalism, and by the hellish life he gave himself thereof. // This verifies what I say about the *plus-de-jouir*. The *Merhwert*, is the *Marxlust*, that is Marx's own *plus-de-jouir*.
>
> *(Lacan 2001: 434)*

Lacan expected practical consequences from this grid while voicing scepticism facing political activism of the leftist type. This appears in an anecdote:

> I remember the uneasiness of a young man who wanted to be Marxist and had gotten mixed up with a group of members of (the one and only) Party who showed up in strength (God knows why) to my paper on 'The dialectic of desire and the subversion of the subject in psychoanalysis'.

I was very nice (I am always nice) and mentioned in *Ecrits* the confusion that I felt before the following response from this audience member,

'Do you think that you can expect to have any kind of effect from writing a few letters on the blackboard?'

Such an exercise, however, had its effects: and I have the proof – my book [*Ecrits*] was rejected by the Ford Foundation that supports such gatherings in order to clean them up. The Foundation found it unthinkable to publish me.

It is just that the effect that is produced has nothing to do with communication of *la parole*, and everything to do with the displacement of discourse.

(Lacan 2001: 407)

The Ford Foundation refused to fund the translation of *Ecrits* into English but funded that of Heinz Hartmann's *Ego Psychology and the Problem of Adaptation*, a book written in the 1930s and published in English in 1957.[3] Not surprisingly, Hartmann saw the ego as a compromise whose good functioning led to accommodation with an unquestioned *reality*. Hartmann was president of the IPA during the years of Lacan's marginalization; the rejection by the American foundation was doubly insulting. Here Lacan also chides the Communist for his naïveté, when demanding 'an immediate effect' in a fantasy of political efficacy. Precisely because he is aware that American institutions exert invisible political effects on post-war intellectual life, Lacan cannot trust leftist tactics of immediacy. This position entails a double refusal: he resists the Marxist call to immediate action and resists changing his theses to suit the humanistic standards of the Ford Foundation which had funded, among many others, his old friend Raymond Aron.

Lacan believed in the possibility of changing the dominant discursive practices that underpin the subtle veil of alienation which we can call 'ideology' by introducing new modalities of 'discourse'. The 'displacement of discourse' Lacan meant to achieve was far from the bombastic belief that society will be changed all of a sudden by a general strike. Lacan refuses the temptation of playing the role of 'baby-sitter of History': 'When one will acknowledge the kind of *plus-de-jouir* that makes one say "Wow, this is somebody!", then one will be on the way toward a dialectical matter maybe more active than the Party fodder [*chair à Parti*, punning both on "chair à canon", cannon fodder, and on "chair à pâté" patty filling) commonly used as baby-sitter of history (*baby-sitter de l'histoire*)]' (Lacan 2001: 415). Even if the articulation of the four discourses may be ultimately credited to the 'cunning' (*List*) of a History that arranges everything, at least understanding its logic should make us aware that it is important as much to refuse to be 'cannon fodder' for its slaughter-bench as to be wary of not playing the nice but deluded role of 'baby- sitter' while the grown-ups continue their seductive tricks or strategies aiming at accumulating power.

Was the key to May '68 and its aftermath another Gainsbourg's song of 1969, the notorious '*Je t'aime moi non plus*' with its sounds of female orgasm? Its graphic lyrics combine eroticism ('I come and go between your hips and I hold back') with

26 Jean-Michel Rabaté

warning ('Physical love is a dead end street'). It is tempting to take this song as a symptom of the pervasiveness of Lacan's teachings at the time.

In France, everything ends with songs. Another consequence of the aftermath of May '68 brought Lacan face to face with another Goldmann, Pierre, not Lucien, this time. Pierre Goldmann had chosen direct action even before '68. He had gone to Cuba to train with revolutionaries and returned to Paris in the fall of 1967. He did not actively take part in the May events but after the triumph of the right, headed off again for Latin America, leaving in September 1968. Seeing himself as a French Che Guevara, he went to Venezuela where he worked for a year with an armed revolutionary group. In September 1969, back in Paris he started a series of hold-ups of pharmacies. Then he planned to hold-up Lacan whom he would subdue with a gun, force him to recite poems by Antonin Artaud, another of 'society's suicides', and make off with his cash, since Lacan extorted fortunes daily from his patients. Goldmann went to Rue de Lille with an accomplice. As they were going up the stairs, Lacan was leaving with Gloria, his secretary. Goldmann, awed by Lacan's face, did not dare attack: 'But when I saw this thinker with his white hair, I was startled, struck, impressed: never could I point a gun at him. I said so to my assistant and we left' (Roudinesco 1997: 343). In April 1970, Goldmann was arrested for the murder of two pharmacists, killed in a botched hold-up. He spent five years in jail where he wrote *Souvenirs d'un juif polonais né en France*. He was acquitted after a second trial. After having been released, on 20 September 1979, he was shot dead by extreme-right terrorists who were never found. His younger brother Jean-Jacques Goldmann, then a French pop star, dedicated a concert to his dead brother. Jean-Jacques Goldmann, who became famous for a hit with a Lacanian title, *'Il suffira d'un signe'*, and whose name is now written with one n only, was to write most of the hits for singers like Céline Dion, Marc Lavoine, Johnny Halliday, Patricia Kaas, Khaled, etc. When Serge Gainsbourg died in 1991, Goldman was the most popular French pop singer.

Notes

1 This is a revised and shortened version of '68 + 1: Lacan's *Année érotique*', published in *Parrhesia*, 6 (2009): 28–45, available online at: www.parrhesia.org.
2 My own translation from the French publication.
3 I owe this point to Catherine Liu.

Bibliography

de Certeau, Michel (1994 [1968]) *La Prise de parole et autres écrits politiques*. Paris: Seuil.
Epistémon (1968) *Ces idées qui ont ébranlé la France*. Paris: Fayard.
Evans, Dylan (1996) *An Introductory Dictionary of Lacanian Psychoanalysis*. New York: Routledge.
Foucault, Michel (2001) *Dits et Ecrits I, 1954–1975*, ed. D. Defert, F. Ewart, and J. Lagrange. Paris: Gallimard.

Lacan, Jacques (1967) *Seminar XIV, The Logic of Fantasy* [1966/67]; unofficial transcript of Lacan's seminars, available online at: www.ecole-lacanienne.net/seminaireVI.php (accessed 12 October 2014).

Lacan, Jacques. *Seminar XV, The Psychoanalytic Act*; unofficial transcript of Lacan's seminars, available online at: www.valas.fr/IMG/pdf/THE-SEMINAR-OF-JACQUES-LACAN-XV_l_acte_P.pdf (accessed 12 October 2014).

Lacan, Jacques (1967/68) *Seminar XV, The Psychoanalytic Act* [*1967/1968*], unofficial translation by Cormac Gallagher, available online at: www.lacaninireland.com/web/wp-content/uploads/2010/06/Book-15-The-Psychoanalytical-Act.pdf (accessed 20 October 2014).

Lacan, Jacques (1991) *Le Séminaire, livre XVII: L'Envers de la Psychanalyse*. Paris; Seuil.

Lacan, Jacques (2001) *Autres Ecrits*. Paris: Seuil.

Lacan, Jacques (2006) *Seminar XVI: D'un Autre à l'Autre*. Paris: Seuil.

Mattonti, Frédérique (2008) 'Structuralisme et Prophétie', in *Mai-Juin 68*. Paris: Editions de l'Atelier.

Mounin, Georges (1969) 'Quelques traits du style de Jacques Lacan', *La Nouvelle Revue Française*, 1 January: 84–92.

Rabaté, Jean-Michel (2003) 'Lacan's turn to Freud', in *The Cambridge Companion to Lacan*, ed. J.-M. Rabaté. Cambridge: Cambridge University Press, 1–24.

Roudinesco, Elizabeth (1997) *Jacques Lacan*, trans. Barbara Bray. New York: Polity Press.

2

POLITICS AND PSYCHOANALYSIS IN THE TIMES OF THE INEXISTENT OTHER

Jelica Šumič

SCIENTIFIC RESEARCH CENTRE OF SLOVENIAN ACADEMY OF SCIENCES AND ARTS

According to theorists from a variety of intellectual traditions, there is no question more burning today than the question of the way out, i.e. the possibility of a radical break with the existing state of affairs capable of initiating change within the late capitalist conjecture. If contemporary thought faces today the growing impasses of the way out, this is partly, at least, due to the fact that the new regime of mastery, knowing no limit, no outside and therefore no exception, seems to annihilate the very possibility of a way out that would articulate the negation of the present with the creation of an alternative to that which exists. Hence, our task can be none other than to examine to what extent contemporary thought, associating psychoanalysis and philosophy, can rise to this challenge. Our departure point is the assumption that, for psychoanalysis and for contemporary political thought, there must be another perspective, another angle under which it is possible to conceive of a way out while breaking with the prevailing conception of a solution in terms of a subversion of the existing hegemonic arrangement. We can find an understanding of the specifically political consequences of this impasse in Lacan's discussion of the relationship between politics and the unconscious. Indeed, it is in one of Lacan's rather startling statements that we find the formulation that will guide us: 'I do not say "politics is the unconscious" but simply "the unconscious is politics"' (Lacan 1966–67: 10 May 1967).

'The unconscious is politics'

What is so striking about Lacan's concessive formulation is that, under the guise of continuity, an unexpected inversion is produced, as politics seems to be occupying, contaminating even, the unconscious itself, the sole domain that is within the competence of psychoanalysis. With this intrusion of politics into the unconscious, the very subject-matter of psychoanalysis, something is surreptitiously added that suspends, ruins even, the classic, Freudian thesis: 'politics is the unconscious'. What this thesis, according to which the unconscious dominates politics, immediately implies is that the social bond at stake in politics is governed by a certain logic that operates unbeknown to men thus brought together, a logic that 'is already operative in the unconscious' (Lacan 2006: 673), namely the logic of the signifier. From such a perspective, it may well appear that the formula: 'politics is the unconscious', merely sums up the two preceding, now classic, definitions of the unconscious furnished by Lacan himself: 'The unconscious is structured like a language' and 'The unconscious is the discourse of the Other'. Yet such a view is rendered extremely problematic from the moment that it appears that the Other itself is challenged, or does not exist at all.

For the claim now seems to be more radical, requiring not just that collective formations in the field of politics be analysed as unconscious formations,[1] but that the unconscious itself must be accounted for as being linked to, indeed, dependent upon, the discourse of the master. Thus, when Lacan in his seminar on *The Other Side of Psychoanalysis* stresses that '[A]s stupid as this discourse of the unconscious is, it is responding to something that stems from the institution of the discourse of the master himself' (Lacan 2007: 91), he thereby implies that any modification of the master's discourse will have decisive consequences for the discourse of the unconscious. To begin with, in fact, it is worth noting that when Lacan claims that 'the unconscious is politics', he is not only taking into account that 'something changed in the master's discourse' (Lacan 2007: 207), announcing in that way a suspension, at least in part, of the validity of Freud's formula, thereby confining it to the era in which the Other still existed. By stating that 'the unconscious is politics', Lacan can be seen to be already suggesting here that in a world in which the Other has become problematic, even non-existent, a new and more radical conception of the unconscious is required. Clearly, it is not the same to designate the unconscious as the discourse of the Other when the latter still existed, or when the existence of the Other is quite obviously, that is to say, at the level of hegemonic discourse, called into question.

This shift in Lacan's theory of the unconscious could thus be seen as a direct effect of the precariousness, in the field of politics, of the very link, the agency of the Other, on which the structural equivalence between the discourse of the unconscious and the master's discourse was founded. Taken further, it is clear that this move from the first to the second formula has direct implications for contemporary theorization of politics. In being articulated to the barred Other, i.e. to the perspective of the not-all, i.e. of the incompleteness of any space of discursivity, the second formula indicates at the same time the possibility of a fundamentally different politics, one which is not restricted to the resistance to and/or the subversion of the Other's discourse by uncovering its radical contingency. For if politics was at the outset viewed by Lacan as the paradigm of the master's discourse, the emergence of a new discourse, the capitalist discourse, problematizes the notion of the Other as a guarantor, thus shaking up the basic laws of the constitution of the social order and changing what constitutes social reality for us.

30 Jelica Šumič

Retroactively, the second formula can thus be considered as a formula forged by Lacan for the era of the non-existent Other, that of a universe without a beyond, an infinite or not-all universe. Indeed, the second formula amounts to the reversal of the first: if the first formula, insofar as it is centred around the famous *point de capiton*, provides us with a formula of metaphorization, the second formula is one of the generalization of metonymy, or, rather, of the general metonymization. Now this concerns our problem directly: to evaluate the contemporary possibility of change in the present conjecture while taking into account the mutation of the master's discourse, that namely which is articulated to the lack in the Other, to the barred Other, and which Lacan, as is well known, designated as the discourse of the capitalist.

What follows is an attempt to outline the space of the problem of the not-all and to show if and to what extent politics and psychoanalysis are able to face and to resist the deadlocks inherent to the generalized metonymization while theorizing and practising new forms of the non-segregationist collectivity. Our aim in this essay is to contribute towards an understanding of this complex issue by bringing into question the seemingly self-evident relationship of the mutual exclusion between politics and psychoanalysis.

From the not-all to the 'for all'

In order to expose an affinity in dealing with the universal in politics and psycho-analysis, it is necessary to move beyond the traditionally hostile polarities of the singular and the universal and to reverse the usual perspective, according to which there is no passage between the domain of the singular and the domain of the universal. We will then move on to consider the relationship between psycho-analysis and politics from the point of view of the collectivity 'for all' constituted through a complex practice of disidentification and production of the generic or, to use Agamben's term, 'whatever' singularities.[2]

Our starting assumption is that politics and psychoanalysis encounter the same structural impasse, that of dealing with some kind of an irreducible heterogeneity or alterity. Indeed, the central issue in analysis is precisely that of a knot which holds the subject together, an instance that links together three registers that would otherwise remain disconnected: the symbolic of his or her representation, the real of his or her enjoyment, and the imaginary consistency of the body's image. What the patient learns at the end of his or her analysis is that nothing holds together these three instances, the real, the imaginary, and the symbolic – except the symptom or sinthome as Lacan termed it in his later teaching. Politics, likewise, irrespective of the regime, of the type of government, confronts a similar impasse that could be formulated in the following terms: how to hold together singularities which have nothing in common. Modern politics, at least from the French Revolu-tion onwards, has treated this impossibility of the social bond by constructing a form of collectivity, which would be 'for all'. It is a paradoxical collectivity since the condition for its very constitution requires the exclusion of the exception, of some otherness that is presumed to be evading the universalization.

From such a perspective, psychoanalysis and politics appear to be two different languages for articulating heterogeneity or otherness that are in confrontation with each other. But is the heterogeneity or otherness in psychoanalysis the same as that which we encounter in politics? What is at issue here is precisely the question: under what conditions is it legitimate to bring together politics and psychoanalysis? Indeed, any attempt to relate psychoanalysis to politics is far from obvious. According to the received idea, there seems to be no common ground permitting their encounter. In this view, psychoanalysis is presumed to be defending the rights of the singular, of that precisely which resists the universal. Indeed, psychoanalysis is by definition the domain of the 'not for all'. As such, psychoanalysis cannot, without losing its competence, force the boundaries of confidentiality imposed by its practice to wander into a domain in which, on the contrary, something is valid only insofar as it applies to all. From this view, psychoanalysis has no competence in the domain destined 'for all'. Politics, by contrast, designed as the order of the collective, deals with the masses, with the multiple. Insofar as politics is pre-occupied with the question of that which is valid for all, it can only turn a blind eye to the singular: the proper object of psychoanalysis. For politics, in which there seems to be no place for the singular, it would be an illegitimate step to make the opposite move: from the 'for all' to that of the 'only for one'. Indeed, if we follow the received idea, what makes their encounter impossible is a double interdiction of the passage from the register of the singular to that of the multiple.

We propose to reverse this perspective and to examine under what circumstances the relation between these two domains, that of the 'for all' and that of the 'irreducible singularity', can be established. Hence, the very fact of posing the question of heterogeneity or otherness in politics and psychoanalysis requires the construction of a site, a scene for their encounter. Our guide in this pivoting of perspective will be Lacan. We will refer, more specifically, to his *Television,* in which he presents both his critique of politics as a way out of capitalism and the task of psychoanalysis in a universe governed by the capitalist discourse. Consider the following remark: 'The more saints, the more laughter; that's my principle, to wit, the way out of capitalist discourse – which would not constitute progress, if it happens only for some' (Lacan 1990: 16).

First of all it should be noted that to propose psychoanalysis as a solution, as the way out of capitalism, is only possible in the very specific circumstance of the collapse of the belief in the emancipatory power of politics to face the growing impasses of the way out of capitalism, i.e. of a regime of mastery that yields to the generalized metonymization. As a consequence, psychoanalysis, according to Lacan, is confronted with a paradoxical task: to find a way out of a discourse which is considered to be limitless, 'eternal', a discourse which precisely knows of no way out. It could, then, be said that, for Lacan, only psychoanalysis is capable of inventing, forcing even, in the situation of an impasse, a radically new solution: that of an immanent way out.

However, it is important to consider how psychoanalysis can emerge as a way out of the capitalist discourse. It is true that Lacan harboured some ambitions

32 Jelica Šumič

concerning the 'duty incumbent upon [psychoanalysis] in our world' (Lacan 1990: 97), as he puts it. From this point of view, it seems that psychoanalysis, according to Lacan, is capable of succeeding there where the politics of emancipation failed: to find a way out of the growing impasses of capitalism. Indeed, one is tempted to say that psychoanalysis emerges as a tenant-lieu, placeholder of the impossible, absent emancipatory politics.

Politics of symptom or politics of love?

What could, then, be a politics proper to psychoanalysis? Indeed, what politics might result from psychoanalysis? Actually, there exist two interpretations of the politics of psychoanalysis respectively termed the 'politics of symptom' and the 'politics of love'. Both of these interpretations, which have their partisans and critiques, are to a certain extent grounded in Lacan's work, in particular since they both take as their point of departure the irreducible heterogeneity inherent in the subject, a kernel of the real resisting the dominant social bond. There is something in the subject that makes him/her other, unlike any other in the community to which he or she belongs. While both of these paradigms refuse the antinomic relation between politics and psychoanalysis, they nevertheless differ in outlining the crucial stake of such a politics proper to psychoanalysis.

According to first reading, the politics of psychoanalysis can only be a 'politics of symptom'. Setting out from the assumption that politics and psychoanalysis are in an antinomic relation, the task of psychoanalysis is to examine contemporary modes of the social bond from the viewpoint of the symptom (Soler 1998: 71–76). The symptom here is conceived as a specific fixing of jouissance proper to each subject, in a word, as that which in the subject resists universalization. The central stake in such a politics of symptom is therefore to uncover the tension between the social bond and the symptom. More particularly, to reveal the incompatibility between the allowed and the forbidden jouissance. Thus, there is, on one hand, jouissance, such as is prescribed by the social Other, and, on the other hand, there is the symptom as a mode of enjoyment, particular to each subject and which is as such irreducible to the standard jouissance. As a result, the jouissance under the guise of the symptom cannot but present a threat to the social bond.

There are two structural consequences that follow from the politics of symptom. The first is that the conclusion to be drawn from the conflict of these two jouissances is that nothing can 'hold together' subjects-symptoms, nothing can bring together these irreducible modes of jouissance. From this perspective then, jouissance can be seen as the impossible-real of the social bond. Jouissance, as a symptom, is that irreducible otherness or heterogeneity on which no collective logics can be grounded. The ultimate lesson to be drawn from psychoanalysis insofar as it ventures into the domain of the social and politics is then the affirmation of what we would propose to call the 'solipsism of enjoyment'.

There is however a problem that such a 'politics of symptom' cannot solve to the extent that the hegemonic social bond today, the discourse of the capitalist,

Politics and Psychoanalysis in Times of the Inexistent Other **33**

brings into question what is supposed to be the capital issue of this politics, namely, the tension between the prescribed, standard jouissance, and jouissance provided by the symptom. Thus the politics of symptom may well have been applicable in Freud's time. Today, however, there seems to be no place for such a politics of symptom precisely to the extent that the capitalist discourse itself dissolves the tension between the singular and the universal. Capitalism is namely an exceptional social bond. Capitalism, in a sense, could be seen as an aberration among social bonds, since it realizes what in all the other social bonds seems to be impossible: its compatibility with enjoyment. The capitalist discourse is namely a social bond, which does not demand that the subject sacrifice his or her enjoyment. Rather, the capitalist social bond is a bond that adapts itself to the 'trifle', the private enjoyment of everybody. It is offered as an apparatus that is able to provide the subject with the lacking enjoyment. So, from this perspective, it could be argued that, not only does enjoyment not threaten the capitalist social bond, but, on the contrary, capitalism presents itself as a discourse in which the solipsistic 'democracy of enjoyment' rules, a democracy whose sole principle is *primum vivere*: one lives for enjoyment. This is because, the capitalist discourse, by situating in the place of the agent, the barred subject that is caught in an infinite quest for the missing signifier, the one which could put an end to the subject's erring, exploits the lack it installs in the subject as a way of reproducing itself. The cunning of the capitalist discourse then consists in exploiting the structure of the desiring subject: by manipulating his or her desire, i.e. by reducing it to demand, the capitalist discourse creates the illusion that, thanks to scientific development and the market, it is able to provide the subject with the complement of being that he or she is lacking by transforming the subject's lack of being into the lack of having. In this view, 'having' is considered to be a cure for the lack of being of the subject of the capitalist discourse. One could then say that, being nothing but the embodiment of the lack of being, the subject of the capitalist discourse can only be completed by products thrown on the market.

This is why Lacan named the subject of the capitalist discourse, 'the proletarian', this being a name for the subject that is inseparable from that which constitutes the complement of his or her being: his or her *plus-de-jouir*, surplus-enjoyment, the object *a*. As the dominant structure of social relations, the capitalist discourse provides the conditions for an obscure subjectivation, one that depends on the conversion of the surplus-value, that is to say, any product thrown on the market, into the surplus-enjoyment, the cause of the subject's desire. Indeed, it is precisely this indistinction between the surplus-value and the surplus-enjoyment which makes it possible for the capitalist production of 'whatever objects' to capture, indeed, to enslave the subject's desire, to sustain its eternal 'this is not it'. It could be claimed that capitalism, insofar as it promotes a sort of an autistic enjoyment, promotes at the same time a particular communal figure, that which Jean-Claude Milner (1983) termed a 'paradoxical class', a collective in which its members are joined or held together by that which disjoins them, namely, their idiosyncratic mode of enjoyment. What is thus placed in question is precisely the social bond. Or to be more precise, the social bond that exists today is one presented under the form of dispersed individuals that is but another name for the dissolution of all links or unbinding of all bonds. For something has radically changed with the globalization of the capitalist discourse. Globalization, in this respect, does not mean simply that nothing is left in its place, as no anchoring seems to be capable of controlling the unending movement of displacements and substitutions. Indeed, in the current space of discursivity, the notion of place itself is strangely out of place. What is more, with the category of place thus rendered inoperative, it is one of the key categories of emancipatory politics, the notion of lack, necessary to the subject for it to sustain itself in the symbolic Other, which as a result becomes obsolete.

Both features of the capitalist discourse, disidentification and the replacement of prohibition of enjoyment with commanded enjoyment through the regulation of desire, could, then, be brought together in a single syntagm of the generalized proletarization. In the words of Lacan, 'there is but one social symptom: every individual is in effect a proletarian, that is to say that no discourse is at the disposal of the individual by means of which a social bond could be established' (Lacan 2011: 18). Ironically, proletarization remains the symptom of contemporary society. Only, this proletarization is of a particular kind, one that, by being articulated with the intrinsically metonymic nature of the capitalist discourse, has lost all its subversive effectiveness, its entire revolutionary potential. Summarizing in this way Lacan's thesis on the contemporary proletarization is to shed some light on the impasses of the present generalized 'metonymization', operated by the capitalist discourse, in order to identify the difficulties of contemporary subjectivity in finding a way out of the present impasse. For the inexistence of the Other, contrary to what might be expected or hoped for, is not in and of itself a liberating factor for the subject, it is not experienced by the subject as liberation from the capture which the Other effects upon him/her. Quite the contrary: in the absence of the master signifier which would render a given situation 'readable', the subject remains a prisoner, not of the Other that exists, but of the inexistent Other, better put perhaps, of the inexistence of the Other.

The second paradigm of the politics of psychoanalysis is to a certain extent the reversal of the first one. What is at issue here is to show that enjoyment, precisely as an irreducible heterogeneity or otherness, is the point at which psychoanalysis encounters politics. Far from precluding all social link, enjoyment appears rather as a foundation for that politics which could be termed, for lack of a better term, the 'politics of love'. At issue in this paradigm is love for one's neighbour rather than the solipsism of enjoyment. The texts of reference here are, of course, Freud's *Civilisation and its Discontents* and Lacan's *The Ethics of Psychoanalysis*, two texts having as their point of departure the presupposition that what constitutes the otherness of the Other is enjoyment insofar as it is evil. For Freud, the evil jouissance I suspect in the Other justifies my reservations with regard to him, the reason why the Other does not deserve my love since I can give my love only to the one who is like me. For Lacan, on the contrary, it is precisely this evil jouissance that the Other and I have in common. This irreducible otherness of jouissance is what joins us together. And this is why Lacan can claim 'that fundamental evil which dwells within this neighbour [...] it also dwells in me' (Lacan 1992: 186). This is why Lacan in his *Kant with Sade* reproaches Sade, but in an indirect way Freud too, with the misrecognition of his own enjoyment. Sade, just like Freud, Lacan says '*refuses to be my neighbour*'.

The reason for this refusal, according to Lacan, is that 'Sade does not have neighbourly enough relations with his own malice [*méchanceté*] to encounter his neighbour in it' (Lacan 2006: 666), backing away, just like Freud, from the Christian commandment: '*Thou shalt love thy neighbour like thyself*'. Nothing then, to follow Lacan, is closer to me than that which I try desperately to avoid, this nameless, evil enjoyment that I encounter not only in the Other but in me too. On the other hand, it is precisely because, like myself, the Other is in the same position in relation to that which Lacan calls '*la chose la plus proche*', that thing which is closest to me being of course jouissance, that I can love the Other. What is difficult to accept here is not the idea that the Other is unfathomable, enigmatic, wholly other. What is unthinkable is this sameness that the Other and me share at the level of enjoyment. That which radically separates me from the Other, his or her absolute particular enjoyment, is at the same time that which we have in common: this otherness in me. Paradoxically, enjoyment as this irreducible otherness is the foundation of sameness.

The crucial point of Lacan's interpretation of the love of one's neighbour, far from a postmodernist exaltation of the irreducible otherness of the Other, is designated here as a strategy for handling this irreducible otherness in me. Love, insofar as it is beyond all transaction, this non-reciprocal love, in the final analysis, as a renouncement of any direct equivalent to that which I give, all promise of payment, this wholly unmotivated, gratuitous love, love as a gift without recompense, is what Lacan proposes as a solution to the impasse caused by the encounter with the enjoyment in the Other, with the otherness of the Other. This 'real' love – real in the sense that it demands the impossible – to love somebody for that which provokes his hatred and aggression and turns them against me – is a possible strategy for handling that otherness in me, for neutralizing it. From the perspective of the second interpretation of the politics of psychoanalysis, only psychoanalysis, by bringing to light enjoyment as the irreducible singularity common to me and my neighbour, as a paradoxical sameness in otherness, can elaborate a theory of the subject appropriate to democracy. Indeed, a theory of subject that is necessary to democracy. It is precisely at this point that the political implications of love of thy neighbour can be drawn out. Love of thy neighbour as a way of dealing with enjoyment is precisely what Derrida perceives as a chance for democracy. According to Derrida, 'there is no democracy without respect for irreducible singularity or alterity'. But, Derrida adds, 'there is no democracy without a "community of friends", without the calculation of majorities, without identifiable, stabilizable, representable subjects, all equal' (Derrida 1997: 22).

A non-reciprocal love for thy neighbour detached from all usefulness is that terrain at which politics and psychoanalysis necessarily meet. Indeed, such a love can be seen as a model for a non-segregationist community. This is because the indifference to the useful, which situates love beyond all altruist utilitarianism, signifies a radical mutation in the field of politics, a mutation that concerns precisely the status of the Other. For the break with the useful characterizes not only love and friendship, but also hatred, as Freud himself points out in his *Civilisation,* because my enemy is not interested in the profit he might gain from the wrongdoing he inflicts on me. This leads to a somewhat unexpected conclusion: if the refusal of usefulness, the indifference as to the possible gain, is what friend and enemy have in common, then the distinction between the friend and the enemy disappears.

The crucial question here is of course: what consequences can be drawn from the disappearance of the demarcation line between friend and foe, in the final analysis, from the collapse of the figure of the Other for the social bond and, consequently, for politics? This is precisely the central issue in Schmitt's theory of politics. As is well known, Schmitt situated the friend/enemy discrimination at the core of politics,[3] signalling in this way that the moment of hatred is essential in politics. The intrinsic complicity between enmity and the Other, more precisely, between the identification of the Other and the domestication of hatred, is embedded, according to Schmitt's fundamental thesis, in the very constitution of a (homogeneous) political community. In Schmitt's view, a mere agglomeration of fellow men can never bring about the desired homogeneity as the recognizable similarity requires the existence of an instance of dissimilarity, an element of otherness or heterogeneity which, at the level of the relationship between mere fellow men, is precisely lacking. At this level, not only is the other not an Other at all, since it is coupled with the ego, in a relation which is always reflexive, interchangeable, but this specular relation itself is governed by a lethal alteration: if it is you, I am not, and if it is me, it is you who are not.[4] In deconstructive terms: in the absence of some radical otherness which makes it possible for individuals grouped together to identify themselves as being in some crucial aspects similar and can thus constitute themselves into a community, the unleashing of a pure logic of identity or equivalence would, instead of bringing about a reconciliation and unification, lead to a total destruction depicted in the Hobbesian fantasy of the state of nature.

Schmitt's greatest merit is to have pointed out the intrinsic complicity between enmity and the Other. If we are to follow Schmitt, for homogeneity to be established at all, the existence of an instance of dissimilarity, an element of otherness is required, that which at the level of the relationship between *semblables*, fellow men, is precisely lacking. Schmitt's introduction of the friend/enemy distinction can thus be understood as an attempt at diffusing the hatred that the fellow men would otherwise vent against one another through the 'exportation' of this inherent aggressivity elsewhere. This externalization of the Other that prevents the slipping into cruelty and total destruction is possible only on the condition that the relationship of enmity is purified of all passion and affects.[5] Hence it is not simply the 'we/they' distinction that would in itself render the checking of the excess of hostility, the measureless violence, possible, but the symbolization of enmity, involving a distance, construction of a remote, external Other, and rules that must be respected by all. Viewed from this perspective, the role of the Other is pacifying.

On the other hand, however, hatred is never completely domesticated. As Schmitt himself is forced to acknowledge, the establishment of such a constitutive beyond is always incomplete since the Other is always contaminated by another figure of the enemy, within the community. This other Other, by being unlocable, indiscernible, corrodes the communal being, threatens the community with its dissolution. From the very start, there are then two figures of the enemy and not simply one: the symbolic enemy that Schmitt calls the political enemy. And there is yet another figure of the Other: the 'real' or internal enemy. Whereas the first figure is essentially pacifying, the second activates the absolute destructive hostility leading to a permanent civil war.

This distinction between the 'good' external, i.e. political, enemy, and the 'bad' unfathomable internal enemy, is patently undermined in present conjecture of globalization. This is because today we are facing a situation in which, strictly speaking, there is no instance that could play the role of the 'constitutive outside', no instance of the 'they' that would render possible the construction of the 'we', since both 'we' and 'they' are always already 'in', included. Hence, it is essential to realize how contemporary otherlessness, paradoxically, opens up the possibility for the emergence of a hatred that nothing can appease.[6] The proliferation of the hated real others in an era of the non-existence of the Other is necessary since – once the figure of the external, political, 'symbolic' enemy is eliminated, once everybody is included – anybody, myself included, can occupy the place of the radical, real other. For what characterizes present-day globalization is namely the denial of all exclusion. The exclusion of the exclusion did not, however, make the exclusion disappear; it has only become internal and thus invisible. It is precisely because the frontier between the included and the excluded is ultimately invisible, as there is no sign, no attribute that would help me determine who is 'in' and who is 'out', that, in a universe without beyond or limit, a universe that knows of no exception, anybody can, in principle, find himself/herself occupying the place of the real, dehumanized Other. This construction of the 'altogether others' in a constellation in which no Other is possible bears some similarities to the movement designated by Lacan as barbarism of all human assimilation. According to Lacan, in order for the subject to attain his/her identity, s/he is compelled to precipitate to her/his self-affirmation: 'I declare myself to be a man for fear of being convinced by men that I am not a man' (Lacan 2006: 174).

This is precisely the reason that the 'politics of love', a politics which aims at the impossible articulation of the otherness and the social bond, the impossibility of counting and the necessity of counting, remains forever contained within the perspective of the promise, it is forever 'to come', '*à venir*', never in the here and now. In other words, such a politics cannot provide us with a satisfactory answer to the question: how is it possible to justify the legitimacy of the move from the singular to the universal? The politics of love is satisfied with the ceaseless affirmation of the singularity of otherness. That is why it cannot indicate a way in which this singularity could be asserted politically, i.e. a way of politicizing the singularity of the singular by introducing another principle of counting: that of counting the uncounted, the uncountable. Ultimately, what such a conception of politics in terms of love misrecognizes is precisely the irreducible gap between counting and the impossibility of counting as the sole site in which contemporary politics of emancipation can be situated. We propose to call the politics of emancipation that politics that organizes a confrontation between counting and the impossibility of counting, an operation that reveals the constitutive impossibility of institutionalizing a collectivity 'for all', a collectivity in which what is at stake is precisely the predicate determining the belonging to the community, the line of demarcation between inside/outside, us/them.

Lacanian School and its politics

It is precisely at this point that contemporary politics of emancipation encounters psychoanalysis. We would argue that psychoanalysis can show us how it is possible, in spite of everything, to think and to practise a collectivity 'for all' as an open, non-segregationist community. For the great merit of Lacan's proposed solution in *Television* consists in recasting the question of the universal, of the 'for all', from the perspective of the not-all, of the infinite. Clearly, the solution proposed by Lacan is a paradoxical solution since we are dealing here with an interior way out, if we may say so, a paradoxical way out which implies no transgression, no forcing of a barrier, since there is no barrier separating the outside and the inside. In view of this interior way out, everything depends, of course, on the way in which we understand Lacan's statement: 'It would not constitute progress if it happens only to some'. Does the expression 'not only for some' imply 'for all' or not? Our claim is that it points in the direction of the 'for all'. To be sure, this is a very peculiar 'for all' since, in the not-all, that is, in an infinite universe in which this 'for all' is situated, it is impossible to state the universality of the predicate.

To fully grasp the political implications of this articulation of the 'for all' to the 'not-all', we must distinguish between two forms of the not-all: the not-all of incompleteness and the not-all of inconsistence. The first not-all is what we usually refer to as the all or the universal, to use its traditional name. This category designates a unity constructed through the limitation, or, more precisely, through the exclusion of an exception. And there is another form of the not-all, the inconsistent not-all which can, paradoxically, be obtained, not through the exclusion of the exception, but through its inclusion. By the very fact of subtracting the exception from a series we render it limitless, non-totalizable. Now, what exactly is the status of the exception seen from the perspective of the not-all? We cannot simply state: there is no exception to the universal function, for instance, 'All A are B'. We should rather say: if there is an exception we don't know where to find it. From the perspective of the not-all, the exception is seen as being erratic. It is everywhere, yet nowhere to be located. It could then be said that the exception is generalized. We could also say, for instance, that we are all exceptions.

The first figure of the not-all is subtractive or segregationist, because the price to be paid for the constitution of the 'all' is the exclusion of those who do not possess the required predicate. A 'true' not-all is non-segregationist because, from the outset, all exception is postulated as being undecidable, indeterminable. Consequently, such a not-all is open, inclusive, in a word: 'for all'. We can see here a solution to the impasse that Schmitt confronted: how to conceive of a community when there is no Other from which the members of the community are to be distinguished. The politics of the non-segregationist not-all is symmetrically inversed compared to that proposed by Schmitt: it consists in including the Other rather than in excluding the Other. Not of course in the name of respecting the rights of otherness, openness to the Other, but in order to bring into question the communal identity, the supposed homogeneity of the group. It is this second aspect of the not-all, one in which it is impossible to determine the existence of a totalizing exception, that can best be illustrated by the politics inherent to Lacan's School: *École de la Cause*. For there is yet another way of considering a politics proper to psychoanalysis, one that is capable of dealing with the problem of the structural non-totalization.

A shift in Lacan's reflections on politics in general and the functioning of a psychoanalytical institution whose principal task would be the transmission of a radically singular experience such as can only be encountered in an analysis, is marked by a paradoxical thesis according to which: a group is the real, that is, according to Lacan's vocabulary, a radical impossibility. The real of the group is that which is precisely at stake in the foundation of his School: *École de la Cause*, School of the Cause. If we propose to consider Lacan's thesis about the real of the group seriously, this is precisely because Lacan, while insisting on the impossibility of the group, by founding his School nevertheless succeeded in demonstrating that there is a way of dealing with this impossibility.

Lacan's solution to the impasse of collectivity consists in opening his School 'to everybody', which is to say 'to anybody'. Setting out from the assumption that there is absolutely nothing to define the analyst, no pre-given predicate or property on which his identification could be grounded, the only viable solution is one that takes into account precisely this impossibility of determining a predicate that would be proper to the (Lacanian) analyst. The solution is then none other than to call on all those who are willing to work in the Freudian field. By inviting to his School anybody, without any qualification, Lacan created an open, empty space destined to be inhabited only by a special kind of work, the work of the 'determined workers',[7] be it analysis or not, as he puts it.

As the expression 'determined worker' suggests, it is the work that decides the belonging to the collectivity. This also implies that this work cannot be standardized. The work to be done is by definition indeterminable since it cannot take place unless there is transference to a cause at hand. This expression, 'determined worker', emphasizes the importance of the fidelity to a cause, the willingness of everyone involved in it to risk himself or herself and his or her desire in the pursuit of what is ultimately unknowable. All that the work to be done by everybody requires, and that despite the fact that neither its quality nor quantity can be prescribed, is a new relation to the cause; in the final analysis: the task that everybody is confronted with is that of inventing psychoanalysis. It is precisely in this sense that in Lacan's School it is impossible to distinguish good, determined workers from idlers. Rather, School of the Cause is to be seen as a collectivity that is profoundly non-segregationist. It is non-segregationist because the presence of an element allegedly heterogeneous to the collectivity, a non-analyst, is not only tolerated but required in order to bringing into question the predicate: to be an analyst.[8]

This Lacanian collectivity 'for all' can serve us as a model for the anonymous egalitarianism required by contemporary emancipatory politics insofar as it renders visible the functioning of both universalist, although incompatible logics: the one that is grounded in the exception, and the other that takes as its departure point the axiom according to which: 'there is none who has not got it', namely the capacity to be a determined worker. The paradox of the politics implied in Lacan's School resides namely in the fact that it is situated precisely at the level of that which cannot be represented nor counted as it is what is left after the completion of identification. In short, it is situated at the level of the pure, whatever singularity. Yet it is precisely this irreducible singularity that Lacan's School proposes to take into account, to 'count'. For the ambition of Lacan's School is not only to find a way out of the traps of identification. It is above all to find, to force, a passage there where there is a non-passage, an impasse, a deadlock, of the group. What is at stake in the foundation of the *École de la Cause* is a paradoxical project: to universalize the singular.

We can see now that what is at stake in the distinction of the two logics of the universal is eminently political. At issue here is the way in which the logics of the not-all is set to work, made operational there where the segregationist logics operate, there where the exclusion, be it visible or invisible, reigns. From this perspective, Lacan's School can be viewed as a special collectivity 'for all', that of workers, a collectivity, which implies the disidentification, practised at the level of the group: everyone ought to become anyone, whatever singularity. This is not to say that one discovers oneself as already being such. On the contrary, one only becomes such: anyone. This is a subjective transformation that everyone has to accomplish for him or herself. This is because the collectivity 'for all' is ultimately grounded in a cause that sets us to work. In this sense it includes in the real a radical novelty: a paradoxical collectivity that is at once not-all, non-totalizable, and yet at the same time 'for all', offered to all.

Such a collectivity 'for all' that is grounded in the real of the group, which is to say in its impossibility, is certainly a forcing: a forcing of saying, because what characterizes such a collectivity is precisely the advent of an allegedly mute, uncounted, invisible instance that starts to speak out and, in so doing, asserts its presence: 'We are here'. But it is also a forcing of all social order and its counting. What is at issue here is not to correct the miscount made by the social order by including those who were left outside, those who did not count, but rather to accomplish, in view of those uncounted and counted alike, the operation of transfinitization, an operation that aims at constituting an open, non-segregationist 'for all'. How many members will count this 'for all' of the not-all? It doesn't matter. It is not about the numbers. On the condition, however, that it remains, just like a Cantorian aleph, indifferent, impervious, to both all addition and all subtraction. So this paradoxical interior way out is nothing other than the constitution of a local, temporary, provisional collectivity 'for all'. It is not to remain forever. All that remains forever, ultimately, is its name and its call.

Notes

1 Freud was indeed the first to show, in his famous *Group Psychology and the Analysis of the Ego*, that for there to be a group, it is necessary that its members are hooked up to the same identificatory signifier.
2 Here we refer, of course, to a notion elaborated in Agamben (1993).
3 'The specific political distinction, to which political action and notions can be reduced is the distinction between friend and enemy' (Schmitt 1996: 26).
4 See Lacan 1988: 169.
5 'The enemy is solely the *public* enemy, because everything that has a relationship to such a collectivity of men, particularly to a whole nation, becomes *public* by virtue of such a relationship. The enemy is *hostis*, not *inimicus* in the broader sense (...) The enemy in the political sense need not be hated personally, and in the private sphere only does it make sense to love one's enemy, that is one's adversary' (Schmitt 1996: 28–29).
6 It should be noted, however, that it is not only due to the changed circumstances that the establishing of the instance of the Other in the present-day constellation of globalization proves to be impossible, thus rendering the relevance of Schmitt's concept of the political questionable. Rather the friend/enemy binary is from the outset self-de(con)structive. Significant in this respect is the conflation of two lines of Schmitt's argument: on the one hand, the identification of the enemy is grounded in a dialectic of the reciprocal recognition since, for Schmitt, one can only recognize one's enemy by being simultaneously recognized as his/her enemy. However, by tacitly assuming that nothing is more proper to self than one's own enemy, indeed, by acknowledging that the enemy is *interior intimo meo*, to say it with Saint Augustine, that is, 'more interior than my innermost being', Schmitt is forced to admit that the line of demarcation between the self and one's own enemy remains radically undecidable. Thus to the question, 'Whom may I finally recognize as my enemy?' Schmitt can provide the only appropriate answer, namely: 'Only myself. Or my brother' (Schmitt 1987: 89).
7 This expression was introduced by Lacan in his 'Founding Act' (see Lacan 1990: 100).
8 See, for instance, Lacan 2001: 270, 272.

Bibliography

Agamben, Giorgio (1993) *The Coming Community*. Minneapolis: University of Minnesota Press.
Derrida, Jacques (1997) *Politics of Friendship*. London: Verso.
Lacan, Jacques (1966–67) *La logique du fantasme*, unpublished seminar.
Lacan, Jacques (1990) *Television*, A *Challenge to the Psychoanalytic Establishment*. New York: W. W. Norton.
Lacan, Jacques (1991) *Seminar, Book II, The Ego in Freud's Theory and in the Technique of Psychoanalysis. 1954–55*. New York: W. W. Norton.
Lacan, Jacques (1992) *Seminar, Book VII, The Ethics of Psychoanalysis*. London: W. W. Norton.

42 Jelica Šumič

Lacan, Jacques (2001) *Autres écrits*, Paris: Seuil.

Lacan, Jacques (2006) *Écrits*. New York: W. W. Norton.

Lacan, Jacques (2007) *Seminar, Book XVII, The Other Side of Psychoanalysis*. New York: W. W. Norton.

Lacan, Jacques (2011) 'La troisième', in *La cause freudienne*, 79.

Milner, Jean-Claude (1983) *Les noms indistincs*. Paris: Seuil.

Schmitt, Karl (1987) *Ex Captivitate Salus, Erfahrungen der Zeit 1945/47*. Pletenberg: Peiran.

Schmitt, Karl (1996) *The Concept of the Political*. Chicago, IL: Chicago University Press.

Soler, Colette (1998). 'La politique du symptôme', in *Quarto*, 65.

PART 2

Lacanian psychoanalysis and the political

PART 2.1

Oedipus and the intricacy of language and sexuality

3

'FREUD'S DREAM'?

Lacan and Oedipus[+]

Philippe Van Haute

RADBOUD UNIVERSITY, NIJMEGEN, THE NETHERLANDS

Tomas Geyskens

BELGIAN SCHOOL FOR PSYCHOANALYSIS

Introduction

In his seminar on *The Other Side of Psychoanalysis* – and more particularly in the chapter entitled 'Beyond the Oedipus complex' (Lacan 2007 [1969–70]: 87–140) – Lacan mercilessly criticizes the Freudian Oedipus complex. In this seminar, he calls the Oedipus complex – one of psychoanalytic theory's major clinical concepts – 'useless' in the clinical setting (Lacan 2007 [1969–70]: 113). He also notes his surprise that this discovery was not made before (ibid.). Lacan writes that clinical experience should have shown psychoanalysts that the Freudian Oedipus complex is unable to adequately account for the relationship between the hysterical patient and the mythical master figure from whom she expects an answer to all her questions. Hysterical patients themselves continuously set up this master figure and seek his counsel and advice … until he fails.[1] One can think here of the famous Dora-case that in many respects plays a paradigmatic role in Freud's theory of hysteria (Freud 1905). Dora categorically dismisses Freud's interventions, exposing in this way the inadequacy of his knowledge. In this regard, Lacan says that the hysterical patient incarnates the truth of the master that she herself sets up, namely, that he falls short structurally and is inadequate.[2] Since the hysterical patient is not herself aware of this, she has no other choice but to stage this truth time and again.

In order to fully comprehend this claim, we must first take a step back. In *The Other Side of Psychoanalysis* Lacan calls the Oedipus complex 'Freud's dream' (Lacan 2007 [1969–70]: 135, 159), by which he means that Freud's formulation of this complex should be interpreted like any other dream. More specifically, it means that the theoretical articulation of this complex reveals, in a disguised way, something about Freud's own unconscious desire[3] that simultaneously obscures his vision of the truth of the Oedipus myth. According to Lacan, this truth is the structural and inevitable castration of the master, which is an effect of language.[4]

48 Philippe Van Haute and Tomas Geyskens

This truth is lost in Freud's interpretation of the myth (Lacan 2007 [1969–70]: 130). The Freudian myth about a primal father who owns all the women and is murdered by his jealous sons should also be interpreted in such a way that its latent content can surface. As in the Freudian reading of Sophocles' Oedipus, the theme of the death of the father and patricide in this myth of the murder of the father also hides the structural and insurmountable character of castration. Had Freud not allowed himself to become blinded by the neurotic problems of his patients in which the murder of the father unconsciously played a crucial role, he might have realized that what is at stake in the Oedipus myth is the truth and impossibility of ever completely merging this truth with knowledge (Lacan 2007 [1969–70]: 134–35). According to Lacan, Oedipus personifies the master figure and his castration.

Lacan's interpretation and critique of the Freudian Oedipus complex has potentially important consequences for a psychoanalytically inspired philosophical understanding of the status of social reality. It could be read as a first step in overcoming the conservative social consequences of the central role of the Oedipus complex that also characterized Lacan's early work. Indeed, Freud's supposedly historical account of the murder of a primal father by his jealous sons that explains the origin of the law and of human society, implies that the structure of this society is essentially patriarchical. However, when the reference to the primal father is nothing but a neurotic phantasy – when there is, as we will see, no Other of the Other (the master is essentially castrated) – doesn't this mean that our (sexual) identities are 'constructed' in the Other without there being an (Oedipal) rule to judge their adequacy (e.g. with the supposed essence of the symbolic or of nature)? The idea that there is 'no Other of the Other' can be read as a crucial element in the critique of the essentialist interpretation of social and political reality that hounds psychoanalytic theory.

I begin by discussing Lacan's idea that the Oedipus complex is 'Freud's dream' and proceed to analyse Lacan's re-interpretation of the Oedipus myth. In so doing I suggest that Lacan's theory of the four discourses replaces the structural role of the Oedipus complex. Next I illustrate the clinical relevance – especially as it concerns an understanding of hysteria – of this new theory through a short commentary on Lacan's remarks concerning the Dora-case in *The Other Side of Psychoanalysis*. This illustration makes clear how far this theory takes us from Freud's text. Finally, I make some suggestions about the political and social relevance of the chapter from *The Other Side*.

1 Freud reads Sophocles[5]

Freud's first reference to the Oedipal problematic occurs in his letters to Fliess (Freud 1986). He writes that he discovered in himself the infatuation with the mother and the rivalry with the father. He further adds that this theme characterizes everybody's childhood, which explains why the Oedipus myth continues to make such a strong impression on us. At one time in our youth all of us were little Oedipuses. Even if we have repressed these infantile wishes, they remain

Freud's Dream? Lacan and Oedipus **49**

active in our unconscious. This makes possible our remaining under the spell of King Oedipus' fate, despite our intellectual reservations against fate's determining our existence (Freud 1986: 272).

Freud returns to this Oedipal theme in *The Interpretation of Dreams* in his chapter concerning typical dreams (Freud 1900, from p. 248 onwards). He devotes a number of pages to dreams about the death of loved ones, not only siblings but also parents, specifically, a parent of the opposite sex than that of the dreamer (Freud 1900: 256). He also connects these dreams with infantile Oedipal desires repressed after puberty but that remain active in the unconscious.

Freud refers to the Oedipus myth and Sophocles' tragedy *Oedipus Rex* to support this argument. He writes that '... a legend ... has come down to us from classical antiquity: a legend whose profound and universal power to move can only be understood if the hypothesis I have put forward in regard to the psychology of children has an equally universal validity' (Freud 1900: 261). Freud rejects the belief that the legend's tragic effect lies in the contrast between the almighty will of the gods on the one hand and humankind's inability to escape the evils that threaten it on the other (Freud 1900: 262). On the contrary, he writes that 'King Oedipus, who slew his father Laius and married his mother Jocasta, merely shows us the fulfilment of our own childhood wishes' (Freud 1900: 262). Freud finds support for this argument in Sophocles' work as well. Jocasta herself mentions to Oedipus a dream dreamt by many people: 'Many a man ere now in dreams hath lain with her who bare him. He hath least annoy who with such omens troubleth not his mind' (line 982ff., cited in Freud 1900: 264). Freud says this dream is but the complement to that regarding the death of the father. Hence, the Oedipus fable is nothing more than our phantasy's reaction to both of these typical dreams (Freud 1900: 264). Since these dreams are unacceptable to adults, this fable must also incorporate fright and self-punishment (Freud 1900: 264). Oedipus gouges out his own eyes when he realizes what he has done.

Notice that in his discussion, Freud fails to draw a distinction between the Oedipus myth, with its different versions, and Sophocles' tragedy (Lacan 2007 [1969–70]: 131). Neither does he question the political or cultural context in which this legend was created. Freud believes reference to the two childhood desires just mentioned provides a sufficient understanding of this tragedy. He limits himself to the most manifest level of the Oedipus myth and its meaning (Lacan 2007 [1969–70]: 130ff.). At this level he most definitely has a point: Oedipus commits two crimes that Freud believes constitute the core of the Oedipus legend, of which he wants to understand the lasting impact. Lacan nevertheless notes that this limitation of the legend's meaning at the same time denudes it of all tragic effect (Lacan 2007 [1969–70]: 131, 134).

One can indeed find in Sophocles' text, as Freud justly remarks, an explicit reference to the desire to sleep with the mother, but desire to kill the father is a much more complicated issue. First, Freud introduces this desire in a chapter about typical dreams that contain references to the death of loved ones, but none that refer to patricide. There is an unexplained gap in his argument here. Nor is this theme as obviously evident in the tragedy of Sophocles as Freud claims it to be. It is true that Laius' murder gives Oedipus access to his mother, but Oedipus murders his father without realizing it. Moreover his father is only his father in the strictly biological sense. Laius only provides the seed from which Oedipus is conceived (Lacan 2007 [1969–70]: 148).

2 A psychoanalytical origin tale: *Totem and Taboo* [6]

The Freudian Oedipus complex cannot be separated from the myth regarding society's origin that Freud himself designs in *Totem and Taboo* (Freud 1913). 'Origin myth' is not in fact a fitting description of the tale Freud tells in that work. He believes the tale describes *the real origin* of human society and history. It has often been argued that the theory of the Oedipus complex is a continuation of this 'origin myth' since this myth can be understood as historical justification for this complex. However, Lacan remarks that it is indeed strange that no one has been concerned with the fact that the content of *Totem and Taboo* differs strongly from Freud's characteristic reference to the tragedy of Sophocles (Lacan 2007 [1969–70]: 131). The role and meaning of the (murder of the) father are indeed central in both the classic Oedipus complex and the origin myth from *Totem and Taboo*, but this role is different in the two cases. In the classic Oedipus complex, the law of the father prohibits intercourse with the mother and, vice versa, Oedipus must first kill his father to sleep with his mother (Lacan 2007 [1969–70]: 139). Here patricide provides access to an incestuous pleasure.[7]

Matters are completely different in *Totem and Taboo*.[8] In that work, Freud conceptualizes a myth about humanity's origin in which the starting point is less the law than an unlimited enjoyment – of the father this time. Freud was himself absolutely convinced of its truth. The original father figure, writes Freud, owned all the women, denying his sons access in the process. This is the reason he is murdered. The sons hoped patricide would ensure their participation in the father's unlimited pleasure. But the murder does not have its intended effect. Following his murder, the sons continue feeling obliged to the father's laws. Freud writes that their behaviour is guided by guilt. They are obedient *in a differed way*, not so much to avoid 'a war of all against all' for ownership of the women, but because they feel guilty about the murder. The sons not only feared and hated their father, they also loved him. In this way, the power of the 'dead father' can be greater than that of the living father (Freud 1913: 149). Hence, this murder results not in access to an incestuous and unlimited pleasure but rather submission to the law of the father.

3 Freud's dream

I already mentioned that Lacan believes the Freudian Oedipus complex should be read as a dream of Freud's. His thoughts on the matter should be interpreted like those of any other dream. We must first ask ourselves: where does Freud's patricidal theme stem from? In this context Lacan refers to the preface of *The*

Interpretation of Dreams (Lacan 2007 [1969–70]: 141), where Freud writes the following regarding this book's significance to him: 'It was, I found, a portion of my own self-analysis, my reaction to my father's death – that is to say, the most important event, the most poignant loss, of a man's life' (Freud 1900: xxvi). We remember that Freud interprets the dream of the father's death from the perspective of a childhood desire to murder the father. This would consequently allow the little child access to the mother.[9] Hence the dream of murdering the father is a reaction to his death: 'Freud,' Lacan writes, 'thus wished to be guilty for his father's death' (Lacan 2007 [1969–70]: 122)

To understand this claim, we should once again turn our attention to Lacan's interpretation of *Totem and Taboo*. The father's murder is central in this case as well. Moreover, Freud understands this murder as a historic event. 'What is there to conceal?' Lacan asks and answers: 'That, as soon as the father enters the field of the master's discourse where we are in the process of orientating ourselves, he is, from the origins, castrated ...' (Lacan 2007 [1969–70]: 101).[10] The theme of patricide is nothing more than a defence against castration. How should we understand this?

In this instance Lacan refers to a patient's dream Freud discusses in his chapter on 'absurd dreams' in *The Interpretation of Dreams*. This dream runs as follows: '*His father was alive once more and was talking to him in his usual way, but* (the remarkable thing was that) *he had really died, only he did not know it*' (Freud 1900: 430, Freud's italics). This dream becomes intelligible, writes Freud, if one adds '*in consequence of the dreamer's wish*' after 'but he had really died'. The same is true of 'He did not know' if it is supplemented with '*that the dreamer had this desire*' (Freud 1900: 430). Lacan says that Freud's introduction of the theme of the murder of the father, this dream, and *Totem and Taboo*'s origin myth all indicate an attempt to obscure the father's castration – in other words, his actual limitations and mortality. As long as we are capable of believing (unconsciously) that the father's death is the consequence of murder, we are also capable of believing that his death is the *exclusive* consequence of this murder. Or, in the terminology of *Totem and Taboo*, as long as we believe that collective patricide terminated the father's enjoyment, we are also capable of misrecognizing the structural character of castration – the impossibility of unlimited enjoyment or jouissance outside the law (Lacan 2007 [1969–70]: 141–43).

4 Castration as the truth of the Oedipus complex

According to Lacan, Freud's emphasis on the historical character of the origin myth in *Totem and Taboo* and, more generally, his emphasis on the father's murder, should be understood as a misrecognition of castration's structural character. *Totem and Taboo* implies a misrecognition of castration as the ultimate truth of desire and the subject. As with any other dream, however, Freud's origin myth not only obscures. Lacan points out that this myth simultaneously highlights an important truth about desire, albeit in a distorted way. By postulating a similarity between the dead father and unlimited jouissance (Lacan 2007 [1969–70]: 143–44), this tale indicates an impossibility. Someone who is deceased cannot, after all, take pleasure. Hence, Lacan equates the dead father with the 'real', according to the formula that 'the real is the impossible' (Lacan 2007 [1969–70]: 143). He means by this that the dead father refers to a dimension that is structurally outside the human realm of all possible meaning. Lacan says it is the father of the primal horde who appears in the dreams of neurotics – more specifically, those of hysterical patients. It is the father who has an answer to any and all questions, and in particular, one who would satisfactorily answer the question *What is a woman?* (Lacan 1994 [1956–57]: 141). Or better still *What does a woman want?*[11]

We already find this theme for instance in the seminar *The Object Relation* (Lacan 1994 [1956–57]).[12] In this early seminar Lacan refers to the familiar criticism that Freud takes little or no account of the actual physical pleasure experienced by women, particularly young girls. Freud believes that the young girl does not, after all, have knowledge of the vagina's existence.[13] In *The Object Relation* Lacan argues that Freud neither attempts to minimize the importance, nor deny the existence, of female pleasure in this way; rather, Lacan says Freud's intention was to show that this pleasure only becomes meaningful within the symbolic order. It is in the symbolic order, Lacan explains, that the phallus serves as the signifier of lack (Lacan 1994 [1956–57]: 141).

In Lacan's discussion, the phallus emerges as the signifier that indicates the desire of the Other, insofar as this desire is submitted to the order of signifiers, in other words, insofar as it ultimately escapes all concrete determinations. Various objects – any object in principle – can appear in the space marked by this signifier and thus obtain a phallic meaning. This implies that these objects momentarily appear to the subject as possible fulfilments of its desire. Nevertheless, such an ultimate fulfilment is impossible. The phallus is the signifier of an irremovable lack in the symbolic: an object capable of fulfilling desire is in reality irretrievable.

For the woman, however, the phallocentric nature of the symbolic implies that in the symbolic her desire can only take shape in terms of a male signifier. Lacan often says that the symbolic has no signifier to indicate female desire per se and 'in itself' – one separate from reference to the phallically structured male desire.[14] Whichever role is allocated to the woman in the Other's desire, this role can only be interpreted from the perspective of the phallus as signifier of lack.[15] The question 'What does a woman want (outside and independent this phallic universe)?' is the logical consequence. The hysterical subject incarnates this question, as well as the search for a father capable of answering.

Symbolically structured reality is, by definition, the world of lack indicated by the phallic signifier (Lacan 2007 [1969–70]: 149). This implies that within this order, there is no possible answer to the question 'What is a woman (outside and independent of this phallic universe)?'[16] Consequently, neither can the father capable of fulfilling desire and answering the hysterical subject's question be found in this reality. He is an impossibility. This father is a dead father, which implies a father no longer defined by lack, a father who cannot fail.

Castration, says Lacan, is an effect of language: '… language … cannot be anything other than a demand, a demand that fails' (Lacan 2007 [1969–70]: 144). Every demand produces a remainder specifically because it is articulated in language.[17] In this sense, every demand 'fails'. More specifically, desire only exists by the grace of our inscription in language, in the chain of signifiers that renew the lack in which it originates time and again. Lacan also then concludes that castration is a truly symbolic function that can only be understood from the perspective of the chain of signifiers (ibid.).[18] In this way, Lacan completely separates the problem of castration from reference to the murder of the father and, in turn, the Freudian Oedipus complex. Only reference to the father – even if he is 'dead' – still stands, but Lacan's re-reading of the Oedipus myth shows that he wants to substantially re-evaluate this reference too.

5 Oedipus as incarnation of the master

We already know that, according to Freud, the Oedipus legend derives its meaning from the fact it shows the realization of two inextricable infantile desires. According to Lacan, however, this is inessential.[19] He says that Oedipus gains access to Jocasta's bed less because he murdered his father – unknowingly, besides – than because he solved the sphinx's riddle ('What first walks on four legs, then on two, and finally on three?'). In other words, Oedipus becomes king because he mastered the sphinx's test of truth, which had claimed the lives of many citizens before.[20] First and foremost Oedipus is someone who deciphers enigmas for the sake of the community. Half human, half beast, the sphinx is also an enigmatic creature. Oedipus solves the riddle – 'Man' – and frees Thebes from the grips of evil forces in this way (Lacan 2007 [1969–70]: 140; Demoulin 2002: 403).

Lacan says that Oedipus assumes the position of the master in this way. He is the one who knows, and is capable of uniting society and protecting it against danger with his knowledge. For Oedipus, truth and knowledge are one and the same; there is no separation or distance between the chain of signifiers and the truth it expresses. In other words, the master denies or represses the split, which inevitably results from inscription in the signifying order.[21] According to Lacan, the tale's continuation proves without a shadow of a doubt that this is Oedipus' significance. When Thebes is hit by the plague the people turn to Oedipus once again to find a solution. The oracle at Delphi tells him that Laius' murderer is in Thebes and the only way to conquer the plague is by unmasking the murderer.

At this point, says Lacan, Oedipus finds himself once again confronted with the problem of the truth, which gives way to something that is at least partially related to the problematic of castration (Lacan 2007 [1969–70]: 140). Bit by bit Oedipus uncovers the truth of what he has done and the circumstances surrounding his ascension to the throne. When Oedipus realizes he is responsible for his predecessor's death, he executes on himself the sentence he pronounced for the murderer. Oedipus gouges out his own eyes. Lacan interprets this act as symbolic of castration (Lacan 2007 [1969–70]: 140–41). In this way, Oedipus demonstrates that the truth of the master is his castration. Since signifiers are differentially determined and only signify in reference to other signifiers, the possible coincidence of knowledge and truth is, in principle, excluded. Every piece of knowledge leaves a remainder. No one can ever fully express truth; structurally it is a 'half-said' (*'mi-dire'*) (Lacan 2007 [1969–70]: 126).

Lacan's re-evaluation of the Oedipus myth topples the Freudian perspective. This myth does not concern access to the mother as desire's ultimate object through the father's murder; rather, it concerns the figure of the master and his structural castration. Consequently this tragedy does not revolve around desire for the mother but a desire to know and the impossibility of this knowledge ever coinciding with truth (Lacan 2007 [1969–70]: 135). In this way the figure of the (castrated) master replaces the figure of the (murdered) father.

6 Dora and the search for a master

The remarks that Lacan makes on Freud's Dora-case in the text we are commenting on here, allows for a further elucidation of Lacan's critique of the Oedipus complex. According to Lacan, Freud positions himself in his relation to Dora as a master through his interventions and interpretations. Freud is the one who knows, and his only task consists in convincing Dora of this knowledge. Several years later Freud himself concedes that his prejudices regarding sexuality – more specifically, what a fully fledged sexual relationship ought to be – made understanding Dora's homosexual ties with Frau K., which turned out to be crucial to understand her problematic, impossible. But perhaps this is not the only thing Freud overlooks. More important than the homosexual object choice is the dynamic that controls the hysterical patient's desire. It has become a common place to say that, in essence, hysterical desire aims at remaining unfulfilled. Hysterical desire is a desire for an unfulfilled desire. Freud relentlessly searches for a *specific* object that answers Dora's (unconscious) desire. He is thus doomed to miss the mark. Hysterical desire does not aim at being fulfilled by any specific object. Not surprisingly Dora is unimpressed by Freud's therapeutic and analytical skills. She abandons her therapy after only a few months. But what then is the dynamic that fundamentally determines hysteria, which Lacan supposedly identifies, but Freud misses?

As in his other commentaries of the same text,[22] in *The Other Side of Psychoanalysis* Lacan highlights the importance Dora attaches to the father's sexual 'impotence' (Lacan 2007 [1969–70]: 108).[23] One cannot claim that someone fails in this way, Lacan continues, without simultaneously measuring him against a symbolic function. Not only is Dora's father what he is in reality – an ill old man – but he is also a father in the way a soldier can be a 'veteran fighter'. The father carries the title 'former begetter' (*'ancien géniteur'*) and continues to carry reference to the possibility of procreation. Even after he has become 'impotent', he retains this symbolic position toward women. This is the origin of the father's idealization, which characterizes and facilitates hysterical discourse. This idealization is necessary to elevate the father to the level of master. Consequently, the hysterical woman seeks the master in the father.[24] A desire to know inspires this master, and she believes he is in principle capable of answering her questions with which she is struggling.

It is not always clear in which way and to what extent we can retrace this search for a master in Freud's case study of Dora. In *The Other Side of Psychoanalysis* Lacan does not read this text systematically; rather, he uses it to illustrate his own views. He only refers to it because of his own theory of hysteria. With regard to the relation to a master, Lacan refers to one of the two dreams that play a central role in Freud's interpretation of Dora (Lacan 2007 [1969–70]: 110). In the second dream Dora is told that her father has died, and her mother writes that she can now return home. After extensive travel Dora returns home, but she discovers her family members are already at the graveyard (Freud 1905: 94 onwards). After Freud explains his interpretation of this dream to Dora, she remembers another piece of the dream: 'she went calmly to her room, and began reading a big book that lay on her writing-table' (Freud 1905: 100). Lacan reads this as illustrating the fact that only the dead father produces the knowledge of sexuality desired by the hysterical woman – Dora in this case. Freud himself gives a somewhat more trivial explanation. The dream realizes a revenge phantasy aimed at her father. Dora's addition fits into this interpretation: 'Dora's father was dead … She might calmly read whatever she chose. Did not this mean that one of her motives for revenge was a revolt against her parents' constraints? If her father was dead she could read or love as she pleased' (Freud 1905: 100). This is a far cry from a frenetic search for a master.

As in other instances where he discusses Dora in *The Other Side of Psychoanalysis*, Lacan concentrates on the scene at the lake (Lacan 2007 [1969–70]: 109–10). He says: 'It is quite true that at this moment the other's *Jouissance* is offered her, and she doesn't want having anything to do with it because what she wants is knowledge as the means of *Jouissance*, but in order to place this knowledge in the service of truth, the truth of the master that she embodies as Dora' (Lacan 2007 [1969–70]: 97).[25] Why does the hysterical woman yearn for knowledge? As we know, the problem of hysteria is dominated by the question 'What does a woman want?' (Lacan 2007 [1969–70]: 150). We might reformulate this issue in terms of the (im)possibility of a sexual relationship. A relationship presupposes two different and above all complementary partners that are capable of engaging in a symmetrical relationship with each other. According to Lacan, however, the relationship between the two sexes cannot be described in this way. He says that ultimately there is but one point of reference – the phallic signifier – in relation to which *both* sexes determine their positions towards each other. This train of thought results in the Lacanian adage that there is *no sexual relationship* (Lacan 2007 [1969–70]: 19, 34).[26]

What attracts Dora to Herr K., says Lacan, is the fact that his organ is functional, as opposed to her father's.[27] But this organ only has meaning insofar as another can rob her of it. Lacan refers to a dream of Dora's in which the house of her family is on fire. Her mother wants to save her jewel-case from the burning house. Herr K. also gave Dora a jewel-case as a present. Lacan says the fact that Herr K. gave Dora a jewel-case and not the jewellery to be kept in the case is crucial to the

56 Philippe Van Haute and Tomas Geyskens

interpretation of this dream (Lacan 2007 [1969–70]: 109–110). In his interpretation of this dream Freud equates the jewel-case with the female genitals (Freud 1905: 91). Consequently, in her relationship with Herr K. Dora is uninterested in his organ (or his 'jewels') – which is to say sexual fulfilment – but in the question of her womanhood. Who am I as woman, beyond the phallic economy to which Herr K. wants to confine me?[28]

The hysterical subject pursues knowledge for the sake of truth. This truth is, however, that the master is defective and essentially characterized by lack.[29] Lacan's thematization of the hysterical patient's strategy now becomes clear. She appoints, as it were, a master – the father, a rabbi, but also the psychoanalyst – from whom she expects an answer to her questions (Lacan 2007 [1969–70]: 150). The hysterical subject, then, presents herself as an enigma to this master.[30] Through everything she says and does the hysterical subject suggests that answering her questions – resolving the enigma she incarnates – substantially aids the master in completing his knowledge and (re)establishing his masterhood. She inspires every psychoanalyst, because she is so 'interesting' and makes such an 'exciting' psychoanalytic patient.[31] She awakens the desire for knowledge. No matter the answer the master produces, however, it is by definition deficient. Every answer reduces the subject to a pure object of the Other's desire for knowledge. Every answer reduces the subject to an illustration of a theory that is structurally incapable of answering the hysterical question – '*What is a woman?*'

The hysterical subject's paradoxical relationship vis-à-vis (the master's) knowledge mirrors a similarly paradoxical relationship vis-à-vis sexual fulfilment. The master is no longer characterized by lack, and he cannot fail. This is only possible when the master no longer desires. Hence, the hysterical patient takes great care in 'choosing' her masters. They are objects that are 'out of reach' – the priest or rabbi, the psychoanalyst or a teacher – so that the hysterical subject is able to pretend for a while that they are indeed 'above' or 'beyond' desire. In this instance, however, the subject presents itself as a mysterious and exciting object that still has the potential to complete the master. Woe to the 'master' who takes the bait and emerges as desiring subject. Rejection is then inevitable. The hysterical patient resists precisely this transformation into a phallicized object that has no other meaning besides facilitating the other's jouissance. The only option left for the unmasked master is endless speculation regarding how it went so terribly wrong or, like Freud ... to write a case study.

Conclusion

In *The Other Side of Psychoanalysis*[32] Lacan unmasks the Oedipus complex as a 'dream of Freud's' that has to be interpreted. At the same time he re-interprets hysteria as an incarnation of 'the truth of the master', namely that the latter is in actual fact characterized by his deficiency and is thus castrated. Hysteria is the continuous staging of this truth. Freud does not understand hysteria from the perspective of a search for a master. But Lacan's theory at the same time sheds an

Freud's Dream? Lacan and Oedipus **57**

interesting light on the course, and more importantly the failure of the analysis of Dora: Freud behaves toward her like the master for whom she has been searching and whose shortcoming she makes painfully clear at the same time.

The Oedipus complex no longer plays a central role in Lacan's theory of hysteria presented in *The Other Side of Psychoanalysis*. As a result, the reference to Lévi-Strauss' structural interpretation of the complex – from which Lacan in his early texts gleaned his view that the woman should be understood as exchange object – also disappears.[33] Henceforth Lacan understands hysteria from the point of view of the relation to a master and he further links it to the impossibility of a sexual relationship that is by nature not exclusive to either sex (Lacan 2007 [1969–70]: 112, 150). In *The Other Side of Psychoanalysis* Lacan still exclusively thematizes this impossibility in terms of the phallocentric character of the symbolic order.[34] In the symbolic, sexual difference can only become meaningful based on a reference to the phallus as signifier of lack. This implies that there is only one single reference point in the symbolic from which both sexes can determine themselves vis-à-vis the other. Hence the impossibility of a sexual relationship.

The passages from *The Other Side of Psychoanalysis* that we commented on illustrate the progressive 'de-oedipalization' of Lacanian theory. This de-oedipalization is first and foremost a disconnection of the Oedipus complex – the reference to an almighty father – and castration. Even if one thinks – for good reasons, I believe (Van Haute 2005) – that Lacan's phallocentric account of the symbolic remains problematic, one can read the present chapter as a first important step in overcoming Oedipal essentialism. If castration – or, more concretely, the 'lack of being' – is the most fundamental characteristic of the subject, then this subject cannot but find its identity in the Other. The Other, so Lacan now seems to think, is a system of signifiers that characterizes a certain group or community. This system has no foundation outside itself and the reference to the father is in the end nothing but a neurotic construction that loses its universal significance. This implies that our sexual identities that, according to Freud and the early Lacan, were determined in and through the Oedipus complex, can only be founded in the shared belief of a certain community. The same is true for the realm of the social as such. In this way Lacan not only seems to take a much more 'constructivist' stance then before with regard to the problem of sexual identity, but he at the same time shows that social reality is essentially contingent and hence subject to critique (Verhaeghe 2002: 154ff).

It also became clear that the theory of the four discourses that Lacan developed at the end of the 1960s plays a crucial role in this context. Can we say that this theory replaces once and for all the Oedipus complex or are things more complicated? Whatever the case may be, in the years following *The Other Side* Lacan further de-oedipalizes his psychoanalytic theory. It is important to mention that in the process Lacan's emphasis is no longer on desire and castration, but rather on the jouissance of the Other and the structural loss of the object *a*. We can interpret this evolution as an attempt to overcome the phallocentrism that still plays a central and determining role in *The Other Side*. In this attempt, the formulas of sexuation as developed in the seminar *Encore* play a crucial role (Van Haute and Geyskens 2012). Whether or not this attempt succeeds is yet another debate ...

Notes

+ An earlier and shorter version of this paper appeared online on Psychomedia Lacaniana in 2012.

1 'What is there to conceal? That, as soon as the father enters the field of the master's discourse where we are in the process of orientating ourselves, he is, from the origins, castrated ... the experience with the hysteric, if not her sayings, at least the configurations she presented him with, should have guided him better here than the Oedipus complex does and led him to consider that this suggests that, at the level of analysis itself, everything is to be put back into question concerning what is necessary from knowledge, in order for this knowledge to be called into question in the site of truth' (Lacan 2007 [1969–70]: 101). We return to this passage at a later stage.

2 Or, in more Lacanian terminology, that he is 'castrated'. We return to this later.

3 This is the equivalent of the latent content of a dream. Freud's explicit interpretation of the Oedipus myth corresponds with the manifest content of a dream.

4 'Castration is a real operation that is introduced through the incidence of the signifier, no matter which, into the sexual relation (*rapport sexuel*). And it goes without saying that it determines the father as this impossible real that we have been talking about' (Lacan 2007 [1969–70]: 129) We return to this passage at a later stage.

5 In this section we are very inspired by a very interesting article by Demoulin (2002).

6 For a detailed discussion of the evolution discussed in this paragraph, see Grigg 2008.

7 Besides, in this case Lacan believes it concerns less desire *for* the mother than desire *of* the mother. From this perspective the law of the father limits the unlimited enjoyment of the mother. This law puts a lid on the desire of the mother. The law of the father prevents the small child from being reduced to the ultimate object of desire of the mother. This also defines the meaning of the law of the father.

8 For a detailed discussion of this evolution, see Grigg 2008.

9 The fact that references to the Oedipus complex and the Oedipal explanations are only included in later editions of *The Interpretation of Dreams* is not without importance to our discussion.

10 See note 4 for the French text. For a detailed discussion of Lacan's theory of the four discourses, see e.g. Fink 1998 and Verhaeghe 1996.

11 'The idea of putting the omnipotent father at the origin of desire is very adequately refuted by the fact that Freud extracted its master signifiers from the hysteric's desire. It must not be forgotten, in effect, that this is where Freud began and that he acknowledged what it is that remains at the center of his question ... It's the question, "What does a woman want?"' (Lacan 2007 [1969–70]: 129). The connection Lacan makes here between the Oedipus complex, *Totem and Taboo*, and hysteria can be challenged from a historical perspective. Indeed, the introduction of the Oedipus complex mainly concerns Freud's growing focus on obsessional neurosis from roughly 1910 onwards (Van Haute and Geyskens 2011, *passim*).

12 For what follows, see Lacan 1994 [1956–57], from p. 141 onwards.

13 For a critique of the philosophical presuppositions on which this theory is based, see Van Haute 2005.

14 For an interesting discussion and critique of this theory see Schneider 2006: 299–340.

15 For the preceding see Mitchel and Rose 1982, Miller 2000, Morel 2002, Soler 2000 and 2002, and Monique David-Ménard 2009, among others. One wonders whether and in what exact way the view that the symbolic lacks a signifier for women and that the women's role in the Other's desire can only be elucidated in terms of the phallus as

signifier of lack is a psychoanalytical reformulation of Lévi-Strauss's view that women are exchange objects between *male* kinship lines (Lévi-Strauss 1949).

16 In his seminar *Encore* (Lacan 1998 [1972–73]), Lacan juxtaposes the limited phallic jouissance governed by the symbolic's laws with another 'female' jouissance that escapes or transcends the symbolic. Moreover, in that work Lacan totally detaches reference to these forms of jouissance from biological reality. This development implies a crucial correction to Lacanian phallocentric thought as it is discussed here. Space is lacking here to discuss this point in more detail.

17 This is the place where Lacan situates object *a* – the 'object-cause' of desire (Lacan 2007 [1969–70]: 144). A detailed discussion would take us too far afield.

18 This is the very reason why in *The Other Side of Psychoanalysis* Lacan introduces a theory of discourses that replaces reference to the Oedipus myth (Demoulin 2002: 410).

19 At this point we could also note the influence of Lévi-Strauss and others on Lacan's interpretation of this myth. However, this would deviate too far from our own argument. For these influences, see Grigg 2008 and Demoulin 2002.

20 'What's important is that Oedipus was admitted to Jocaste's side because he had triumphed at a trial of truth' (Lacan 2007 [1969–70]: 117).

21 For a more technical discussion of the master's discourse in relation to the three other discourses Lacan distinguishes in his seminar *The Other Side of Psychoanalysis*, see Verhaeghe 2001 and Fink 1998, among others.

22 See e.g. Lacan 1993 [1955–56]: 181–206 and Lacan 1994 [1956–57]: 95–147; for an overview, see Voruz 2007.

23 Our subsequent commentary concerns the following passage: 'It is implicitly to proffer that the father is not merely what he is, that it is a little like "ex-soldier" – he is an "ex-sire". He is a father, like the ex-soldier, until the end of his life. This implies that in the word "father" there is something that is always in fact potentially creating. And it is in relation to this fact that, in this symbolic field, it must be observed that it is the father, insofar as he plays this pivotal, major role, this master role in the hysteric's discourse, that, from this angle of the power of creation, sustains his position in relation to the woman, even as he is out of action. This is what is specific to the function from which the hysteric's relation to the father stems, and it is very precisely this that we designate as the idealized father' (Lacan 2007 [1969–70]: 95).

24 Later she does the same thing with other figures – the priest or rabbi, the doctor ... the psychoanalyst.

25 It is not quite clear why Lacan refers to 'pleasure of the Other' and not 'phallic pleasure', since it is precisely the latter that Herr K. 'offers' Dora.

26 For further commentary on this problem and its orientation within the history of psychoanalysis, see Van Haute 2000: 136ff. This issue is central in the seminar *Encore* (Lacan 1996 [1972–73]).

27 'What suits Dora is the idea that he (Herr K) has the organ...not so that Dora can find happiness in it, if I can put it thus, but so that another woman should deprive her of it' (Lacan 2007 [1969–70]: 96, translation slightly changed).

28 That this is the determining factor of Dora's pathology also emerges, according to Lacan, from the 'theoretical contemplation' ('*contemplation théorique*') (Lacan 2007 [1969–70]: 110) of Frau K. and of her 'adorable white body' (Freud 1905: 61), which flourished during a visit to Dresden when Dora spent two hours 'in front of the Sistine Madonna, rapt in silent admiration. When I asked her what had pleased her so much about the picture she could find no clear answer to make. At last she said: "The Madonna"' (Freud 1905: 96).

29 'And this truth, to say it at last, is that the master is castrated' (Lacan 2007 [1969–70]: 97).

30 The hysterical patient volunteers up symptoms, the meaning of which she does not understand. These symptoms can all be connected to the question of womanhood.

31 'She wants the other to be a master and to know lots of things, but at the same time she doesn't want it him to know so much that he does not believe that she is the supreme price of all his knowledge. In other words, she wants a master she can reign over' (Lacan 2007 [1969–70]: 129).

32 It is clear that the evolution of the place and meaning of the Oedipus complex from Lacan's first series of lectures to *The Other Side of Psychoanalysis* can and should be studied in more detail than has been done here.

33 See on this Van Haute and Geyskens 2011.

34 Lacan takes in this regard a further major step in his seminar *Encore* (Lacan 1998 [1972–73]). There he positions the limited phallic jouissance that is subject to the laws of the symbolic opposite another 'female' jouissance that escapes or transcends the symbolic. We don't have place here to develop this idea further. For the relation between the 'formulas of sexuation' and the problematic we introduced in this article see Van Haute and Geyskens 2012: *passim.*

Bibliography

David-Ménard, M. (2009) *Les constructions de l'universel. Psychanalyse, philosphie.* Paris: PUF.

Demoulin, C. (2002) 'L'Oedipe rêve de *Freud'*, *Psychoanalytische perspectieven*, 20: 397–414.

Fink, B. (1998) 'The Master Signifier and the Four Discourses', in *Key Concepts of Lacanian Psychoanalysis*, ed. D. Nobus. New York: Rebus Press, 29–47.

Freud, S. (1900) *The Interpretation of Dreams*, SE IV–V.

Freud, S. (1905) *Fragment of an Analysis of a Case of Hysteria*, SE VII.

Freud, S. (1913) *Totem and Taboo*, SE XIII.

Freud, S. (1986) *Briefe an Wilhelm Fliess 1887–1904*, ed. J. M.Masson. Frankfurt am Main: S. Fischer Verlag.

Grigg, R. (2008) *Lacan, Language and Philosophy.* New York: Suny Press.

Lacan, J. (1993 [1955–56]) *The Seminar of Jacques Lacan, Book III, The Psychoses*, ed. Jacques-Alain Miller, trans. Russell Grigg. New York and London: W. W. Norton and Company.

Lacan, J. (1994 [1956–57]) *La relation d'objet. Le seminaire de Jacques Lacan, Livre IV*, ed. Jacques-Alain Miller. Paris: Seuil.

Lacan, J. (1998 [1972–73]) *The Seminar of Jacques Lacan, Book XX, Encore, On Feminine Sexuality, the Limits of Love and Knowledge*, ed. Jacques-Alain Miller, trans. Bruce Fink. New York and London: W.W. Norton and Company.

Lacan, J. (2007 [1969–70]) *The Seminar of Jacques Lacan, Book XVIII, The Other Side of Psychoanalysis*, ed. Jacques-Alain Miller, trans. Russell Grigg. New York and London: W.W. Norton and Company.

Lévi-Strauss, C. (1949) *Les structures élémentaires de la parenté.* Paris: PUF.

Miller, J.-A. (2000) 'On Semblances in the Relation between the Sexes', in *Sexuation*, ed. R. Salecl. Durham, NC and London: Duke University Press, 13–27.

Mitchel, J. and Rose, J. (1982) *Feminine Sexuality. Jacques Lacan and the Ecole Freudienne.* New York: W.W. Norton and Company.

Morel, G. (2002) 'Feminine Conditions of Jouissance', in *Reading Seminar XX. Lacan's Major Work on Love, Knowledge, and Feminine Sexuality*, ed. S. Barnard and B. Fink, New York: SUNY, 77–92.

Schneider, M. (2006) *Le paradigm feminine.* Paris: Flammarion.

Soler, C. (2000) 'The Curse on Sex', in *Sexuation*, ed. R. Salecl. Durham, NC and London: Duke University Press, 39–53.

Soler, C. (2002) 'Hysteria in Scientific Discourse', in *Reading Seminar XX. Lacan's Major Work on Love, Knowledge, and Feminine Sexuality*, ed. S. Barnard and B. Fink. New York: SUNY, 47–56.

Van Haute, P. (2005) 'Infantile Sexuality, Primary Object-love and the Anthropological Significance of the Oedipus Complex: Re-reading Freud's "Female Sexuality"', *International Journal for Psychoanalysis*, 86(6): 1661–1678.

Van Haute, P. and Geyskens, T. (2012) *Towards a Non-Oedipal Psychoanalysishe Art of an Impossible Jouissance. Clinical Anthropology of Hysteria in Freud and Lacan.* Leuven: Louvain University Press.

Verhaeghe, P. (2001) 'From Impossibility to Inability. Lacan's Theory of the Four Discourses', in *Beyond Gender. From Subject to Drive.* New York: Other Press.

Verhaeghe, P. (2002) 'Vers un nouvel Oedipe: pères en fuite', *Revue française de psychanalyse,* 1: 145–158.

Voruz, V. (2007) 'A Lacanian Reading of Dora', in *The Later Lacan: An Introduction* (Series in Pyschoanalysis and Culture), ed. V. Voruz and B. Wolf. New York: SUNY.

4

NOT EVEN

The politics of Oedipus

Mladen Dolar

UNIVERSITY OF LJUBLJANA

Oedipus – what a strange idea. Maybe the strangest thing is that something that appeared so utterly shocking, scandalous, preposterous, and bizarre when Freud first proposed it has become so utterly domesticated and commonly received in the *Zeitgeist*. It takes a great effort to restore its scandalous value. Freud first came upon this idea in his correspondence with Wilhelm Fliess (in the letter dated 15 October 1897), in the process of his own self-analysis, which was carried out in close companionship with his venerated friend:

> So far I have found nothing completely new, but all the complication to which I am used [...] Only one idea of general value has occurred to me. I have found love of the mother and jealousy of the father in my own case too, and now believe it to be a general phenomenon of early childhood. [...] If that is the case, the gripping power of *Oedipus Rex* [...] becomes intelligible [...] The Greek myth seizes on a compulsion which everyone recognizes because he has felt traces of it in himself. Every member of the audience was once a budding Oedipus in phantasy, and this dream-fulfillment played out in reality causes everyone to recoil in horror, with the full measure of repression which separates his infantile from this present state.
>
> *(Freud 1954: 221–24)*

This is the place from where this modern saga of Oedipus stems, a new edition of the ancient saga. It all sounds rather naïve – everybody is a budding Oedipus, everybody can unwittingly recognize himself in it, everybody, of course, lives to kill the father and sleep with the mother; what else would a man ultimately want? At the end it all comes down to a number of assumptions: to the incest and its prohibition as the universal condition upon which the culture is constituted; to the name of the conflict that it secretly holds at its core; to the emergence of desire coupled with the prohibition, to the doom of our childhood, to the irresolvable drama of subjectivity, and to the paradigm and the parable of human condition.

The idea of Oedipus had not abandoned Freud for the rest of his career; he persistently kept returning to it as something which constitutes the very core of psychoanalysis. In the *Interpretation of Dreams* (1900) he expounded it at length:

> If *Oedipus Rex* moves a modern audience no less than it did the contemporary Greek one, the explanation can only be that its effect does not lie in the contrast between destiny and human will, but is to be looked for in the particular nature of the material on which that contrast is exemplified. There must be something which makes a voice within us ready to recognize the compelling force of destiny in the *Oedipus* [...] His destiny moves us only because it might have been ours – because the oracle laid the same curse upon us before our birth as upon him. It is the fate of all of us, perhaps, to direct our first sexual impulse towards our mother and our first hatred and our first murderous wish against our father. Our dreams convince us that that is so. King Oedipus, who slew his father Laius and married his mother Jocasta, merely shows us the fulfilment of our own childhood wishes.
>
> *(Freud, SE 4: 262)*

Thus we might think that we know everything about human desire. This suggestion was perhaps the most scandalous part of psychoanalysis at the beginning,[1] but shocking as it initially was, it soon became the most widespread, the most commonly known idea that psychoanalysis proposed, to the point that it obtained the status of a truism, a cliché, a triviality which easily lends itself to caricature.

I do not wish to linger with this understanding of Oedipus any longer; instead I want to address another kind of Oedipus that seems to be completely obfuscated from this traditional narrative. Nevertheless a quick remark is perhaps necessary. To put it in a nutshell, Oedipus is not an answer but a question. It is not some universal answer to the impasse of human desire, its passepartout key or the naming of its secret aims (to kill the father, to sleep with the mother), rather Oedipus questions the dislocation of human desire, the impossibility to locate and root it. Oedipus, after all, was a dislocated subject par excellence, expelled from his home at birth, a voluntary exile from Corinth, expelled from Thebes, an exile from human society at Colonus, and finally dislocated at the moment of his death when he was deprived of a grave. Oedipus, rather than being an easy solution, presents a field of conflicts and tensions, which prevents from any simple assumption of our desire and of our symbolic mandate. As Shoshana Felman put it: Oedipus is a signifier, not a signified,[2] not some generally valid meaning of desire, but desire's way to elude meaning. This misunderstanding further constitutes and enables the anti-Oedipal criticism of psychoanalysis, which largely sees in the psychoanalytic account a reduction of the subject's entire socio-political field to a family romance, to the story of the 'mummy and daddy', which supposedly bereaves desire of its nomadic nature. But one would be hard put to see Oedipus, the member of the most dysfunctional family in history, as a proponent of a familial reduction, it rather displays the impossibility of any such reduction, undermining any assumption of family roles. As Balibar aptly put it:

> [...] the family structure is not based on Oedipus, but Oedipus, to the contrary, inscribes the conflict and the variability of subjective positions into its core and thus hinders any possibility for the family to impose the roles which it prescribes as simple functions for individuals to fulfil 'normally'.
>
> *(Balibar 1997: 337)*

Thus Oedipus is not a reduction to the family, but rather the inner disruption of the family. But what is even more important, crucial for our purpose: Oedipus is not the rule, but an exception. This is what makes him most interesting for psychoanalytic theory. If everyone is supposed to be burdened with the unconscious guilt for transgressive incestuous and patricidal desires, then Oedipus is unique for refusing to assume such guilt. The one who actually did what all others are supposed to desire is the one who persists in the position of a 'waste' or abandonment, in a refusal of his destiny, and in accepting the role of its unwitting agent.

To see Oedipus in this 'exceptional yet abandoned' light one must turn to the text *Oedipus at Colonus*. As a short historical comment, Sophocles wrote *Antigone* first (*c.* 442 BC), while chronologically this is the last part of the saga of the Oedipus. In *Antigone* the protagonists are Oedipus's children, Eteocles and Polyneices who kill each other, and Antigone who buries her banished brother Polyneices in defiance of the Theban ruler (one should just point out that Antigone, as opposed to Oedipus, knows exactly what she is in for, she nevertheless heroically commits her act and bears all the consequences). *Antigone* was followed by *King Oedipus* (*c.* 429 BC), which chronologically is the first part of the saga, where Sophocles recounts the notorious and gruesome events; and finally the *Oedipus at Colonus*, written in 406 B.C., in Colonus, Sophocles' own birthplace, where he died in the same year and before its first performance. *Oedipus at Colonus* is chronologically the second part, recounting the events following Oedipus's expulsion from Thebes and preceding Antigone's act. The two parts *King Oedipus* and *Antigone,* preceding and following *Oedipus at Colonus,* are part of general culture and part of basic education, but how come hardly anyone knows about *Oedipus at Colonus*? It is as if some general amnesia set in regarding this crucial second part of the Oedipus story; Lacan throughout his teaching insisted on the importance of the second part if we are to understand the full relevance of Oedipus and the scope of its intervention.

What happens at Colonus? Oedipus, blind and expelled, is accompanied by his faithful daughter-sister Antigone, his only help, wandering around, not finding a place of abode. He is known to everyone, notorious for his horrible fate, but as nobody would want to have him, he is the source of abomination and embarrassment; yet on the other hand an oracle predicted that the place of his burial will secure peace and prosperity to the polis, so he is also a desired presence and a political asset. Finally Theseus, the Athenian king, will accompany him to death, and as Colonus

Not Even: Politics of Oedipus **65**

was under the Athenian jurisdiction, this would secure the future of Athens. Most importantly, Oedipus insists throughout the play on his innocence, while at the same time occupying the position of an outcast of fate, a figure of total expropriation, bereft of everything. When chorus raises the reproach of incest, this is what he says:[3]

CHORUS: Thou hast done …
OEDIPUS: I did no deed!
CHORUS: No deed?
OEDIPUS: I took a gift the City gave.
      Oh, why should she have given me that,
      The City that I sought to save?

(vv. 539–41)

He has saved the city from the sphinx and he merely received the queen in marriage as the gift of gratitude in return. When Chorus reproaches patricide:

CHORUS: Didst thou not slay?
OEDIPUS: I slew. But there
      Mine innocent heart hath answer, too.
CHORUS: What answer?
OEDIPUS: 'Twas but Justice.
CHORUS: How?
OEDIPUS: 'Tis simply told. The man I slew
      Would have slain me. In will, in law,
      Unstained I did what I must do.

(vv. 545–48)

Even more:

    If, here and now, some stranger came and sought
    To kill thee, thee, so strict in deed and thought,
    Wouldst question: 'Is this unknown man by chance
    My father?' or strike quickly in defense.
    Smite him, I think, if still thou lov'st the light,
    Not look around thee for thy legal right.
    In such a pass, by God bewildered, then
    I strove. Oh, were my father risen again
    I think, I think, himself would pardon me.

(vv. 991–98)

Imagine being confronted by a dangerous stranger – who would ask a thug if he is by chance one's father? Even the father's soul would have to agree with him.

There is a maximal opposition between his position here and in *Oedipus Rex*. There he was the king who has obtained and acquired everything, he was at the height of his power; here he has fallen into the darkest pit, bereft of everything, identifying precisely with this decrepit, impotent, repulsive refuse. *King Oedipus* is the tragedy of appropriation, and the price one has to pay for it, *Oedipus at Colonus* is the tragedy of utter and absolute expropriation, and of stubborn persistence in it. The unique trait of Oedipus is his adamant unwillingness to subjectivize his guilt, his insistence in his dislocation, so that one might say that he is an object rather than a subject, an abject object. As a subject he seems perfectly rational and transparent, even modern: I cannot be responsible for the will of gods, I did a terrible deed but nobody can hold me accountable for it. Not only does he keep coming up with legal argument for his non-guilt, he also adamantly insists that his desire was not implicated, he refuses his conscious or unconscious desire to be in any way part of it. There was no complicity on his part, conscious or unconscious. Not only he did not know, he also did not desire. Oedipus is an exception, everybody else is the rule.

But his clear conscience does not turn him into a hero, anything but. Hegel says somewhere, apropos Greek tragedy, that for great characters it is a point of honour to be guilty and that one could not offend them more than to consider them innocent (Hegel 1970: 546). They have done a deed, but through a tragic flaw (*hamartia*), a fatal blindness, they produced unintended tragic consequences, and they can only prove that they are worthy heroes by heroically assuming their guilt and facing the consequences. Oedipus is an anti-hero. The best way to describe his position would be: not only did I commit a terrible crime, I cannot even be guilty for it. I am expropriated even of this dignity.[4] Let us mark this structure of the argument: 'not only … but even not …'. I will come back to it.

This is why Lacan, from his early times on, since Seminar II (1991 [1954–55]), insisted so much that *Oedipus at Colonus* was the key to Oedipus. One has to go beyond Oedipus, and what is beyond Oedipus is Oedipus himself, namely Oedipus at Colonus. It is Oedipus himself who is anti-Oedipus. If Freud's introduction of Oedipus in *The Interpretation of Dreams* was inscribed in the framework of the pleasure principle in its conflict with the reality principle (incestuous desire striving for pleasure and satisfaction, the paternal law sustaining the reality principle prohibiting the striving for satisfaction), then Oedipus at Colonus is placed precisely 'beyond the pleasure principle' (and hence equally beyond the reality principle, beyond the apparent conflict of the two), into the realm that Freud marked by introducing the notion of the death drive. Death drive is the persistence of life beyond the framework of pleasure and reality.

This is what the most famous passage in *Oedipus at Colonus* aims at, the notorious verses pronounced by Chorus, witnessing Oedipus' fate:

> Not to be born, by all acclaim,
> Were best; but once that gate be passed,
> To hasten thither whence he came
> Is man's next prize – and fast, Oh fast!
> *(vv. 1223–27)*

The best thing is not to be born at all, and the second best, once born, to return to where one has come from. (Make oneself unborn? This seems to be even less feasible than not to be born.) The first thing to note is that Sophocles is not saying something original here, he is actually plagiarizing, transcribing the very famous lines by Theognis written a century and half earlier, around 550 BC:

Best of all for mortal beings is never to have been born at all
Nor ever to have set eyes on the bright light of the sun
But, since he is born, a man should make utmost haste through the gates of Death
And then repose, the earth piled into a mound round himself.

Theognis had already used the crucial wording *me phynai*, 'not to have been born', as did Sophocles. Theognis' verses are notorious for they have often been presented as the quintessence of the Greek tragic view of the world. One can find analogous lines in Bacchylides and in Euripides, both preceding *Oedipus at Colonus*.

The best thing is not to be born – how can one say this? What is it in life that makes it possible to set oneself against life, to put life in question, negate it, degrade it, to rank it second in relation to death? How can one subvert this hierarchy, the spontaneous and self-evident presupposition of being alive at all? What Chorus is saying is: life, life as such, is not worth living. Better not to be born. This looks like the ultimate complaint, the complaint of all complaints, the biggest grievance imaginable against one's own existence. All other complaints and protests against the world, its injustice and troubles, appear as banal in comparison. What is wrong is not this or that particular evil, but ultimately the very fact of being born at all. Other grievances concern particular misfortunes and calamities, personal, social, political, even cosmic, but they are in the end only partial, limited, and fragmentary metonymies of this highest complaint. What are all disasters compared to the ultimate disaster of having been born? The best commentary on this was provided by Aaron Schuster, the greatest theorist of complaining: 'The train is late … best not to be. Unpaid bills … best not to be. I accidentally murdered my father and slept with my mother … best not to be.'[5] This is the biggest lament against an irreparable wrong, but it can only be uttered by someone who has already endured that wrong. Suicide, as Schuster remarks, is an act of impotence: it can merely end life, but not repair the ultimate trouble of having been born.

There is something comical in this most tragic of all pronouncements, and what I am aiming at is this trajectory from Oedipus to comedy, in order to find the proper way to speak of life, in becoming, and of childhood. Lacan commented on this for the first time in his Seminar II and then on a number of occasions throughout his career, always pointing out the comical aspect:

It would be better not to be born. Of course! This means that here there's an unthinkable unity [namely us as unborn], about which absolutely nothing can be said before it comes into existence, from which time it may indeed insist, but one could imagine it not insisting, so that everything passes into the

68 Mladen Dolar

universal rest and silence of the stars, as Pascal puts it. That is true enough, it may be so at the moment when one says it, *it would be better not to be born*. What is ridiculous is saying it and entering into the order of the calculus of probabilities. Spirit is only spirit because it is close enough to our existence to cancel it with laughter.

(Lacan 1991 [1954–55]: 233–34, translation modified)

The source of the comical in this sentence is an impossible evaluation between how is it not to be born as compared to having been born – from where can one consider this, weigh the pros and cons? What is the probability of partaking in this highest happiness of not being born? The spirit in question is the spirit of *mot d'esprit*, the word of spirit, the spirit of wit, of a joke, the capacity of a word to virtually do away with our existence and make it unhappen, as it were.

This is the spirit in which Freud comments on this. On the one hand he considers *King Oedipus* in all seriousness in *The Interpretation of Dreams* (and in many other places), on the other hand he takes up this most notorious sentence from *Oedipus at Colonus* in his book on jokes:

> Never to be born would be the best thing for mortal men. 'But,' adds the philosophical comment in *Fliegende Blätter*, 'this happens to scarcely one person in a hundred thousand'.

(Freud, SE 8: 57)

So Freud takes up this famous sentence with an appendix, taken from a Munich satirical journal, as an example of a certain technique of jokes, where a seemingly commonsensical appendix subverts the initial statement and displays its untenable nature. Freud comments on this joke as follows:

> This modern addition to the ancient wisdom is an obvious nonsense which by the apparently cautious 'scarcely' becomes even more obtuse. This appendix is added to the first sentence as an irrefutably correct limitation; it can open our eyes to the fact that this venerable wisdom is hardly any better than nonsense. Anyone who is not born is not a mortal man at all, and there is no good or best for him. The nonsense in the joke here serves to reveal and present another nonsense.

(Ibid.)

In sum, the old Greek wisdom is ultimately nonsense, it is uttered from an impossible position of enunciation, it contains a pragmatic paradox (in the technical linguistic sense of the word): if it were to be true, it could not be uttered at all, it can be proffered only by someone already born, thus having missed the best, the retroactive conclusion is absurd, for the best is impossible given that this sentence exists at all. He who has not been born is not in a position to proclaim that the best possible has happened to him.

Not Even: Politics of Oedipus **69**

But this joke is perhaps not so innocent, it circumscribes some basic impasse of human life, or life at large. Life is presented through the spyglass of having survived not being born, and only by surviving our own non-being can we retroactively posit it as the best. Or to put it in a short slogan: being is a failed non-being. We may know full well that it is best not to be born, in general that non-being is better than being, but we failed to achieve this. Perhaps in this light one should consider life (in becoming) as a Freudian slip: it would be best not to be, but oops, we failed, there was a slip causing that we are, some Freudian slip happened already at our birth, our birth was like a slip of non-being, conditioning our coming into the world in the first place. To quote Schuster's brilliant formulation: 'The human being is the sick animal that does not live its life but lives its failure not to be born.'

To put it in more general terms: being is the slip of non-being – and one should take slip in the sense of the etymology of the Latin word, *lapsus*, as the fall, the lapse, the fall of non-being into being. We have always already fallen into being, we are the result of having lapsed, of a *lapsus* of that non-being which would have been the best that could have befallen us. The non-being must have been a bit inattentive so in a moment of its distractedness it has lapsed into being.[6] Finally, the most famous philosophical question 'Why is there being instead of nothing?' (from Leibniz to Heidegger) has the same structure. In line with Freud's joke one could say: there would rather be nothing, but it scarcely happens once in a hundred thousand times. We were unfortunately not so lucky.

Let me point out a certain form of the argument that I am after and give some more examples. With Oedipus we have already seen the formula 'not only did I commit the most horrible crime, but I can't even be guilty for it'. Another example can be taken from Alenka Zupančič's book on comedy, where she argues against the widespread idea that comedy is based on the revenge of our finitude on the high ideals and striving for infinity. Comedy opposes the ideals by our human finitude and banality, it dethrones, unmasks, and ridicules the high ideals. As opposed to this she proposes a truly excellent formula: 'Not only we are not infinite, we are not even finite' (Zupančič 2008: 53). Our finitude is a finitude with a failure, a slip, with a hole in it, a failed finitude, it leaks a bit and this is the driving force of comedy. The point of comedy is not to play out our finitude against the infinity, but to aim at the fact that we can't even be finite. 'Not only non-X, even not X.' In the register of comedy we can find another example with analogous structure, the proposal to sum up Lubitch's comedies by this adage: 'Human beings do everything to sabotage their own happiness, but they fail even at that.' In sum, happiness is the slip of unhappiness, its lapse, its inadvertent misfortune, its fall. We strive hard to be unhappy – and psychoanalysis presents the best evidence of countless complex strategies and tools invented by humans, with boundless creativity, to block and sabotage their happiness – but even that they do not manage, not always, they occasionally botch it. This adage presents an inversion of 'the best is not to be born' – striving for misery produces happiness by a slip, happiness is the result of a failure. The ambiguity of this proposal perhaps stands at the heart of human condition: happiness always fails, or happiness is subject to failure. One can

70 Mladen Dolar

read it in a commonsensical manner of striving for happiness that always goes awry in one way or another, or in a far less naïve psychoanalytic sense of striving for unhappiness which fails, and thus produces our fragmented access to happiness. The ultimate example of this structure of argument is 'The best is not to be born – but even that fails' it has always already failed. But the fact that we can say this – putting into suspense our lives and our being, scrutinizing it from the perspective of non-being – has sizeable consequences for our life and being. This is a life that can set itself against life and makes it possible to live our lives on the basis of non-being, through non-being at their core.

One should consider life in this light, and this is precisely where Freud's notion of death drive comes in, not through the tragic perspective of death that undercuts life or presents its bleak goal in relation to which life is but a detour, but through the comedic outlook of our failure to have access to the best, the non-being, but which is what provides an access to our being at all. There is perhaps at the core of psychoanalysis something that one could call the failure of negation. What is repression but an attempt to negate and repress certain problematic content, but a negation that fails so that the repressed makes its return? What is after all the very notion of the unconscious but a negation of the conscious, the other of consciousness, but a failed negation of un- in the unconscious comes back in slips, dreams, jokes, tiny cracks where it keeps coming back, at least for a moment, displaying the very impossibility of consciousness ever closing up on itself? What is death drive but a failure of death as the negation of life, death that does not manage to negate life but keeps being inscribed in it, insisting at its core as an excess of life, that in life which is more than life, more than survival, more than finitude, negation as a surplus that gives us access to enjoyment, as opposed to pleasure, an enjoyment beyond the pleasure and the reality principles? And what is finally life in becoming but the failure of non-being, failure of not having been born, negation that fuels becoming in the midst of life, something in life that is not a mere life function?

Thus the ultimate formula of human misery, 'the best is not to be born', rejoins the very possibility of what provides splinters of enjoyment and happiness in human life, in a short-circuit between tragedy and comedy.

Notes

1 'None of the findings of psychoanalytic research has provoked such embittered denials, such fierce opposition – or such amusing contortions – on the part of critics as this indication of the childhood impulses towards the incest which persist in the unconscious' (Freud, *SE* 4: 263).
2 One of the sources of inspiration for this paper is 'Beyond Oedipus: The Specimen Story of Psychoanalysis', in Felman 1987: 99–159. 'For Lacan, the Oedipus complex is not a signified but a signifier, not a meaning, but a structure. What Freud discovered in the Oedipus myth is not an answer but *the structure of a question*' (ibid.: 103).
3 I am using the George Murray translation available online as a Project Gutenberg Canada e-book.
4 For this reading of Oedipus I am very much indebted to Alenka Zupančič (2000: 175–200).

5 For many insights I am deeply indebted to Aaron Schuster's unpublished manuscript.
6 This could serve as a basis for a larger framework of a subtractive ontology whose origin can be traced back to Democritus. Heinz Wismann, one of the greatest authorities on Democritus, comments on his position as following: 'Being, one could say, is just a privative state of non-being [*l'être* (...) *n'est qu'un état privatif du non-être*]; its positivity is a lure. It is a kind of subtraction operated on nothing [*soustraction opérée à partir de rien*, subtraction executed on the basis of nothing], atom can be thought as the avatar of the void [*avatar du vide*]' (Wismann 2010: 65).

Bibliography

Balibar, Étienne (1997) *La crainte des masses*. Paris: Galilée.
Felman, Shoshana (1987) *Jacques Lacan and the Adventure of Insight*. Cambridge, MA: Harvard University Press.
Freud, Sigmund (1954) *The Origins of Psychoanalysis*. New York: Basic Books.
Freud, Sigmund (2001) *The Standard Edition of the Complete Psychological Works of Sigmund Freud*. London: Vintage Press.
Hegel, Georg Wilhelm Friedrich (1970) '*Vorlesungen über die Ästhetik III*'. in *Werke*, Vol. 15. Frankfurt am Main: Suhrkamp Verlag.
Lacan, Jacques (1991) *The Seminar, Book II, The Ego in Freud's Theory and in the Technique of Psychoanalysis*. New York: W. W. Norton and Company.
Wismann, Heinz (2010) *Les avatars du vide*. Paris: Hermann.
Zupančič, Alenka (2000) *Ethics of the Real*. London: Verso.
Zupančič, Alenka (2008) *The Odd One In*. Cambridge, MA: MIT Press.

5

LACAN'S IMAGINARY

A practical guide

Juliet Flower MacCannell

UC IRVINE, USA

Imaginary, Symbolic, Real

To understand the Imaginary in the theory of Jacques Lacan, we must begin with his unique view of the ego. Lacan's conception differs greatly from that of ego psychology, which like him claims a basis in Freud. For ego psychology, the ego is a positive force, a bulwark against the unconscious drives that threaten the personality's integrity: our id must be controlled by our ego, and later by our super-ego, to make us fit for society. Freud's ego was not so simple, however. Indeed, he says our ego may well consider itself an independent whole, but this is to deny its actual dependence on others: 'In the individual's mental life someone else is invariably involved, as a model, as an object, as a helper, as an opponent [...]' (Freud *SE* 18: 69). The integral, self-contained ego is a delusion: individual psychology is always already, Freud says, social psychology – although he makes an exception of narcissism (ibid.).

Lacan took up Freud's position on the illusions of the ego but extended his conception: for Lacan 'the narcissistic moment' is precisely when the *ego* is born. And it is born not as *single*, but as *double*, as both itself and another. According to Lacan, the initial formation of the ego comes from the infant's encounter with its own image in the mirror. In his early 'The Mirror Stage' (1949) and 'The Aggressivity of the Ego' (1948) Lacan details the process by which the infant's ego is alienated in and from its own mirror image. What appears in the mirror materializes before the infant's eyes, a being that seems infinitely superior to what the child knows itself to be: an inchoate jumble or a 'body in pieces'. Its mirror image is a clearer, more fully formed self than what the infant experiences as its own.

The *Imaginary* is thus the very basis of the *ego* for Lacan. The infant's mirror image shapes its self-image, and in no simple way. For out of this uneven pairing of *the ego* and its *mirror-image (imaginary) other* grows a quasi-Hegelian rivalry. The ego opposes itself to this other who seems to be an *ideal ego*. As Lacan explains, the mirrored other appears to possess a special 'it' that grants it superiority, a singular object that Lacan subsequently names object *a*: an object the ego feels it must have lost, and whose loss it attributes to thievery by its rival.[1]

The destructive hostility that ensues from this imaginary tug of war between ego and other is and must be tempered, according to Lacan, by an invisible third party that comes *between* the imaginary rivals. This third party is *symbolic* in character and it announces itself as an enigmatic *signifier* (the root form of language) that calls the infant to speech and thus to society. Entering the *Symbolic* alters the ego, the two-dimensional, imaginary body it inhabits. At the same time, the rival *other* is transformed from an ideal ego *who has what the ego lacks* into an other *who is equally wanting*. In other words, 'control' of one's aggressive drives is not exercised by a 'healthy ego' *à la* ego psychology, but rather by the subjection of the ego to the *symbolic order*. How does that happen?

Lacan says 'structure carves a body' out of animal substance (Lacan 1990: 6). It splits the *ego* into two parts, conscious and unconscious, forming a *speaking subject* (*parlêtre*). The conscious part, under the dictates of language and society places its original passions and aggressions under the rule of a primal law: Oedipus, or the 'no' of the Father. This law is installed as an *ego-ideal* (usually modelled on the Father) in the newly formed subject's *unconscious*.

The subject's *body* is also modified by language. It is no longer shaped exclusively by its two-dimensional mirror image. Instead it is 'carved' or shaped by a language that cuts away animal and imaginary pleasures (MacCannell 2013). Language alters the body, originally centred on satisfying organic needs and appetites, by ordering it according to a linguistic logic: the human body becomes the infamous '*body without organs*' (Deleuze and Guattari 1977). Indeed, Lacan characterizes the dominion of the *symbol* as endowed with the power to insert *productive voids* (MacCannell 2013) into the *real* of one's anatomical body – voids that shape the speaking subject, channel its sexuality, and make its social order into an arena of creative outlets for the *drives*.

What are the *drives*? Privation of organic satisfactions can never, of course, be total. Indeed, the very fact of the original loss leaves an unconscious residue: satisfactions denied haunt the body in unconscious *fantasy* form, 'repetitive' *jouissance* returns to the body, investing it in the 'erogenous' zones. (Erotism sometimes escapes these localized zones, as when body parts other than the genitals become fetishized.)

The *body without organs* represents a *loss* of simple satisfactions for us, but a *gain* for culture, civilization, and the *Symbolic*: the removal of simple, animal satisfaction drives us, Freud said, to strive to fill in for this lack: to *sublimate* it and find ways of enjoying, despite the ban against it (Freud *SE* 7: 168). *Desire* is thus born: Oedipal desire; *symbolic desire* or *jouissance* deferred. Like language, which always promises a 'meaning' it can never finally deliver, desire promises a satisfaction that it is itself instrumental in deferring.

So it is that right from the start of his clinical research and teaching Lacan formally opposed the *Imaginary* (which grows from and defines the ego as originally

74 Juliet Flower-MacCannel

aggressive) to the *Symbolic* (wherein *subject* and *other* are born into a non-rivalrous relation). He opposed both *Symbolic* and *Imaginary* to the *Real,* which is the absence of these elementary human forms. The *Real* is that which is not subject to the laws of speech or the constraints of Oedipus: it is the realm of *jouissance* or absolute fulfilment, ultimate satisfaction, and finally death. The true virtue of the *Symbolic* is not only that it supplants the *Imaginary* but it also makes a 'hole' in the *Real.* That is, the *Symbolic* remodels our natural impulses potentially destructive to human life, and thus protects us from the devastating force of the *Real.*[2]

Lacan's very clarity about the role of the *Imaginary* has lured many into believing his conception of it is largely limited to the mirror stage (Lacan 2006: 75–81). They see his *Imaginary* as a flat, two-dimensional world of rivalry between the *ego* and *ideal ego* that sets up an anti-social hostility detrimental to Oedipal norms. If this were all there is to Lacan's analysis of the *Imaginary*, it would make him just one more moralist critiquing its illusions in the vein say, of Adorno. It would mean that Lacan believed Oedipus was indeed the ideal solution for the subject, the only desirable norm.

Such a view is simply incorrect. (Lacan is reported to have pronounced *normal* as *norme male* meaning 'evil norm', or 'male norm', the French pronunciation of either would be indistinguishable.) Lacan is well aware that while entrance into the *Symbolic* moderates the ferocity of the ego's hostility to the other, it does not fully eradicate it. The original hostility to the other remains, albeit driven into the unconscious: the primal scene of rivalry with the ideal ego becomes unconsciously elaborated as a fantasy scenario in which the ideal other, who has deprived you of the coveted object *a*, is finally bested, leaving you free to enjoy the object. This fantasy *underlies* Oedipus just as it *undermines* it. It drives our actions, and is the ultimate support for our desire.

Lacan is thus well aware that the *Symbolic-Oedipal* solution to the problem of hostility to others has never been resolved, the aggressivity toward the other originating in the *Imaginary*. His cue was in Freud's *Civilization and its Discontents*, where Freud says that every human is hostile to the 'civilization' it depends on to make it human (the animal brought under the sway of language and society). We know that we must depend on and join with others in constructing this civilization and enjoying its fruits, but we resent it in our deepest psyche. Lacan's striking refinement on Freud was to reduce the kernel of this conflict to a formal, identifiable moment (the mirror stage) in the unfolding of the subject, its subversion, and the dialectic of its desire.

Early readers of Lacan and Freud believed that both men thought the subject's Oedipal trajectory and the installation of its complex made us submit to the regime of social discourse. They often failed to note that the power of Oedipus inevitably wanes; the child rebels against parental prohibitions on enjoyment; its inner voice encourages the child to go ahead and just 'Enjoy!' (Lacan 1992: 6–7; 1998: 3).[3] A commandment *to* pleasure presents the child with a double bind. If it obeys, it faces castigation for indulgences that are socially punished. More often its transgressions simply embarrass it and leave it guilty. While analysts like Anna Freud thought the superego was thoroughly benign, a 'voice of moral conscience', her rival Lacan saw it as a manifestation of the pernicious presence of a hostile other in the unconscious, an *'extimate'* other within. It becomes a voice issuing simulated Oedipal imperatives that command us *to* and also prohibit us *from* at the same time, inducing thus new forms of repressive guilt.

Lacan's emphasis in Seminar VII on the ethics of (dis)obeying superego imperatives led the early Slavoj Žižek to depict our political era as that of the *obscene or sadistic superego*, in which an 'anything goes' mentality combines with intensifying self-imposed regulations against (guilty) pleasures (e.g. the various fads for 'giving up' eating sugar, fat, or meat). The limitation of Žižek's approach is that it remains insightful at the level of *individual psychology* without addressing corresponding alterations in the constitution of *society* itself – material changes in what Lacan called *discourse* or varying *forms of the social link*.[4] The fact that Oedipus, desire, and our social links no longer seem to compel us subjectively indicates less the reign of the superego than the rise of the *Imaginary* which now has the power to determine what only the *Symbolic* once determined: the shape of *society itself.*

The long slow decline of symbolic authority over the social order and the growing sway of the Imaginary over group psychology have to be considered for their broadest social and political, not just individual implications. We can no longer assess society and its politics, and their inherent conflicts, by relying exclusively on symbolic terms. As Deleuze and Guattari long ago divined in their *Anti-Oedipus* (1977: n. 27), Lacan was the first to clear a path for understanding ours as a truly *post-Oedipal condition*, whose imaginary basis is recalcitrant to analysis and remains largely unchallenged in any convincing theoretical way. (Despite assiduous efforts by the Frankfurt School's Adorno, the Neo-Frankfurt School's Marcuse, and impassioned critics like Antonio Negri and Guy Debord.)[5] Žižek has come closest with his focus on the sadistic superego but the results are not entirely satisfactory.

Lacan knew that desire, lack, unfulfilled longing – all these still rest on the primal passions originally installed (and 'satisfied' fantasmatically) in the unconscious. Making the case for how psychoanalysis uses the signifier to free the subject from bondage to its phantasms, Lacan said that fantasies couldn't survive being spoken (Lacan 1992: 80). Yet, we must wonder if such articulation is even possible any longer in a social order now dominated more by the Imaginary than by symbolic speech?

In his later seminars Lacan began paying specific and sustained attention to the role of the Imaginary as it shapes *society* as it once shaped the *ego*. Psychoanalysts and social analysts alike have underutilized Lacan's insights here. In Seminar XVII he hewed closely to Freud's *Group Psychology* tracing the outlines of its Imaginary social order. He created algorithms for the social discourses and tracked the 'revolution' from the discourse of mastery (*Symbolic-Oedipal*) to the discourse of the university, a discourse that places accumulated knowledge in the dominant position (and which Lacan links to that of capitalism, whose dominant is accumulated wealth). In Seminar XXIII he will add something else: an unheralded revolution in discourse, working its way through the Imaginary, to new forms of the social link (MacCannell 2006; 2014).

Society of the Imaginary

Imaginary social order

Much thinking about society today – certainly the popular account of it – assumes it to be a set of *autonomous individuals* bound to their fellows by means of *visible images* rather than by *abstract symbols* (e.g. law, morality, ethics). It also assumes that image-based *social link* bind *discrete egos* together into a *unified whole* through *mutually reflecting self-images*. Finally, it is thought that those who are party to this mirroring exchange are and must be *like one another*.

Human society defined as a *commerce of images* appears to have a major advantage over societies formed through *symbolic exchange*: because it develops as a singular totality, a whole composed of individual egos acting as visual mirrors for each other, it can call upon the resources of *self-love* to ensure the attachment of each ego to every other in the society. Inter-ego conflict is muted by the deepest imperative of what Freud (*SE* 18, 1922: 93ff.) called 'the artificial group' (bound together by mirroring self-images): *the command to conformity and uniformity*: 'Everyone must have the same and be the same' (ibid. 120–21).[6] Society pretends to be all, ending the need for interpersonal conflict.

This cohesion is, of course, a two-edged sword. Take the contemporary grouping of like egos in 'identity politics'. *Identity politics* were originally the political action arm of minorities in a larger society for pleading their sub-group's special legal needs for greater rights and recognition. Yet no matter how specifically historical, cultural, and legal their demands, an identity that had earlier been defined by our actual ethnic or religious affiliations, ended by being defined culturally, mainly through *imagery*. Visible characteristics like skin colour or attire, became the hallmark of identity politics. However, anyone antipathetic to such groups could also mobilize images to demonstrate that 'those' people simply do not fit in – they deviate too far from a nation's ideal ego, its *imago*.

When the Sarkozy government in France singled out the Roma for deportation, news outlets began publishing pictures of the gypsies' shabby lifestyle, their dark looks, their suspicious dexterity as making manifest that they were not really part of the French nation. The implication? That the 'whole' French nation would be better off – more homogeneous, more harmonious – without *those* people.[7] For a large, pluralistic society to pretend to a singular self-image that excludes all unlike 'others' is perhaps the most troubling political outcome of an image-dominated social discourse.

Imaginary economy

The *economic* corollary to a society of the Imaginary is (the claim of) the inherent superiority of Western *capitalism*: capitalism is said to be unique in its power to create the wealth of nations and individuals, and thus everyone under its regime has an even chance of obtaining said wealth. All are free to enjoy. Yet accumulating wealth is hardly a feature of most people's experience under capitalism. So capitalism must force masses of people to adopt and ardently espouse an economic ideology that does not necessarily benefit them.

It deploys well-crafted images of a vast *wealth-available-to-all* that links us libidinally to the one-sided world of capitalism, designed as much to inhibit the free exercise of our imagination to oppose it as to incite our devotion to it. The populist appeal of late capitalism seems to spring most from a media saturation of images of immense wealth – a wealth that vast numbers of people are unable, in reality to access, let alone accumulate. These include dramatized portrayals of wealthy families (e.g. *Dallas*), advertisements for luxury goods (where ordinary items like purses, watches, or shoes magically turn into exorbitantly expensive, unattainable fetishes), and the inordinate attention television and the Internet pay to the lifestyles of the rich and famous.

If money was once deemed an 'external' or objective measure of one's social worth, it was because money itself was *symbolic* in character, tied to a specific social contract to represent a certain *value*. The Symbolic dimension to money has however yielded to the Imaginary: one enriches oneself now with virtual money, Bitcoins, accumulated without any societies authenticating their worth.

Glaring illustrations of wealth and luxury can stifle our freedom to dream of alternative futures, to contemplate different social arrangements, or to devise other economies than those defined exclusively by wealth accumulation, the cardinal feature of capitalism. The image of superabundant wealth (recall Scrooge McDuck swimming in his gold) is the powerful binding ideological force in the economy of the Imaginary; the more such images contradict the reality of people's economic condition, the more they become attached to it. Lacan thus asked, 'What is wealth?' and the answer was a tautology: 'Wealth is an attribute of the wealthy.' He then asked why those without wealth support the wealthy: the answer is *identification* (Lacan 2007: 94–95). Despite actual disparities of wealth, each person must be convinced that the wealthy are really *just like you and me*. Mesmerizing images of the wealth-touting capitalism erase the poor or demonize them for insufficiently identifying with the affluence of the whole.[8]

Identification: the link that binds

Identification powers the solidarity of the whole: no differences may appear; no gaps in the social totality may be recognized.

Consider how today's cultural and political leaders project images that show them being just like us – not remote authorities invested with mysterious symbolic power. Reviewing Tony Blair's memoirs, Peter Stothard asks this question:

> Are politicians different from the rest of us? Do they live by the same rules? Should they live by the same rules? When we are told about their personal lives and habits […] are we being persuaded that they are more like us than they really are? Is that useful for either side? Blair is drily candid on the

pretences required for modern politics, the need to appear like a normal person during election campaigns, buying items in front of the TV cameras from security-vetted salesmen in security-cleared shops and learning the prices of grocery items he would never buy lest he be accused of not knowing the cost of corn flakes.

(Stothard 2010: 10)

In the Imaginary social order, configured around a unified ego as site of mastery and control, the unconscious paternal *ego-ideal* of Oedipus is replaced by a visible *object* with which all egos are equally linked together libidinally and through which all egos identify *'themselves with one another in their ego'*, as Freud remarks (*SE* 18: 116).

The image-object fuses everyone's *ideal ego* with that of others through identification with the Leader. Instead of a three-dimensional relation to a Symbolic Other, there is a flat mirroring of all by all. The symbol, neither a *having* nor a *being*, meets its dialectical antithesis in this image-object, which asserts we can both *have* (the object) and *be* (the object) – and can do so not despite, but because of our social obligations. Analytic protocols that assume the Oedipal-symbolic premise of a successful installation of the ego-*ideal* in each member of a society yield little insight.

Only an undivided, unified individual ego can be the basic unit of a social order formed by identification. There is undeniably a deep appeal in the idea of joyously reunifying the split ego and joining that whole ego to an equally unified social group with no need for sacrificing satisfactions to the collective. Equally alluring is its promise of equality: 'Every one must be the same and have the same' (Freud *SE* 18: 120–21). Such a social order is no longer formed by efforts to bridge the gaps between us opened by the symbol. No gaps are tolerated in the whole: if the other is you, the very same as you, with the same value, the same being, no language or metaphor need bridge any distance nor grant symbolic passage from subject to the other.

The paradox of a society based on the self-image of a unified ego, not a divided subject is that this requires the ego to be an isolatable unit, discrete and countable, while this 'undivided' ego only exists as a unit by virtue of its inclusion in the whole, the bounded totality of a social order whose oneness and singularity mirrors

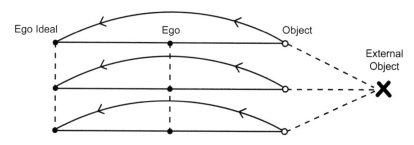

FIGURE 5.1 Identification

and sustains it. In an Imaginary order only the One can support a multitude of ones. *Identification with the whole society* is both required and assured by the fact that the society itself is strictly modelled on the individual as a unified ego, one and whole and at one with the whole. Reconciling ultimate individual differences by submerging them in the empire of the images, has, of course, its dark side: recall Freud's picture of the exploited plebeian in Ancient Rome: 'No doubt one is a wretched plebeian, harassed by debts and military service; but to make up for it, one is a Roman citizen, one has one's share in the task of ruling other nations and dictating their laws' (Freud *SE* 18: 13).

Banishing reality in favour of fantasy and abandoning the basic idea of a symbolic social contract puts the Imaginary in the driver's seat. If it curtails freedom of the imagination and impoverishes human discourse, reducing the richness of life to being measured by a single dominant (wealth), one might still ask, 'What harm a regime of the Imaginary?' True, at the dawn of Imaginary society, we experienced a terrible politics of race and religion that deployed visual imagery to stir conflict, war, persecutions, and genocides (like the infamous intercutting of pictures of vermin with 'Jewish' faces in Nazi propaganda films). Such abuses were somewhat curtailed after World War II. Still, post-war thinkers and planners firmly believed that creating small homogeneous *societies of likes* (called 'garden cities' or 'suburbs') would generate greater cohesion than traditional societies ever had[9] (Abrams 1949: 38). The widely held belief that the individual (Negri: the 'singularity'; Marcuse: the 'autonomous', 'private' individual) is the building block of society and its supposed solution to social antagonism is highly questionable. Can inter-ego hostility, set off by the dominance of the *Imaginary* in the single psyche, be sufficiently controlled in a universal society of the *Imaginary*? Freud thought not.

Sublimation, Symbolic and Imaginary

For Lacan, as for Freud, the original basis of human life in common (civilization, society) was an inescapable *lack*. *Everything held in common is nothing* – except for what each subject yielded claim to for itself. The entirety of one's relation to others is structured by the *recognition of mutual lack* – the other's lack is equal to one's own. (Recall that in the pre-social mirror stage you assume the other *has* the 'it' you lack.) From religion as sacrifice to love, what counts in the Symbolic social order is that each offers the other precisely *what they do not have*: their nothing, their desire, their lack.

The constitutive lack at the heart of the Symbolic grants it a crucial openness to change, to creating meaning, to becoming rather than being, or winding down to the entropy or death that ensues when full satisfaction (the lowering of tension to zero) is achieved. For Lacan all drives are partial but all relate to what he says is the only substance in psychoanalysis: *jouissance,* satisfaction literally unfulfillable for a *parlêtre* in its human experience. *Sublimation* is its answer to the allure of the 'Nirvana principle' where the absence of tension is deadly. Oedipal society, with '*Thou shalt not*', bans certain enjoyments. Since no subject can give up all pleasure, Symbolic *sublimation* simulates fulfilment of forbidden wishes in art and drama where

80   Juliet Flower-MacCannel

proscriptions on drive satisfaction are provisionally lifted – we stage murder, incest, and other illicit passions. There is a knot tying *abstract symbols of mutual lack/desire* to *unconscious fantasy enjoyment*. The *sine qua non* social life requires, is an art that makes it tolerable.

In the long run, all societies promise individuals a measure of satisfaction for forbidden wishes – otherwise that portion of us which is 'enemy' to civilization would have long since prevailed. Where drive satisfaction is not strongly proscribed, Symbolic sublimation is ineffective. In the post-Oedipal what was once consigned to the unconscious rises to the surface. Drives appear on the verge of satisfaction: recall the 1960s slogan, 'Just *do* it!' What then protects the Imaginary order from entropy?

Imaginary society can no more dispense with sublimation than the Symbolic one: no society can exist without limits on the enjoyment of all by all. Lacan discovered where sublimated satisfaction exists in the post-Oedipal: in *fantasy objects* as spurious as symbolic substitutes for the mother under Oedipus (2007: 95ff.). The difference is not of kind, but degree. In post-Oedipal society there are what Lacan calls *jouissances en toc*, counterfeit enjoyments, mock fulfilments (Lacan 2007: 95; MacCannell, 2006). Whereas simulating drive satisfaction was once the province of great writers, talented dramatists, and outstanding artists, today we automate the production of image-objects promising full enjoyment (blockbuster action movies, video games) that easily displace the sublime pity and fear of Aristotle's stage. The fake or simulated enjoyment, *jouissance en toc*, appears in all those gadgets swirling all around us (Lacan 2007: 188). Well before the advent of the i-objects that now surround us (iPod, iPhone, etc.) Lacan predicted that our new social reality, which is a realm of images or appearances (*aléthosphère*), would soon be overfilled with gadgets (*lathouses*) busy 'fulfilling' us – in a fake manner (again *jouissance en toc*).

Lacan suspected that the true function of *jouissance en toc* was to reassure us, by dint of an overwhelming accumulation of these gadgets, that our drives are fully satisfied and under control – and that the ego is secure in its wholeness, unity, and mastery.

Psychoanalysis of the Imaginary?

A revolution – in discourse, from Oedipal to post-Oedipal – has set the *positive image of fulfilment* above the *negative symbol* founded on lack. This means that the image must be engaged on its own terms. We can no longer take for granted the effectiveness of the symbol for safeguarding the creative openness necessary to defend against the drives and the ultimate entropy giving in to them entails. Let us therefore turn directly to the image, to the symbol's opposite, for analytic breakthrough. The challenge is to trace a path to an open and creative social contract by *going through the Imaginary*, rather than setting ourselves against it, vainly trying to turn back to an Oedipal-symbolic.

Can Imaginary society provide the necessary openings to prevent sclerosis and stasis or entropy, given its unity, solidarity, and virtual seamlessness? Or is the tendency to one-sidedness and closure in the image-based social order rather a fundamental weak spot psychoanalytic criticism can exploit as new grounds for critique?

How can we open up the Imaginary's self-enclosed, rigidifying, and increasingly entropic existence and make a *breach* in it wide enough for *something else* to appear in it, *something new* to emerge from it, and for *something other* to touch it and move it from without?[10]

Symptom to sinthome: from symbolic speech to signifying image

In the theory offered by Saussure the linguistic sign is an *image plus a concept* or a *signifier* and its *signified*. But is the picture of the tree Saussure provides the *image*, or is the written *word 'tree'* the image? Which is the *concept*: the *image* or the *sound–image of the word 'tree'*? Either part of the sign can be deemed the signifier – or the signified. And that is precisely the point. The signifier mobilizes images and concepts to structure meaning in a way that eludes most theorists' grasp of the working of the image (e.g. Adorno).

The signifier is ultimately the *only* operative concept in language – a language that is and remains the model for the Symbolic. The reason: the unfathomable *division between signifier and signified* is of far less importance to its *meaning* than is any sign's *difference from other signs*. Even though one might want to believe that an established language is finished, a closed lexicon, the differentiating process from signifier to signifier is an unending process of promising but not delivering *final* meaning. The supposed *whole* of a language is never really whole.

Language is by definition, incomplete; we must keep renewing it with more signifiers, producing more possible meanings. As Lacan puts it in one of his later seminars:

> In the long run, this language, we create it. This is not reserved to the stages or phases where language is created: at each and every instant we give it some sense, we give it a little push, without which language would not be living. It is not living except that at each instant one creates it. It is in this that there is no collective unconscious. There are only particular unconsciouses insofar as each one, at each instant, gives a little push to the language he or she speaks.
> *(Lacan 2005: 133)*

Language is thus the *Symbolic* par excellence: an open, self-generative system of meaning creation based on adding yet one more signifier to another with productive gaps between them. It is a body ever in need of new appendages, new limbs, new signifiers if it is to be what it is. But as with the Oedipal–symbolic there is another side to language.

We imagine we enjoy an immense body of words and meanings, much as Hegel imagined 'total-knowledge' would be enjoyed at the end of history. While in reality each signifier requires a *next* – an *other* signifier to grant it provisional meaning, we fantasize that somewhere every signifier is just part of a vast treasury available to us:

> This other signifier is not alone. The stomach of the Other, the big Other, is full of them. This stomach is like some monstrous Trojan horse that provides

the foundations for the fantasy of a knowledge-totality. It is, however, clear that its function requires something coming and striking it from the outside, otherwise nothing will ever emerge from it. And Troy will never be taken.

(Lacan 2007: 33)

The promise of a full meaning and a place in the lexicon of established socio-symbolic meanings for the subject can never be fulfilled, and this promise ends unhappily with the poor subject lodged in 'the stomach of the big Other', unmoved, and unmoving. The signifier's failure to finalize meaning is a blessing in disguise: it protects us from death drive; it keeps us moving onwards instead of backwards or staying stuck. This 'belly' is like Imaginary society, the illusion of a container, not round but flat, centred on an ego that has expelled from its purview whatever does not fit its ideal. It lacks dimensionality; its logic is that of 'the sack and the cord' (Lacan 2005: 146), the dead end of social discourse.

Lacan's four discourses, the various forms of the social link, are the following: *master, university, hysteric,* and *analyst.* Each exhausts the universe of possible human links within them, but with some impediment, some obstacular knot that cannot be articulated or linked into the discourse. Each algorithm symbolizes this blockage in the lower left quadrant of the discourse.

Where does the impediment arise? The gaps between signifiers generate ever-changing meanings. But in speech there is also a permanent gap where one particular signifier has been 'dropped' from the productive chain. Its *meaning stays fixed* (as fantasized enjoyment/pain), and while it plays no part in conscious social discourse it is an impediment *to* that discourse. It is *the thing that cannot be said.* This dead signifier is the *symptom,* a subjective obstruction.[11] For all the Imaginary's dream of undoing the primacy of the signifier, the central problem of the symptom/obstacle remains or increases daily: consider how taboos on speech have multiplied to the point now where casually tactless words are deemed racist 'micro-aggressions'.

The image-object blocks us as vexatiously as the symbolic symptom. After Lacan in *Seminar XVII* sought alternatives to the current form of our social link (*identification with image–objects*) he decided to engage the Imaginary directly. What he found, beyond the opposition of symbolic-symptomatic/identification with *image–objects* or *ersatz* ego-ideals, was less a new model *for* identification than a way to *undo* identification altogether. Lacan had not considered that the Imaginary could ever in itself provide any way of escape from that closed 'identity' sack it puts us in – until the concept of the sinthome, in which he finds a new freedom for the subject in the effectiveness of a link that suddenly comes *undone*.

A different model for the post-Oedipal: late Lacan and the discovery of a dialectic in the Imaginary

Lacan begins a *two-dimensional* flattening operation that reveals to him that the Symbolic, which we have long assumed to be the sole locus of the 'hole' or the opening that allows for change, creativity, etc., is *no longer the 'true hole'* (2005: 134). That opening is now there where the *Imaginary* (and not just the *Symbolic*) confronts and breaches the *Real*. To make an opening in the ostensible seamlessness of the *Imaginary* totality by *Imaginary* rather than *Symbolic* means is something new in Lacan's theory. I believe it is linked to his understanding of how much Freud's *Group Psychology* with a particular ego at the centre of it has come to define our social order.

By locating a structural void *even in* the Imaginary, Lacan's thesis offers a creative openness, a potential fracturing of the image's received totalitarian meaning. The apparent meaning must have, we might say, a bit of *non-meaning* inserted into its perfection. The 'true hole' marks where the *Imaginary* meets up with *Real*, and *makes a hole in it*, just like the Symbolic – a hole, which enables other images to start interacting with the image present before the eyes, a hole that voids the pretence of the image to be all and to end all.

Recall that an internal *symbolic* limit opened the *ego* to the world and reduced its quotient of hostility to others – the gap between *I and you* and that intangible third person, the *Symbolic Other*. The Imaginary order rejected symbolic identification with the others *lack* and substituted for it the overt *identification* with what others possess: an ideal *image–object*. No gaps, no change, and thus insufficient resistance to death drive. But to discover a 'true hole' in the Imaginary is to open a new discursive possibility, an alternative social link that deploys *both identification and lack*. The knot must come undone.

Lacan articulated his vision in his early 'Rome Discourse' (1953) where he invoked 'the subjectivity of his time':

> Let whoever cannot meet at its horizon the subjectivity of his time give it up then. For how could he who knows nothing of the dialectic that engages him in a symbolic movement with so many lives possibly make his being the axis of those lives? Let him be well acquainted with the whorl into which his era draws him in the ongoing enterprise of Babel, and let him be aware of his function as an interpreter in the strife of languages.
>
> *(Lacan 2006: 264)*

Rather than assume Lacan is merely caught up in the then current lingo of phenomenology and the 'intersubjective relation', it is wiser to see his imperative to identify with one's fellow subjects as a transindividual in the light of the Imaginary's ascendance to discursive dominance. Lacan speaks of 'the ongoing enterprise of *Babel*', not of the formal structure of *a* single language, but of a discordant interlocution *among* languages. Babel is no traditional linguistic order, but like the Symbolic one, it can disrupt false plenitudes and the dream of a completed lexicon of meanings. 'An ongoing enterprise' means movement, not entropy.

A static Imaginary frames the horizon as a *boundary*, an enclosure; Lacan proposes it as *ever-receding line*. Lacan's *transindividual* unties us *from* Imaginary society more than it ties it *to* any specific society; and it unties the subject from its shackling to a fixed articulation within a *pseudo-horizon*. Thus it offers us another sort of linkage to others, based on experience. To reach for that ever-receding horizon, the analyst

84 Juliet Flower-MacCannell

has first to be situated within the closed one, inside that box, a consumer of the very images that bind us too tightly together. Lacanians often short-circuit the laboriousness of this task with pop culture references (movies, the media, and politics). But discussion of *the method* such analysis requires and the *systematic* analysis of discourse and its alienation of the subject have lagged. The real task of the analyst is to grasp precisely how discourse situates and alienates *all* of its subjects, including oneself.

Lacan says the domain of psychoanalysis 'is that of concrete discourse qua field of the subject's transindividual reality; and its operations are those of history, insofar as history constitutes the emergence of truth in reality' (Lacan 2006: 214), and that this means we must recognize that 'it is not at the subject's disposal in reestablishing the continuity of his conscious discourse' (ibid.). The fiction of our order as a self-enclosed whole has to be deconstructed (MacCannell 2014).

Urging images (even or especially self-images) into 'the ongoing enterprise of Babel' breaks apart the seamless 'perfection' of Imaginary society and its egos. The Imaginary can and must shatter its own unity and open up a space for encountering (and countering) the Real. Only in that space will we find ways of escape. A parallel opening of the ego itself is also necessary (Lacan 2005: 152; MacCannell 2014).

The opposition *subjective symbolic lack* (once thought to be confined only to the Oedipal order) to *egocentric identification with imaginary plentitude* (so clearly delineated by Freud in his *Group Psychology*) has been to some degree rendered moot by the triumph of the Imaginary ego. Only if that ego might finally see itself as something other than a closed circle can the jerry-built structure of group psychology be brought down, and the social link be re-conceived. One must, as in Baudelaire's beautiful phrasing, know how to 'take a bath of multitude' – to be in the crowd, but not at one with it. Only when the ego is open to others, open to desire, passion, and creativity can we figure a serious alternative to Oedipal repression as our means of living together and co-creating our world.

Notes

1 Unchecked, the 'primitive rivalry' over the 'it', excited in the ego by its encounter with the imaginary other, develops as *psychosis*: the rival other becomes a fixture in one's own mind, an internally hostile and eternally terrifying object within (Lacan 1993: 39–40).
2 In the formation of the human subject, all three realms are linked together, although not always in the same way. The 'link' is Lacan's *Borromean knot*, in which Symbolic, Imaginary, and Real are linked together with voids or 'holes' between them, openings without which there is no knot.
3 Noting how complex the generation of the superego is in Freud, Lacan writes: 'Will it [the ego] or will it not submit itself to the duty that it feels within like a stranger, beyond, at another level? Should it or should it not submit itself to the half-unconscious, paradoxical, and morbid command of the superego [...]? If I may put it thus, isn't its true duty to oppose that command?' (Lacan 1992: 7).
4 The theory of social link is developed systematically in Lacan's Seminar XVII (2007 [1969–70]) and in subsequent seminars. Seminar XX presents its final form.
5 Guy Debord's 1967 *Society of the Spectacle* also opened this topic, but he attributes it to commodity fetishism and narcotization. Lacan and Freud show the mechanics of imaginary identification.

6 Freud notes that even gender distinctions are not desirable in the artificial group. Later Lacan would note that capitalism begins by 'getting rid of sex'.
7 At the time, President Nicolas Sarkozy launched a campaign to get his compatriots to define 'Frenchness' by making checklists of what they considered 'real' French attributes.
8 Right-wing conservative candidates freely and viciously attack the poor, comparing them to calves sucking at the state's teats and to monkeys.
9 Nineteenth International Conference for Housing and Town Planning, held in 1948, Zurich, Switzerland, and attended by delegates of 30 countries (Abrams 1949: 38).
10 In Seminar XXIII, Lacan showed the way in his concept of the *sinthome*, a word-image that permits the subject's *jouissance* to flow through it, rather than being repressed by verbal expression. Recall that speech excises *jouissance*. The *sinthome* is something else, and in my view, quite the opposite of 'psychotic', but is rather the essence of the experience of art (MacCannell 2014).
11 'The symptom [...] inscribes the symbol in letters of suffering in the subject's flesh' (Lacan 2006: 252).

Bibliography

Abrams, C. (1949) 'Human Relations and City Planning', in *Human Relations in Chicago*. Chicago, IL: City of Chicago.

Debord, G. (1967) *La société du spectacle*. Paris: Buchet Chastell.

Deleuze, G. and F. Guattari (1977). *Anti-Oedipus*. New York and London: Continuum Books.

Freud, S. (1948–74) *The Standard Edition of the Works of Sigmund Freud*, Vols 1–24. London: Vintage.

Lacan, J. (1990) *Television. A Challenge for the Psychoanalytic Establishment*. New York: W. W. Norton and Company.

Lacan, J. (1992) *Seminar, Book VII, The Ethics of Psychoanalysis*, trans. D. Porter, New York: W. W. Norton and Company.

Lacan, J. (1993) *Seminar, Book III, The Psychoses*, trans. R. Grigg. New York: W. W. Norton and Company.

Lacan, J. (1998) *Seminar, Book XX, Encore*, trans. B. Fink. New York: W. W. Norton and Company.

Lacan, J. (2005) *Le Séminaire. livre XXIII, Le sinthome*. Paris: Éditions du Seuil.

Lacan, J. (2006) *Écrits*, trans. B. Fink. New York: W. W. Norton and Company.

Lacan, J. (2007) *Seminar, Book XVII, The Other Side of Psychoanalysis*, trans. R. Grigg. New York: W. W. Norton and Company.

MacCannell, J. F. (2006) 'More Thoughts for the Times on War and Death: Lacan's Critique of Capitalism in Seminar XVII', in *The Other Side of Psychoanalysis*, ed. J. Clemens and R. Grigg. Durham, NC and London: Duke University Press, 194–215.

MacCannell, J. F. (2013) 'The Abyss of Mind and Matter: Sexuality on Edge', in *Erogene Gefahrenen Zonen: Aktuelle Produktionen des (infantile) Sexuellen*, ed. Insa Härtel. Berlin: Kadmos, 73–89.

MacCannell, J. F. (2014) 'The Open Ego: Woolf, Joyce and the "Mad" Subject', in *Madness, Yes You Can't: Lacan on Insanity*, ed. M. Steinkoler and P. Gherovici. Abingdon: Routledge.

Stothard, P. (2010) 'Review of Tony Blair, A Journey: My Political Life', *The Times Literary Supplement* (10 September), 10.

6

SEXUAL IS POLITICAL?

Alenka Zupančič

SCIENTIFIC RESEARCH CENTRE OF SLOVENIAN ACADEMY OF SCIENCES AND ARTS

The quandary of the relation

In John Huston's movie *Freud: The Secret Passion* (1962) a very powerful scene pictures Freud presenting his theory of infantile sexuality to a large audience of educated men. His brief presentation is met with strong and loudly stated disapproval, interrupted by roaring almost after every sentence; several of the men leave the auditorium in protest, spitting on the floor next to Freud. At some point the chairman, trying to restore the order, cries out: 'Gentlemen, we are not in a political meeting!'

This is a very intriguing remark, pointing us straight in the right direction: that of a strange, surprising coincidence between politics and (the Freudian, as well as Lacanian) theory of sexuality. It is as if every time one reopens the question of the latter, something is decided that is of a political order. This was certainly true for the politics of the psychoanalytical movement itself, and for the chasms that it produced within the movement. But it might also be true in the more specific sense of politics as referring to what can be articulated around some fundament social antagonism(s).[1] What was, and still is, disturbing about the Freudian discussion of sexuality is not simply sexuality itself – this kind of resistance, indignant at psychoanalytical 'obsession with dirty matters', was never the strongest one and was soon marginalized by the progressive liberalism of morals. Much more disturbing was the thesis concerning the always problematic and (ontologically) uncertain character of sexuality itself. To the Victorians screaming 'sex is dirty', Freud did not answer something like 'no, it is not dirty, it is only natural', but rather something like: 'What *is* this "sex" that you are talking about?'

It is my strongest conviction that it is precisely here, with the question of sexuality and what it does with it (conceptually), that one has to situate the properly political dimension of the Freudo-Lacanian psychoanalysis. This thesis may sound counter-intuitive, especially since what is at stake is not at all a claim about how politics is something that, deep down, has to do with sexuality. What is at stake is not the kind of psychological level as implied in claims about sexual motivation of politics (and politicians). The claim is different, and stronger; it has to do with the ontological status of politics and sexuality (or, rather, of their objects).

When speaking about psychoanalysis and politics today, one usually does one of two things. One either leaves sexuality out, puts it aside, and pursues other concepts, such as the (barred) Other, surplus-enjoyment, the Lacanian theory of the four discourses, the Lacanian contribution to the ideology critique ... All of these are of course crucial, yet they cannot be exempted from the issue of the sexual without losing something central, namely a conceptual articulation of a negativity at work at their core, sustaining them as well as relating them to one another. There is also another attitude which, in tune with the prevailing (Western) ideology of our time, combines liberalism of morals (anything goes and should be tolerated as far as there is no abuse involved) with political conservativism (of the status quo, in which every zealous political engagement is by definition 'pathological', unbefitting 'normal', 'non-neurotic' human beings). These two attitudes share a symmetrical (albeit not identical) mistake. The philosophical and politically more radical reading of Lacan dismisses sexuality *as something* that only has a secondary, anecdotic, or 'regional' relevance. And the liberal psychoanalytic reading dismisses politics *as something* necessarily pathologic (blind to the impossibility at work in it). The mistake of the first is not that it misreads the relevance of sexuality, but that it considers it *as something* (something which simply *is,* and can be considered of lesser or bigger importance). In the same way, the mistake of the second is not that it fails to see that an essentially different politics is nevertheless possible, but again that it takes politics *as something,* as a fully blown entity with certain characteristics. In other words, it fails to see that politics is by definition politics of the impossible (relation).[2] What relates sexuality and politics is that they are not simple ontological categories, but essentially imply and deploy something which is not of the order of being, and which Lacan refers to as *the real.* The real is precisely not being, but its inherent impasse.

The Lacanian concept of the sexual is not something that provides a best description so far of a certain reality (called sexuality), what it does is that it develops a unique model of thinking a fundamental non-relationship as dictating the conditions of different kinds of ties (including social ties, or 'discourses'). For this is what the Lacanian concept of sexuality is primarily about. It conceptualizes the way in which a fundamental impasse of being is at work in its structuring (as being). It is important, however, to stress the following: by insisting that the Lacanian concept of the sexual is not simply about any kind of sexual *content* (or sexual practice), we are in no way aiming at its 'purification', trying to produce something like its pure form or pure (philosophical) idea, and hence making it philosophically more acceptable. The point is that beyond all sexual content and practices the sexual is not a pure form, but refers instead to the *absence of the latter* as that what curves and defines the space of the sexual. In other words, this is an 'absence' or negativity that has important consequences for the field structured around it. How to understand this?

The paradoxical status of sex is the opposite of, say, the status of unicorns: it is not about an entity that is nowhere to be found empirically, although we know exactly what it would look like if found empirically; rather the opposite: empirically, sex exists very well (and we are pretty able to recognize, 'identify' it); what seems to be missing – to put this in Platonic terms – is the Idea of sex, its essence: what exactly is that we recognize when we say 'this is sex'? Plato went as far as to say that even the lowest things like mud and dirt have their corresponding ideas (ideal essences), but what about sex? Is there an Idea, a pure form of sex? The answer seems to be negative. And this is not because sex would be situated even 'lower' on the chain of beings than mud or dirt, but for some other reason. Presenting sex as low and 'dirty' is already a response, a 'solution' to its more fundamental scandal – namely that we don't even know what it *is*. The embarrassment at and the covering up of sexuality, as well as its controlling and regulating, should not be taken as self-explanatory, that is as explained by the 'traditional' cultural ban on sexuality, but rather the other way around, this ban should be explained by an ontological lapse involved in sexual as sexual. The cause of embarrassment in sexuality is not simply something that is there, on display in it, but on the contrary something that is not there – something which, if it existed, would determine what sex actually is, and name what is 'sexual' about sex. Sex is all around, but we don't seem to know what exactly it is. We could perhaps go as far as to say: when – in the human realm – we come across something for which we have absolutely no clue what it is, we can be pretty certain that it 'has to do with sex'. This formula is not meant to be ironic. *Il n'y a de sexe que de ce qui cloche.* Sex is only in what does not work.

In this precise sense culture is not simply a mask/veil of the sexual, it is the mask or, rather, a stand-in for something in the sexual which 'is not'. And it is also in this precise (indirect) sense that culture, civilization, is – as the classical Freudian stance goes – sexually driven, 'motivated'. It is not driven by that in the sexual which is, but rather by that which is not.

That in the sexual which is not is the relation: *there is no sexual relation.* This famous Lacanian claim is often understood too hastily as a learned and clever sounding formulation of that what people, poems, literature, films have always known and kept repeating in different ways: 'true love is impossible (to last)', 'love is mostly unhappy', 'Men are from Mars, women are from Venus', 'relationships don't work', 'there are only series of (missed) encounters', 'there are only elementary particles'. It is easy to show where this kind of understanding moves too quickly and overrides, covers up the real written by Lacan's formula. What it does is that it immediately moves to ontologize the non-relation(ship). And so we exclaim: 'But of course, there is no sexual relation(ship)! This explains it all (and especially the history of our love life).' The fundamental ontological category, 'being as being', is the non-relation, and this is why we are where we are! The truth is admittedly not very pleasant, but this is how it is, and at least we can understand why things are as they are.

In this way the non-relation is understood as the ultimate truth, the ultimate code or formula of reality. We are led to conclude that the non-relation is the *cause* of oddities and difficulties of all concrete relationships. More precisely: the ontologically stated non-relationship is seen in this perspective as the obstacle to the formation of any 'successful' concrete, empirical relationship. Lacan's point, however, is paradoxically almost the opposite: it is the inexistence of the relation that only opens up the space for relations and ties as we know them. In Lacan's own words: 'the absence of the relationship does of course not prevent the tie (*la liaison*), far from it – it dictates its conditions' (Lacan 2011: 19). The non-relationship gives, dictates the conditions of what ties us, which is to say that it is not a simple, indifferent absence, but an absence that curves and determines the structure with which it appears. The non-relation is not the opposite of the relation, it is *the inherent non-logic (a fundamental 'antagonism') of the relations* that are possible and existing.[3]

This represents a new and original conceptual model of the discursive space as being generated out of, and around, a missing link in the ontological chain of its own reality. Biased by its constitutive negativity this structure is always more or less than what it is, that is to say more or less than the sum of its elements. Moreover, the causal link between these (signifying) elements is determined by what appears at the place of this negativity as both heterogeneous and inseparable from the signifying order: the impossible substance of enjoyment, conceptualized by Lacan in terms of the (partial) object *a*. Object *a* is not a sexual object. Rather, it is *a*-sexual. It is the objective counterpart of the non-relation (it is non-relation as object).[4] Yet it is also what is at work in all forming of ties, in the very structuring of (discursive) being qua being. With this in mind it is more than a pun, a play on words, to suggest that what follows from this Lacanian conceptualization is an '*object-disoriented ontology*'. If there is an ontology that follows from psychoanalytic (Lacanian) theory, this can only be an ontology 'disoriented' by the object *a*.

So, again, what is most valuable in the Freudo-Lacanian concept of sexuality is that it introduces a conceptual model of thinking of a non-relation as dictating the conditions of different kinds of ties, including social ties (or discourses).

It is in this precise sense that one could reaffirm the well-known slogan 'sexual is political' and give it a new, more radical meaning. 'Sexual is political' not as a realm of being where political struggles also take place, but in the sense that a true emancipatory politics can only be thought on the ground of an 'object-disoriented ontology' as sketched above – that is ontology that pursues *not* being qua being, but the crack (the real, the antagonism) that haunts the latter from within, informs it.

In what follows we will develop this with reference to an example which can help us explore and articulate more closely what is at stake in these claims. The example is that of a most peculiar encounter between sexuality and politics as staged in an ingenious text by Russian Marxist author Andrei Platonov, *The Anti-Sexus*, situated at the very heart of the 20th century's discussions of a possible emancipatory politics.

'The global human problem of sex and the soul'

As Aaron Schuster pointed out in his introduction to the recent English (re)publication of Andrei Platonov's *The Anti-Sexus*:

90 Alenka Zupančič

If part of the twentieth century's revolutionary program to create a radically new social relation and a New Man was the liberation of sexuality, this aspiration was marked by a fundamental ambiguity: Is it sexuality that is to be liberated, delivered from moral prejudices and legal prohibitions, so that the drives are allowed a more open and fluid expression, or is humanity to be liberated from sexuality, finally freed from its obscure dependencies and tyrannical constraints? Will the revolution bring an efflorescence of libidinal energy or, seeing it as a dangerous distraction to the arduous task of building a new world, demand its suppression? In a word, is sexuality the object of or the obstacle to emancipation?

(Schuster 2013: 42)

As already suggested by Schuster, this may be a wrong alternative, in the sense that it misses something crucial about the psychoanalytic take on sexuality – as well as, we may add, about its take on emancipation. Whereas the latter is most often conceived in terms of freeing ourselves of the (social) non-relation – or else as approaching the Ideal of the Relation, even if unattainable – Lacan puts us in a very different perspective. The aim of abolishing the non-relation (and replacing it with a relation) is rather the trademark of all social repression. Sexual difference and oppression of women are very good examples of this. The most oppressive societies have always been those which axiomatically proclaimed (enforced) the existence of sexual relation: a 'harmonious' relation presupposes an exact definition of essences (involved in this relation) and of roles pertaining to them. If there is to be a relation, women need to be such and such. A woman who *doesn't know her place* is a menace to the image of the relation (as totality of two elements that complement each other). To this psychoanalysis does not respond by saying that woman is in fact something else to what these oppressive orders make her out to be, but with a very different, and much more powerful claim: the Woman does not exist. (Which is precisely another way of saying 'there is no sexual relation'.) If we look at the history of political (and class) oppression we can also see how the enforced idea of a 'harmonious' system has always been accompanied by the most brutal forms of exclusion and oppression. The (Lacanian) point, however, is not simply something like: 'Let's acknowledge the impossible, and instead of trying to "force" it, make do with it.' This, indeed, is rather the official ideology of the contemporary 'secular' form of social order and domination, which has abandoned the idea of a (harmonious) *totality* to the advantage of the idea of a non-totalizable multiplicity of singularities forming a 'democratic' network. In this sense it may even seem that the non-relation is the dominant ideology of 'capitalist democracies'. We are all conceived as (more or less precious) singularities, 'elementary particles', trying to make our voices heard in a complex, non-totalizable social network. There is no predetermined (social) relation, everything is negotiable, depending on us and on concrete circumstances. This, however, is very different from what Lacan's non-relation claim aims at, namely the (acknowledged) absence of the relation does not leave us with a pure neutrality of (social) being. This kind of acknowledging of the non-relation does not really acknowledge it. What the (Lacanian) non-relation means is precisely that there is no neutrality of (social) being. The non-relation is not a simple absence of the relation, but refers to a constitutive curving of the discursive space – the latter is 'curved' by the missing element of the relation. In this sense, to conceive democracy, for example, as a more or less successful negotiation between elements of a fundamentally neutral social being is to overlook – indeed, to *repress* – this consequential negativity, operative at the very core of social order. It is in fact just another form of the *narrative of the relation*, which becomes quite clear if we think about how the political and economic ontology of the non-totalizable multiplicity of neutral singularities is usually accompanied by the idea of some kind of political and economical of *self-regulation*. The invisible hand of the market is the showcase example of this, and we'll be returning to it later.

For Lacan the non-relation is a priori in the precise sense that it appears with every empirical relation as its inherent condition of possibility, and not as its Other. The choice is never that between relation and non-relation, but between different kinds of relations (bonds) that are being formed in the discursive space curved by the non-relation. The non-relation does not mean that there is no (fixed, pre-determined) relation *between* particular elements, but refers to a declination, a twist in these elements themselves: 'in themselves' they already bear the mark of the non-relation (and this mark is the surplus-enjoyment generated by the signifiers). To acknowledge the non-relation does not mean to accept 'the impossible' (as something that cannot be done or abolished), but to see how it adheres to all things possible, how it informs them, what kind of antagonism it perpetuates in each concrete case, and how. This is the kind of acknowledgement that – far from closing it, only opens up the space of political invention and intervention.

But let us return to the *The Anti-Sexus* and how it can help us see and define the core of the problem. So, what is this text? To sum it up, I rely once more on Schuster's presentation:

> In 1926, Russian Marxist author Andrei Platonov composed *The Anti-Sexus*, a remarkable text which remained, like so many of his other writings, unpublished during his lifetime. The work is a fictional brochure, issued by the company Berkman, Chateloy, and Son, Ltd. and 'translated' from French by Platonov, that advertised an electromagnetic instrument promising to relieve sexual urges in an efficient and hygienic manner. The device, available in both male and female models, had a special regulator for the duration of pleasure and could be fitted for either personal or collective use. The purported occasion for the pamphlet was the company's expansion into the Soviet market after its success in many other parts of the world. The brochure includes a statement touting the virtues of the 'Anti-Sexus' and the company's mission to 'abolish the sexual savagery of mankind,' and is followed by testimonials by a number of illustrious figures, from Henry Ford and Oswald Spengler to Gandhi and Mussolini. The Anti-Sexus, we are told, has many benefits and

92 Alenka Zupančič

applications: it is perfect for maintaining soldiers' morale during wartime, for improving the efficiency of factory workers, for taming restless natives in the colonies. It also fosters true friendship and human understanding by taking sexual folly out of the social equation. The 'translator' has added a critical preface where he condemns the cynicism and vulgarity of the enterprise, even while praising the pamphlet's writerly merits. He explains that the reason he decided to publish the text was to openly reveal the bourgeoisie's moral bankruptcy. No Bolshevik can read this capitalist drivel without a hearty laugh. The Anti-Sexus thus advertises itself as the surest form of 'contra-"antisexual" agitprop.'

(Schuster 2013: 42–45)

We will not go into the (very interesting) question of where Platonov stands in this debate, staged as it is in a multilayered and multi-genre way, in which a text of literary fiction is presented as *translation* of an advertising *pamphlet* accompanied by *comments* of prominent men (yes, they are all men) and by a critical *introduction* from the 'translator'. We will simply take it at its face value, and start by interrogating the presuppositions and paradoxes of the device (called the Anti-Sexus) advertised and discussed in this pamphlet.

These are the presuppositions of the Anti-Sexus device: sexuality is problematic because it involves the Other who, as everybody knows, is utterly unpredictable, unreliable (has her own will, caprices, indispositions ...), or simply unavailable. On the other hand and *at the same time*, our relations with others are complicated and conflict-ridden because the expectations and demands concerning sex are always in the air, complicating things: sex stands in the way of good social relations. This is the double quandary presumably resolved by the Anti-Sexus, which is claimed to be able to isolate, extirpate what is sexual about enjoyment from all other pleasures and relations in which it appears, distillate as it were the pure essence of sex (and then administer it in just the right dosage). In this way, the Anti-Sexus provides an 'Other-free' enjoyment (enjoyment free of the Other) and at the same time makes it possible for us to relate to others in a really meaningful way: to create real, lasting bonds (pure spiritual friendship).

It is clear that *two* operations are at stake here, or two aims: on the one hand, the aim is to exempt, extract sex from the Other and, on the other hand, it is to exempt the Other from sex. This way one gets two separate entities: as the result of the first operation, we get a sexless Other (to whom one can now relate in a friendly and non-problematic way); as the result of the second operation, we get a pure substance of sex, which we can enjoy directly whenever we want.

The Anti-Sexus is said to accomplish both things:

We have been called upon to solve the global human problem of sex and the soul. Our company has transformed sexual feeling from a crude elemental urge to an ennobling mechanism, we have given the world moral behavior. We have removed the element of sex from human relationships and cleared the way for pure spiritual friendship. Still, keeping in mind the high-value instant pleasure that necessarily accompanies contact of the sexes, we have endowed our instrument with a construction affording a minimum of three times this pleasure, as compared to the loveliest of women used at length by a prisoner recently released after ten years in strict isolation.

(Platonov 2013: 50)

As much as we can be tempted to laugh here, this addresses a problem that has been all but constantly raised in the modern debates concerning possible (and radical) emancipation of humankind: the crucial obstacle to the global human emancipation is humanity ('human nature') itself. Human emancipation is actually emancipation from the human. Human nature is the weak link in the project of social emancipation. In this line of thought we usually get a harder and a softer mode of ensuring this: either to build a New Man, or to 'canalize' the disruptive factor of humanity, and 'satisfy' it in a way that cannot interfere with building and maintaining the social relation.[5]

The proposition of the Anti-Sexus is to canalize the disruptive element. But, here is the problem: can this 'disruptive element' really be thought of in terms of an *element*, that is in terms of something that one can define, circumscribe, isolate? The answer seems to be negative and this is best seen in the way in which the basic operation of the Anti-Sexus immediately falls into two different operations: exempting, removing sex from the Other, and exempting, removing the Other from sex. Not much is said about how the first is done, the device basically provides the solution to the second. It exempts the other from sexual pleasure, and the idea is, it would seem, that this automatically accomplishes the other task as well: it exempts, removes sex from the Other, or produces a sexless Other, ready to form spiritual bonds with me. Since the sexual needs of the Other are always perfectly satisfied, she or he becomes sexless (sex is not a player in the relationship between people). This, of course, is a strange presupposition to say the least. Other is sexless if he or she 'is being masturbated' most of the time.

And here we hit against the very formula of the Anti-Sexus device, which I propose to formulate as follows: 'to make oneself masturbated', '*se faire masturber*' – to paraphrase the grammatical form used by Lacan in his conceptualization of the drive.[6] In order to properly conceptualize the drive as something that escapes the active/passive opposition, Lacan proposes a formula that introduces something active at the very heart of passivity, and vice versa. In the case of the scopic drive, for example, he dismantles what looks like reversal(s) between *seeing* and *being seen* with the formulation *making oneself seen*. In this sense the Anti-Sexus and its formula (*se faire masturber*) could be said to provide the formula of the 'sexual drive'. We saw how its task is actually twofold and twisted: in order to remove enjoyment from the Other one has to remove the Other from enjoyment. This suggests in fact that enjoyment and the Other are structured like babushka: enjoyment is 'in' the Other, but when we look 'in' the enjoyment, there is also the Other 'in' it, and so on … Enjoyment is in the Other, and the Other is in enjoyment. This is perhaps

94 Alenka Zupančič

the most concise formulation of the structure of non-relation, the non-relation between the subject and the Other. If enjoyment is what disturbs this relation, it does so not simply by coming *between* them (and hence holding them apart), but rather by *implicating*, placing them one in the other.

Let us take a moment here and look more closely at both sides of this configuration.

What we have on the one hand is this: all enjoyment already presupposes the Other, regardless of whether we 'get it' with the help of the 'real Other' (another person) or not. Even the most solitary enjoyment presupposes the structure of the Other (if it is to register as enjoyment, *jouissance*). Which is also why the more we try to get rid of the Other and become utterly self-dependant, the more we are bound to find something radically heterogeneous ('Other') at the very heart of our most intimate enjoyment. There is no enjoyment without the Other because all enjoyment originates at the place of the Other (as the locus of the signifiers). Our innermost enjoyment can only take place at that 'extimate' place. (And this is something else than to say that enjoyment is *mediated* by the Other, or that we 'need' the Other in order to enjoy.) It is of utmost importance to grasp that the radical heterogeneity, incommensurability, and antagonism of the signifier and enjoyment is not due to their heterogeneous origins (for example, that one comes from the body and the other from the symbolic order), but on the contrary to the fact that they *originate at the same place*. The Other is both the locus of the signifier and the locus of enjoyment (mine, as well as the enjoyment of the Other).

On the other hand (and by way of an illustrative digression), what we find for example at the very heart of the most sex-free, spiritual (Christian) love, is a proliferation of partial objects and their enjoyment. Far from being disruptive of the Christian social bond — as it is often mistakenly believed — what psychoanalysis identifies as partial objects (objects carrying the surplus-enjoyment) are the very *stuff of the communion*.

Christianity is usually taken as the magisterial example of the kind of attitude that bans the drive sexuality related to partial objects and promotes only 'purposeful' reproductive coupling. Yet, it suffices to shift the perspective just a little bit (and at the right end), as Lacan does in the following passage, to get a completely different picture:

> Christ, even when resurrected from the dead, is valued for his body, and his body is the means by which communion in his presence is incorporation — oral drive — with which Christ's wife, the Church as it is called, contents itself very well, having nothing to expect from copulation.
>
> In everything that followed from the effects of Christianity, particularly in art — and it's in this respect that I coincide with the 'baroquism' with which I accept to be clothed — everything is exhibition of the body evoking jouissance — and you can lend credence to the testimony of someone who has just come back from an orgy of churches in Italy — but without copulation. If copulation isn't present, it's no accident. It's just as much out of place there as

it is in human reality, to which it nevertheless provides sustenance with the fantasies by which that reality is constituted.

(Lacan 1999: 113)

Indeed, as favoured as it is in the religion's doxa, 'natural (procreative) intercourse' is utterly banned from the religious imaginary, whereas the latter does not recede from, for example, images of canonized saints eating the excrement of another person.[7] If we take a look at eminent stories (and pictures) of Christian martyrdom, they are surprisingly full of partial objects in the strict Freudian meaning of the term. A real treasury of images of objects relating to different partial drives. St. Agatha's cut-off breast and St. Lucy's gouged-out eyes are just two of the most well-known examples, portrayed hundreds of times by different artists.[8] Partial drives and the passion or satisfaction they procure are abundantly present in many aspects of Christianity and constitute an important part of its official imaginary. The pure enjoyment, 'enjoyment for the sake of enjoyment' is not exactly what is banned here; what is banned, or repressed, is its link to sexuality.

It is clearly of utter importance for the Christian religion *not* to acknowledge these ('polymorphous perverse') satisfactions of the drives *as sexual*, while not banning them in themselves. But why exactly? Why this necessity not simply to fight all enjoyment, as it is often wrongly believed, but to *separate enjoyment from sexuality* (to de-sexualize the enjoyment) as neatly as possible? Because its connection with sexuality exposes the non-relation at the very heart of every relation (and thus exposes an irreducible element of contingency at work in all forming of bonds). As all religions, Christianity presupposes and enforces the relation. The idea of a 'non-sexual sexual enjoyment' that we find here is actually the same as the one at work in the Anti-Sexus device. What is needed for the relation to exist is a 'sexless sex', or an 'Otherless other' (an Other free of otherness).

(So, instead of saying that pure sex and pure love are equality impossible, we should perhaps go a step further and say that if they existed, they would be indistinguishable. What distinguishes, even opposes them, is their non-existence. Yet if there were, in fact, something like pure love, it would be indistinguishable from the pure essence of sex. Whereas the less they exist as fully blown ontological categories, the more different they are.)

This then is the double paradox that we are trying to formulate: if we remove the Other from enjoyment, we find the Other at the very heart of the most auto-focused, masturbatory enjoyment. On the other hand: if we remove enjoyment from the Other, we find enjoyment at the very heart of the (most spiritual) bond with the Other. The Other and enjoyment are 'extimly' related. Which is why in order to remove enjoyment from the Other a second operation is immediately called for, that of removing the Other from enjoyment. The two 'elements' imply each other, each carries the Other 'in' itself, and this is what curves, what may look like a symmetry (or relation) in a way that resembles some of Escher's drawings of impossible objects. I would claim that the sexual relation is 'impossible' in precisely this way, the impossible at stake is of the kind of these impossible objects.

'The invisible "handjob" of the market'

Lacan's point is that, as one with the discursive order, the non-relation is at work in all forms of social bonds, it is not limited to the 'sphere of love'. (The latter is rather distinguished by the fact that in its field it actually happens, from time to time, that the relation 'stops not being written'). And his further point is that the social relations of power – domination, exploitation, discrimination – are first and foremost exploitations of the non-relation.

This is a delicate point, for it seems to contradict a point made earlier, namely that the most authoritarian social orders are those which aim at freeing the social from the non-relation, that is to say social orders built in the name of the relation. Yet this is not necessarily contradictory. Perhaps we even find here a good way of distinguishing between the abolition of the non-relation as an emancipatory project, and what we may call 'narratives of the Relation' which are actually in the service of the most vicious (social and economic) exploitation of the non-relation. Abolition of the non-relation has been in fact the way in which the authentic revolutionary projects of the 20th century often understood the path to radical emancipation. The catastrophic results of this kind of politics were built in the very *honesty* of the attempt to abolish the non-relation. The modus operandi of engineering a New Order has been that of exposing the non-relation and attempting to force it out of the social equation, by all means possible. And this is very different, in its logic, from what we may call the exploitation and segregation of people by presenting a given form of social antagonism as the ultimate Relation, supposedly protecting us from the utter Chaos of the non-relation. Here, social injustice directly translates into a higher Justice. At work is not a crazy attempt to abolish the non-relation as the fundamental negativity, but *disavowing* it while at the same time *appropriating* it as the productive point of social power. This is a truly political lesson of psychoanalysis: power works by *first* appropriating a fundamental negativity of the symbolic order, its constitutive non-relation, while building it into a narrative of a higher relation. This is what constitutes, puts into place, and perpetuates the relations of domination. And the actual exploitation is based on, made possible (and fuelled) by this appropriation, this 'privatization of the negative'. This is what distinguishes – to take the famous Brechtian example – the robbing of a bank (usual theft) from the founding of a bank (a double theft which appropriates the very lever of production and its exploitation).

In no place is this better visible than in the case of capitalism, which starts off with two revolutionary ideas: 'economic relation does not exist' and 'the non-relation could be very profitable'. The first idea corresponds to the 18th-century economists, led by Adam Smith, putting into question the previous 'mercantile' doctrine and belief that the amount of the world's wealth remained constant and that a nation could only increase its wealth at the expense of another nation. The latter is the image of a 'closed' totality in which the relation ensures the visibility of the difference (in wealth): if you want more, you have to take it from somewhere, so someone else has to lose. The relation is that of subordination (of the weak to the powerful), but it is still a relation. The new economic idea undermines this (totality-based) relation, while at the same time prizing the productivity of the newly discovered non-relation. The wealth can also increase 'by itself', with the Industrial Revolution and the new organization of labour being the primary sources and carriers of this increase. I'm deliberately putting this in crudest and most simple terms, so as to expose the most salient structural traits of this shift. What is the fundamental 'discovery' of capitalism? That non-relation is profitable, that it is the ultimate source of growth and profit. And with it comes the idea that, this being so, there is no reason why everybody couldn't profit from it. This way we got the narrative of a new, higher Relation, the foundational myth of modern capitalism, known as 'the invisible hand of the market'.

Adam Smith's 'capital' idea starts out from positing a social non-relation as a fundamental state also on another level: as elements of social order, individuals are driven by egotistic drives and pursuit of their self-interest. But out of these purely egotistic pursuits grows a society of an optimal general welfare and justice. It is precisely by ruthlessly pursuing one's own interest that one promotes the good of society as a whole, and much more efficiently so than when one sets off to promote it directly. As Smith puts it in a famous quote from the *Wealth of Nations*: 'It is not from the benevolence of the butcher, the brewer or the baker, that we expect our dinner, but from their regard to their own self interest. We address ourselves, not to their humanity but to their self-love, and never talk to them of our own necessities but of their advantages' (Smith 2012: 19).

What is interesting about this idea in the context of our previous discussion is how it makes a first step in the right direction and then stops short. Put in the terms we were using earlier, the idea is that what we find at the very core of the most selfish individual enjoyment is actually the Other (looking after a general welfare). What is missing is the next step: ... and what we find, at the same time, at the core of this Other is a most 'masturbatory' self-enjoyment. Adam Smith's mistake is not so much that he saw the dimension of the Other possibly at work in the most selfish pursuits of individual interests – all in all, this thesis is not simply wrong: with our actions we never do just what we think we are doing and what we intend to do (this is even a fundamental lesson of both Hegel and Lacan). His mistake was that he didn't follow this logic to the end: he failed to see where and how the Other and its invisible hand also do not do only what they think they are doing ... This is what comes forward with every economic crisis, and is becoming more and more overwhelmingly clear: left to itself the market (the Other) is bound to discover the 'solitary enjoyment'. At some point in his (spoken) comments[9] on Platonov's *Anti-Sexus*, Aaron Schuster used the expression: 'the invisible "handjob" of the market', which I'm borrowing here, since one could hardly find any better way of putting what we are trying to articulate here.[10]

Adam's Smith's idea could indeed be formulated in these terms: let's make the non-relation work for everybody's profit. And one could hardly deny the fact that what we consider as wealth has increased in absolute (and not only relative) terms since the 18th century. Or, as we often hear, that everybody, even the poorest, are

98 Alenka Zupančič

living better than two centuries ago. Yet the price of this modern economic relation is, again, that the differences (between rich and poor) are also exponentially huger.

What are the reasons for the non-relation being so productive and profitable? Marx already saw it perfectly: in order for the non-relation to be economically productive and profitable, it has to be built in the very mode of production. He situated this at the precise 'structural' point when labour appeared on the market as yet another commodity for sale. This is a key point in what he analyses as 'the transformation of money into capital'. Put very simply: that what *makes the products* (labour-power) also appears with them on the market as *one of the products*, objects for sale. This paradoxical redoubling corresponds to the point of structural negativity and its appropriation as the locus of market's 'miraculous' productivity. The money-owner finds on the market a commodity whose use-value possesses the peculiar property of being a source of value, and whose actual consumption is a creation of value. (How would Escher draw this particular 'impossible object'?) This is why it is too simple to say, that what the capitalists have 'more' of, they have 'stolen' from the workers. This kind of claim still presupposes the old, 'closed', relation-based economy. … What capital exploits is the point of negativity ('entropy') of the social order, with the workers situated at this precise point. Capitalists are not so much 'stealing' from the workers as employing them to make the negativity/entropy of the system work for them, the capitalists. Or, in other words: 'they are making themselves enriched'…

This then is what Marx recognized as the concrete structural point of the non-relation in capitalism, serving as the condition of its type of production and exploitation. Labour-power *as commodity* is the point that marks the constitutive negativity, gap of this system, the point where one thing immediately falls into another (use-value into source of value). Labour is a product among other products, yet it is not exactly like other products: there where the latter have a use-value (and hence a *substance* of value), this particular commodity 'leaps over' to the source of value. The use-value of this commodity is to be the source of value of (other) commodities. It has no 'substance' of its own. This could also be put in a formula: 'the Worker does not exist'. What exists – and must exist – is the person whose work is sold and bought. Which is why it is essential according to Marx that the person working does not sell himself (his person), 'converting himself from a free man to a slave, from an owner of commodity into a commodity. He must constantly treat his labour-power as his own property, his own commodity' (Marx 1990: 271). This also shows how the usual humanist complaint about how, in capitalism, 'we are all just commodities' misses the point: if we were indeed just commodities, capitalism wouldn't work; we need to be free persons selling the labour-power as our property, our commodity.

The Marxian concept of the proletariat could be seen precisely as formulating the fact that, in capitalism, the Worker doesn't exist (the Worker that existed would actually be a slave). Which is why proletariat is not simply one of the social classes, but rather names the point of the concrete constitutive negativity[11] in capitalism, the point of the non-relation obfuscated and exploited by it. Proletariat is not the sum of all workers, it is the concept that names the symptomatic point of this system, its disavowed and exploited negativity. And this general Marxian idea has lost none of its pertinence today.

In conclusion we can return to the invisible hand, its other side and its criticism: is it enough to claim that it does not exist, and to try to put in its place a better, truly operative Other? As a matter of fact, this is precisely the theoretical question that we see today rising on the left: is it tenable to bet one's cards on the side of distribution? In other words, is there a way in which we could make the non-relation-based profit really profitable for all? Can we keep the profitable side of the non-relation while keeping its negative side under control (by means of different social correctives and regulations concerning the distribution of wealth)? How exactly? Or else do we have to renounce to the very idea of making profit out of the non-relation, which may very well equal the renunciation of profit (as we know it) tout court? But again, how? How to 'renounce' this, on the basis of what kind of global act of self-determination? These questions are indeed too 'theoretical', in the sense that in social reality we never get to answer them in this way, directly. But the fact remains that there could be no emancipatory politics without introducing and insisting on the question of the non-relation, and of its (im)possible place and role *within* the social order, and not only as its concealed/repressed, yet fully exploited presupposition. Which is why the points where something 'impossible' happens, takes place, occurs, are the best compass in the search and the capacity to recognize the unpredictable contingencies that no emancipatory politics can afford to ignore in the name of its pre-established ideas about what the emancipation is and how it looks.

Notes

1 For an exhaustive commentary on these questions, see Dolar 2007: 14–38.
2 One should be careful how to understand this, however. It is not to say that true politics – as different form socio-economic management – always strives for the impossible, for example for the impossible ideal of full justice and equality, but rather that true politics as such is the impossible at work, or the working of the impossible.
3 Which is why the only way to approach sex, to talk about it, is to take it as a logical problem (or as an onto-logical problem). This way we perhaps stand a chance to get at something real. On the other hand, if we approach it as a problem of the body and its sensations, we are bound to end up in the imaginary (or in the metaphysics).
4 See also Slavoj Žižek's powerful discussion of the non-relation in Žižek 2012: 794–802.
5 To some extent the more recent idea of the 'post-human' also belongs to this tradition of conceiving the emancipation as emancipation from the 'human'.
6 See Lacan 1998: 194–96.
7 See for example *The Autobiography of Saint Margaret Mary* (Charlotte, NC: TAN, 2009).
8 For a really impressive collection of these images it suffices to search the Internet for Saint Agatha (and Saint Lucy) – images.
9 'One or Many Anti-Sexes?', *What is To Be Done With Sexuality?* conference, Slovenian Academy of Sciences, Ljubljana, 27 May 2014.
10 And with this formulation in mind it is difficult not to get some further ideas, such as 'the invisible "blowjob" of the real-estate market …'

11 The formulation 'concrete constitutive negativity' requires a further explanation. In general theoretical terms of this configuration we should say it is not that there is one fundamental non-relation and a multiplicity of different relations, determined by the former in a negative way. It is rather that every relationship also posits the concrete point of the impossible that determines it. It determines what will be determining it. In this sense we could say that all social relations are concretizations of the non-relation as universal determination of the discursive, which does not exist anywhere outside these concrete (non)relations. This also means that the non-relation is not the ultimate (ontological) foundation of the discursive, but its surface – it exists and manifests itself only through it. Put differently: it is not that there is (and remains) a fundamental non-relation which will never be (re)solved by any of the concrete relations. Rather: every concrete relation de facto resolves the non-relation, but it can only resolve it by positing ('inventing'), together with itself, its own negativity, its own negative condition/impossibility. The non-relation is not something that 'insists' and 'remains', but something that is repeated – something that does not stop not being written. It is not something that resists all writing and that no writing can actually write – it is inherent to writing and repeats itself with it.

Bibliography

Dolar, Mladen (2007) 'Freud und das Politische', in *Texte. Psychoanalyse, Ästhetik, Kulturkritik* [Wien], Vol. 4, 14–38.

Lacan, Jacques (1998) *Seminar, Book XI, The Four Fundamental Concepts of Psycho-Analysis*. New York: W.W. Norton and Company.

Lacan, Jacques (1999) *Seminar, Book XX, Encore*. New York: W. W. Norton and Company.

Lacan, Jacques (2011) *Le séminaire, Book XIX, … ou pire*. Paris: Seuil.

Marx, Karl (1990) *Capital*, Vol. I. London: Penguin Books.

Platonov, Andrei (2013) 'The Anti-Sexus', *Cabinet Magazine*. Issue 51.

Schuster, Aaron (2013) 'Sex and Anti-Sex', *Cabinet Magazine*. Issue 51.

Smith, Adam (2012) *An Inquiry into the Nature and Causes of the Wealth of Nations*. Ware, Hertfordshire: Wordsworth Editions.

Žižek, Slavoj (2012) *Less than Nothing*. London: Verso.

7

OBJECT *A* AND POLITICS

Dominiek Hoens

RITCS (BRUSSELS), BELGIUM

In one of his later seminars, looking back on a life's work devoted to 'a return to Freud', Lacan considers object *a* as something he invented (Lacan 1973–74: lesson of 9 April 1974). Despite Lacan's repeated statements (e.g. 1981 [1980]) that one should consider him as a Freudian and that his structuralist reading of Freud is thoroughly based in and on the work of the Viennese psychoanalyst, with the addition of object *a* something novel was introduced into this mere 'return to Freud'. Object *a*'s novelty raises at least three questions: where does it occur within Lacan's work, why does he need to invent it, and how does the notion relate to other aspects of Lacan's theory? These questions will be addressed in section one. In section two of this chapter we will examine the political dimension and implications of the notion.

The genesis of object *a* in Lacan's work

The question of where to locate the emergence of object *a* in Lacan's teaching may inspire a reading of his early work (1936–53) as already containing, if not the notion itself, then at least the place where it might have occurred or formulations that anticipate it. Despite the interesting results this exercise may possibly deliver, we will not engage here in that sort of speculation. The more obvious path starts with reminding us of a strange turn Lacan's analysis of *Hamlet* takes in Seminar VI (2013 [1958–59]).

In the preceding seminars Lacan had been able to distinguish between the registers of the imaginary and the symbolic, between the (conscious) ego and the subject (of the unconscious), between mirroring demands and triangular desire, between the frustrated aspiration to fullness and the assumption of one's castrated lack of being, between the other and the Other. Lacan not only made crucial distinctions between those two registers, but also argued that the symbolic precedes the imaginary and functions as its hidden, that is unconscious, condition of possibility.

102 Dominiek Hoens

Lacan's 'symbolic' is a rearticulating of Freud's famous depiction of the unconscious as the other scene (*andere Schauplatz*), that is an unconscious dimension that adds itself to the conscious domain of signification and mutual recognition. Lacan understands this Freudian 'other scene' as the Other, that is as a space containing the signifiers that precede and determine any subjectivity. In that sense one could imagine the Other to exist without a subject, yet – and this is Lacan's point in the 1950s – psychoanalysis can only take place when a subject is supposed *to* the Other, as support and bearer, not to be confused with the patient's ego (*moi*).[1]

On a clinical level, this supposition is the precondition to any psychoanalytical work. Analysis can start with the uncanny feeling that an obscure, blind determination is at work in the problem one presents to the therapist – a fate one cannot escape or does not know how to control – *and* that one is somehow subjectively involved in the very thing one complains about. If transference is the principle of psychoanalysis, then it first and foremost concerns the supposition of a knowledge one has no immediate access to, but the supposition of which is provoked by the symptoms, the dreams, the slips, etc.: how am I involved in this? What and where am I in this seemingly absurd and unwanted problem that makes life difficult?

However, as Freud already noted in his essay on 'Negation' (1961 [1925]), to know what is repressed or to become conscious of what was, before analysis, an unconscious thought does not result in the removal of 'the repressive process' (*Verdrängungsvorgang*). One may arrive at a full intellectual acceptance (*volle intellektuelle Annahme*) of a certain, initially repressed thought, yet that does not alter the mechanism of repression. What is lacking in order to arrive at the removal (*Aufhebung*) of repression is the reconnection of the representation (*Vorstellung*) with the affect. How this reconnection is brought about should not concern us here,[2] and although Lacan does not follow Freud's and most of the post-Freudians' division between representation and affect, the idea that knowing does not suffice to undo or alter the mechanism of repression is the starting point of Lacan's take on *Hamlet*.

In contradistinction to Oedipus, Hamlet knows. He knows his father was killed and from quite early on in the play he knows who the perpetrator is. Moreover he knows what is expected from him – to exact revenge on the murderer, uncle Claudius – and no external conditions stand in between his intention and the act to perform. As Freud (1953 [1906]) put it, *Hamlet* is not a psychological drama, in which the hero is divided between two conscious, contradictory desires, but a psycho*pathological* one, as Hamlet knows everything he needs to know regarding the murder and murderer, with the exception of the reason for his own procrastination. Freud identified this reason with illicit, Oedipal desires – namely killing the father and having sexual intercourse with the mother – which Claudius acted upon, hence Hamlet's equally unconscious identification and sympathy with the villain. And as Freud considered the Oedipal conflict as universal, this also explains the fascination the play has continued to exert on audiences until today.

In that sense, it is no surprise that Lacan turned to *Hamlet* in *Seminar VI*, after having spent five years of his teaching to a structuralist rearticulation of the Freudian Oedipus. Within the post-Freudian legacy of his times Hamlet was considered as one of the best examples of the neurotic struggling with unconscious, Oedipal desires. And although it is clear that Lacan hardly ever used works of literature as mere illustrations of his theses, *Hamlet* must have been one of the crucial plays to 'test' his theoretical apparatus.[3] This testing neither consisted in a mere application of psychoanalytic theory, nor in its verification by a literary example. Although space is lacking here to explore this in detail, one can argue that Lacan often turned to literature when he experienced a certain impasse or deadlock in his theorizing, eventually resulting, via a literary work, in changes to the former.

The commentary on *Hamlet* takes up no less than seven sessions of the *Seminar VI* (2013 [1958–59]: 279–419) and this is mainly due to a hesitation in determining the precise status of Ophelia. As mentioned above, at the start of his lessons on *Hamlet* Lacan can rely on a particularly strong theoretical framework, elaborated during the preceding years of his seminar. In order to answer the main question – why does Hamlet procrastinate? – Lacan initially makes use of the distinction between the imaginary ego and the subject (of the unconscious). Hamlet, the ego, avoids the dimension of desire, an avoiding which is revealed in the relation towards Gertrud, his mother. She testifies to a desire that does not concern Hamlet, yet he remains puzzled by the question of what directs and limits this desire when it is obviously no longer his father who could function as the third element in the Oedipal triangle. That explains why Hamlet mercilessly denounces this desire, as much as he needs it within the quest for his own position as a subject. Here Lacan points out that Hamlet seeks to be the imaginary phallus of the Other's desire, namely the object that would undo the lack inherent in the dimension of desire. This positioning oneself as the imaginary phallus implies the misrecognition of lack as structural and an interpretation of desire as a demand (for love). This, however, can barely be considered as a stable solution, as is made evident by the play and condensed in the famous question *To be or not to be* … 'the phallus', Lacan adds. If Hamlet has lost his position as a subject and therefore ends up as entirely dependent on the others whom he actually despises, criticizes, and ridicules, the obvious question is if and when Hamlet can leave this fatal, imaginary dialectic and become the subject of desire.

The shift from being the object of an imaginary demand to the subject of symbolic, that is castrated, desire, occurs near the end of the play at the famous graveyard scene, in which people gather around the grave of Ophelia, who took her own life. Hamlet sees Laertes, Ophelia's brother, mourning and engages in a competition on the magnitude of their mourning. Ophelia, whom he rejected in a most callous way, becomes the object of rivalry, not as a positivity – something one could enjoy, or that would make one more complete – but as a lost love. Although Hamlet enters the competition with Laertes in an imaginary way, which usually entails the jealous supposition of fullness the other enjoys, the aspect of Laertes he identifies with is a lack and Laertes' mournful expression of it. Bidding against Laertes, what Hamlet discovers is not a supposed plenitude, but a lack that he identifies with and eventually considers as a sum 'forty thousand brothers could not, with all their quantity of love [make up]' (V, 1, 259–61). Eventually he will be able to exact the long postponed revenge on his uncle, Claudius, and thus perform his task. He even authors this act, as in the same scene he exclaims 'This is I, Hamlet the Dane' (V, 1, 246–47). For the first time the subject of a signifier appears – to be a Dane or a Danish prince is a symbolic identity which is granted, not chosen – a subject that can come into being on the basis of the recognition of a fundamental non-being or desire.

The question that seems to puzzle Lacan, however, concerns Ophelia. Is she *o-phallos*, a signifier that signifies the lack of an ultimate signifier within the field of the Other? And does her appearance within the love of Laertes as a lack to be mourned, allow Hamlet to subjectify this lack and to consider it as a constitutive lack of being? This would be the reading one would have expected Lacan to present to his audience and which he unfolds to a large extent. Yet, eventually, he equates Ophelia with the letter *a* he had been using in the formula of phantasm: $ \diamond a$.[4] This means that Ophelia qua signifier may have a phallic function, but that, as causing Hamlet to desire, she seems to have neither a symbolic, nor an imaginary status.

In those sessions on *Hamlet* we find the first articulation of an object that corresponds to the subject qua desire and that actually precedes it. This supplement to Lacan's teaching is surprising, for, as suggested above, at the time Lacanian theory was a theory of desire, of a structural lack caused by the inscription of the subject into the order of the symbolic. Within the symbolic the subject finds socially determined objects (signifiers) which can both fix and metonymically defer desire. Therefore the logical question is, roughly put, why did Lacan need to add the object *a* to this encompassing theoretical edifice? As Lacan hardly ever discussed his own theory from a metatheoretical perspective, the answer to this question can only be tentative and open to debate.

From the preceding seminar, Seminar V (Lacan 1998 [1957–58]), it was already clear that phantasm, $ \diamond a$, has the function to unconsciously produce pleasure. Desire may be open, unfulfilled, and metonymically slide from one signifier to another, this is only possible when it is supported by an unconscious scenario that stages the fulfilment of desire. In the first commentaries on phantasm Lacan argues that phantasm produces pleasure, because it consists in transferring one's own castration ($) onto an other (a). This is in accordance with the usually perverse nature of unconscious phantasies, which have to 'prove' that the subject is not marked by an insurmountable lack but a fellow human being. The notation with the Lacanian algebra for this 'other' is 'a', the first letter of the French *autre* (other). Later on Lacan will italicize this 'a' and refer to it as object *a* in order to highlight the difference with the imaginary other. The difference between a and *a* resides in their status: a qua other situates itself on level of the imaginary, *a* as object is neither symbolic nor imaginary, but real. One of the crucial implications of considering the object *a* as real resides in the impossibility of recuperating this object within the orders of the symbolic or the imaginary. In that sense, phantasm, $ \diamond a$, not only indicates how one may imagine an object fulfilling and hence cancelling out desire, but also how desire gets caused by the object. The object as radically lost and absent gains a sole 'positivity' in its capacity to stir and provoke desire. Therefore,

Object *a* and Politics **105**

phantasm has the paradoxical quality to produce an unconscious pleasure, that is the satisfaction of desire, and to function as the condition of possibility for any desire.[5] This paradox is inherent to the formula of phantasm, where ◇ indicates, amongst other things, the conjunction, ◇, of $ and *a*, and the disjunction, ◇, of the two. From this we can conclude that object *a* is both the phantasmatic object which supports the production of pleasure and the kind of object that causes desire.

The loose formulation with which the paragraph above ended – object *a* as a 'kind of object' – reveals the second element of the answer to the question why Lacan introduced object *a*. Being neither symbolic, nor imaginary Lacan will eventually qualify it as real. Here we cannot go into an explanation of the notoriously difficult category of the real,[6] but highlighting some of object *a*'s qualities may allow us to grasp why it is real.

After *Seminar VI*, whose sessions on *Hamlet* we have been discussing, *Seminar VII* deals with the ethics of psychoanalysis (Lacan 1986 [1959–60]) in which the notion of *das Ding* (the Thing) plays with the role of naming the realm beyond the signifier at which desire ultimately aims. Although one should not conflate *das Ding* with object *a*, it is clear both notions are closely related and indicate the transgressive aspect of desire. In *Seminar VIII* (Lacan 2001 [1960–61]) one finds another articulation of object *a* as *agalma*, which refers to what makes an object valuable beyond its obvious, tangible qualities. Here again we find the idea that something may provoke desire, although one may not be able to pinpoint (consciously) what quality turns an object into a desirable one. In the same seminar one finds another important indication how object *a* may be considered as a cause, namely in Lacan's discussion of a trilogy, *The Hostage/Crusts/The Humiliated Father*, by Paul Claudel (1979). Reduced to its minimum, the play – at least in Lacan's interpretation of it – unfolds the dissolution of a symbolic universe and the creation of a new one. With respect to the latter Lacan emphasizes the importance of the character of Pensée, a blind woman who attracts other characters' desiring gaze. The issue of a last (or first) signifier and its relation to object *a* is further discussed in *Seminar IX* (Lacan 1961–62), where Lacan argues that object *a* is a cut that precedes any lack or gap in the symbolic. In *Seminar X* (2004 [1962–63]), object *a* is identified as the object of anxiety, which occurs when lack is lacking, or, put differently, when the subject gets too close to what causes its desire. In the same lessons Lacan presents a new version of his mirror stage, and through a complex device of mirrors it is shown how a particular element, object *a*, is not specular and cannot be discerned within the scopic field. The dialectic of distance and proximity is a central issue in *Seminar XI* (Lacan 1973 [1964]). There it is argued that what supports seeing is an object, both most intimate and exterior to the seeing subject, i.e. its own gaze. Further developments of object *a* include passages in *Seminar XVI* (Lacan 2006 [1968–69]) where Lacan discusses object *a* in the context of Marx's *Mehrwert* and Pascal's notorious 'wager'. Inspired by Marx he names object *a* a *plus-de-jouir*, a wordplay on *plus* that contains both the dimensions of loss (*plus*), and of enjoyment (*jouir*) turned into a surplus (*plus*).[7] The idea that object *a* both is lost and functions as a surplus one cannot get rid of, reappears in the discussion of Pascal's *pensée* on the

106 Dominiek Hoens

wager. The fragment, in which it is argued that it is reasonable to bet on the existence of God, allows Lacan to question the stake: as soon as one enters the game one has to consider the stake as lost – in this case one's life – yet what is lost haunts the game as an expected outcome, that is a second, yet infinitely happy life. Finally, in *Seminar XX* (Lacan 1975 [1972–73]), he develops the logical and ontological status of object *a* via a rearticulation of Aristotle's square of opposition and an introduction of the notion of *pas-tout* (non-all). Briefly put, ontologically speaking object *a* is an ex-sistence (as Lacan prefers to write it) without an essence, that is its 'being' cannot be expressed in assertions of the form 'All x Px'.[8]

This rough overview proves first and foremost how, after its introduction in *Seminar VI*, the conceptualization and exploration of object *a*'s implications continued to preoccupy Lacan. We can deduce from it a series of qualities that clarify its 'real' status. It is a) non-specular, b) partial, without being part of a whole, c) acts as the cause of desire, d) lost, but not absent, as it e) provides enjoyment on a phantasmatic level, and f) it is singular, in the sense that it resists universalization. Taken together these features provide us with the second part of the answer to our guiding question, as will be shown in the next section of this chapter.

The political implications of object *a*

As indicated above, the wager of psychoanalysis, its fundamental hypothesis, concerns the *subject* of the unconscious. Hamlet may be very conscious and testify to a melancholic perspicacity with which he discerns all that is rotten in the State of Denmark, he is at the same time blind for his position as a subject. This does not mean he has repressed it or does not dare to confront it, but simply that he has lost it. Not only mourning for the loss of his father – which requires a social time of mourning that no one seems to observe – he also faces a task and bears a responsibility he is not up to. In Lacanian terms, this means he lacks the symbolic coordinates that could orient his thoughts and actions. This implosion of the Other – exemplified by a father who appears as a ghostly, weak figure who died 'in the blossoms of his sin' and is betrayed by his wife – makes Hamlet position himself with imaginary means. As we have seen, he needs to discover his subjective position qua subject of the signifier. This inscription of the subject into the symbolic and the recognition of the Other as marked by castration and desire, bears some striking resemblances with the political subjectivity democracy relies on.

From the primacy attributed to the symbolic Other one may derive at least three intertwined political principles that support the current and widely shared idea about democracy. The first one consists of taking as a starting point that the subject is not an autonomous ego that uses language and other media to give meaning to the world. A person may think he is and doing that, but from a Lacanian point of view the realm of the ego is unconsciously and structurally supported by an Other which precedes the subject and onto which the latter is dependent. In political terms this means that the subject is the subject of an order of mediation and representation that precedes it. In that sense a democracy is not and cannot be the direct expression of one's desires, but involves a structural gap between the order of political representation and the personal. In a democracy one gets represented and this inevitably entails alienation in the sense that the realm of politics can only function at a distance from what it is supposed to represent, to take care of, and listen to, i.e. the people. From this perspective representation is not an accidental, unfortunate quality of some (bad) forms of democracy but a necessary and essential element of any democracy. The second principle concerns those who have political power. This power is castrated in the sense that one only has it to the extent that it has been given (via elections) for a limited time within a limited domain. In Lacanian terms, one can only have the phallus on the basis of not having it. In that sense democratic political power is by essence finite and one of the tasks a democracy should carefully observe is to consider this place of power as empty: no one can directly claim it and whoever happens to occupy it, does this by the grace of contingent election. The third and most fundamental premise of democracy consists in abandoning any claim on truth. A democracy is characterized by an organized clash of more or less well-informed opinions. Any political idea, programme, or project, can be promoted, but this implies endorsing one fundamental rule of the game: it does not claim to be a politics of truth.

These three principles could be further developed in dialogue with a Lacanian view on subjectivity as subjectivity of an Other which comes first (representation), is organized around a lack (castration), and operates with signifiers which are by definition neither rooted in being, nor supported by an ultimate guarantor of their truth.

This point of view indicates one of the main possible political implications of Lacanian theory, which can be summarized as: democracy and Lacanian psychoanalysis, *même combat*. In that sense the psychoanalytic cure can be considered as a training in democracy, meaning that the aim of psychoanalysis – to be able to deal with castration as a lack of being that gets located and operative via signifiers – coincides with the kind of political subjects democracy needs.[9]

Yet, referring back to *Hamlet*, we have seen that this political culture of the symbolic is only made possible through a construction of a phantasm in which a subject $ relates to an object *a*. This means that a subject is never merely a subject of the symbolic, but is caused, on another level, by a real, non-symbolic element. The subject is – making use of a rhetorical figure dear to Lacan – not without (*pas sans*) an object.[10] This little *a* obstructs the seamless translation of Lacanian psychoanalysis into the democratic principles outlined above. Before discussing the implications of this, we can now understand why Lacan needed to introduce object *a*. This object prevents from conceiving the subject as a mere subject of the Other, which represses and hence unconsciously identifies with its lack. The lack-of-being (*manque-à-être*) characteristic of the subject does not coincide with the lack in the desiring Other. The subject as a subject of desire needs to realize itself in relation to the symbolic Other whose principle is the paternal law, castration and lack, but what causes the subject is an object. From the point of view of the subject the object is the answer to the lack in the Other, that is the element mediating between its own lack and the Other's, $ ◊ *a* ◊ Ⱥ.

108 Dominiek Hoens

This can also be observed from *Hamlet*. To consider this tragedy as a *modern* tragedy, may lead one to highlight Hamlet's experience of an Other no longer guaranteeing and supporting the symbolic, political order. The Other appears as flawed and as demanding from Hamlet to do what the Other cannot do. In brief, God or father no longer function as the support of a universe, hence human beings themselves need to take up this role. In that sense *Hamlet* is the tragedy of a modern human being struggling with this responsibility, fully realizing he is completely alone.

Yet, this advent of modern subjectivity has its obscure, spectral side. As Greenblatt (2013: 212) puts it: '*Hamlet* is a play of contagious, almost universal self-estrangement'. The self-estrangement starts with the appearance of Hamlet Sr., who is neither real nor mere illusion, which provokes amongst the other characters the question of where to put the line of demarcation between what is real and what is unreal; a question one quickly applies to oneself: *am* I or do I *resemble* myself? One can argue that this ontological questioning starts with the ghostly appearance of Hamlet's father – as a voice without tangible body, that is a disincarnated invocative object – and ends with Ophelia, a lifeless body, another object that is both there and not there. In brief, the modern subject does not only relate to a ghostly dimension which proves to be difficult to silence or ignore, moreover it could not be a modern subject without this 'objective' double.

This can sound hardly surprising to any reader of Lacan. The subject is not without an object does not only refer to the structural intertwinement of subject and object, but also to a necessary work of substitution of the one for the other. Positioning oneself as a subject implies that one emerges from an object position. Logically speaking one is always and foremost the object of the Other's desire and to become a subject of desire means leaving this objectal position behind. From early texts like *Logical Time* (Lacan 2007 [1945]), to the reflection on love in *Seminar VIII* (Lacan 2001 [1960–61]), to later developments on phantasm, one finds, on a formal level, the same argument: subjectivity emerges as a substitution for object *a* and is able to persist only at a distance from object *a*.

The above attempt to argue for an analogy between Lacanian psychoanalysis and some of the characteristics often considered as constitutive for any democracy, are problematized by the inclusion of object *a* in our considerations. For indeed one may be tempted to argue that the inclusion of the problem of object *a* makes even more clear how Lacanian psychoanalysis is an apology of our modern, democratic subjectivity: direct enjoyment is relocated to an unconscious, phantasmatic level which supports desire as an open-ended quest within a symbolic order. Yet, as we have seen, according to Lacan, this symbolic order and its subject is principally based on and caused by an object that cannot be included with the symbolic. This non-inclusion is not to be understood as the plain and simple exclusion of a non-symbolic, superfluous element, but as the marginal, spectral appearance, functioning as the condition of possibility for any symbolic subjectivity.

This supplementing of his earlier theory with object *a* is to be considered as a materialist turn. Despite the earlier and repeated emphasis on the materiality of the signifier, and, following Stalin, the depiction of language as infrastructure (Lacan

2007 [1956]: 344), the proper Lacanian field as Lacan once invited his audience to name it, is the field of enjoyment (1991 [1969–70]: 93). This does not mean that the notion of enjoyment is meant to cover a field of supposedly pre-symbolic drives, libidinal energies, and bodily, hence more 'material', substances. It means – the first and ultimate lesson of Freud – that whatever happens to the subject, enjoyment is continuously produced. Imagine a psychoanalytic politics aiming to curtail enjoyment, to create conditions for desire instead of fake consumerist ideals, and to promote cooperation instead of competition, etc., for any truly psycho-analytically inspired politics this would only be possible by taking into account the rather disappointing idea that change can only be brought about when it touches upon the way subjects 'headlessly' enjoy.

In that respect Lacanian psychoanalysis is needed more than ever. Despite the widely spread conviction that we have entered a time of austerity, that fewer will be able to live a life of untroubled material wealth, and that for many life will be precarious, with lurking unemployment and generalized poverty, our times are also clearly most inviting to all forms of enjoyment. The most obvious examples are the unremitting suggestions to consume. These can be considered as an exploitation of human subjects as subjects of a structural lack and as ways to stir and to direct their desire. Here the dimension of enjoyment is mainly imaginary: one does not only buy a product, but one also gets sold the dream that one will be able to enjoy it like the people do in the advertisement. In short, to consume means to sacrifice an object to an unconscious God who is capable of enjoying all those shiny, yet useless gadgets, unread books, empty swimming pools, and so on.

Moreover, the financial means needed for consumption are to be earned via a successful professional life. The ideology underpinning this duty, generally referred to as neoliberalism, argues that one needs to take responsibility for one's own life and that the degree of success (material wealth, social esteem, …) is dependent on each individual's effort. This meritocratic line of reasoning leads to the bleak con-clusion that one has to love a system of production and of distribution of wealth that owes you nothing in return. The value of one's life is entirely dependent on the function it has within that system; a function it can easily lose. Borrowing a line from David J. Blacker, after the age of exploitation we now shift into 'a mode of elimination that targets most of us … as waste products awaiting managed disposal' (Blacker 2013: 1).

How this relates to jouissance and object *a* can be derived from Lacan's repeated discussion of Christianity. Following Koyré and Kojève on this point, Lacan understands Christianity as essential to the advent of modernity and hence as part of any reflection on our modern, political condition. By way of example, in *Seminar X* (Lacan 2004 [1962–63]) masochism is considered as the Christian's 'second nature'. This second nature resides in a readiness to self-effacing sacrifices in the name of the commandment to love, which is, according to Lacan, a maso-chist strategy to provoke God's anxiety. The masochism may be present in the acts performed out of love (for the neighbour), but the *perversity* of them is a matter of where one locates oneself with regards to castration. The perverse position is an

110 Dominiek Hoens

object-position that transfers the constitutive lack of the symbolic order onto another being, that is, God. That is why both the sadist and masochist equally desire the Other's anxiety, for it is a proof of the Other's split and castrated subjectivity, which makes it possible for the pervert to keep up the (unconscious) illusion he is not subjected to castration. To the masochist the Christian God may appear as indifferent, absent, or silent, but sacrificing oneself may provoke Him to show concern and care, in brief, to get scared about what people do out of love for Him.

If Lacan discusses Pascal and other Christian thinkers, it is also meant to discover and open up onto desire where Christianity locates love. Lacan qualifies this love as perverse and his oeuvre can be read as a warning against the exploitation of it, as it currently happens each time one seems to get addressed as an individual but is actually asked to sacrifice oneself, that is to love the mute capitalist mode of production.

The difference between desire and Christian love, allows us to pinpoint the difficulty of a Lacanian politics. Our brief sketch of what is at stake with object *a* showed how subjectivity cannot emerge without this objectal enjoyment. This conflation of subject and object in enjoyment forms at least a 'logical' moment one cannot overlook when dealing with politics and political transformation. The 'rationality' of the symbolic order is supported by an 'irrational' enjoyment, and changes of the former can only occur if one passes via the latter. On a therapeutic level that is exactly the starting point of Lacanian psychoanalysis. Someone, the analyst, pretends to occupy the position of the object in order to allow the analysand to reconstruct a phantasmatic scenario, which, in a second step, allows him or her to emerge as a subject of desire.

If there is a politics of object *a*, the obvious starting point is the analytical discourse, which is a social bond that situates the object *a* as the agent. The question is whether this discourse can operate beyond the confines of the analyst's cabinet. That seemed to have been Lacan's ambition, although he only expresses it at the moment he points out its failure: '[It] is at this point that I am questioning the fruitfulness of psychoanalysis. You have heard me more than once saying that psychoanalysis did not even succeed in inventing a new perversion. That is sad. Because, after all, if perversion is the essence of man, what kind of unfruitfulness in this practice' (Lacan 2005: 153). The 'new perversion' means that psychoanalysis would succeed in giving desire a place in a society under the spell of enjoyment and intervene by installing a culture where enjoyment, our endless sacrifices to an obscure God, can be questioned. There is no reason not to share Lacan's pessimism on this point, just as much as there is only reason to continue to think *with* the analytical discourse.

Notes

1 One should keep in mind that when Lacan discusses the subject, he is not referring to the individual (human being), but situates this notion within a long philosophical tradition starting with Aristotle who introduced the term *hypokeimenon*, literally 'underlying thing'.
2 A first step to answer this question would reside in discussing the idea of working-through (*Durcharbeitung*) as different from a mere recollection of repressed material; see Freud, 1958 [1914].

3 Lacan may have been reminded of the play *via* his reading of the works of Ella Sharpe, whose *Dream Analysis* (1988 [1937]) was discussed in the opening sessions of *Seminar VI*.
4 This occurs in a lesson aptly entitled by the editor as 'The Ophelia object'; see Lacan 2013 [1958–59]: 367.
5 One can argue that melancholy, the state within which one is no longer able to desire, is caused by the disintegration of the phantasm as a frame needed for objects to appear as desirable. Leader (2003) presents a convincing exposition of this thesis.
6 See Eyers (2012) for a detailed overview.
7 For more about this see the illuminating discussion between Tomšič (2012) and Bianchi (2012).
8 'Object *a* has no being' (Lacan 1973–74: lesson of 9 April 1974).
9 And most probably only a democratic culture enables psychoanalysis to do its work of questioning the ideals and empty signifiers that organize one's subjective life; cf. Miller (2003).
10 Joan Copjec (2006: 99) argues that this *pas sans* is Lacan's way of telling us '[…] that it would be an understatement to say it has an object'.

Bibliography

Bianchi, Pietro (2012) From Representation to Class Struggle, *S: Journal of the Circle for Lacanian Ideology Critique*, Vol. 5. www.lineofbeauty.org (accessed 1 September 2014).

Blacker, David J. (2013) *The Falling Rate of Learning*. Winchester and Washington, DC: Zero Books.

Claudel, Paul (1979) *L'Otage suivi de Le Pain Dur et de Le Père Humilié*. Paris: Gallimard.

Copjec, Joan (2006) 'May '68, the Emotional Month', in *Lacan: The Silent Partners*, ed. Slavoj Žižek. London and New York: Verso, 90–114.

Duras, Marguerite (1977) *Le Camion*. Paris: Minuit.

Eyers, Tom (2012) *Lacan and the Concept of the Real*. Basingstoke: Palgrave Macmillan.

Freud, Sigmund (1953 [1906]). 'Psychopathic Characters on the Stage', *The Standard Edition of the Complete Psychological Works of Sigmund Freud*, Vol. 7, trans. James Strachey. London: The Hogarth Press and the Institute of Psycho-Analysis, 305–310.

Freud, Sigmund (1958 [1914]) 'Remembering, Repeating and Working-Through', *The Standard Edition of the Complete Psychological Works of Sigmund Freud*, Vol. 12, trans. James Strachey. London: The Hogarth Press and the Institute of Psycho-Analysis, 147–156.

Freud, Sigmund (1961 [1925]) 'Negation', *The Standard Edition of the Complete Psychological Works of Sigmund Freud*, Vol. 19, trans. James Strachey. London: The Hogarth Press and the Institute of Psycho-Analysis, 235–239.

Greenblatt, Stephen (2013) *Hamlet in Purgatory*. Princeton, NJ and Oxford: Princeton University Press.

Lacan, Jacques (1961–62) *Le Séminaire, Livre IX: L'Identification* (unpublished).

Lacan, Jacques (1973 [1964]) *Le Séminaire, Livre XI: Les Quatre Concepts Fondamentaux*, ed. Jacques-Alain Miller. Paris: Seuil.

Lacan, Jacques (1973–74) *Le Séminaire, Livre XXI: Les Non-Dupes Errent* (unpublished).

Lacan, Jacques (1975 [1972–1973]) *Le Séminaire, Livre XX: Encore*, ed. Jacques-Alain Miller. Paris: Seuil.

Lacan, Jacques (1981 [1980]) 'Le Séminaire de Caracas, *L'Âne*. 1: 30–31.

Lacan, Jacques (1986 [1959–1960]) *Le Séminaire, Livre VII: L'Ethique de la Psychanalyse*, ed. Jacques-Alain Miller. Paris: Seuil.

Lacan, Jacques (1991 [1969–1970]) *Le Séminaire, Livre XVII: L'Envers de la Psychanalyse*, ed. Jacques-Alain Miller. Paris: Seuil.

Lacan, Jacques (1998 [1957–1958]) *Le Séminaire, Livre V: Les Formations de l'Inconscient*, ed. Jacques-Alain Miller. Paris: Seuil.

Lacan, Jacques (2001 [1960–1961]) *Le Séminaire, Livre VIII: Le Transfert*, ed. Jacques-Alain Miller. Paris: Seuil.

Lacan, Jacques (2004 [1962–1963]) *Le Séminaire, Livre X: L'Angoisse*, ed. Jacques-Alain Miller. Paris: Seuil.

Lacan, Jacques (2005 [1975–1976]) *Le Séminaire, Livre XXIII: Le Sinthome*, ed. Jacques-Alain Miller. Paris: Seuil.

Lacan, Jacques (2006 [1968–1969]) *Le Séminaire, Livre XVI: D'Un Autre à l'autre*, ed. Jacques-Alain Miller. Paris: Seuil.

Lacan, Jacques (2007 [1945]) 'Logical Time and the Assertion of Anticipated Certainty: A New Sophism', in *Écrits: The First Complete Edition in English*, trans. Bruce Fink. New York: W. W. Norton and Company, 161–175.

Lacan, Jacques (2007 [1956]) The Freudian Thing, in *Écrits: The First Complete Edition in English*, trans. Bruce Fink.New York: W. W. Norton and Company, 334–363.

Lacan, Jacques (2013 [1958–1959]) *Le Séminaire, Livre VI: Le Désir et Son Interprétation*, ed. Jacques-Alain Miller. Paris: La Martinière and Le Champ Freudien.

Leader, Darian (2003) 'Some Thoughts on Mourning and Melancholia', *Journal for Lacanian Studies*, 1(1): 4–37.

Miller, Jacques-Alain (2003) 'Lacan et la Politique', *Cités*, 16: 105–123.

Sharpe, Ella (1988 [1937]) *Dream Analysis*. London: Karnac.

Tomšič, Samo (2012) 'Homology: Marx and Lacan', *S: Journal of the Circle for Lacanian Ideology Critique*. 5, available online at: www.lineofbeauty.org/ (accessed 1 September 2014).

PART 2.2

Politics and Lacan's theory of discourses

8

ON THE MASTERY IN THE FOUR 'DISCOURSES'

Peter Klepec

SCIENTIFIC RESEARCH CENTRE OF SLOVENIAN ACADEMY OF SCIENCES AND ARTS

Jacques Lacan's conception of discourse is one of the most interesting theoretical tools for the analysis of ideology, power relations, and politics we have today, yet to see its full richness and analytical potential one has to overcome some obstacles, prejudices, and misconceptions that sometimes accompany psychoanalysis and Lacan's thought in more particular. Written down in the form of four mathemes (see Figure 8.1), it might at first seem, at least for an uninitiated reader of Lacanian theory and praxis, either too abstract or simply too complicated. Another reason that obstructs its grasp is that, for some Lacan's theory of four discourses appears too historical and in itself also historically (out)dated, for others it is either too formalistic, too structuralist, or simply too dedicated to the theses concerning the role of language and communication that has by now become a part of common knowledge. With all the above in mind one might not see why one should bother with it at all. The focus of this contribution is the problem of mastery in Lacan's four discourses, while more or less leaving aside other important points concerning politics in this theory: for example, their consideration of 'enjoyment as the political factor',[1] as the paradoxical cement which simultaneously binds and unbinds every social link.

Throughout his teaching Lacan used the term 'discourse' in many different ways. From rather linguistic connotations at the very beginning in the early 1950s,[2] it is only later, in the late 1960s and early 1970s,[3] that the term discourse refers to the social link or social bond. This is also how we should understand it in the context of the theory of the four discourses. Although the discourse theory enterprise coincides historically with the events of May '68 and its aftermath, it would simply be wrong to see in it a historically conditioned project which could today transpire as being completely outdated or surpassed. Lacan's first point concerning the conception of the 'discourse' seems to be the opposite of what was the dominant view in Lacan's time and what still is the dominant view today in the age of

116 Peter Klepec

globalization, namely, that there are no (strong) social links, and that there are only more or less dispersed individuals able to make decisions and (free) choices. With the term 'discourse' Lacan wants to emphasize that *there are* (social) links of which strength, persistence, and scope we are perhaps even unaware of: 'there are structures'[4] (Lacan 2007: 13). This means that there are intersubjective *relations*:

> discourse can clearly subsist without words. It subsists in certain fundamental relations which would literally not be able to be maintained without language. Through the instrument of language a number of stable relations are established, inside which something that is much larger and goes much further than actual utterances.
>
> *(Lacan 2007: 13)*

Discourse is therefore another name for a social link:

> [I]n the final analysis, there's nothing but that, the social link. I designate it with the term 'discourse' because there's no other way to designate it once we realize that the social link is instated only by anchoring itself in the way in which language is situated over and etched into what the place is crawling with, namely, speaking beings.
>
> *(Lacan 1998b: 54)*

So, there is discourse and the sooner one tries to find out how it works and how one is embedded in and instated by it the better:

> Each of you – I am speaking even for the leftists – you are more attached to it than you care to know and would do well to sound the depths of your attachment. A certain number of biases are your daily fare and limit the import of your insurrections to the shortest term, to the term, quite precisely, that gives you discomfort – they certainly don't change your world view, for that remains perfectly spherical. The signified finds its centre wherever you take it. And, unless things change radically, it is not analytic discourse – which is so difficult to sustain in its decentring and has not yet made its entrance into common consciousness – that can in any way subvert anything whatsoever.
>
> *(Lacan 1998: 42)*

Although it seems that here Lacan is expressing a conservative view. By stating that any subversion necessarily fails and that in the end all insurrections are futile, he is only warning us about the range and the scope of our daily praxis, customs, habits, and attachments rather than speaking of some impossibility or necessity of failure. To an extent this implies that what we consider as a radical change is for Lacan not radical enough, that is they often retain the same logics of operation/conduct. One can therefore change his/her discourse, one can evolve from one discourse to another, yet the real question is *how* the *real* change *can* occur? That is a change that breaks with the logics we are fighting against. It would be wrong to say that Lacan excludes the possibility of a radical change. Nevertheless he writes: 'unless things change radically' (Lacan 1998: 42), or, to put it differently – it is not Copernicus, but Kepler's solution that is more radical for 'it throws into question the function of the centre' (Lacan 1998: 43). So, when Lacan cautions: 'Do not haste to serve you with the word *revolution*' (Lacan 2007: 11), the real question for him is the question of a *radical change*. One could say that from the very beginning of his teaching Lacan is concerned with such a change and preoccupied with the question of how psychoanalysis might represent one. Everything in his teaching, from the role of the analyst and the end of an analysis (if there is one) to his battle with IPA, from his opposition to philosophy and ego-psychology to all that stands under 'the myth of the *I* that masters' and what he calls *Je-cratie/I-cracy* (Lacan 2007: 63), might be conceived in this light. Why else would he try in *Seminar XVII* to present psychoanalysis as the obverse, the other side of the master's discourse? Why else would his motto for the ethics of psychoanalysis in *Seminar VII* be 'Do not give up on your desire',[5] do not give up on your desire of the analyst? And last but not least, if the ethics of psychoanalysis as the 'ethics of the real' (Zupančič 2000) is also about the ethics and *real change*, then Lacan knows well that such a change or 'not giving on your desire' is all but simple. That is precisely why he states that the 'analytic discourse [...] is so difficult to sustain in its decentring' (Lacan 1998: 42).

The same reasoning and arguments can be applied to the thesis we started with: there is discourse and one cannot do away with it (too simply).[6] Why is that so and what is 'discourse' after all? Discourse is 'social link, founded on language' (Lacan 1998: 17) as Lacan states. Or, more precisely, every social link and every social organization: 'is a link between those who speak' (Lacan 1998: 30). This accentuation, especially in light of the linguistic turn of 20th-century philosophy, can hardly be seen as something new or original; on the contrary, there are not many major contemporary thinkers (with a notable exception of Alain Badiou, perhaps) who would deny that language has an all-important role. But, as always with Lacan, all is in the detail. His engagement with language and speech depart from common understandings and would require a detailed account and explanation that exceed the scope of this contribution.[7] For the intended intervention it suffices to highlight Lacan's following statement: 'Language is the condition of the unconscious – that's what I say' (Lacan 2007: 41).[8] The last part 'that's what I say' means 'that's what I, Jacques Lacan, say' and throughout Lacan's early teaching this was condensed in guidelines such as 'the unconscious is structured like a language' or 'a signifier represents the subject for another signifier'. With the advent of the concept of discourse both of these basic guidelines underwent certain revisions. But before delving any further into this, two short comments concerning linguistics and structuralism need to be made. If, for quite some time, Lacan does see linguistics as a scientific ally of psychoanalysis, he later distances himself from these claims by speaking about 'linguistricks' (Lacan 1998: 15). If he claims that discourse is the structure which goes beyond speech and which can subsist without words, he is, contrary to all appearances and conjunctions, not a structuralist. A controversial statement, yet Lacan from the very beginning retains the concept of the subject, which in a strict sense remains incompatible with structuralism. Furthermore, both seminars in which his concept of the discourse plays a major role, *Seminar XVII* and *Seminar XX*, contain important discussions and critiques of his friends, contemporaries, and allies, namely Claude Lévi-Strauss and Roman Jakobson. Perhaps one could even say that Lacan's theory of the discourses elaborates on the limits of the notion of structure.

The departing point for the concept of the discourse as a 'link between those who speak' could thus be simplified in the following way: from the fact of speaking (to each other) stem a number of consequences. Those are: that from the very beginning we enter in *relations* with others through the medium of speech and language; that this medium (speech; language; symbolic order; structure) has a *formative* function for us and thus brings certain consequences (we are not masters of language, but on the contrary, we are spoken by it; the Other precedes the subject, 'the desire is the desire of the Other') and certain products (the split subject, $, the object *a*, and its vicissitudes, *jouissance*), which are condensed in the theses Lacan developed over the course of time ('the unconscious is structured like a language', 'the subject is the subject of the signifier', 'signifier represents the subject for the other signifier', 'the sender receives his own message from the receiver in an inverted form', 'there is no metalanguage', 'there is no Other of the Other', etc.).

To say 'there is discourse' means therefore to introduce its *formative* functions and consequences. The discourse 'structures the real world' (Lacan 2007: 18) and that's why for Lacan, strictly speaking, *outside* it there is nothing: 'there is no such thing as a pre-discursive reality. Every reality is founded and defined by a discourse' (Lacan 1998: 32). In this way the discourse is conceived as a necessary structure that conditions and determines every act, action, affect, thought, meaning, sense, etc. of the speaking being. The discourse shapes, defines, and creates reality itself: 'it's already inscribed in what functions as this reality I was speaking about before, the reality of a discourse that is already in the world and that underpins it, at least the one we are familiar with. Not only is it already inscribed in it, but it is one of its arches' (Lacan 2007: 14–15). This reality, however, is not a complete or a full one, it is not Whole.[9] In contrast there is not only one discourse, there are for Lacan four different discursive forms: the discourse of the Master, the discourse of the University, the discourse of the Hysteric, and the discourse of the Analyst. From their very names we can already see that three of them are named after their principal actor or agent, whereas one (the University) is a name of an institution (but it does not stand for an institution, it could be equally applied, for instance, to the European bureaucratic machinery, Stalinist Soviet Union, world of surveillance, biopolitics, etc.). Herein lies an ambiguity in the notion of the discourse itself, for it sometimes names an institution, a relationship, a praxis, or a place one assumes in a speech or any other act, at other times it stands for an arrangement and an apparatus. Furthermore, one and the same individual can act or speak simultaneously in different discourses – as, for instance, in Hegel's case, where he sometimes utters from the discourse of the Master, at others he is the Professor of the University or a Philosopher of Prussian State, and yet, for Lacan, he is also 'the most sublime hysteric' (Lacan 2007: 35).[10] The discourses themselves, as it will be demonstrated later, can change and following certain logics and certain conditions, revolute to other discourses. It seems that for Lacan the claim 'there is discourse' means that there is always already one form of the discourse, the discourse of the Master. All other discourses were invented at a certain point in history: the discourse of the University in the 17th century and the discourses of the Hysteric and Analyst only later – with no guarantee at all that the latter (and its praxis, namely, psychoanalysis) will continue to exist. However, the fact that one discourse 'may have appeared longer ago than the others is not what is important here' (Lacan 1998: 16). The discourses change over the course of history ('Something changed in the master's discourse at a certain point in history [...] (Lacan 2007: 177)), but they *do not* describe the movement of history itself: 'My little quadrupedal schemas – I am telling you this today to alert you to it – are not the Ouija boards of history' (Lacan 2007: 188).

One consequence of the above described formative function of the discourse is that ultimately for every speaking being there is no way out of the discourse as such,[11] except perhaps for psychotics, where the main operation is foreclosure of the symbolic and of the signifier, where 'the unconscious is present, but not functioning' (Lacan 1993: 208). That is why Lacan says somewhere that 'a madman is the only free man',[12] whereas all other speaking beings are subjected to discourse. Or, as the late Lacan put it – 'the non-duped err'. The claim that a human being 'has to "speechify"' (Lacan 2007: 51) means that discourse is also a blending of language and apparatus into one. The wordplay 'speechify', or in the French original 's'apparoler' goes simultaneously in several directions: 'parole', word, 'appareil', apparatus, 's'appareiller', pairing/coupling, to form a couple, etc. What is important in this context is that Lacan's claim: 'Every reality is founded and defined by a discourse' (Lacan 1998: 32) cannot be read alone and is properly understood only when linked with another claim: 'Reality is approached with apparatuses of jouissance' (Lacan 1998: 55). Thus if Lacan claims that 'what dominates [society] is the practice of language' (Lacan 2007: 239), his conception of discourse is not just about language and communication, but also about enjoyment or jouissance and its alliance with the signifier: 'This, then, is the relationship between these terms that are four in number. The one I have not named is the unnameable one, because the entire structure is founded upon its prohibition – that is to say, *jouissance*' (Lacan 2007: 176). It is here, exactly, that one finds the relation between politics and psychoanalysis: 'The intrusion into political can only be made by recognising that the only discourse there is, and not just analytic discourse, is the discourse of *jouissance* at least when one is hoping for the work of truth from it' (Lacan 2007: 78).

The enjoyment or jouissance for Lacan is the intense and the extreme pleasure beyond pleasure principle, which denotes satisfaction in dissatisfaction. Whereas before Lacan conceived enjoyment as impossible and unattainable,[13] and accentuated his transgressive character ('jouissance is prohibited to whoever speaks' (Lacan 2006: 696), as prohibited it is said between the lines, 'inter-dit'), he later changed the tonality and states that:

120 Peter Klepec

> there is no transgression here, but rather an irruption, a falling into the field, of something not unlike *jouissance:* surplus. [...] But perhaps even that has to be paid for. That is why I told you last year that in Marx the *a,* which is here, is recognized as functioning at the level that is articulated − on the basis of analytic discourse, not any of the others − as surplus *jouissance.* Here you have what Marx discovered as what actually happens at the level of surplus value.[14]
>
> *(Lacan 2007: 20)*

In other words: 'Moreover this is why I'm describing what appears here as "surplus *jouissance*" and not forcing anything or committing any transgression' (Lacan 2007: 19). That is why Lacan from there on began to accentuate that a signifier and a signifying chain as such are in the function of enjoyment. But the enjoyment is the 'strange kind of a master', as it 'serves no purpose' (Lacan 1998: 3), a simple endless repetition and his real 'master' is an obscene one − the superego: 'Nothing forces anyone to enjoy except the superego. The superego is the imperative of jouissance − Enjoy!' (Lacan 1998: 3).

Nobody knows where this will end: 'I have already said enough to you for you to know that *jouissance* is the jar of the Danaids, and that once you have started, you never know where it will end. It begins with a tickle and ends in a blaze of petrol' (Lacan 2007: 73). Jouissance is nothing but a waste:

> In fact, it is only through this effect of entropy, through this wasting, *that* jouissance acquires a status and shows itself. This is why I initially introduced it by the term '*Mehrlust*', surplus jouissance. It is precisely through being perceived in the dimension of loss − something necessitates compensation, if I can put it like this, for what is initially a negative number − that this something that has come and struck, resonated on the walls of the bell, has created *jouissance, jouissance* that is to be repeated. Only the dimension of entropy gives body to the fact that there is surplus *jouissance* there to be recovered. And this is the dimension in which work, knowledge at work, becomes necessary, insofar as, whether it knows *it* or not, initially stems from the unary trait and, in its wake, from everything that can possibly be articulated as signifier [...] This knowledge is a means of *jouissance.* And, I repeat, when it is at work, what it produces is entropy. This entropy, this point of loss, is the sole point, the sole regular point at which we have access to the nature of *jouissance.* [...] This has little to do with his speaking. It has to do with structure, which gets fitted out. The subject, who is called human, no doubt because he is only the humus of language, has only to speechify himself to its fittings.
>
> *(Lacan 2007: 50–51)*

Thus jouissance 'necessitates repetition' the latter is 'based on the return of jouissance' (Lacan 1992: 45, 46), because 'there is a loss of *jouissance:* And it is in the place of this loss introduced by repetition that we see the function of the lost object emerge, of what I am calling the *a*' (Lacan 2007: 48). With this we come to

On the Mastery in the Four Discourses **121**

the point: 'where things raise questions, that is, at the level of putting something into place that can be written as *a*' (Lacan 2007: 179). Consequently, the four discourses are not about what functions in our intersubjective relationship and in our daily communication, but about what in the strict sense *does not* function: what cannot be mastered, or what does not work. At least from his *Seminar XI* on, Lacan began to highlight the cause and its role. He speaks of it in the following way: 'In short, there is cause only in something that doesn't work' (Lacan 1987: 22). And if *Seminar XI* accentuates the gap, discontinuity, obstacle,[15] the discourses themselves highlight the categories of *impossibility* and *powerlessness*, 'impuissance' in French: 'Whatever way you come at things, whatever way you turn them, each of these little four-legged schemes has the property of leaving its own gap' (Lacan 2007: 203). In other words:

> In supposing the formalization of discourse and in granting oneself some rules within this formalization that are destined to put it to the test, we encounter an element of impossibility. This is what is at the base, the root, of an effect of structure.
>
> *(Lacan 2007: 45)*

Armed with the above preliminary remarks, a move towards the mathemes of the four discourses can finally be made.

As Figure 8.1 demonstrates, the mathemes are written in the form of four algorithms – they each stripped of all content and can be passed in the exact same form. Such representation is not coincidental; in fact it speaks of Lacan's politics of knowledge and mastery. Lacan for one claimed that with the mathemes there is no master's interpretation – in other words there is no right interpretation. This is the political lesson of Lacan's matheme – 'you are permitted/allowed to know', *scilicet*: and there is no one who is not permitted or allowed to know.

Lacan's theory of discourses consists of four discourses, four places, and four elements.[16] As seen in Figure 8.1, four places construct every discourse: the place of the agent, the other, the truth, and the product/loss. Sometimes Lacan makes minor alterations – the place of the agent, for instance, is sometimes also the place of the desire (see Lacan 2007: 106), the place of production is by the same passage designated as the place of loss. The places themselves are positioned left and right, top and bottom, whereas a bar divides the upper and lower positions. They form an imaginary square similar to a square of oppositions in logics or to a Greimasian square. The agent is placed in the upper left position that is also a place, which is dominant in every discourse. One starts (similar to where we in our Western culture start to write) at the top left position and continue to the right. If one interprets this diagram as a scheme of communication, then all positions to the left are occupied by what is active in the discourse that is speaking or sending a message, whereas those receiving a message occupy all positions to the right. Places or positions at the top represent something that is manifested, whereas those at the bottom stand for the latent, the hidden, or repressed. The place most active and

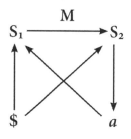
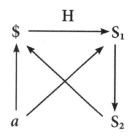
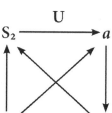
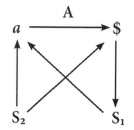

FIGURE 8.1 The four discourses

most powerful in every discourse is the top left position of agency, agent, or dominance, whereas all positions at the bottom, divided with the bar, signify a (hidden) truth and/or the loss/product. Another rather apparent segment of the discourse is that the agent is, despite its dominance, separated from the other and from the truth, and that the latter – the truth – is not the same as the product. Which, for example, implies that in a speech-act something is uttered in a particular name or from a given place. The act of speech and utterance imply an agent, yet the agent of speaking is not necessarily identical with the person of utterance. When we speak we always address the other, though for Lacan, this other is not identical with a person, it can be a locus, a locus of the other. The very logic of the positions presented above introduces a standard Freudian psychoanalytical theme concerning the analysis of unconscious formations (dreams, jokes, linguistic slips). In every discourse there is a manifested (upper) and latent (bottom) level. Here one encounters a lot of classical Lacanian themes such as that nobody can master the language, speech, and their effects ('the sender receives his own message from the receiver in an inverted form', 'there is no metalanguage', 'there is no Other of the Other'). In other words – what Lacan is saying is that every communication is misunderstanding (or ends as such): we try to communicate with the other, but every communication has effects and products that cannot be mastered, as well as its hidden truth.

A similar point can be made for the elements occupying these places. They too produce different effects as they exchange positions or places. The four elements of every discourse – S_1 (master-signifier), S_2 (the battery or chain of signifiers or knowledge), a (*objet petit a* or surplus-enjoyment), $ (divided subject) – always

On the Mastery in the Four Discourses **123**

remain in the same order. In that way we get four, instead of 24 possible combinations. The fixed order in which the elements appear can be interpreted in various ways. For example, one can add to the classical Lacanian thesis – 'a signifier represents the subject for another signifier' (sequence: $, S_1, S_2) – the relationship of the signifier to jouissance – 'the signifier is situated at the level of enjoying substance [...] The signifer is the cause of jouissance' (Lacan 1998: 24; sequence: $, S_1, S_2, a). From the set sequence of elements certain impossibilities also follow – the $ and S_2 are always diagonal, never one after another, for the subject is always a split subject, one who does not know, whereas knowledge does not represent the Whole or a Totality. Similarly S_1 and *objet petit a*. The signifier cannot master the object a as every attempt to recapture, as Lacan says, 'this paradoxical, unique, specific object, that we call object a' would be an ill founded rumination (see Lacan 1998: 268). In other words, psychoanalysis is not a mastery and neither a hypnosis: 'For the fundamental mainspring of the analytic operation is the maintenance of the distance between the I – identification – and the a' (Lacan 1998: 273).

Turning the elements in the above formulas, keeping them in the same order, clockwise or counter-clockwise creates the mathemes of four discourses. For instance, if the discourse of the master is turned counter-clockwise the formation is transformed into the discourse of the university, but if the same is done in the clockwise direction the discourse of the hysteric appears. By another 'turn of the screw' either counter-clockwise in the direction of the discourse of the university or clockwise in the direction of the discourse of the hysteric, one ends in the discourse of the analyst. Such a movement from one discourse to another, in a clockwise or counter-clockwise direction indicates that a direct passage from the master discourse to the discourse of the analyst is impossible. That is also why Lacan insists that the 'master's discourse has only one counterpoint, the analytic discourse' (Lacan 2007: 99). The question central to this movement of and between discourses is what makes one discourse change into another discourse and what pushes it to perform this logical exercise? Lacan's answer is that something 'hystericises the discourse' (Lacan 2007: 34). Later he adds that: 'there is some emergence of psychoanalytic discourse whenever there is a movement from one discourse to another' (Lacan 1998: 16).

While there are four discourses that appear as equal there is nevertheless one discourse which seems to have a very special place. In *Seminar XVII* Lacan explains its role and places it in the centre: that is the discourse of the master. That is of no surprise, as in Lacan's entire oeuvre there is no single line of thought or a single thesis which does not stand for an attempt to counter the effects of mastery. The topic of the master is permanently present in Lacan, and one could consequently claim that the entirety of the four discourses concerns nothing else but the mastery and its vicissitudes. At first this might seem strange as Lacan has been accused of many things, one of which is of being an 'absolute master'[17] himself. But if all the anecdotes and stories are put aside, and attention is given solely to Lacan's major theses concerning the role and the position of the analyst (in the seminar in question, for instance, the analyst position is 'substantially made from the object a'

(Lacan 2007: 42), this concerns 'an effect of a discourse that produces a reject' (Lacan 2007: 43)), or attention is given to his general theses on language whereby nobody is a master of language and speech as everyone undergoes a symbolic castration, including the master. Lacan clearly stated that: 'the master is castrated' (Lacan 2007: 97). In other words, there is no master strictly speaking, everybody has to go through a medium of language and face the consequences. Furthermore, a master is always a product of an intersubjective relation; it is the other who makes the master who he is, as the conduct of the bondsman in Hegel makes a lord for his master. The position of the master is simultaneously more fragile and yet more solid than it appears at first. More fragile and uncertain because the master's position does not really depend on the master. He is nothing but a function; thus he depends on the fate of the master-signifier and has nothing in himself that would permanently guarantee his position of mastery (its fate depends upon the *object petit a* or that very same elusive object, love, sought in a loved one), but even here the master is hystericized (or put in a position of a hysteric). He questions himself: 'Do I still/really have something special in me?' There are numerous political examples illustrating precisely this point of hysterization of the master; to only mention the notorious case of Ceauşescu. As is well known, his confidence 'that he had still got it' let him down at a fatal public meeting in 1989. Another and a similar problem with the master in modern politics is, as Lacan writes:

> A radical decline of the function of the master, a function that obviously governs all of Aristotle's thought and determines its persistence over the centuries. It is in Hegel that we find expressed an extreme devalorization of the position of the master, since Hegel turns him into the great dupe, the magnificent cuckold of historical development.
>
> *(Lacan 1992: 11)*

Yet despite its demise and its devalorization – as the two examples above testify – the figure of the master continues to function; and even more, as Lacan never forgets to add that it is not (and will not be) easy to get rid of it.

The strategic reasons as to why the discourse of the master is set as a point of departure for the remaining three discourses are not only historical but equally structural. The upper level in the master's discourse epitomizes Lacan's thesis that 'a signifier represents a subject for another signifier': S_1, master-signifier or unary trait, represents the master for all other signifiers (S_2). However, this thesis later underwent some important specifications, which point in the direction of mastery: 'The signifier is first and foremost, imperative' as Lacan writes (1998: 32). The statement links every discussion about ontology with the discourse of the master (here Lacan uses wordplay maître/m'être, master/my-being). For the signifier as such commands, and this links it on the one hand with stupidity (as 'the signifier is stupid' (Lacan 1998: 20)) and on the other hand with jouissance (as 'the signifier is the cause of jouissance' (Lacan 1998: 24)). This explanation of the relations between the signifiers and the master discourse is still congruent with the Hegelian matrix of

On the Mastery in the Four Discourses   **125**

master/slave dialectics where, in the fight for the recognition, which is also a 'fight to the death', the one who gives up and surrenders to the other becomes a slave and in turn recognizes the victor as his master. The master or the lord for Hegel is ignorant or even stupid, for he does not know; all he does is enjoy himself. In contrast to enjoyment, the knowledge remains on the side of the bondsman, the servant or the slave, who is forced to work and who will for Hegel one day triumph in the course of history. In contrast, Lacan is quite sceptical of the Hegelian/Marxist solution:

> The work, Hegel tells us, to which the slave submits in giving up jouissance out of the fear of death, is precisely the path by which he achieves his freedom. There can be no more obvious lure than this, politically or psychologically. Jouissance comes easily to the slave, and it leaves work in serfdom.
>
> *(Lacan 2006: 686)*

One could read the matheme of the discourse of the master through a Hegelian matrix of the master/slave dialectics, where the left side $S_1/\$$ would represent the master, the right side S_2/a the slave. In this reading, the master (S_1) takes up the position of the agent who puts the slave (S_2) to work, and who appropriates the surplus (a) as a result of that slave's work.

But Lacan is very clear that his conception is not about the *person* of a master, but about what he *does*:

> In the master's discourse, for instance, it is effectively impossible that there be a master who makes the entire world function. Getting people to work is even more tiring, if one really has to do it, than working oneself. The master never does it. He gives a sign, the master signifier, and everybody jumps. That's where you have to start, which is, in effect, completely impossible. It's tangible every day.
>
> *(Lacan 2007: 174)*

What the master does is provide a signifier, a master-signifier.[18] 'S/he gives a sign' and all of his powers depends on that sign (or on some sort of insignia). On the political level the same situation appears in a fight for what Gramsci called 'hegemony', that a need never to chase to provide signifiers which account and make sense of the situation.

If S_1 or the master-signifier is the strongest part of the master discourse, then how come that in the discourse, under the bar (if one is to look at the schema again), one finds $\$$ or a split subject? At least three readings of this situation should be considered: first, one could say that for Lacan the subject, $\$$, does not have an identity and thus has to identify with something. Thus: 'Wo $\$$ war, soll S_1 werden' means that one has to enter the symbolic order, choose his unary trait, and in turn his master-signifier. Second, this $\$$ can also be read as a retroactive act which cuts off the signifier, and represses a gap and a loss introduced by its own

126 Peter Klepec

intervention. And third, it can be said that the strongest is also the weakest – that the truth of the master is not only that he is castrated, but also that he is an impostor, bluffer, make-believer 'that he has it'. 'That he has what?' one might ask. The lost object, the object that was, strictly speaking, never lost for the subject never had it. That is how one could also understand Lacan's claim that the product of the master discourse, the *objet petit a*, masks the truth, that is 'the division of the subject' (Lacan 2007: 118).

But what else is the product of the master discourse? It cannot be simply the work of the other, but the work of a slave, of labour, or a surplus work. 'A real master, as in general we used to see until a recent era, and this is seen less and less, doesn't desire to know anything at all – he desires that things work. And why would he want to know? There are more amusing things than that' (Lacan 2007: 24). The master, and this is a constant in Lacan's work, only wishes to see that 'the work goes on'. Lacan states:

> As far as that which is of interest to us, namely, that which has to do with desire, to its array and disarray, so to speak, the position of power of any kind in all circumstances and in every case, whether historical or not, has always been the same. What is Alexander's proclamation when he arrived in Perse-polis or Hitler's when he arrived in Paris? The preamble isn't important: 'I have come to liberate you from this or that.' The essential point is 'Carry on working. Work must go on.' Which, of course, means: 'Let it be clear to everyone that this is on no account the moment to express the least surge of desire.' The morality of power, of the service of goods, is as follows: 'As far as desires are concerned, come back later. Make them wait.'
>
> *(Lacan 1992: 315)*

Is there a way out of this impasse of mastery? Do other discourses represent an alternative? In other words, where do we encounter mastery in the other three discourses? The discourses of the hysteric and of the university, which logically follow from the discourse of the master either clockwise or counter-clockwise, both possess some affinities with the master. The discourse of the hysteric has the split subject (the subject who does not know, the desiring subject) placed in the position of the agent. 'The hysteric's desire is to have an unsatisfied desire' as Lacan (2006: 620) claims, and continues that the desire is hysterical in its nature, for the desire of a man is not his but the other's desire. That, however, does not mean that either the other or the analyst are the master. Instead one could say that the hysteric is allergic to mastery be it in the form of a master-signifier, of another person or of the other: the hysteric is prone to prove that any authority or any mastery is ill-founded and that the master does not really know. Thus Lacan's motto 'do not compromise on your desire' could also be rephrased into: 'do not seek out the master (of your desire)'. What a hysteric wants is precisely the master who would match his/her task: that is the hysteric 'wants the other to be the master, and to know lots of things, but at the same time she doesn't want him to know so much that he does not believe she is the supreme price of all his knowledge. In other words, she wants a master she can reign over. She reigns, and he does not govern' (Lacan 2007: 129). Thus the hysteric wants to be the master of the master and thus a real master! This is perhaps one of the reasons why Lacan links (hysterical) revolt with the call for a master: 'What the hysteric wants is a master' (Lacan 2007: 129), and why he retorts to 1968 protesters: 'You want a revolution? Voilà! You'll get it, things revolve just so, and you'll get a new form of master, state socialism' (Lacan 2007: 34, 37). It is exactly this new form of mastery, the new, perverted form of the master that is present in the discourse of the university. In the university discourse the dominant position is occupied by knowledge (that is *savoir* and not *connaissance*), whereas in the position of truth one finds the master-signifier. Such positioning signifies that behind all knowledge there is power, mastery, the mastery of knowledge, and the domination of the other to whom this knowledge is imparted. From the a-morphic mass or masses (the object *a* in the place of the other) the university produces the subject, $, in the place of the product. Though the discourse of the university represents the hegemony of knowledge, well visible in today's hegemony of science, in the scientific discourse, and in the triumph of bureaucracy, it is interesting what Lacan says about knowledge albeit in the context of the hysteric rather than the university: 'the desire to know is not what leads to knowledge. [Rather w]hat leads to knowledge is – allow me to justify this in the more or less long term – the hysteric's discourse' (Lacan 2007: 23).

Thus can psychoanalysis facilitate 'a way out of mastery'? There are no easy answers to this crucial question, which ultimately Lacan left open to the very end. To attempt an answer, one has to first remember that for Lacan there are no easy solutions. He says explicitly not to 'expect anything more subversive in my discourse than that I do not claim to have a solution' (Lacan 2007: 70). Second, due to its occupational nature (it is a clinical and an individual experience) psychoanalysis cannot 'constitute progress, if it happens only for some'.[19] Third, there are numerous theoretical and practical ways with which Lacan in his late thought continues to counter-effect the mastery. There is a claim in *Seminar XVIII* that psychoanalysis is the only discourse, which is not of the semblance. Moreover, although very much in passing and thus underdeveloped, Lacan seems to introduce the fifth – capitalist – discourse,[20] and persists in a search for a new form of a master-signifier[21] (and hence the orientation 'towards a new signifier').[22] On the practical/clinical level there are numerous attempts of transgressing the mastery: from the introduction of different procedures, such as the one of the 'pass', to Lacan's dissolution of his own School and the founding of a range of new forms of psychoanalytic associations. Ultimately there is no end in questioning the analytic discourse as 'the social bond determined by the practice of an analysis' (Lacan 1990: 18), in which the analyst 'positions himself as the cause of desire. This is an eminently unprecedented position, if not a paradoxical one, one that is validated by a practice' (Lacan 2007: 152). This praxis depends on the role one ascribes to the *objet petit a*,[23] but that opens a whole new problematic and stands for the beginning of another debate.

Notes

1 To use the phrase Slavoj Žižek (1991) uses in the subtitle of his second book published in English. In a certain, simplifying way, of course, one could even say that practically every one of Žižek's works in the last 30 years or so presents nothing but the variation on this theme.

2 For instance: 'The unconscious is the discourse of the other' (which first appears in 1953, and later becomes 'the unconscious is the discourse of the Other'; see Lacan 2006: 689, etc.).

3 The 'discourse' first appeared in Lacan's *Seminar XVI, From an other to the Other*, which started in November 1968; a year later it came to the centre in *Seminar XVII, The Other Side of Psychoanalysis*. Some of its important conceptual changes were introduced later, especially in *Seminar XX, Encore*, which ended in June 1973 and was published as a book in 1975. Among Lacan's published works centred on the conception of discourse one should mention his radio interview *Radiophonie* (especially Question VII) which was partially aired several times in June 1970, published in issue 2–3 of the then newly founded journal *Scilicet*, as well as Lacan's only public appearance on French television filmed in 1973, broadcast finally just to escape scandal after trying to muscle in on its final form at the beginning of 1974. In the same year it was published as a rewritten transcription simply as *Television*.

4 During discussion after Michel Foucault's lecture 'What is an Author?' held on 22 February 1969 (the first lecture of his XVIIth seminar began on 3 December 1968), Lacan retorts to Lucien Goldmann and others who claimed that 'structures do not march on the streets': 'If the events of May '68' prove anything, then they prove that the structures descended to the streets' (Foucault 2001: 848).

5 More on that in Lecture XXIV 'The paradoxes of ethics or have you acted in conformity with your desire' in *Seminar VII* (see Lacan 1992: 311ff.).

6 Yet another way of saying this for Lacan, but one that would demand detailed and extensive detour into ontology, would be: 'There's One', 'Y a de l'Un'. For a detailed reading we would here subscribe to Zupančič (2011).

7 More on that in Milner (1995).

8 Perhaps one should mention what, in this context, Lacan says about the relationship between the unconscious and discourse: 'I do not base this idea of discourse on the ex-sistence of the unconscious. It is the unconscious that I locate through it – it ex-sists only through a discourse' (Lacan 1990: 18).

9 By the way, the very idea of the Whole has consequences for politics too: 'The imaginary idea of the whole that is given by the body, as drawing on the good form of satisfaction, on what, ultimately, forms a sphere, has always been used in politics by the party of political preaching' (Lacan 2007: 31).

10 See Dolar 2006: 129–55.

11 This question of 'the way out' concerns further development of the conception of discourse and the introduction of the fifth discourse, discourse of *The Capitalist*. For more on that see the Samo Tomšič's chapter in the present volume.

12 Or 'the truly free men are precisely the madmen' as Lacan puts it in his talk on 10 November 1967 given to psychiatrists. See Lacan (2011b).

13 See Miller 2000: 46.

14 More on that Zupančič 2006: 155–178.

15 More on that in Miller 1989: 30–50.

16 Why four? Hegel in his *Science of Logics* had already spoken about the four elements necessary for dialectics; Lacan himself does speak on numerous occasions about number four, quarter turn, and quadripodes: 'I have been speaking about this notorious quarter turn for long enough, and on different occasions – in particular, ever since the appearance of what I wrote under the title "Kant with Sade" – for people to think that perhaps one day it would be seen that this isn't limited to what the so-called Schema Z does [...]' (Lacan 2007: 14). See also Lacan 2006: 653, 657; 2014: 104, 177; 2007: 14,

On the Mastery in the Four Discourses **129**

20, 36, 92, etc.; 2007b: 15; 2011: 65ff., etc. The logics of number four in Lacan was brilliantly exposed in Jacques-Alain Miller's unpublished seminar *1,2,3,4* (1984–85).

17 See Borch Jacobsen 1991.

18 Lacan elaborated this topic in his *Seminar III* with the concept of the quilting or anchoring point (see Lacan 1993: 293ff.).

19 This is also linked with, if one can say so, the universal dimension of emancipation, which Lacan is well aware of: 'The more saints, the more laughter; that's my principle, to wit, the way out of capitalist discourse – which will not constitute progress, if it happens only for some.' (Lacan 1990: 20). See also Jelica Šumič's chapter in this volume.

20 For more on that see Samo Tomšič's chapter in this volume.

21 'And, as I was saying last time when I was leaving Vincennes, perhaps it's from the analyst's discourse that there can emerge another style of master signifier' (Lacan 2007: 176).

22 'Vers un signifiant nouveau' is the title of five lectures Lacan gave in 1977. See Lacan 1979: 7–23.

23 For Jacques-Alain Miller's thesis that today the discourse of the analyst is no longer the obverse side of the master's discourse, see Žižek 2006: 110ff. and 2006b: 298–308.

Further reading on Lacan's discourse theory

Evans, Dylan (1996) 'Discourse', in *An Introductory Dictionary of Lacanian Psychoanalysis*. London and New York: Routledge, 44–46.

Grigg, Russell (2001) 'Discourse', in *A Compendium of Lacanian Terms*, H. Glowinski, Z. M. Marks and S. Murphy. London and New York: Free Association Books, 61–70.

Chemama, Roland (ed.) (1995) 'Discours', in *Dictionnaire de la psychanalyse*. Paris: Larousse, 87–90.

Krutzen, Henry (2003) 'Discours', in *Jacques Lacan. Séminaire 1952–1980. Index référentiel*, 2nd edition. Paris: Anthropos, 199–204.

Fink, Bruce (1995) 'The Status of Psychoanalytic Discourse', in *Lacanian Subject. Between Language and Jouissance*. Princeton, NJ: Princeton University Press, 129–146.

Bracher, Mark, Alcon Marshall W. Jr., Corthell Ronald J. and Massardier-Kenney, Françoise (eds) (1994) *Lacanian Theory of Discourse. Subject, Structure and Society*. New York: New York University Press.

Clemens, Justin, and Grigg, Russell (eds) (2006). *Jacques Lacan and the Other Side of Psychoanalysis: Reflections on Seminar XVII*. Durham, NC and London: Duke University Press.

Bibliography

Borch Jacobsen, Michel (1991) *Lacan: The Absolute Master*. Redwood City, CA: Stanford University Press.

Clemens, Justin and Grigg, Russell (2006) *Jacques Lacan and the Other Side of Psychoanalysis: Reflections on Seminar XVII*. Durham, NC: Duke University Press.

Dolar, Mladen (2006) 'Hegel as the Other Side of Psychoanalysis', in *Jacques Lacan and the Other Side of Psychoanalysis: Reflections on Seminar XVII*, ed. J. Clemens, and R. Grigg. Durham, NC and London: Duke University Press, 129–155.

Foucault, Michel (2001) *Dits et écrits I, 1954–1975*. Paris: Gallimard.

Lacan, Jacques (1979) 'Vers un significant nouveau', *Ornicar*, 17–18.

Lacan, Jacques (1987) *The Four Fundamental Concepts of Psycho-Analysis*. London: Penguin.

Lacan, Jacques (1990) *Television/ A Challenge to the Psychoanalytic Establishment*. New York: W. W. Norton and Company.

Lacan, Jacques (1992) *The Seminar, Book VII. The Ethics of Psychoanalysis, 1959–1960*, ed. Jacques-Alain Miller, trans. Dennis Porter. New York: W. W. Norton and Company.

Lacan, Jacques (1993). *The Seminar, Book III. The Psychoses*, ed. Jacques-Alain Miller, trans. Russell Grigg. New York: W. W. Norton and Company.

Lacan, Jacques (1998) *The Seminar, Book XI, The Four Fundamental Concepts of Psycho-Analysis*, ed. Jacques-Alain Miller, trans. Alan Sheridan. New York: W. W. Norton and Company.

Lacan, Jacques (1998b). *The Seminar, Book XX, Encore: On Feminine Sexuality, the Limits of Love and Knowledge*, ed. Jacques-Alain Miller, trans. Bruce Fink. New York: W. W. Norton and Company.

Lacan, Jacques (2006) *Écrits*. New York: W. W. Norton and Company.

Lacan, Jacques (2007) *The Seminar, Book XVII, The Other Side of Psychoanalysis*, ed. Jacques-Alain Miller, trans. Russell Grigg. New York: W. W. Norton and Company.

Lacan, Jacques (2011) *Le Séminaire, livre XIX, ...ou pire*. Paris: Seuil.

Lacan, Jacques (2011b) 'Psychoanalysis and the Formation of the Psychiatrist', *The Letter. Irish Journal for Lacanian Psychoanalysis*, 47.

Lacan, Jacques (2014) *The Seminar, Book X. Anxiety, 1962–1963*, ed. Jacques-Alain Miller, trans. A.R. Price, London: Polity Press.

Miller, Jacques-Alain (1989) 'To Interpret the Cause. From Freud to Lacan', *Newsletter of the Freudian Field*, 3, 1 & 2.

Miller, Jacques-Alain (2000) 'Six paradigms of jouissance', *Lacanian Ink*, 17.

Milner, Jean-Claude (1995) *L'Oeuvre claire. Lacan, la science, la philosophie*. Paris: Seuil.

Žižek, Slavoj (1991) *For They Know Not What They Do. Enjoyment as a Political Factor*. London: Verso.

Žižek, Slavoj (2006) 'Object a in Social Links', in *Jacques Lacan and the Other Side of Psychoanalysis: Reflections on Seminar XVII*, ed. J. Clemens, and R. Grigg. Durham, NC and London: Duke University Press, 107–128.

Žižek, Slavoj (2006b). *The Parallax View*. Cambridge, MA: MIT Press.

Zupančič, Alenka (2000) *Ethics of the Real. Kant, Lacan*. London: Verso.

Zupančič, Alenka (2006) 'When Surplus Enjoyment meets Surplus Value', in *Jacques Lacan and the Other Side of Psychoanalysis: Reflections on Seminar XVII*, ed. J. Clemens, and R. Grigg. Durham, NC and London: Duke University Press, 155–168.

Zupančič, Alenka (2011) *Seksualno in ontologija*. Ljubljana: Analecta.

9

DISCOURSE AND THE MASTER'S LINING

A Lacanian critique of the globalizing (bio)politics of the *Diagnostic and Statistical Manual*

Colin Wright

UNIVERSITY OF NOTTINGHAM

If a single concept could claim to underlie the diverse innovations in post-Marxism, postcolonialism, critical race studies, feminism, queer theory, and gender studies over the last 30 years, it would surely be Michel Foucault's notion of 'discourse', understood as the productive commingling of power and knowledge. And yet, relatively few have seen that Jacques Lacan's work offers arguably even richer resources for a theory of the interweavings of discourse, power, and knowledge. Well before Foucault's work made such an impact, Lacan had been developing a nuanced theory of discourse that drew on Saussurean linguistics, game theory, and cybernetics, as well as Freudian psychoanalysis. It was to discourse, too, that Lacan returned in a novel way in *Seminar XVII* as a response to the radicalism of May '68 (Lacan 2007). However, what Lacan meant by discourse was never what Foucault meant.

In what follows, I want to outline what is specific about Lacan's psychoanalytic rather than sociolinguistic concept of discourse; what separates it from but also allows it to usefully supplement Foucault's; and what it contributes to the key problematic within all truly political theories of discourse: the role of the subject in the dialectic between structure and agency (a question dramatically posed by May '68). My overall claims are that: if we follow *Seminar XVII* closely, the relationship between psychoanalysis and politics can be seen to be irrevocably linked to its clinical practice; that this link to the clinical is what prevents the co-opting of psychoanalytic theory by 'university discourse'; and that the clinical link also focuses Lacanian political theory on the contemporary discourse of health, something Foucault himself recognized as the 'biopolitical' core of neoliberalism (Foucault 2010).

To outline the implications of this juxtaposition of a Foucaultian and a Lacanian approach, I will undertake a brief critique of the *Diagnostic and Statistical Manual of Mental Disorders* (*DSM*), the textbook which governs the application of psychiatric theory and practice in many parts of the world. Following this example, I will then

132 Colin Wright

reflect more generally on what the Lacanian theory of discourse offers to the critique of capitalism.

Political discourse theory in the academy

May '68 was arguably a fork in the path for the concept of discourse. As we shall see, it prompted Lacan to reinvent his understanding of discourse. But it was also the moment when a broadly Foucaultian notion of discourse took off in the academy.

Foucault's first major publication, *Madness and Civilization* (1961), had referred to madness as an historically variable 'discourse' rather than an ontological invariant, and was received largely as a structuralist intervention into the history of ideas. This was also the case with *The Order of Things* (1966) which studied the changing discursive conditions of the disciplines of linguistics, biology, and political economy, in order to outline an archaeology of the sciences of Man. Foucault was then seen to be at the centre of structuralist anti-humanism alongside Louis Althusser and, indeed, Lacan himself – though Foucault came to dispute this characterization of his work (Foucault 1980, 114). And yet the Foucaultian concept of discourse really rose to prominence as part of the *critique* of structuralism, initiated by Jacques Derrida in 1967, but in full swing after May '68.

Althusser's structuralist Marxism had seemed bereft before the novelty of the May movement, and his stubborn adherence to the *Parti Communiste Française* (PCF) condemned him in the eyes of many (Ross 2002). The refreshing combination of Maoist and also Situationist ideas during May '68 (Feenberg and Freedman 2001) paved the way for the replacement of Althusser's structuralist concept of 'ideology' – which only an intellectual vanguard of Marxist 'scientists' could supposedly identify – by the Foucaultian concept of 'discourse' – which was already equipped to critique the social construction of scientific truth-claims, including Marxist ones. Jacques Rancière's very public break with Althusser was based on exactly this issue of the veiled violence of supposedly scientific knowledge. For Rancière, any institutionalized, 'objective' knowledge, whether validated by a university system or a political party, endorses a hierarchical distribution of intellects and roles, so that Althusser's version of ideology critique was actually a 'return to order' (Rancière 2011: xv). The term 'discourse' then, maintained the links between power and contestation but it also ameliorated the reduction of agency to sociological definitions of class on which the supposed 'scientific' legitimacy of Althusser and the PCF rested. Though Foucault himself was considerably more nuanced – *The Archaeology of Knowledge*, for example, is clear that discourse is fragile in its very imposition (Foucault 2003) – the dominant understanding of discourse to emerge from this moment was a version of 'social constructionism' that would later feed into the so-called Science Wars and postmodernism.

Nor was this an exclusively French affair. For British Cultural Studies, particularly under the influence of the late Stuart Hall, a turn to discourse in the 1970s was part of a related shift to the so-called New Social Movements, and thus to a broad-based identity politics. Hall himself combined semiotic approaches to 'encoding/decoding' with a Gramscian understanding of a hegemonic cultural politics (Hall 1973). Paradoxically, it was also at this time that Lacan's work began to be taken up in Anglophone academia precisely as a 'discourse theory' that could explain the mechanisms of ideology. This is very clear in the psychoanalytic film theory of the *Screen Studies* group, most famously exemplified by Laura Mulvey's notion of the 'male gaze' (Mulvey 1975). Picking up on Althusser's own use of it in the 'Ideology and Ideological State Apparatuses' essay (Althusser 1971), these semiotic critics of film, advertising, and mass visual culture used Lacan's early paper on the 'mirror stage' (Lacan 2006a) to explore the construction of sexed, gendered, and raced 'subjects' in capitalist society.

But already, something crucial had been lost in this turn to a constructionist understanding of discourse: the sexed/gendered/raced subject of Anglo-Saxon Cultural Studies had ceased to be a recognizably *psychoanalytic* subject in the Lacanian sense. The fundamental point about Lacan's mirror stage argument is that the foundation of the illusory ego lies not simply in the reflective surface of the imaginary, but also in the validating function of a symbolic Other: it is the (m)Other that confirms the infant's *imago*. The elementary psychoanalytic consequence of this is that the egoic individual who (mis)recognizes himself in the mirror never coincides with or exhausts the topologically distinct subject of the unconscious because his being, as it were, comes from the Other. Lacan was always diametrically opposed to the idea that power positively produces 'subjects' without remainder, whether via Althusserian interpellation or Foucaultian discourse. For him, the very fact of speaking introduces an excess or leftover because the speaker has a real body of drives which cannot be symbolized in speech. Once speech is assumed, desire becomes possible, but as what persists (and insists) in the lack produced when need is subtracted from demand (Lacan 2006b). The infant, for example, might seem to demand the breast to satisfy his need for nourishment, but more fundamentally he desires, insatiably, the love of the Other. Lacan's related opposition between the 'subject of the signifier' and the 'subject of the signified' (see Lacan 2006c: 430) demonstrated that while discourse, understood as a Foucaultian truth-regime, can indeed produce subjects as objects of statements, the *Lacanian* subject evades any such reduction because of its excessive character. To take the simplest example, when in English we invoke the personal pronoun 'I' to try to convey what is most intimate to our sense of self, it is obvious that we rely on a mere signifier that everyone speaking English also leans on for the same paradoxical purpose. In any statement with the structure 'I am x', there is a referent at the level of propositional content and this is the 'subject of the signified' which attempts to fix a meaning. But there is also the excessive moment of enunciation itself, which Lacan calls 'the subject of the signifier', and which makes its presence felt not *as* but *in* speech, often as a break in meaning (the famous 'Freudian slip' for example). Moreover, as the difficult concept of the real comes to the fore in Lacan's later teaching, the subject is more and more indexed to a radically singular mode of enjoyment outside symbolic law, though not outside language in its meaningless materiality.

Reading very early Lacan through a Foucaultian notion of discourse, as many in Anglophone academia did, evacuated this all-important distinction between the imaginary individual, with an apparent identity amenable to 'construction', and the real subject of the unconscious which is not a 'social construction' but a singular creation or invention which makes use of the common discourse. Conceptualizing the subject as nothing other than its hailing by power is absolutely incompatible with any psychoanalytic understanding of the subject, even on the most orthodox, biologistic reading of Freud in which 'instinct' exceeds and undermines the demands of social repression.

Nonetheless, it was from British Cultural Studies that the most overtly 'Lacanian' political discourse theory emerged in the mid-1980s. Ernesto Laclau and Chantal Mouffe's *Hegemony and Socialist Strategy* (1985) brought Gramsci and Lacan together in an anti-essentialist post-Marxism that put 'discourse' at the centre of political change. However, the version of Lacan they appealed to was dry and formalistic and entirely divorced from clinical practice. They took from early Lacan two key concepts: the 'empty signifier', and *points de capiton* or 'quilting points'. The 'empty signifier', they argued, operates like a master signifier ordering the relations between the other elements in a symbolic system, but only because it is ontologically empty. They had in mind the kind of abstract nouns that do indeed organize much ostensibly political debate, such as 'freedom', 'nation', and 'democracy'. Lacan's other notion of *points de capiton* was then used to refer to the always provisional 'quilting' of the social text(ile), stabilizing a semiotic flux by means of certain privileged signifiers. They interpreted this 'quilting' as a hegemonic filling of these empty signifiers in order to create 'chains of equivalence' encompassing more and more actors in the discursive social space. Official representational politics, they contended, colonizes these empty signifiers in ways that preserve a particular group's vested interests behind the rhetoric of universalism. Yet they also held out a hope for a radical form of democracy that exploits this universalism in order to extend equivalence to minority groups. Yannis Stavrakakis (1999) has highlighted precisely what was Lacanian in particularly Laclau's political discourse theory, while Slavoj Žižek (Butler et al. 2000) has pointed out the ways in which it has never been Lacanian enough. Nonetheless, Laclau and Mouffe's nominally 'Lacanian' discourse theory did spawn an approach to 'texts', influential in Media and Cultural Studies, called Critical Discourse Analysis (Wodak and Meyer 2009). Thanks to the dominance of the hard sciences, there is some debate about whether this can be considered a methodology at all, but it is certainly taught as if it were one.

From the point of view of psychoanalytic clinical practice, it is clear that many crucial concepts are lost in this translation of Lacanian ideas into social and political theory, and into transmissible methodologies serviceable to academic knowledge-production. What becomes, for example, of the unconscious itself, as an enjoying knowledge that does not know itself (Lacan 1999)? Laclau and Mouffe effectively claim to master the unconscious as a structure of lack whose effects can be formalized, predicted, and even mobilized as part of a political programme of increased inclusivity. In all rigour, this cannot be found in Lacan. For related reasons, academic discourse analysis seems to reduce speech to two modes: either the speech of the big Other imposing hegemonic power, or an attempt by the subject to make their voice heard by addressing to that Other a demand for recognition. Clinically speaking, this reduces speech to its self-reinforcing imaginary dimension. In analytic practice, Freud's 'fundamental rule' of free association aims to enable the speaker to hear the Other already in their own speech. Certainly with neurotics, analysis moves in exactly the opposite direction of any 'politics of identity', even one based on a structural lack assumed to be democratically empowering. One of Lacan's most succinct definitions of the aim of analysis is the attainment of 'absolute difference' (Lacan 1998a: 276), meaning the singularity of the analysand's mode of enjoyment as radically distinct from wider social norms. Such absolute difference is incompatible with the 'multicultural' or 'rainbow' version of difference dreamed of by the liberal pluralism that Laclau and Mouffe's approach comes dangerously close to resembling.

I would suggest that this tendency to remain at the level of the imaginary stems from a problematic conflation of speech and discourse within academic discourse analysis. This is due probably to the discipline's origins in conversation analysis and sociolinguistics, where discourse is indeed conceptualized primarily as 'talk', as well as its recourse to a constructionist reading of Foucault. From a Lacanian point of view however, the structural gap between discourse and speech is a prerequisite for any notion of the unconscious, and thus for any topology of the relationship between subjectivity and the 'social link'. One of the underlying problems in all of this work therefore, is a deeply non-psychoanalytic conception of the link between psychoanalysis and politics, in which the former becomes a theory appropriable by the latter. However, by turning now to *Seminar XVII* (also a response to May '68), we can explore Lacan's psychoanalytic understanding of 'discourse' and, in the process, reconfigure the psychoanalysis–politics relation by foregrounding clinical practice.

A closer look at the other side

The Other Side of Psychoanalysis is one of the most startling innovations in Lacan's teaching. Loosely, it can be situated as an auto-critique of aspects of *Seminar VII* on ethics, as a continuation of the concern with the foundations of psychoanalysis in *Seminar XI*, and as paving the way for the renewed focus on knowledge in *Seminar XX*. Most famously however, it is where he chooses to formalize the 'four discourses': the discourse of the Master, the Hysteric, Analysis itself, and the University. I am going to say less about each of these individually, and more about what they reveal regarding Lacan's approach to discourse in general, since from the outset it was productively different from Foucault's.

The profound consistency in the way Lacan uses the term 'discourse' was already evident in his interpretation of three key theoretical resources during the 1950s: Saussurean linguistics, Lévi-Strauss' concept of myth, and cybernetics and information theory.

First, from Saussurean linguistics Lacan takes the distinction between *parole* as speech, and *langue* as the underlying system of differences invoked in every speech-act. *Langue*, then, would be the linguistic unconscious into which we are constitutively thrown by dint of our prenatal induction into a particular speech community. Crucially however, one can never point at or circumscribe *langue*: even in Saussure's *Course in General Linguistics, langue* represents a limit to positivist knowledge, linking it, in Lacan's view, to the unconscious. Whenever Lacan speaks of 'discourse' then – as in the famous aphorism 'the unconscious is the discourse of the Other' – he is invoking the Saussurean point that *langue* only exists in the social conventions of speakers. Discourse is thus an intrinsically *social* bond not only because it involves, minimally, two subjects, but also because it distributes relations between them prior to any particular act of speech: for there to *be* speakers, this distribution must already have taken place. Even when one speaks to oneself, the symbolic Other is present. To express this using one of Saussure's favoured examples, if it is possible to play oneself at chess, the rules of chess must be in place as a 'third' that facilitates the turn-taking of the 'two' which, in purely chess terms, are indeed at play even in this scenario.

Second, this emphasis on discourse as a chess-like combinatory is explored further through Lacan's reading of structuralist anthropologist Claude Lévi-Strauss (1969). In his approach to myth, Lévi-Strauss argued that the diverse cosmologies invented by different cultures around the world are effectively imaginary treatments of underlying symbolic systems. What Lévi-Strauss contributes over and above Saussure, however, is the additional idea that myths are responses to fundamental logical contradictions which cannot be resolved: again, we see a constitutive relation to impossibility that gets mythic systems underway, as reaction formations to what Lacan would call the real. For example, Lévi-Strauss shows that the elaboration of Oedipal themes in many cultures reflects a 'treatment' of the incest taboo regulating exogamous kinship structures (Lévi-Strauss 1969). By such means, a contradiction which can be formally expressed 'X:Y' is, not resolved, but sublated by myth into a narrative form that re-presents that contradiction at another level, as 'Y:X'. Mythic speech is thus secondary to a preceding symbolic discourse.

Third, Lacan further separates discourse from speech with reference to developments in cybernetics and information theory. Taking his lead this time from Roman Jackobson who was tangentially involved in the famous Macy conferences on cybernetics, Lacan parses a distinction between 'message' and 'code' (Lacan 1998b). Any meaningful message, he recognized, is but the epiphenomenal result of an underlying logical system of encoding which is absolutely without meaning. In this sense, if a discourse can be said to be 'common' (p. 16) it is only by 'saying' absolutely nothing (just as, in our digital era, the fact that binary code means nothing whatsoever is the very quality fuelling the information revolution). Lacan's early challenge to psychological theories of communication predicated on intention, therefore paralleled developments in information theory at this time, thanks to which messages were being re-conceptualized as patterned randomness or organized 'noise'. For Lacan, there is always a failure in the imagined circularity of human communication, and it is precisely this that discourse explains.

One can see these traits of discourse coming to the fore in a new way in *Seminar XVII* where Lacan declares that 'discourse can clearly consist without words' (Lacan 2007: 13) but that '[t]he deployment of speech [...] has been confused with what discourse is' (ibid.: 167). Was this critique already directed at a simplistic conception of Foucaultian discourse? Echoing Lévi-Strauss, Lacan also clarifies that discourse is structured around something opaque and irresolvable. Early on in the seminar, this relates particularly to the S_1 as a unary trait which intervenes into the 'battery of signifiers', written S_2, in order to construct a coherent field of knowledge, but one which is henceforth marked by this initial meaningless inscription (ibid.: 13). As the seminar unfolds, it becomes clearer that this opacity at the kernel of all discourse is ultimately the real of *jouissance* (in relation to which the unary trait is already a treatment, a regulation via the repetition of the signifier). Discourse of any kind is therefore an attempt to order the disordered real.

Here we could contrast Lacan's assertion that 'the impossible is the real' (ibid.: 165) with the famous Situationist slogan circulating around the same time: 'Be realistic, demand the impossible!' Though the latter invokes a critique of dominant conceptions of both 'reality' and what is possible within it, Lacan's intervention implies that every demand is already indirectly addressed to an impossibility, but one that, as real, can never be granted by the Master still implied within the Situationist slogan (for to whom but a Master could such a rebellious demand be addressed?). This is where the stakes of the distinction between speech as talk, and discourse as *structure*, become apparent. Although Lacan acknowledged that, historically, the Hysteric's critique of the Master has led to displacements of discourse (ibid.: 94), he also recognized, in the wake of May '68, that no amount of breathless pseudo-Maoist chatter at the level of speech could *in itself* produce change at the level of the real of discourse. It was the old astronomical notion of 'revolution', as a heavenly rotation returning to its starting point, that Lacan had in mind when he said to one of the radicalized *soixante-huitards*: 'What you aspire to as revolutionaries is a new master. You will get one' (ibid.: 207).

It would be a major mistake, however, to conclude that Lacan was a conservative reactionary. As a psychoanalyst, he was necessarily committed to the notion of change. But also as a psychoanalyst, he was committed to the *specificity* of that change within a mode of discourse like no other: psychoanalysis itself as a clinical practice. Defining psychoanalysis as a discourse and thus a social bond between analyst and analysand, and *not* as a mode of technical talk reserved for expert initiates, indicates that just because the phrase 'the unconscious' is being used, it by no means follows that the unconscious is at work. Indeed, the reverse would be a safer bet. Such a distinction was already at play in Lacan's critique of the 'other psychoanalysis' of ego psychology and Kleinian object relations. But *Seminar XVII* goes further by formalizing the structure of analytic discourse itself, as a response, I would argue, to the risk that psychoanalysis would be pulled into the vortex of the various 'philosophies of desire' then fuelling aspects of May '68. Is this not a genuine danger the moment psychoanalytic knowledge is abstracted from clinical practice where its discourse is operative? Psychoanalytic talk is cheap, but a discourse that can sustain transferential effects is rare and precious.

One particularly widespread understanding of the relationship between psycho-analysis and politics is what I would call *the politicization of libido*. By this I mean that seductive fantasy of the violent return of repressed sexual instinct against the forces of social control broadly shared by thinkers coming out of the Frankfurt School's Freudo-Marxist tradition, such as Wilhelm Reich, Herbert Marcuse, and, later, Deleuze and Guattari (to whose *Anti-Oedipus*, of course, Foucault wrote such an affirmative preface). Significantly, many in this Freudo-Marxist tradition, Theodor Adorno most notably, viewed clinical psychoanalysis negatively as a disciplinary mechanism for imposing bourgeois norms, despite seeing great revolutionary value in psychoanalytic *theory* and its account of libido. Lacan would agree that libido – or, in his terms, *jouissance* – is political, but not in this vitalist sense. Despite appearances then, the assertion in *Seminar XVII* that 'the only discourse there is, and not just analytic discourse, is the discourse of *jouissance*' (2007: 78), represents a crucial shift *away* from this naïve politicization of libido which coincides (but hardly coincidentally) with a downplaying of the clinic.

Ten years earlier in *Seminar VII*, Lacan had argued that the symbolic and *jouissance* are fundamentally opposed, though he presented transgression, via the figure of the Marquis de Sade, as a roundabout way of attaining it from the dialectic between law and desire (Lacan 1997). But here in *Seminar XVII*, he shows that the symbolic and *jouissance* have merged under capitalism. He does so by developing a theory of 'surplus *jouissance*' which draws on, but also adds to, Marx's notion of surplus-value. His key insight is that far from inaugurating a loss of enjoyment through alienation from one's 'species being' – as the early Marx of the *1844 Manuscripts* argued – with labour's transformation into a commodity, work in fact becomes enjoyment itself, rendering loss and surplus two sides of the very same coin. As Lacan puts it, 'the important point is that on a certain day surplus *jouissance* became calculable, could be counted, totalized' (Lacan 2007: 177). The Master suddenly takes an interest in counting, in knowledge itself as a means of accumu-lation. The feudal lord, blissfully happy in his ignorance of practical life so long as his serfs took care of all that, is replaced by the bookkeeper, the bureaucrat, the statistician, and today perhaps the performance reviewer. This culminates in what Lacan calls, not without calculated irony, the 'university discourse', in which knowledge comes to occupy the place of mastery. By *Seminar XVII* then, knowl-edge becomes not the mortifying enemy of *jouissance*, but the 'sister of *jouissance*' (ibid.: 67), i.e. the vehicle of its production and transmission, its blood relation.

This new simultaneity of knowledge and *jouissance*, and the related under-standing of all discourses as apparatuses of *jouissance*, means that we are no longer dealing with a simplistic model of libidinal repression as the psychosocial core of civilization. Repression persists, but it is not of affect as some kind of substance or *élan vital*: it is of and through signifiers (ibid.: 144). Lacan takes us beyond the tra-dition in political philosophy of 'social contract theory'. For with figures like Hobbes, Rousseau, and indeed a certain Marx, do we not see a consistent recourse to problematic figures of what might be called 'enjoying nature', whether sublated in a sovereign Leviathan (Hobbes), corrupted by the absence of a general will

(Rousseau), or quashed by the division of labour (Marx)? And in each case, can it not be said that these images of enjoying nature play a part in presenting the structural fact of the impossibility of the real *as if it were merely a contingent loss*, getting a whole massive effort of recuperation underway? Nor does Lacan spare Freud from this kind of critique: a third of *Seminar XVII* is taken up with a discussion of Freud's Oedipal 'dream' (2007: 117) about the 'father of the primal horde' in *Moses and Monotheism*, which similarly situates loss in a primordial past, and projects backwards the fantasy of an uncastrated man who can enjoy all women.

A quite different topology of the 'other side' becomes discernible with this reading of discourse as an apparatus *of*, rather than against, *jouissance*. Analytic discourse is very precisely the 'other side' of the Master's discourse in that the former results from a 90° counter-clockwise rotation of the latter's matheme. Certainly, Lacan believes there is something subversive in this turn. But his title also parodies metaphysical notions of the 'other side' characteristic of what I have called the 'politicization of libido'. The topology he has in mind is much closer to a moebius strip in which psychoanalysis is the 'other side' of the Master's discourse only as a twist in the very same discourse. *Seminar XVII* suspends all simplistic notions of a pure before or beyond or outside of discourse, and yet also of total discursive determination on the 'constructionist' model. In the fourth session, Lacan gives us another way of thinking of the psychoanalysis–politics relation:

> But the fact that the analytic discourse completes the 90° displacement by which the three others are structured does not mean that it resolves them and enables one to pass to the other side. It doesn't resolve anything. The inside does not explain the outside.
>
> *(Lacan 2007: 54)*

Here, Russell Grigg provides a useful translator's note that reminds us that *l'envers* can also mean 'the lining' 'as in the lining of a jacket' (ibid.: 54). Is this not an excellent figure for the kind of topological twist Lacan is describing? A lining offers a surface that follows the innermost contours of a jacket tailor-made to embody the Master (in the midst of May '68 we can perhaps think of the uniform of *les Flics*, the academic's no-doubt corduroy jacket, or today the business suit). Nevertheless, such a lining also introduces folds, slippages, little wrinkles of excess that help the jacket sit on the body it borrows as a framework, but can lead to uncomfortable furrows. These furrows also relate to knowledge, for precisely as a *lining* of the Master's discourse, analytic discourse is too internal to provide a transcendental (masterful) knowledge of the whole. Far from being a mode of ignorance however, this awareness of the lack in the Other is the positive form of psychoanalytic knowledge. For a long time, Lacan had been saying 'there is no such thing as a meta-language' or, differently put, that 'there is no Other of the Other'. This is at once an ethical and a logical proposition. It is logical to the extent that, as Bertrand Russell pointed out to Frege, there cannot be a set of all sets that do not belong to themselves, a structural fact that Gödel articulated for the field of mathematics. For psychoanalysis, however, that there is no Other of the Other is also an ethical proposition insofar as it bars a global knowledge of the unconscious that would somehow be outside of, or uncontaminated by, the unconscious itself, a pure knowledge free from the effects of the signifier or of *jouissance*. An analyst, for example, who both listens and interprets from such an imaginary position of ideal or transcendent knowledge is entirely deaf to the unconscious, and his interventions will inevitably close it down. In a culture that sustains dreams of masterful metalanguages, such as the Human Genome Project as the overarching 'Book of Life', this insistence on a lack, limit, or lacunae in knowledge, goes very much against the positivist grain. Lacan's invocation of the lining here, however, suggests that unconscious knowledge will always exist in the intimate folds of the Master's discourse which needs its lining to clothe the body-politic.

But to repeat, this knowledge emerges from analytic discourse itself. It is not disseminated by institutional power, which is why Lacan gave such careful thought to the structure of the psychoanalytic school (see Section V of Lacan 2001). As a critical and cultural theory, psychoanalysis certainly has an important place in the academy. But as a practice, it is inseparable from a discourse in which masterful knowledge is only an initial supposition that must ultimately be discarded: this is the famous 'subject supposed to know' which, at least in the case of the symbolic transference of neurotics, instantiates in analysis an Other deemed to have the answer to one's existential questions. But crucially, such a subject supposed to know is precisely a supposition internal to the transferential address, and not an ontological fact: like Socrates, the analyst is only wise to the extent that he knows he knows nothing. The subject supposed to know is thus what Lacan calls a *semblant*, an appearance that, although essential early on, is destined to fall away. In this sense, though the matheme of the analyst's discourse *in Seminar XVII* places the cause of desire in the position of agency, it would be a category error to promote analytic discourse to a 'science of desire' because the kind of knowledge it produces is not of the scientific kind. The link between psychoanalysis and politics rests, rather, on a claim to being the only discourse capable of showing the desire – or better, the *jouissance* – at work in the others, particularly university discourse and its reification of, precisely, science.

The biopolitics of the DSM

One would be hard-pushed to find a better example of university discourse than the *Diagnostic and Statistical Manual of Mental Health Disorders* (DSM). Yet, as a nodal point linking an ensemble of deterritorialized institutions, it is also a quintessential example of Foucaultian discourse operating at the nexus of power and knowledge (see Rose 1998, 2006). Globalization of any kind obviously profits from standardization, whether English as the 'language of business' or of GDP as the 'universal' measure of good governance: the globalization of mental health is no different, and the DSM is its primary instrument.

Clinical psychiatrists, psychologists, counsellors, and even social workers around the world now use the DSM as a standard diagnostic assessment tool, shaping hospital admissions, care 'pathways', and regimes of pill-based treatments. Academics within and without the 'psy' fields use the DSM's categories to organize their empirical research and interpret their findings. The multibillion dollar global pharmaceutical industry tailors its research and development to the DSM's latest classifications. That industry also has a very substantial role in the formation of those classifications in the first place: members of the DSM committees have been forced to declare very significant ties to 'Big Pharma', from holding shares, to serving as paid researchers, to endorsing the most recent off-the-shelf anti-depressant or anti-psychotic drugs. These same companies undertake aggressive marketing campaigns in order to shift cultural frameworks around mental distress: witness GlaxoSmithKlein's intervention in the 1990s into Japanese perceptions of depression (Watters 2011). In the wake of this cultural manipulation, health insurance companies – more and more prominent within the neoliberalization of various health care systems – administer their claims through DSM categories. There is even worrying evidence of a strong correlation between the size of a health insurance claim and the likelihood of the payout diagnosis being given (Moloney 2013). Legal systems in various countries now base convictions and sentencing on 'expert' advice from criminal psychiatrists and psychologists whose authority rests upon their invocation of the DSM. Therapists of various persuasions know to utilize DSM vocabulary when called upon to write court reports, even when it does not inform their clinical work. And by locating itself at the centre of this web of productive global power, the DSM is a serious money-spinner: the *American Psychiatric Association* makes over $5 million a year from the sale of this 'textbook', totalling an estimated $100 million over the DSM's 60-year existence (Angell 2011).

A detailed genealogy of the emergence of the DSM is out of the question here, yet a quick sketch will show its 'Foucaultian' dimensions. It is inseparable from the rise of statistics as an instrument of governmentality, having its origins in census data from the 1880s when an attempt was made to measure levels of 'idiocy' in the American population (notably, many towns in the south automatically placed all their African-American residents under this heading). Just as stereotypically Foucaultian is the fact that the first DSM was explicitly based on a 1943 War Department technical bulletin entitled 'Medical 203', shifting the locus of the production of psychiatric knowledge from asylums and hospital settings to the US Army and its concern with the psychological robustness of soldiers. The DSM has since specialized in the exponential proliferation of new mental disorders. The first 1952 edition listed 106 disorders; the second in 1968 listed 182; and the massive revisions involved in the third edition of 1980 led to no less than 265 disorders. This third edition explicitly abandoned Freudian psychopathology and the related categories of classical psychiatry, basing the etiology of mental disorders instead on the catch-all notion of 'chemical imbalance' (to which, of course, pills could best respond). The 1987 revision of DSM-III once again increased the number of disorders, this time to 292. The fourth edition published in 1994 listed almost triple the number identified in the first edition, at a whopping 297. The general upward trend has continued with the most recent, and controversial, DSM-V, as has a very problematic tendency to dramatically reconfigure previous categories. Autism has ceased to be a 'spectrum' and 'Asperger's' has disappeared completely, though, confusingly, those who have received that diagnosis are permitted to keep it (American Psychiatric Association 2013). Very much in keeping with Foucault's later theorization of biopolitics, the DSM can be seen as pivotal in placing a certain understanding of health – at once affective and connected to economic productivity – at the centre of neoliberal modes of social control (Foucault 2010).

So what might a Lacanian notion of discourse add to these Foucaultian insights into the DSM? Immediately, it encourages us to look beyond the technical vocabulary the DSM utilizes and even the institutional contexts that implement it, to focus on the structure of the social link it implies, and relatedly, at the relationship to knowledge and *jouissance* it maintains.

As a diagnostic tool, the DSM inscribes a social link that fits perfectly into Lacan's formalization of university discourse. We can take each of the four quadrants of its matheme in turn. First, in the place of agency, the DSM relies on a classificatory form of 'neutral' knowledge that kicks its machinery into motion prior to any medical professional's speech: if a diagnosis has performative efficacy it is because of the preceding primacy of this 'evidence-based' knowledge. Yet this supposedly 'neutral', self-reinforcing 'evidence base' covertly relies on the incorporation of the DSM's own epistemological limits into its very diagnostic logic, as indicated by notions such as 'co-morbidity' and various 'not otherwise specified' disorders (see Hacking 2013 for a critique of this problem). Second, in the place of truth, this neutral yet dominant knowledge, or S_2, conceals its roots in a new S_1, a now distributed form of statistical mastery linked to the uncoupling of expertise from individual experts (is this disembodying of clinical knowledge not one effect of 'evidence-based medicine', such that we now have Cognitive Behavioural Therapy that can be delivered entirely online?). Third, as a discourse, the DSM produces individuals marked by the label of a disorder which can often stay with them for a very long time, a lifetime in some cases. No longer the castrated neurotic of Freud's era however, this is a subject ordered, as it were, by their disorder: DSM labels often support group identities based on medicated subject positions, as with the role of Ritalin in Attention Deficit and Hyperactivity Disorder. Fourth then, the DSM is paradigmatic of what Lacan calls 'university discourse' insofar as it puts *objet a* to work not as desire (metonymically passing along a signifying chain and given imaginary coherence by a fantasy framework), but rather, as an object of consumption produced by the market. Such objects plug directly into bodily *jouissance* without passing by way of the Other of language, often in the form of mood-stabilizing 'happy pills'.

This elevation of a real rather than a symbolic treatment of *jouissance* even suggests that the DSM is barely definable as a *social* link at all: the psychiatrist merely enacts the pre-given logic of the standardizing system with little or no clinical judgement of their own entering into the process. Speech in general is suppressed to the extent that DSM diagnoses are known to take a matter of minutes (Verhaeghe 2004). The 'subject' of this diagnosis, moreover, is effectively silenced as the object of a knowledge they do not possess: they become what Foucault presciently theorized as the neoliberal subject that simply responds, flexibly and without friction, to biopolitical forms of social control (Foucault 2010). Is this not also exemplary of the imbrication of capitalism and science which Lacan coins, in *Seminar XVII*, the 'alethosphere' (Lacan 2007: 182)? With this term, Lacan was already describing an atmosphere or environment characterized by gadgets and instruments of consumption, developed by the market in order to stuff the mouths of subjects before they can articulate a desire that would be distinct from (supply and) demand. And does this machinic discourse of the DSM that simply 'works' – grinding subjects, psychiatrists as well as patients, up into its cogs – not imply that each individual is left alone with their own monetized *jouissance*-object, with no overarching Other through which to encounter even imaginary others, let alone the desire in their own speech? If Lacan always defined discourse as a social link, it may not be correct to refer to the *discourse* of the DSM, which seems to sever such links.

The discourse of the capitalist

During a conference in Milan in May 1972 entitled *Du Discours Psychanalytique*, Lacan drew on the board the four discourses he had elaborated two years previously, but then added a fifth: the discourse of the capitalist (see Figure 9.1).

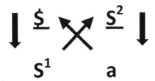

FIGURE 9.1 The Discourse of the Capitalist

Lacan does not say much about this new matheme, and never makes use of it again to my knowledge. However, he does say two significant things – that it is 'insanely clever' (*follement astucieux*) but that 'it is bound to puncture' (*voué à la crevaison*) (Lacan 1972). Its diabolical cleverness is quickly apparent, for unlike the other discourses which are marked by a disjunctive impossibility, the orientation of the vectors here describes a figure eight, symbol of infinity, and thus an infernal circuit. There is also an inexplicable rupture with the combinatory logic of the other four discourses: this configuration cannot be derived even from the Master's discourse which it most closely resembles. This is because Lacan has swapped the $ and the S_1 from the lower and upper registers respectively in the Master's discourse, so that the divided subject here takes the place of truth and is animated by a new master signifier. What Lacan seems to have in mind is the idea that under capitalism the agent ($) addresses his lack to the S_1 of the market, which then produces some knowledge (S_2) that can respond to this lack, which in turn informs the production of an object (a) that satisfies the subject's demand. In fact, there is no gap or excess in this circuit, because unlike the other discourses it is not organized around an impossibility: it seems to model a 'consumer satisfaction' without remainder, insofar as, rather like the drug Soma in Aldous Huxley's *Brave New World*, everything is provided for, all needs are met, all wishes fulfilled.

Why then is Lacan so blithely confident that 'it is bound to puncture'? It can have nothing to do with a labour of the negative, for it is as if the capitalist Master has found a way to respond to the old Situationist slogan by making the impossible possible: castration is excluded from this circuit. Its propensity to deflate seems instead to have something to do with spinning too fast – an update it would seem of the vicious circle Freud had already recognized in *Civilization and its Discontents*. Lacan says of the discourse of the capitalist that 'it works like clockwork, but precisely it works too fast, it consumes itself, it is consumed so well it consumes itself/ burns' (*ça se consomme si bien que ça se consume*) (Lacan 1972). In other words, the consumer of goods comes to be consumed by them. But it is precisely here, at this internal limit of capitalism borne of its reliance on desiring human bodies, that we find a suffering subject inextricably linked to clinical phenomena. Lacan's late matheme of the discourse of the capitalist bespeaks a deflation or exhaustion that registers itself not in the overheated economic cycles of the markets per se, adept as they are at turning crises into opportunities, but in the new symptoms that we see today of anxiety, addiction, depression, and eating disorders.

For this reason, if Lacanian psychoanalysis is to contribute to political theory and political practice, it will have to be not simply at the level of a theoretical speech amenable to University discourse, but as an Analytic discourse which, against the dominant therapeutic culture constructed by the DSM, produces a singular social link between analyst and analysand by means of which to de-suture the subject from its neoliberal individuation.

Bibliography

Althusser, Louis (1971) 'Ideology and Ideological State Apparatuses', *Lenin and Philosophy, and Other Essays*. trans. Ben Brewster. New York: Monthly Review Press, pp. 127–186.

American Psychiatric Association (2013) 'Autism Spectrum Disorder', available online at: www.dsm5.org/Documents/Autism%20Spectrum%20Disorder%20Fact%20Sheet.pdf (accessed 24 March 2014).

Angell, Marcia (2011) 'The Illusions of Psychiatry', *New York Review of Books*. 14 July, available online at: www.nybooks.com/articles/archives/2011/jul/14/illusions-of-psychia try/ (accessed 17 March 2014).

Butler, Judith, Laclau, Ernesto and Žižek, Slavoj (2000) *Contingency, Hegemony, Universality: Contemporary Dialogues on the Left*. London: Verso.

Feenberg, Andrew and Freedman, Jim (2001) *When Poetry Ruled the Streets: The French Events of May 1968*. New York: SUNY Press.

Foucault, Michel (1980) *Power/Knowledge: Selected Interviews & Other Writings, 1972–1977*. New York: Pantheon.

Foucault, Michel (2003) *The Archaeology of Knowledge*. trans. A. M. Sheridan Smith. London: Routledge.

Foucault, Michel (2010) *The Birth of Biopolitics: Lectures at the Collège de France, 1978–1979*. trans. Graham Burchell. Basingstoke: Palgrave Macmillan.

Hacking, Ian (2013) 'Lost in the Forest', *The London Review of Books*, 35(15, August): 7–8.

Hall, Stuart (1973) 'Encoding and Decoding in the Television Discourse', Centre for Cultural Studies, University of Birmingham, Stencilled paper No. 7: 505–517.

Lacan, Jacques (1972) 'Du discours psychanalytique', available online at: http://espace.freud. pagespro-orange.fr/topos/psycha/psysem/italie.htm (accessed 20 March 2014).

Lacan, Jacques (1997) *Seminar VII: The Ethics of Psychoanalysis*, trans. Denis Porter. London: W. W. Norton and Company.

Lacan, Jacques (1998a) *Seminar XI: The Four Fundamental Concepts of Psychoanalysis*, trans. Alan Sheridan. London: W. W. Norton and Company.

Lacan, Jacques (1998b) *Le Séminaire, livre V: Les formations de l'inconscient*. Paris: Éditions du Seuil.

Lacan, Jacques (1999) *Seminar XX: On Female Sexuality, the Limits of Love and Knowledge*, trans. Bruce Fink. London: W. W. Norton and Company.

Lacan, Jacques (2001) *Autres écrits*. Paris: Éditions du Seuil.

Lacan, Jacques (2006a). 'The Mirror Stage as Formative of the I Function', *Écrits: The First Complete Edition in English*, trans. Bruce Fink. London: W. W. Norton and Company, 75–81.

Lacan, Jacques (2006b). 'The Signification of the Phallus', *Écrits: The First Complete Edition in English*, trans. Bruce Fink. London: W. W. Norton and Company, 575–584.

Lacan, Jacques (2006c). 'The Instance of the Letter, or Reason in the Unconscious since Freud', *Écrits: The First Complete Edition in English*, trans. Bruce Fink. London: W. W. Norton and Company, 412–443.

Lacan, Jacques (2007) *Seminar XVII: The Other Side of Psychoanalysis*, trans. Russell Grigg. London: W. W. Norton and Company.

Laclau, Ernesto and Mouffe, Chantale (1985) *Hegemony & Socialist Strategy: Towards a Radical Democratic Politic*. London: Verso.

Lévi-Strauss, Claude (1969) *The Elementary Structures of Kinship*, trans. James Harle Bell, John Richard von Sturmer and Rodney Needham. London: Eyre & Spottiswoode.

Moloney, Paul (2013) *The Therapy Industry: The Irresistible Rise of the Talking Cure and Why it Doesn't Work*. London: Pluto Press.

Mulvey, Laura (1975) 'Visual Pleasure and Narrative Cinema', *Screen*, 16(3): 6–18.

Rancière, Jacques (2011) *Althusser's Lesson*, trans. Emiliano Battista. London: Continuum.

Rose, Nikolas (1998) *Inventing Ourselves: Psychology, Power and Personhood*. Cambridge: Cambridge University Press.

Rose, Nikolas (2006) *The Politics of Life Itself: Biomedicine, Power and Subjectivity in the Twenty-First Century*. Princeton, NJ: Princeton University Press.

Ross, Kristin (2002) *May '68 and its Afterlives*. London: University of Chicago Press.

Stavrakakis, Yannis (1999) *Lacan and the Political*. London: Routledge.

Verhaeghe, Paul (2004) *On Being Normal and Other Disorders: A Manual for Clinical Psychodiagnostics*. London: Karnac Press.

Watters, Ethan (2011) *Crazy Like Us: The Globalization of the Western Mind*. London: Robinson.

Wodak, Ruth and Meyer, Michael (eds.) (2009) *Methods of Critical Discourse Analysis*. London: Sage.

10

PSYCHOANALYSIS, CAPITALISM, AND CRITIQUE OF POLITICAL ECONOMY

Toward a Marxist Lacan

Samo Tomšič

HUMBOLDT UNIVERSITY, BERLIN, GERMANY

Psychoanalysis as critique of libidinal economy

Since its very beginnings, psychoanalysis assumed a critical stand toward the established social order. For this reason, it was repeatedly targeted, discredited, or silenced by various governing ideologies, even the leftist ones. But while the Freudian theories and concepts were declared outdated or pseudo-scientific (or both) they nevertheless continued to provoke malaise and resistance. It is curious to observe that Freud was not always insisting an absolute originality of his theses, claiming that every parent, nurse, or doctor could observe, say, the expressions of infantile sexuality or the presence of sexual motives in the development of mental illnesses. Why, then, did his theories provoke such outrage within and without scientific circles, despite all the private and medical observations? And how could psychoanalysis preserve its scandalous dimension even in times of a more liberal cultural attitude toward sexuality?

Lacan's definition of the unconscious as a specific form of knowledge – 'knowledge that does not know itself' (Lacan 1998: 96, trans. changed) – offers an explanation. On the one hand it suggests that knowledge is not reflexive throughout, which means that a decentralized form of knowledge insists and operates beyond conscious cognition; on the other hand, Lacan's formulation addresses the main critical point of Freudian theories, according to which cognition always involves a specific filter, resistance, refusal to know, the negative of what Foucault (1976) famously called the 'will to know'. This resistance hence testifies that there is no thought without censorship and that thought procedures always-already contain repression. The above-mentioned parents, nurses, and doctors might indeed have encountered manifestations of infantile sexuality but they nonetheless refused to take its appearance, as an indication of what the actual nature of human sexuality might be like, seriously. Instead they continued to stick to the established scenario of sexual development from puberty onward, as well as to the anatomical anchoring of 'normal' sexual desire – two features that psychoanalysis entirely abolished. The constitution of sexuality remained for them an 'unknown known', as well as for scientists, who saw in Freud's sexual etiology of neuroses a 'scientific fairy-tale' (Freud 2000: 52). It therefore makes perfect sense that, once psychoanalysis shed light not only on sexuality but also on the mechanisms of repression, which operate independently of human consciousness and determine thinking from within, its accounts automatically met cultural and scientific resistance. By uncovering the loose and ambiguous anchoring of sexuality in biology and anatomy, the latency period that separates the genital phase from the oral and the anal, Freud did much more than preach 'pansexualism' – a reproach that is still often associated with his theories. He has proven that sexuality is constitutively denaturalized and decentralized, meaning that he revealed in its core a radical absence of a pregiven or fixated sexual norm. The immediate conclusion was that there is nothing natural about sexuality, that sexuality is antinature par excellence, which, however, does not make it less real, i.e. its loose ties to anatomy do not make of sexuality a cultural construction or performative effect. For psychoanalysis, sexuality is reducible neither to nature nor to culture, an ontological and political scandal, which makes of sexuality the privileged target of theoretical sublimation and cultural resistance.

Lacan condensed these lessons in his notorious one-liner 'There is no sexual relation', which can be translated in the following way: there is no central norm or transcendental model, no sexual a priori, around which sexuality would be constituted and which would stabilize its field. Consequently, heterosexuality is no exception or natural model, from which other sexual orientations and identities would deviate – sexuality, as such, is a deviation from an inexistent norm. Differently put, it is the inexistence of sexual relation that makes sexuality exist, only that its mode of existence is inevitably stained with negativity (for this reason Lacan wrote 'ex-sistence'; the Freudian name for the negativity that constitutes sexuality is castration). This was the main critical take of Freud and Lacan on what one could call 'libidinal economy'.[1]

With regard to social reactions to the psychoanalytic revelation of the central role of sexuality in the etiology of neuroses, it is not surprising that resistance became one of the fundamental Freudian concepts, which also assumes a highly particular position. It covers both defence mechanisms of individual psychic apparatus and symbolic mechanisms that constitute and reproduce social reality. In a famous passage, Freud spoke of three scientific insults of human narcissism, thereby indicating that the notion of resistance should be extended to the study of society and not restricted solely to individual clinical experience. When treating a neurotic, the analyst has an entire culture lying on the couch. The idea of human narcissism suggests that resistance is not simply psychological and cannot be univocally located in the mental life of individuals. It comes from the 'inner outside' of the mental apparatus and is inscribed in the symbolic structures that support the subjective and the social reality. According to Freud, this problematic resistance not only strives to sabotage the psychoanalytic treatment but also hinders consequent deployment of scientific, political, and other revolutions, which all confront thinking and society to its immanent deadlocks and contradictions. Consequently every significant transformation of reality necessitates the understanding of formal mechanisms, which, in the given order, determine everyone as subjects. The question here is not to generalize psychoanalytic contents to social contexts and psychologize politics. Lacan's accent on the *logical* connection of the unconscious with social structures, and of psychoanalysis with politics, suggests that the object of psychoanalysis stands beyond the dichotomy of individual and society, as well as beyond simple analogies between libidinal economy and social reality. Following this line, psychoanalysis inverts the relation between resistance and cultural institutions (church, family, hospital, or political party): it is resistance that grounds these cultural institutions, and not the other way around, as Lacan occasionally pointed out. Resistance, too, is decentralized, impersonal, and non-psychological. Its localization on the border between the subjective inside and the social outside – again, in the (symbolic) structure that supports both orders of reality – provides a more accurate image of political struggles and proposes a new topology of political space. Confronting the institutions is undoubtedly necessary for challenging resistance to revolutionary changes, but one should keep in mind that these institutions are merely localizations of a systemic resistance (again what Freud called human narcissism, which is both personal and impersonal, preventing the subject from acting and society from change), the overcoming of which necessitates permanent political organization. Hence, Lacan's engagement in creating a school that would not be grounded on 'institutional transference' and on the figure of the master. Lacan's institutional experiment failed, but its lessons as well as Lacan's accompanying texts remain relevant for raising the question of political organization.[2]

Lacan's notion of discourse addresses the intermediate space, where the binary oppositions such as subjective–social, internal–external, private–public turn short. The discourse designates the structure, articulated in individual speech, as well as the network of formal relations, which support the constitution of social links. While Freud still addressed the political problematic with the more general and neutral sounding term 'culture', Lacan made a step further by openly engaging in a critique of capitalism. It is not surprising that his theory of discourses will eventually meet Marx's critique of political economy, in which Lacan recognized a silent partner of Freud's extension of modern scientific revolution in the field of human objects (language, sexuality, thought). I will return to this connection in the later sections of this paper.

When it comes to sexuality, we cannot ignore that times have changed since Freud first presented his etiology of neuroses. In contemporary Western democracies sexuality appears to be far from controversial.[3] However, the liberal attitude did not overcome the sexual deadlocks, it merely amounted to its commodification. Lacan made an important point here, which is related to his redefinition of the superego as 'imperative of enjoyment' (Lacan 1998: 3). Far from prohibiting, the superego should be envisaged as the instance that articulates an insatiable demand of enjoyment, bombarding the subject with impossible tasks. This obscene superego, whose cultural and political role has been repeatedly thematized by Slavoj Žižek, strikingly differs from its schoolbook image. Freud emphasized its prohibitive aspect, which is not unrelated to the historical context and the broader cultural atmosphere of his time. The puritanism of the Austro-Hungarian Empire, but also of Victorian England, seems to be the perfect environment for the prohibiting and condemning superego. After the 20th-century sexual revolution and with the rise of neoliberalism, the superego, *the* instance that represents cultural demands in the mental life of individuals, appears in a different light. As imperative of enjoyment, the superego comes significantly closer to the demands of continuous economic growth, creation of value, mobility of labour, adaptability of interests, etc. The imperative of enjoyment is the true inscription of liberalism and neoliberalism into the 'mental apparatus'.

If under these conditions – when sex is commodified and branded on every street corner, in cultural industry, media, art, and theory, and everyone is encouraged to realize the creative potentials of their desire – sexuality remains a deadlock; this means that liberalism merely proposed its own version of repression, which did not resolve or liberate anything, precisely *repression through commodification*. The claim that commodification is *the* capitalist form of repression, not only of sexuality but moreover of subjectivity, can be immediately associated to commodity fetishism, in which Marx uncovers a specific 'mystification' of the source of value and which also conceals the social contradictions, the inexistence of social relation, behind abstractions such as freedom (of the market), equality (in exchange), and private property, to which Marx adds the name 'Bentham', the generic name for hard-line utilitarianism and the rule of private interest.[4] Yet repression through commodification no less fails to achieve its goal, for sexuality is no more reducible to commodity form than it is to a presupposed natural model. It can only be commodified for the price of excluding its antagonistic character, or to use Žižek's well-known example, commodified sexuality (sexuality reduced to sex) is like coffee without caffeine: sexuality without the inexistence of sexual relation. The following excerpt from Lacan indicates how to understand this repression and why it makes sense to speak of contradiction (rather than compatibility) between capitalism and sexuality:

> What distinguishes the discourse of capitalism is this – *Verwerfung*, rejection from all fields of symbolic, with all the consequences that I have already mentioned, and rejection of what? Of castration. Every order, every discourse that relates to capitalism leaves aside what we will simply call matters of love.
>
> *(Lacan 2011: 96)*

Commodification thus strives to reject castration, this privileged psychoanalytic name for negativity in sexuality, and even for sexuality as negativity. The same rejection of castration can be associated to financialization, in which the predominance of financial capital creates the illusion that the capitalist abstractions are endowed with a vital force, which enables them to engender more value (something that Marx already submitted to critique), thereby creating the appearance that exploitation, social inequalities, and class struggle ceased to play every part in the production of value and in social reality. I will return more extensively to this aspect of rejection of negativity in the final section of this paper.

What counts for capitalism is only sex, which stands for pure enjoyment without negativity and for a production of more enjoyment through enjoyment itself, whereby the task of commodification is to 'free' sex from sexuality, to create the fantasy of their equivocity and interchangeability. Lacan's remark nevertheless seems to confirm the usual critiques (e.g. Deleuze and Guattari or Foucault), according to which Freud neuroticized sexuality by imposing Oedipal castration as its universal model. However, Lacan's teaching contains a significant reinterpretation of castration. For Freud castration had predominantly biological signification, designating the presence and the absence of penis, and, correspondingly, the so-called 'penis envy' in women and 'castration anxiety' in men, suggesting the opposition of 'having and not having', 0 and 1, as the underlying binary opposition of human relation to sexuality. Lacan argued against this reductionism. For him castration is a symbolic operation, which concerns the constitution of the subject in relation to the signifier. His definition of the signifier as what 'represents a subject to another signifier' (Lacan 2006: 713) contains a hint, how castration should be understood. Lacan departs from Saussure's definition of the sign as an arbitrary relation of the signifier to the signified and as difference to other signs. What forms the difference in the regime of signs is precisely the signifier. The duality of the signifier and the sign is then related to the duality of the subject and the individual. A sign represents something for someone: Lacan's common example is that of smoke, which can represent fire but potentially also signals the presence of another person, for instance a smoker. In any case, signs always correlate to a psychological subject, in the given case an observer, who perceives and interprets smoke. The signifier, on the other hand, taken in its absolute autonomy, as pure difference to another signifier, cannot but represent a non-psychological subject, not for a psychological subject but for another signifier. And since the signifier is not only relational difference to another signifier but also pure difference, non-identical to itself, it can only constitute a split and decentralized subject, which is metonymically represented in the chain of differences that form language on its most formal level. This metonymy of the subject's being, the fact that its being is not stable but involves movement and becoming (to use Deleuze's term, which is usually opposed to metonymy), this precisely is what psychoanalysis addresses with the concept of castration: not presence and absence of an organ, but instability and dynamic in the subject's becoming, a movement that involves decentralization caused by the dependence of the subject's being on the chain of signifiers (pure differences).

The movement in being is hence not without negativity (difference when it comes to the signifier, split when it comes to the subject, metonymy when it comes to the processes of becoming). Lacan emphasizes that, in relation to sexuality and enjoyment, the subject always confronts imbalance. Enjoyment is essentially non-homeostatic and can only be experienced either as incomplete or as excessive, too little – the *this-is-not-it* that relates to the metonymic and chain-like structure of desire – or too much – the unsatisfiable *encore* that concerns the repetitive and circular structure of the drive. The subject assumes an impossible position: either the attempt of satisfaction leads to dissatisfaction, lack of enjoyment because the object escapes the subject's grasp, or it amounts to an intrusion of enjoyment into the body, like in the case of Christian mystics that Lacan discusses in his later seminars (see Lacan 1998: 76). A similar process takes place in Joyce's writing, where language loses its grammatical consistency and abolishes the bar (Saussure's sign for the arbitrary relation) that separates it from the signified. The signifier becomes its own signified, thereby actualizing its autonomy in the production of enjoyment and pushing the productive dimension of language in the foreground. This discursive production becomes a major topic in Lacan's later teaching, and as already mentioned, the shift toward it is accompanied by a systematic reference to Marx, in whom Lacan believed to have found a theory of discursive production that structural linguistics failed to provide.[5]

Lacan's talk of the capitalist rejection of castration suggests that sexuality is one of the privileged targets of social resistance. Instead of acknowledging its non-normative character it imposes its naturalized or commodified version, where sexuality is precisely not considered a field of political subjectivation. Rejection of castration also suggests that the return of castration through psychoanalysis is equivalent to what Freud called return of the repressed, making of psychoanalysis a *social symptom*. In this we encounter the dimension of critique, which strives to show that libidinal economy is an inevitable component of political economy. Lacan continues his critique of capitalism by saying that, after centuries of mystification, 'castration finally made its irruptive entrance in the form of analytic discourse' (Lacan 2011: 96). Psychoanalysis, as such, *is* a return of castration, not simply because it introduces the concept through its theory of sexuality but because, being a discourse that is not grounded on a mystification of sexuality, enables it to determine the rootedness of 'subjective problems' in the same structures that support the given social reality: there is no private symptom, just as there is no private language. In another passage, Lacan will even claim that one of the main psychoanalytic aims is to engage in finding an exit from the capitalist discourse,[6] precisely because the symptoms analysis encounters are, in the given condition, nothing other than structural articulations of the subjective protest against the 'capitalist mode of enjoyment'.

The move, through which Freud reintroduces castration, inscribes psychoanalysis in the critical tradition. It is no coincidence that in this tradition Lacan privileges Marx. An essential part of Marx's science of value consists in showing how capitalism constitutes everyone as labour-power, which is the depsychologized and deindividualized subject of value (see Milner 2011: 90). Both production of value and production of enjoyment can be accurately explained only by addressing the way the autonomy of value (exchange-value as pure difference to another value) and the autonomy of signifier (also pure difference to another signifier) produces a strictly determined figure of subjectivity. This is the meaning of the reintroduction

152 Samo Tomšič

of castration. Marx accomplishes this move in his reinterpretation of the labour theory of value, recalling the seemingly banal fact that what is bought and sold on the market is not labour, which is a process, but labour-power, a particular commodity that, in the abstract act of exchange, appears to be equal to other commodities but actually forms an exception, since it is the only commodity that produces other commodities and actually creates more value than it entered the production process. Marx thereby encounters an inconsistency in the commodity universe and a constitutive subjective alienation, which will enable Lacan to conclude that the proletarian embodies the only universal subjective position in the universe of capitalism (Lacan 2011b: 18). For capitalism everyone is 'translatable' into labour-power, a quantifiable subjectivity.

Freud, too, explains the mechanisms that produce unconscious formations through the consumption of labour-power, thereby proposing a *labour theory of unconscious*. His theory is supposed to account for discursive production of *Lustgewinn*, which literally means profit in pleasure, pleasure as profit, a term that Lacan translated as surplus-enjoyment, in homology with surplus-value. In Freud this unconscious production still appears to be without a subject, and it was only Lacan's introduction of the notion that completed the picture, thereby unveiling the full political importance of Freud's theories. Theory of the subject is the privileged terrain, where psychoanalysis meets Marx's critique of political economy and leads toward emancipatory politics. The reintroduction of castration thus makes of psychoanalysis a *critique* of libidinal economy.

Fetishism and castration: Marx's lesson

As already said, for Marx labour-power is the commodity, in which the capitalist big Other – the Market as the apparently autonomous space of exchange, where commodities, values, and humans interact – encounters its inconsistence. This inconsistence concerns the fact that labour-power is in the position of internal exclusion: in the register of exchange-value (the system of pure differences) it is equated to other commodities. But because exchange necessarily abstracts from use-value, it conceals that the consumption of labour-power entails extraction of surplus-value, the latter being equivalent to unpaid surplus labour. In this gap between use-value and exchange-value Marx exposes the repressed truth of production, but also the constitutive split of labour-power. Through the notion of fetish Marx then shows how this gap is rejected from the field of political economy. The rejection of inconsistency makes the capitalist universe of commodities, but also capital as such, appear as a self-regulating entity, endowed with the mystic power to engender value. We immediately meet Adam Smith's invisible hand of the market, which continues to guide today's neoliberal ideology.

Revealing the structural gaps and contradictions that capitalist ideology censors in the global picture of social relations was surely not the ultimate goal of Marx's critique, just like psychoanalysis did not stop at the deadlocks of sexuality. Both critical projects strive to mobilize the subjectivity, from which radical politics should depart in order to produce fundamental, revolutionary, structural change. In neither case is this subjectivity reducible to a psychological instance (be it the conscious ego or proletarian class consciousness). Psychoanalysis and critique of political economy therefore do not aim at simple cognition of structural relations but rather outline a radical critique of all the attempts to reduce politics to cognition, thereby showing that the revolutionary politics requires a *critical* epistemology, and one could even claim that they propose some sort of 'epistemo-politics'.[7]

This engagement is nowhere more explicit than in critique of fetishism. When Marx translates surplus-value into unpaid surplus labour, his point is not simply that one should introduce a more 'adequate' representation of labour-power, for instance allowing workers to participate in created profit, reducing labour time, distributing wealth in a just way, etc. This reformism does not resolve the contradictions of capitalism, which are not solely empirical (between capitalists and workers) but above all structural (between capital and labour-power). It would be naïve to determine the moment where production of commodities (paid labour) ceases and production of surplus-value (unpaid labour) begins. This border is everywhere and nowhere in production but also in circulation, distribution, and consumption of commodities. Marx's labour theory of value thus cannot be interpreted in the sense that surplus-value is some lost part of labour-power. Again, surplus-value emerges from the structural gap between representation of labour-power in terms of exchange-value and its consumption in production processes. Marx's point is that the two discursive axes, representation and production, cannot be brought into relation, which would amount to a happy reunion of the split subject with the surplus-object.

Such reunion, however, is professed by fetishism, where the three central capitalist abstractions (commodity, money, and capital) appear as self-engendering subjects and as *the* source of value. Consequently, liberalism and neoliberalism insist that the Market is an autonomous and rational entity, grounded on stable and predictable laws. The subjects that enter the economic relations are viewed as embodiments of *homo oeconomicus*, the political-economic version of the subject of cognition, a subject that is supposed to possess knowledge of her private interests, while also having insight in the supposed self-regulating rationality of the market. Marx indicates this epistemological aspiration of economic liberalism when he criticizes the four cornerstones of the capitalist world view, the already mentioned freedom (of the market), equality (in the abstract act of exchange), (private) property, and Bentham as the general name for the political-economic nexus of empiricist epistemology and economic liberalism. Contrary to this homeostatic vision of social relations, Marx continuously demonstrates their fantasmatic kernel, claiming that in order to understand the blind spots and fictions of political economy one needs to recur to the notion of fetish, which served colonial ideologies to describe the 'primitive' forms of religion, where natural phenomena like thunder, storm, etc. are presumably worshipped directly as deities. Marx transformed this ideological use of fetish by applying it back to the societies, from which it was projected on the colonial Other.[8]

Fetishism reveals a gap between knowledge and belief, which, in the political-economic sphere, amounts to the already mentioned attitude that practically treats commodities as if they were intrinsically endowed with value, despite theoretically claiming to know better. We can recall that for Marx fetishism contains a dialectical movement, which comprises three stages: commodity form, general equivalent, and financial abstractions. The critical account of fetishism uncovers in this dialectic a circular structure, a *fetishist circle*, which connects the highest and the lowest level, the apparently immediate materiality of commodities and the immateriality of fictitious capital (financial capital, credit, interest...). In the latter case the surplus product no less needs to be thought not only as substance but also as subject, to put it with Hegel. For if we think it merely as substance, we repeat the error of classical political economists, ending in essentialism, where value appears as the positive quality of objects, supposedly possessing the power to engender more value. Only if we think of capitalist abstractions in their relation to the subject they *produce* (labour-power, indebted subject), can we understand the interdependency of excessive wealth and excessive misery, profit and debt, surplus and lack.

This relation indeed situates all inhabitants of the capitalist universe in the position of indebted subjects. In his discussion of primitive accumulation, Marx outlines a complex picture, in which the genesis of national debts and of modern credit system brings about a new form of debt, not toward a moral instance, King or God, but toward Capital as such – an *abstract debt*, the social implementation of which turns everyone into a priori indebted subjects: indebted in advance because born into a social condition, in which social production and national indebting are inseparable. Marx detects in this modern debt a negative form of wealth, 'the only part of the so-called national wealth that actually enters into the collective possession of a modern nation' (Marx 1976: 919). The created surplus joins capital, which appears to be its self-engendering subject, while the created negative joins the populations, turning them into labour-power, those who are forced to labour. Abstract debt thus becomes the motor of the modern transformation of society and subjectivity, constituting everyone as measurable and calculable commodities. As soon as the question of production of capitalist subjectivity enters the picture, pure loss appears as the censored truth of the presumable vitalism of capitalist abstractions. Recall that for Marx the production of an industrial reserve army was the necessary flipside of creation of profit: on the one hand excessive wealth, the 'immense collection of commodities' (Marx 1976: 125), and on the other hand excessive poverty, the 'immense collection' of unemployed, precarized, and indebted subjects.

Antiquity and Christianity embodied the greed for profit in the figure of the miser, whose uncontrollable lust for value destabilizes and even threatens to dissolve the social link, pushing free citizens into slavery and dependence. But there is one crucial difference between the old spirit of miser and the modern spirit of capitalism. The miser's lust for money is still his private obsession, whereas the capitalist embodies the social externalization of the drive for profit, and the drive for generalized social indebting, an imperative that is imposed on all and places everyone in the object position (a commodity that is said to be equal to all other commodities). The difference between the premodern miser and the modern capitalist is thus that the latter manages to externalize the unsatisfiable drive for enrichment, making it the central component of the capitalist social link. The imperative of indebting becomes a social process, while in premodern times it was still perceived as deviation, which needs to be morally condemned and legally controlled if not forbidden. Here one should avoid the typical social-democratic trap, according to which all problems with financial capitalism would be solved if we bring economy from the heights of financial speculation to the solid ground of the real sector. Just like there is no economy that would be grounded on barter, the immediate exchange of goods, which would historically precede mediated exchange,[9] there is, this time within capitalism, no 'real' economy, which would not always-already be colonized with capitalist abstractions. The dialectic of fetishism begins with commodities, these apparently innocent objects, which are supposed to satisfy human needs, but the crucial lesson of this dialectic is that these objects are already abstractions, as soon as they enter exchange, as they always-already do. The dichotomy between real economy – economy dealing with 'real' products – and financial economy – economy dealing with 'abstractions' – is fundamentally false, just as the opposition between objects that satisfy human needs and those that create value. Both aspects constitute one object and one production.

This is due to the fact that the dialectic of fetishism is a two-way road, simultaneously moving in two opposite directions. The apparently rudimental form of fetishism lies in commodity form, where the object of fetishization is every commodity on the market. Here value is perceived as the positive quality of things rather than a symbolic relation. The next stage concerns the general equivalent, where the fetish-object is money or any valuable metal, which serves as the material support of exchange. Being the object for which all other objects can be exchanged, money is *the* embodiment of value. Here, value no longer appears merely as an objective quality, like in the case of commodity fetishism, where the commodity's use-value still limits the fetishization because it presupposes a human need. In money, the sphere of exchange is efficiently isolated and its autonomy materialized. Marx's critique unveiled the ontological, epistemological, and political consequences of this autonomy, thereby anticipating, as Lacan will claim, the structuralist isolation of the signifier, where human language, its communicative dimension, its use-value, is no less reduced to an abstract system of differences, which arbitrarily relates to the signified, just as value arbitrarily relates to commodities and commodities to human needs. Finally, the most abstract stage of fetishization is the capital-fetish, where objectivity is stripped of all empirical materiality and becomes a bare number, an apparently infinite growth of value without any labouring subject involved; or as Marx will write, capital now *appears* as *the* subject of the valorization process. Here we can detect another expression of the difference between the miser and the capitalist. The old spirit of miser still refers to empirical materiality and builds a treasure of valuable objects, thereby appearing as a form of hoarding. The capitalist, on the other hand, merely counts.

156 Samo Tomšič

His treasure is not a collection of objects but a number. Here we are in our financial economies with their fantasies of infinite growth and living forces of capital.

It would be wrong to read this dialectic of fetishism historically, where the emergence of commodity form would bring about the first form of fetishization, the introduction of paper money the second, and the shift of capitalism toward financialization the third. The movement concerns the abstraction that traverses all stages and finds its ultimate expression in what Marx calls fictitious capital. This dialectic cannot begin without concrete embodiment in commodities, which support the movement toward absolute autonomy of financial abstractions, nor can it begin without financial abstractions, which determine the way everyone relates to commodities. It is, indeed, a closed circle, in which commodity, general equivalent, and capital mutually presuppose each other's existence, while also determining their specific value-generating appearance. Marx's critical move, on the other hand, consists in suspending the efficiency of fetishism (that he attributes to classical political economy) through the logical deduction of surplus-value. Unlike fetishism, logic no longer addresses capital as object (which would eventually appear as subject) but as structure, which always-already contains subjectivized negativity.

The essence of Marx's critical move resides in the rigorous determination of the subject of capitalist discourse (or capitalist mode of production). By detecting the return of the repressed subject, Marx invented the notion of the symptom,[10] the conceptual opposition of the fetish, because it represents the distorted social contradictions and antagonisms and simultaneously reveals a form of subjectivity that counteracts the philosophical and political-economic theories of cognition (consciousness, transcendental subjectivity, *homo oeconomicus*). Marx's critique of fetishism anticipates Saussure's isolation of the signifier, yet with an important difference: for Saussure the system of differences did not involve other than production of meaning, while for Marx the abstraction from use-value produces not only a strictly determined subjectivity, labour-power, but also a new form of discursive enjoyment, surplus-value. Both products stand outside meaning and assume the status of *real* discursive consequences.

These insights produce a break in Lacan's teaching, orienting him toward a *second* return to Freud, in which the reference to Marx entirely substitutes the authority of structural linguistics. The formalization of the capitalist discourse will consequently become one of the central efforts in this theoretical turn.

A brief overview of Lacan's formalization of capitalism

Lacan's use of formalization stands in direct continuity with Marx's dialectical method. It is employed, not in order to fixate the formal relations that support the constitution of social and subjective reality, but to demonstrate the structural deadlocks, instabilities, and possibilities of change, just as Marx used his materialist dialectics in order to unveil the antagonistic and contradictory nature of social relations behind the different layers of fetishization. In what follows, I will briefly outline the main dilemmas of Lacan's formalization of the structure of capitalism.[11]

Given Lacan's focus on discursive production after May '68 and the increasing role of Marx's *Capital* in this development, one can notice that the notion of discourse overlaps with what Marx calls the mode of production. Far from discussing the rigidity and transhistoricity of structures, Lacan insists that political events, such as May '68, demonstrate that 'structures descend to the street'.[12] Through Marx the theory of discourses elaborates a dynamic structuralism, which stands beyond the binary oppositions of 'structure and dialectics', 'structure and history', or 'structure and event'. The point of departure is a formal dispositive, which comprises four elements that can be isolated in the functioning of language: the difference of signifiers, resumed in the minimal couple S_1 and S_2, the subject that a signifier represents for another signifier, $, and the object produced in the discursive functioning, a.

The scheme is contextualized in strict homology with Marx's deduction of surplus-value, where the difference of signifiers stands for the autonomy of exchange-value, the subject of representation for labour-power, and the object of production for surplus-value. In this respect, capitalism merely transforms the elements of old relations of domination, replacing the feudal lord (S_1) with the capitalist and the serf (S_2) with the proletarian. This is not without resonance with certain of Marx's statements in *Capital*, but the complexity of transformations introduced by the capitalist modernity clearly counteracts such a simple scenario. One should also keep in mind that the capitalist and the proletarian are to be understood as social embodiments of capital and labour-power, and not simply as empiric and psychological individuals.[13]

Looking at the relations between the discursive places and their elements we can notice that the circulation is disrupted, meaning that representation of the subject and production of the object cannot be brought into relation and continuity – unless

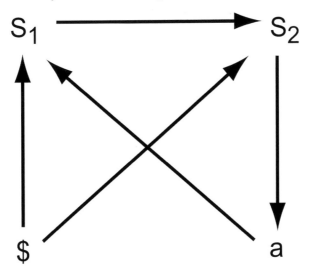

FIGURE 10.1 The Master's Discourse

one fetishizes capital (S_1) as the subject of the valorization process. This break highlights the structural disclosure, which enables Lacan to deduce other discursive formations, which all affirm the logic of the signifier as their common background. For this reason, Lacan does not simply identify capitalism with the master's discourse but instead speaks of capitalism as the 'replacement', 'perversion', or 'transformation' of the old relations of domination, thereby referring to the historical change introduced by modernity, also through the implementation of scientific knowledge, into the social and subjective reality.

Already a year after elaborating the homology between Marx's deduction of surplus-value and Freud's analysis of unconscious production of enjoyment, Lacan started associating capitalism with what he called the university discourse, thereby acknowledging the immediate consequences of May '68, when the university reform introduced an education model based on the system of credit points – in French *unites de valeur,* units of value.

This quantification and commodification of knowledge turned the university into a factory, whose goal is to produce subjects of value, which join the established regime of knowledge (the vector $ \$ \rightarrow S_2 $). In a contemporary university these subjects are most often economically indebted, which is more than evident today, when the student loans are a common practice of obtaining education. Of course, Lacan's point is more general and addresses the historical production of capitalist subjectivity, which is possible through the quantification of labour and the isolation of labour-power in living bodies with the help of disciplines like energetics and thermodynamics.[14] From this perspective, the historical intertwining of commodification of labour with natural sciences ended up producing a calculable and measurable subjectivity.

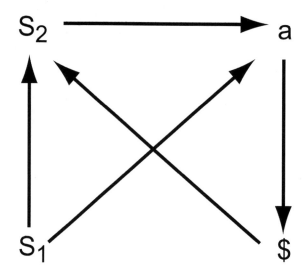

FIGURE 10.2 The University Discourse

Lacan later proposed a third formula of the capitalist discourse, which is usually considered an exception. This development is rather surprising, given that Lacan's theory is grounded on a strict order, which supports only four discursive formations: the master, the hysteric, the university, and the analyst. While the four discourses depart from a quarter turn, which passes from the fundamental scheme to other immediate structures and allows only four such turns, without altering the places and their mutual relations, the capitalist discourse implies a turn that does not displace the elements but instead alters the places and their mutual relations: it turns the place of the subject and that of the master-signifier. This *torsion* then establishes a relation between the subject of representation and the object of production. The subject of capitalism is now no longer located in labour-power but in capital itself. In this way Lacan formalizes the central thesis of political-economic fetishism: money labours (in both meanings of the word).

The immediate consequence of the torsion is rejection of the split that marks the *place* of the subject in the master's discourse, the split that echoes Lacan's definition of the signifier ('the signifier is what represents a subject to another signifier'). In capitalism the subject appears to be in immediate and univocal relation both to the signifier and to enjoyment. There is no gap between representation (the triangle S_1, S_2, $) and production (the triangle S_1, S_2, a). In a way Lacan's formula of the capitalist discourse anticipates the lessons of financialization, which would suggest something like a substitution of the contradiction between capital and labour with the productive split of capital. We could also say that the proposed torsion of the master's discourse translates Marx's abbreviation of the circulation (M – M'), in which money immediately engenders more money and value-representation coincides with value-production.

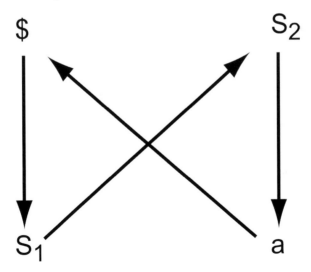

FIGURE 10.3 The 'Fifth Discourse'

160 Samo Tomšič

As said, the formula is often considered as the fifth discourse, in which the subject assumes the position of agent, as if the discursive shift would concern the elements and not the places. However, the relations between the elements show that we are dealing with a transformed master's discourse, from which negativity is rejected: the subjective split between two signifiers is replaced with the previously absent relation between the subject and the surplus-object: the subject now appears to stand in immediate and unproblematic relation to surplus product (enjoyment, surplus-value), finally achieving its self-realization and completion. Rather than experiencing a castrating lack, it exhibits automatic and vital growth. This fantasy of completeness undoubtedly echoes Marx's point regarding fetishism, and for this reason cannot represent an actual discursive formation but formalizes the appearance of capital as a self-engendering entity, the appearance that traverses all stages of fetishism and that echoes the rejection of castration, which nevertheless persists behind this fantasmatic veil. Moreover, castration, i.e. the rejected negativity, returns in the form of the crisis, which, as the European debt crisis has shown, necessarily involves production of surplus populations, the masses of unemployed and precarious citizens, the social embodiments of labour-power. Lacan's formula of the fifth discourse should therefore be considered from the viewpoint of fictitious capital and in strict reference to Marx:

> In truth however, value is here the subject of a process in which, while constantly assuming the form in turn of money and commodities, it changes its own magnitude, throws off surplus-value from itself considered as original value, and thus valorizes itself independently. For the movement in the course of which it adds surplus-value is its own movement, its valorization is therefore self-valorization. By virtue of being value, it has acquired the occult ability to add value to itself.
>
> *(Marx 1976: 255)*

Marx then describes fictitious capital as *übergreifendes Subjekt,* dominating and self-exceeding subject, which is capable of expanding, multiplying, and valorizing itself.[15] This apparently vital subject, subject-capital as a living force, clearly has nothing in common with the negative and alienated subject that Marx finds socially embodied in the proletarian. While the labour theory of value situates labour-power as the rejected negativity of capital, fetishism claims capital to be the true labouring power. The subject both represents itself ($\$ \rightarrow S_1$) and grows from itself ($a \rightarrow \$$). Both meanings of *übergreifen* address the continuity of representation and production, self-representation and self-valorization. But there is a more appropriate critical term for these operations: self-fetishization, the ultimate obscenity of capitalism.

This spectrality, however, insists also in the master's discourse. Not only is capital (S_1) pure difference, like the Saussurean signifier, but also the appearance of self-valorization immediately follows from the structural disclosure. In the master's discourse this appearance is resumed by the vector ($a \rightarrow S_1$), which designates the joining of surplus-value to capital. The torsion of the master's discourse displaces this relation to the fantasmatic immediacy between the subject and the object ($a \rightarrow \$$), thereby concealing the internal break that determines the capitalist structure and the heterogeneity of labour-power and surplus-value. In the fetishist scenario the subject of politics is capital, which means that politics is entirely subsumed under the economic demands and to private interests of a capitalist class. In Marx and Lacan's critical scenario, the subject of politics is heterogeneous to the presumed vital forces of capital, and its social embodiment, the proletarian, indicates the possibility of reversing the relation between politics and economy and to detach the subject of politics from its commodified version.

Marx addresses the capitalist rejection of negativity, still present in the circulation money – commodity – money (M – C – M'), where the mediating commodity in question is precisely labour-power, in the abbreviated formula (M – M') and through the metaphor of spectrality of capital.[16] The analysis of this spectrality and of the political-economic belief it sustains (the invisible hand of the market and the quasi-natural necessity of economic laws, the absolute autonomy of fictitious capital etc.) not only denounces the circulation (M – M') as appearance but also and above all questions the epistemological status of economic knowledge. Political economists, these scientists of value, treat capital as a vital subject and in the same move situate their own economic discipline as a subject supposed to know. The belief in economy is not limited to economists only but makes of everyone an amateur economist in the shared belief that economic knowledge can analyse not only past events (retrospection) and present state of the market (diagnostic) but also foretell the future of financial flows (prognostic). The presupposition is that economy is a rigorous and positive science of value, with privileged insight into the 'spirit of capitalism', and consequently that the rationality of economy is the same as the rationality of financial markets. The ongoing crisis once again unmasked the rootedness of governing economic-political ideologies in this speculative belief and denounced liberal and neoliberal economy as a pseudo-science.

Marx's analysis of fictitious capital assumes a careful position in relation to the apparent self-valorization of capital. He does not denounce this structural appearance as a pure and innocent fiction since it has destabilizing and devastating social consequences. And as already said, the very same abstraction is at work on the apparently more immediate level of commodities. The movement of capital finally seems to overcome all dependency on social labour but the negativity is not entirely eliminated from the system, since it returns in the form of systemic instability. The tendency of structural appearance to absolute autonomy is another description for crisis.

The indebtedness of Lacan's theory to Marx's critique reveals that the psychoanalytic engagement with social reality, too, necessarily amounts to a structural theory of crisis. As soon as this question emerges, the imperative to search for an exit, not only from the crisis, but from capitalism, is around the corner. The task of psychoanalysis, today more than ever, is not to forget that the Freudian epistemological revolution participates in the same epistemo-political horizon as Marx's critique of political economy. In the end, beyond all appearances and more or

162 Samo Tomšič

less trustworthy anecdotes, Lacan's teaching still stands for the recognition and fundamental affirmation of this radical political alliance:

> Marx and Lenin, Freud and Lacan are not coupled in being. It is via the letter they found in the Other that, as beings of knowledge, they proceed two by two, in a supposed Other. What is new about their knowledge is that it doesn't presume the Other knows anything about it.
>
> *(Lacan 1998: 97)*

Notes

1 An expression made famous by Jean-François Lyotard (1974). For a detailed account of political implications of psychoanalytic theory of sexuality, see the contribution by Alenka Zupančič in the present volume.

2 See notably Lacan 2001: 229–41, for the founding act, and 317–19 for the dissolution of the school. For further discussion of the psychoanalytic school, see the contribution of Jelica Šumič in the present volume.

3 Of course, this, too, is not always the case. Resistance against equal marriage in 'progressive' countries like the United States can exist side by side with permanent branding of sex and porn industry. In East Europe and Russia the influence of Catholicism and Orthodoxy continues to engage in a struggle against sexual emancipation, not only of homosexuals but often enough also of women. Claiming that the old scenarios of resistance have vanished would therefore mean voluntary blindness.

4 See Marx 1976: 280.

5 Just as in Marx surplus-value is heterogeneous to the use-value of produced commodities and can be correctly situated only through the autonomy of exchange-value, for Lacan the produced enjoyment is heterogeneous to signification and can be envisaged only after we abstract from the communicative aspect of language. Consequently, psychoanalytic critique of libidinal economy ends up repeating the logic of Marx's deduction of surplus-value. The idea of homology between Marx and Freud is introduced and elaborated in the first three lessons of *Seminar XVI* (Lacan 2006b).

6 'The more saints, the more laughter; that's my principle, to wit, the way out of capitalist discourse – which will not constitute progress, if it happens only for some' (Lacan 1987: 16).

7 I borrow the expression from Colette Soler (2014: 213). Soler rejects the idea that psychoanalysis amounts to a critical nexus of epistemological and political problematic, but one could explain this rejection with the fact that her reading bypasses the importance of Marx in Lacan's teaching, notably after 1968.

8 For a well-pointed historical discussion of fetishism see Iacono 1992.

9 As, for instance, David Graeber has recalled in his bestseller *Debt: The First 5000 Years* (2011).

10 For the various aspects of Marx's invention of the symptom, see Žižek 1989: 11–53.

11 For a detailed discussion of Lacan's theory of discourses, see the contribution by Peter Klepec in the present volume.

12 See Lacan's contribution to the discussion in Foucault 2001: 848.

13 'To prevent possible misunderstandings, let me say this. I do not by any means depict the capitalist and the landowner in rosy colors. But individuals are dealt with here only in so far as they are the personifications of economic categories, the bearers of particular class-relations and interests. My standpoint, from which the development of the economic formation of society is viewed as a process of natural history, can less than any other make the individual responsible for relations whose creature he remains, socially speaking, however much he may subjectively raise himself above them' (Marx 1976:

Psychoanalysis, Capitalism, and the Critique of Political Economy **163**

92). This remark leaves absolutely no doubt that Marx depsychologizes the individuals, which can only be achieved by focusing on the formal structure of capitalist social relations.

14 For a detailed discussion of the role of energetics in the history of capitalism and in Marx's theory of value, see Rabinbach 1992.

15 In the original German passage Marx describes the relation between capital-as-subject and capital-as-surplus with repulsion; not repulsion, which would presuppose an external other, of which value is repulsed, but the repulsion of value from itself as its inner other. Capital collides with itself and thereby produces its own surplus. The inevitable consequence of this repulsion is the appearance of capital as a split subject: $.

16 For further discussion of this spectrality, see notably Derrida 1993 and Vogl 2010.

Bibliography

Derrida, Jacques (1993) *Spectres de Marx*. Paris: Gallimard.

Foucault, Michel (1976) *La volonté de savoir*. Paris: Gallimard.

Foucault, Michel (2001) *Dits et écrits*. Vol. I. Paris: Gallimard.

Freud, Sigmund (2000) *Studienausgabe*. Vol. VI. Frankfurt am Main: Fischer Verlag.

Graeber, David (2011) *Debt: The First 5000 Years*. New York: Melville House Publishing.

Iacono, Alfonso (1992) *Le fétichisme. Histoire d'un concept*. Paris: P.U.F.

Lacan, Jacques (1987) *Television*. New York and London: W. W. Norton and Company.

Lacan, Jacques (1998) *Seminar. Book XX, Encore*. London and New York: W. W. Norton and Company.

Lacan, Jacques, (2001) *Autresécrits*. Paris: Seuil

Lacan, Jacques (2006) *Écrits*. New York and London: W. W. Norton and Company.

Lacan, Jacques (2006b) *Le Séminaire. Livre XVI, D'un Autre à l'autre*. Paris: Seuil.

Lacan, Jacques (2011) *Je parle aux murs*. Paris: Seuil.

Lacan, Jacques (2011b) 'La troisième', in *La cause freudienne*. 70. Paris: Navarin.

Lyotard, Jean-François (1974) *Économie libidinale*. Paris: Minuit.

Marx, Karl (1976) *Capital*. Vol. 1. London: Penguin Books.

Milner, Jean-Claude (2011) *Clartés de tout*. Paris: Verdier.

Rabinbach, Anson (1992) *The Human Motor*. Berkeley and Los Angeles: University of California Press.

Soler, Colette (2014) *Lacan. The Unconscious Reinvented*. London: Karnac Books.

Vogl, Joseph (2010) *Das Gespenst des Kapitals*. Berlin and Zürich: Diaphanes.

Žižek, Slavoj (1989) *The Sublime Object of Ideology*. London: Verso.

11

WHY SHOULD DREAMING BE A FORM OF WORK?

On work, economy, and enjoyment[1]

Mai Wegener

TECHNICAL UNIVERSITY OF BERLIN

Work today

Be it a worker with a jackhammer, at the university or as artist, an intellectual or a manual worker, they all, no matter if they work with 'fist' or with 'brain', as Heidegger wrote,[2] want to call their respective activities *work*. Work is a matter of recognition. It provides an individual with a place in a society. Those who do not work, it is commonly said, stand in debt. They pose a double burden of unemployment: first, they are in debt to others for not having a position and thus no place in a society, and second, they are in confrontation with the notion of free time, which, for them, stands for a devalued time, freed of its meaning and purpose. Nowadays many professions see the world of work as one which is losing a clear, repetitive yet interchanging rhythm between leisure time and work time. Such blurring of the lines, or disturbance of a work/leisure rhythm, is noticeable not only in the academic field (sitting in a café with a laptop, having professional conversations at a party, etc.), but there is a wider logic of deregulation at work, which makes the difference between work and non-work (leisure) unrecognizable.[3] Carmen Losmanns' film *Work Hard Play Hard* (2012) captures many of such new work environments.

Friedrich Nietzsche writing in 1882 commented on the enormous increase of work:

> More and more, *work* gets all good conscience on its side; the desire for joy already calls itself a 'need to recuperate' and is starting to be ashamed of itself. 'One owes it to one's health' – that is what one says when caught on an excursion in the countryside. Soon we may well reach the point where one can't give in to the desire for a *vita contemplativa* (that is, taking a walk with ideas and friends) without self-contempt and a bad conscience. Well, formerly

it was the other way around: work was afflicted with a bad conscience. A person of good family *concealed* the fact that he worked if need compelled him to work. The slave worked under the pressure of feeling that he was doing something contemptible.

(Nietzsche 2001: 184)

Nietzsche addresses a historical break in relation to work, which he describes in both vague and broad terms; yet his general frames sufficiently question the self-evident changes that address the attitude to work in present-day society and differentiates it from feudal and slaveholder ones in the past.

The Grimm dictionary of German language links the earlier meaning of the word *Arbeit* [work] with plague, torment, and servitude.[4] Michael Glawogger's film *Working Man's Death* (2005) speaks of work precisely with this connotation in mind. According to this old meaning, if one is to speculate, a possible definition of work would be: 'Every waste of lifetime accompanied by inner repulsion, the only inner meaning of which is the physical survival of the worker. More cannot be saved from the notion.'[5] The German writer Josef Bierbichler admits that: 'An overall valid definition probably cannot be found', notably because the term work 'is likely to belong to the most self-evident concepts and therefore remains as such both self-evident and unreflected. Except in Marx' (to whom we shall return).[6]

Work did not always have the value and the position that we ascribe to it today. What we know today is work as understood in the capitalist system. Jacques Lacan explicitly refers to the historical re-evaluation of work in his *Seminar XVII*. He states that:

Work has never been given such credit ever since humanity has existed. It is even out of the question that one does not work. This is surely an accomplishment of what I am calling the master's discourse. [...] I am speaking of this capital mutation, also, which gives the master's discourse its capitalist style.[7]

In the time of Sigmund Freud, work already had its capitalist character, albeit under different technological conditions. So what does Freud's conscious decision to resort to the term work mean, and, moreover what did he mean to achieve by allocating it a central place in his theory? His composites *dream-work, joke-work*, and *mourning-work* are well known, but their false fluency hides the tension and even scandals their practice contains. What then, in these cases, does work mean? What do these terms put together? Does it mean that one goes to *dream-work* after the daily work? Is there continuity between these two? And finally what does *working-through* − a central concept for psychoanalysis − in analysis connote?[8] If psychoanalysis and unconscious are inscribed to a tendency whereby work covers all areas of life and in turn becomes indistinguishable from everything else (including itself), then is there an outside of work at all? If psychoanalysis does not clarify where it stands on this issue, does it then fit with the flexible world of neoliberalism and with the culture of working-on-oneself, which is more or less openly inspired and driven by the laws of the market?[9] Avoiding this question also points to an ignorance as to what happens with the term *work* in psychoanalytic theory. Once placed in the *unconscious* economy, the meaning of work does not remain the same. It is at the level of the unconscious and psychoanalysis that this contribution intervenes. This paper outlines the function and the meaning of work in psychoanalysis as introduced in the thoughts of Sigmund Freud and Jacques Lacan. Beginning with Freud, the contribution moves to Lacan, and correspondingly, from Freud's notion of *work* to Lacan's concept of *enjoyment*. My intervention will turn from a discussion of psychoanalysis within the coordinates of modernity to a psychoanalytically grounded commentary on modernity. The aim of this contribution is to shed a different light on the relation work and enjoyment have in the modern capitalist economy. Thus this intervention does not do politics by means of psychoanalysis, but instead, and much more importantly, thinks of the political field through psychoanalysis. As Lacan heavily emphasizes:

> The intrusion into the political can only be made by recognizing that the only discourse there is, and not just analytic discourse, is the discourse of jouissance, at least when one is hoping for the work of truth from it.
>
> *(Lacan 2007: 78)*

Lacan's remark above is a critical milestone for this text. Another milestone is historical and concerns a close intertwining of work and exploitation throughout history, and in particular German history and the concern of the excess of work under National Socialism. In his seminar on the *Ethics of Psychoanalysis* Lacan appeals to *work* as the position of sovereign power:

> As far as that which is of interest to us, namely, that which has to do with desire, to its array and disarray, so to speak, the position of power of any kind in all circumstances and in every case, whether historical or not, has always been the same. What is Alexander's proclamation when he arrived in Persepolis or Hitler's when he arrived in Paris? The preamble isn't important: 'I have come to liberate you from this or that.' The essential point is 'Carry on working. Work must go on.' Which, of course, means: 'Let it be clear to everyone that this is on no account the moment to express the least surge of desire.' The morality of power, of the service of goods, is as follows: 'As far as desires are concerned, come back later. Make them wait.'
>
> *(Lacan 1992: 315)*

All varieties of political power are keen to ensure that regardless of what is going on, work is never interrupted; it continues as usual. Lacan sees the main and thus the most effective point of interruption in the place of desire. As something that cannot be governed or kept in check, desire is the opposite of work. He further points to the tension of opposition between the two. Desire – similar to Freud's unconscious wish – is one of Lacan's fundamental concepts, whereas work is not.

But does this neglect of the idea of work in Lacanian theory hint to its absence? Or is a psychoanalytical intervention into the field of the political about something other than the all-encompassing and always-already present (as seen in the 'Introduction') practice of work? Can psychoanalysis be about something radically other yet maintain a position on work and its role in modernity?

The context in which Hitler and National Socialism was mentioned was to denote something more than just the conjunction of power and work; that moment stands for something sharper or more radical, perhaps something that can even be called the excess of work. The glorification of work under National Socialism was historically the highest (or the lowest) point in work value. At the back of three texts: Hitler's speech on 1 May in 1933, Heidegger's speech in October 1933 to 600 unemployed workers, and Jünger's book *The Worker*, which appeared a year earlier, Werner Hamacher reconstructed the system of work in fascism. Central to his reconstruction were the terms *formation* and *homologation*. The National-Socialist ideology saw in work a formative process that shapes the thing, and this understanding of work was homologically applied to the workers themselves. Work became a condition for the creation (and realization) of man. But the valuation of work under National Socialism contains two extremes: from 'I work, therefore I am, up to: Death through work', as Bierbichler argues. The National Socialist Workers' Party departed from the promise of the power produced by (and through) work. Through the pathos of work the latter was presented as a means to create a people and make the German people 'resurrect'. However, the ultimate end of the power of work and its pathos of re-creation was the slogan *Arbeit macht frei* (Work liberates) put on the front gate of Auschwitz and other concentration camps. National Socialism thus ended up organizing work as raw violence. In his study Hamacher therefore wonders if it makes sense to describe the attempt of freeing oneself from the system, of understanding how it functions, to really oppose it, with the term *Aufarbeitung* or *Durcharbeiten* (both terms mean working-through and are thus central to psychoanalysis). Is work then still useful for instances where 'freedom' or freeing is attempted; can it be reclaimed from this heavy historical burden for a description of a more liberating practice?

Nowadays the system of work has taken on a different path and certainly reformulated itself from the times of National Socialism. The pathos is gone, and the relation to work is rather unremarkably ubiquitous. However, a remark from Werner Hamacher, according to which 'international capitalism is the continuation of the system of work in National Socialism with barely changed means' (Hamacher 2002: 180), can make us pause and wonder if the difference between the notion of work now and its emancipatory claim in the times of National Socialism is indeed as stark as it is portrayed.

The work in Freud

To grasp the full significance of the term 'work' in psychoanalysis, and in the field of politics and modernity, and nevertheless to assess if the implied significance is justified, attention has to be given to Freud. Although for us the term is burdened with the aforementioned recent violent history and governing practices, the same historicity should not be assumed for Freud. At a certain point the question, on which historical context Freud's use of the word leans, should be answered. After all, it can be said that psychoanalysis 'emerged at a time when the economic activity (*Erwerbsarbeit*) became a normal form of working life while simultaneously and increasingly it were the machines which accomplished the work' (Tyradellis and Lepp 2009: 156).

In the context of psychoanalysis, the work in analysis is clearly *psychical*. But what does this mean? The psychical work is no doubt different from mental work as the entire body, not just the brain, is involved. Think of the laughter caused by jokes, the expenditure of mourning, or the effects of dream-life. It is therefore more accurate to speak of the *unconscious* rather than the physical work, as the existence of the unconscious is psychically impossible without a bodily side; yet the access to it can only be gained through speech or the *talking cure* (as Joseph Breuer's patient Anna O famously put it). The unconscious work thus brings together the physical and the symbolic (or mental) which otherwise seem to remain separate.

To understand the work of the unconscious one needs to begin with *dream-work*. The following question immediately arises: who is working in *dream-work*? Unlikely that it is the person who is asleep. Yet something continues to work and to produce. The correct wording of this work would be: *It* works, it dreams to me. Lacan called the unconscious an acephalous or a headless subject, for in this situation, no one can say 'I' and utter their existence. The unconscious, it is said elsewhere, is a 'knowledge that is at work without a master' (Lacan 1990: 14). That is, it works and produces something without direction and with no particular purpose.

With the expression *dream-work* Freud describes the ensemble of mechanisms that cooperate in the formation of a dream. The aim of *dream-work* is thus to bring the unconscious desire past censorship. It therefore accomplishes a particular translation – and deformation – work, thereby creating a manifest dream from latent dream-thoughts. Freud once wrote, 'the whole mass of these dream-thoughts is brought under the pressure of the dream-work, and its elements are turned about, broken into fragments and jammed together – almost like pack-ice' (Freud *SE* 4: 312). The formulation fits well the two central mechanisms and achievements of unconscious work – condensation and displacement – to which Freud added two more: consideration of representability and secondary elaboration (these two are of lesser importance for the present discussion). Lacan, in an attempt to highlight the linguistic nature of these mechanisms (thus the symbolic or mental work), later theorized condensation and displacement as a metaphor and metonymy. Freud further elaborates by saying that:

> The dream-work is not simply more careless, more irrational, more forgetful and more incomplete than waking thought; it is completely different from it qualitatively and for that reason not immediately comparable with it. It does not think, calculate or judge in any way at all; it restricts itself to giving things

Why Should Dreaming Be a Form of Work? **169**

a new form. It is exhaustively described by an enumeration of the conditions which it has to satisfy in producing its result. That product, the dream, has above all to evade the censorship.

(Freud SE 5: 506)

For this very purpose, to bring the unconscious desire across censorship, the *dream-work* makes use of the above-mentioned procedures, whereby Freud's description leaves no doubt that we are dealing with an 'abstract' character of work, from which all positive qualities are evacuated.

The headless capitalist

The crucial question remains: who or what organizes the work in dreams? It cannot be the ego for there is no master in the household. But if the master is absent, from where then, does the *dream-work* receive its driving force and authority? Freud in a passage of *The Interpretation of Dreams* sets out a surprising response. He names the capitalist as this organizer or donor (who provides the necessary means for the dream production). He continues with the impulse for a dream, which is, as Freud insists, mostly in an event of the day that just passed, often in broken lines of thought. However, the day's residues alone are insufficient for producing a dream, they must receive a reinforcement from the unconscious. Freud writes:

The position may be explained by an analogy. A daytime thought may very well play the part of *entrepreneur* for a dream; but the *entrepreneur*, who, as people say, has the idea and the initiative to carry it out, can do nothing without capital; he needs a *capitalist* who can afford the outlay, and the capitalist who provides the psychical outlay for the dream is invariably and indisputably, whatever may be the thoughts of the previous day, *a wish from the unconscious*. Sometimes the capitalist is himself the *entrepreneur*, and indeed in the case of dreams this is the commoner event: an unconscious wish is stirred up by daytime activity and proceeds to construct a dream. So, too, the other possible variations in the economic situation that I have taken as an analogy have their parallel in dream-processes. The *entrepreneur* may himself make a small contribution to the capital; several *entrepreneurs* may apply to the same capitalist; several capitalists may combine to put up what is necessary for the *entrepreneur*. In the same way, we come across dreams that are supported by more than one dream-wish; and so too with other similar variations, which could easily be run through, but which would be of no further interest to us. [...] The *tertium comparationis* in the analogy that I have just used [is] the quantity put at the disposal of the *entrepreneur* in an appropriate amount.

(Freud SE 4: 560–61)

Just as the capitalist possesses a sum of money, the unconscious desire has the available power – or something that translates into such – for the production of a dream. The initiation for the process to begin can be someone or something else, but the capital always comes from the unconscious.

Here, however, an immediate difference to economic life should be marked. First, the work with its capitalist driving force produces a dream as it produces a product or capital; yet the two processes are not the same factually, what they share is the logic of operation and exchange. Second, in the unconscious subject the capitalist and the worker are both divided and united. Freud says, the unconscious desire brings the machines of the unconscious to run in the same way in which the capitalist finances production. Nonetheless, the capitalist as well as the worker are both part of the unconscious; thus they belong to the same order and the same ordering logic. The desire dominates work as something that is part of it and it drives it as a 'headless master'; that is the *dream-work* has no master, for the master's head, or the ego, is asleep. The 'head' or the sleeping person can later only say: 'That was not I. I was not there, where this was made or where it was worked out.' *It* desires *and* works elsewhere.

The currency of the unconscious

The dream takes its capital from the unconscious desire. Freud speaks of *quantity* and thereby reveals his scientific orientation, thus it is unsurprising that the formulation of psychoanalysis is embedded in the upheaval of life sciences, which was accentuated by the change in the concept of force. The principle of 'force conservation' or, as it was also called, 'the conservation of work' (known as the first law of thermodynamics), grounded in 1847 with the physical precision by Hermann von Helmholtz, abolished the old notion of a causal, teleological life force. The Berlin physicalist school that Freud's teacher Brücke had co-founded, adopted such notion of force in physiology. From there on the force in the body was conceived as axiomatic, explicitly fictional and thus of a decomposable magnitude. As Du Bois-Reymond insisted in his pamphlet against the life force:

> There are absolutely no forces, and if one wants to speak of them, at least one should do it in the way that this fiction will actually do the service, to which it is called upon.
>
> *(Du Bois-Reymond 1887: 18)*

This is how force has become a measure of work and in itself a quantity. Freud adopted the scientism of this school. In fact at that time the notion of 'psychic work' began to circulate and there were attempts to establish it, in strong analogy to the physical concept of work, as a fundamental concept of psychology.[10] Freud, too, spoke of work but in relation to phenomena that psychologists of consciousness explicitly described 'as "psychological non-work"'.[11] His varied work-compositions *association-work, dream-work*, etc. thus embody the disputes over the scientificity of these phenomena, in particular over the scientific value of work that Freud so strongly emphasized. By outlining his concept in relation to the one of

W. Robert – who coined the term back in 1886 and understood dream-work as the elimination of the daily impressions – Freud insisted on the interdependence of work and wish. The 'recognition of the existence of dream work' (Freud *SE* 14: 64), according to Freud, testifies of two things: first: 'Dreams are psychical acts of as much significance as any other act'; and second, 'their motive force is in every instance a wish seeking fulfilment' (Freud *SE* 5: 533).

Freud's conceptualization of *dream-work* silently passes from the economic to the physical concept of work. In the scope of psychoanalysis, both, as explained earlier, are closely related. The physical conception of mechanical work and the modern capitalist notion of work – where work is understood as a commodity whose exchange-value, detached from the concrete use-value producing work, is calculable – have the same historical presupposition: that is the emergence of machinery as a condition for the quantification of work. In 1955 Lacan stated: 'The era of the steam engine, its industrial exploitation, and administrative projects and balance-sheets, were needed, for us to ask the question – what does a machine yield?' (Lacan 1991: 61). And later adds:

> Energy […] is a notion which can only emerge once there are machines. Not that energy hasn't always been there. Except that people who had slaves didn't realize that one could establish equations for the price of their food and what they did in their *latifundia*. There are no examples of energy calculations in the use of slaves. There is not the hint of an equation as to their output. Cato never did it. It took machines for us to realize they had to be fed. And more – they had to be looked after. But why? Because they tend to wear out. Slaves do as well, but one doesn't think about it, one thinks that it is natural for them to get aid and croak. And later on, it dawned on people, something which was never thought of before, that living things look after themselves all on their own, in other words. They represent homeostasis.
>
> *(Lacan 1991: 75)*

The history of exploitation, where Lacan placed the return of the energy concept, has, with the exponential use of machines, for the first time taken its modern – calculating, scientific – form. Psychoanalysis, if its reliance on science and form is taken seriously (as explained earlier) can only now come to existence. Its conceptual network is depended and aliened with the differentiations that support the existence of modern sciences and capitalism. For example if one is to look at psychoanalytic terminology, it bears numerous traces of this interdependence: the talk of 'unconscious mechanisms', 'psychic apparatus',[12] etc. The mechanical and scientific are at the core of psychoanalytic terminological apparatus. Of course the translation is not direct. Freud turns scientific terminology into something that accounts for the unconscious forces. The concept of force in Freud's theory does not lead to drive produced by a steam machine, naturally, and nor does the talk of economy amount to the assumption that the psychic apparatus works 'economically' in the sense of their viability or 'demand'. Yet, what Freud adopts from the scientific mechanism of the 19th century is the importance of the functional aspect of force and the fiction of the fundamental concepts. The mechanisms of force and fiction align psychoanalysis with politics and open it to a structural reading.

'One is bound to employ the currency that is in use in country one is exploring' (Freud *SE* 12: 225) writes Freud when he wants to emphasize that in psychoanalysis, unconscious fantasies are to be taken at face value. A fantasy fulfils here the same task as an actual memory. The currency of the 'other scene', as Freud also described the place of the dream-production, unrelentingly calls for the recognition of fiction.

The scientific terminology permeates Freud's theorization. For example, he names *libido* the quantity that psychoanalysis has to deal with. He writes: 'We have defined the concept of a libido as a quantitatively variable force which could serve as a measure of processes and transformations occurring in the field of sexual excitation' (Freud *SE* 7: 2017). The libido is characterized by its quantification – it becomes something that *could* be measured, and is as such given its fictional component. With Lacan, who sharpened this point on quantification and fictionality,[13] one can say that Freud's concept of libido functions as a unification of the psychoanalytic field. It is, in this functional sense, indeed comparable to the function of the money, which, through its circulation in the social field, functions as a form of value. The libido, following Freud's and Lacan's logic, would thus be the psychoanalytic currency. However, this currency has its own laws of circulation, which follow the logic of the *un*conscious. It is a specific logic, for it works as a negation; that is, it does not function as a plus, a gain, or a having, but always as a minus. In the analogy of labour, negation is perhaps a form of a strike. It is about the circulation of a loss or a 'demand for work', as Freud says. The latter – the circulation of a demand as a loss – is crucial. When Freud refers to the drive as 'a measure of the demand made upon the mind for work in consequence of its connection with the body' (Freud *SE* 14: 122), he emphasizes that the drive requires work; moreover, that it creates a compulsion to work. The body, despite its physicality, is not an energy supplier, but merely the *cause* for the work of the unconscious. The mental is connected to the body and it is this operation that is the cause and the driving force of the psychic apparatus.

The limit of dream-work, or: what is the dream working on?

In Freud the object of dream-work is the unconscious desire – the unconscious desire as a tension or a 'strike'. For the desire is always unfulfilled, unsatisfied, castrated, call it what you will, it has the power to set the unconscious mechanisms in motion, and its lack or negativity forms the basis of this motion. Thinking or dreaming – which can be called the work of the mental apparatus – is always triggered by differences, and addressing those differences is becoming more and more complex as the person moves from infancy to adulthood, yet a difference remains a determinant of the unconscious work. If this is turned into terminology of psychoanalysis one can say that the castration is not external to desire but inscribed into it as its internal edge, an end point or a limit. Desire and castration are thus inseparable. What a dream works on is castration, or if one prefers a political analogy, it works on exclusion. At this moment and to this rather technical and mechanical set Freud introduces the Oedipus complex. Initially, perhaps, this is an intervention from the 'outside', however, the 'Oedipal phenomenon' works on desire. It opens and keeps the desire opened. A true, and we can also say a capital, desire can only be the one that does not close, which equally, following Freud, is turned into a forbidden desire. To recall the myth of the Oedipus; when Oedipus' desire closes, when he sexually 'consumes' his mother, he encounters the ultimate end, an edge or a prohibition, masked as a prohibition of incest. If the dream-work is maintained by the unconscious desire, the dream it brings forth is built on a fundamental exclusion (on the ultimate prohibition of incest as in the case of the Oedipus). The unconscious work masked the desire, articulating and covering it at the same time, and in short, repressing it. In this respect, the dream-work is productive: it creates a formation of the unconscious, which brings together the demands of the repressed tendencies and those of reality (e.g. the prohibition), thereby amounting to a compromised formation that is supposed to satisfy both. Thus the dream can be considered as rebus (Freud) or as construction of signifiers (Lacan).

At one point, Freud was forced to distance himself from his postulate that 'the dream is a wish-fulfilment'. The statement could not be maintained because there are dreams in which this type of formation fails – some dreams are not wish-fulfilling. These dreams are traversed by something that dismantles the pleasure principle, something that Freud now began to regard as something closer to its origin. The dreams that repeat anxiety or trauma, for example, belong to those which are traversed, and which guide Freud in *Beyond the Pleasure Principle* to a fundamental revision of his theory, a revision that culminates in the adoption of the death drive. The concept of the death drive – one of its forms of appearance being the compulsion to repeat – is an attempt to theorize something that cannot be integrated, and where the unconscious formation fails again and again. Here, Freud takes on various difficulties that were noticed earlier in his work. In the text itself, there is an impression that Freud struggles with something that exceeds his powers or where his theoretical construction evidently encounters its limits. In the attempt to integrate something that somehow breaks the order, his theory encounters something mythical and/or pseudo-biological. Something real and traumatic persists in the mental apparatus, something that cannot be said. Freud thus makes the assumption that decidedly deviates from the initial statement that dreams are wish-fulfilling. Instead he states that the mental apparatus works on trauma.

With such a radical shift a question of whether we can still speak of *dream-work* has to be posed. What does work in this new constellation mean? Freud conceived work as something formative. From the raw material of thought, from the unconscious signifiers, it creates a dream, a joke, or the like: *formations* of the unconscious. If Freud reserves the term 'work' also for psychoanalysing, this only apparently points in the opposite direction. He writes:

174 Mai Wegener

> I shall describe the process which transforms the latent into the manifest content of dreams as the 'dream-work'. The counterpart to this activity – one which brings about a transformation in the opposite direction – is already known to us as the work of analysis.
>
> *(Freud SE 5: 641)*

The analytical work, as we can read, is dissolving, but it does not strive towards decomposition. It aims at a transformation and thereby contributes to what Freud calls with another famous composite *cultural work*: 'Where id was, there ego shall be. It is a work of culture – not unlike the draining of the Zuider Zee' (Freud *SE* 22: 80). Freud wrote this statement in 1933, at a time when the decisive stage of the reclamation of the Zuider Zee (now Ijsselmeer) was completed. Joris Ivens' film *Nieuwe Gronden* (New Earth) documents this work and portrays the workers struggling with nature, especially with the sea, as the heroes of the draining process and the reclamation of the land. In this context, the work has a strong cultural or cultivating element; it transforms something not yet cultivated or wild – nature – into culture.

If read at the back of this transformation from wilderness into culture, Freud's concept of work reveals a proximity to the definition proposed by Marx:

> Labour is, first of all, a process between man and nature, a process by which man, through his own actions, mediates, regulates and controls the metabolism between himself and nature. He confronts the materials of nature as a force of nature. He sets in motion the natural forces which belong to his own body, his arms, legs, head and hands, in order to appropriate the materials of nature in a form adapted to his own needs. Through this movement he acts upon external nature and changes it, and in this way he simultaneously changes his own nature.[14]

Marx highlighted the changes and the appropriation of nature, the outer, and the inner, through work, whereas his compatriot Engels even more pointedly accentuated the effect of work on the nature of a worker as such:

> Labour is the source of all wealth, the economists assert. It is this next to nature, which supplies it with the material that it converts into wealth. But it is also infinitely more than this. It is the primary basic condition for all human existence, and this to such an extent that, in a sense, we have to say that labour created man himself.[15]

It is through the means of the work that man placed himself out of nature. Thus, as such, the work is culture-forming.

Yet there is – and this is where the analysis turns to now – the unbridgeable tension between a definition that emphasizes the formative, appropriating, integrating, even humanizing aspect of work, and its other aspects marked by destruction and destructiveness. That latter deconstructive element should be taken into account when the word is about the *Beyond the Pleasure Principle* or when the dream (or something else) deals with this beyond. In *Beyond the Pleasure Principle* Freud introduced something that remains Other, dead, impossible to integrate, something that does not go away and cannot be turned into dust through dream-work, but on the contrary (as in the repetition of the drive) it returns and insists in dreams as something unelaborated, excessive, dangerous, thus the death drive itself.

In other words, we are faced with a choice, either to deny the dangerous or destructive site of the dream-process, the function of 'work' or admit that work is not formative and cultivating per se, as it appeared in the readings of Freud we have looked at so far.

Jouissance

It is at the point in psychoanalysis where work is split between the drive and its formative function that Lacan's intervention comes in handy. The *jouissance* or enjoyment comes to great use as it lies beyond the pleasure principle mentioned earlier. As such and in contrast to pleasure, *jouissance* includes displeasure and can be experienced as pain. In fact the ultimate experience of pleasure is limited or met by the fear of death, whereas enjoyment transgresses the limit. The field of sexuality shows the possibility of this inversion most clearly, but it is not the only one. Enjoyment exceeds the tension that can be experienced as pleasure; it carries the possibility of excess in itself. The term *jouissance* thus solves the dichotomy that seemed to exist in Freud's work between wish-fulfilment on the one hand and beyond the pleasure principle on the other hand. If the dream-work realizes enjoyment, then there is 'a beyond' already present in the unconscious desire. If the lust for enjoyment is traversable, it turns out that desire is neither peaceful nor striving for pleasure. In a sense, Lacan with the term *jouissance* translated the quantitative aspect (the sum of excitation). He employs this term at the place where Freud spoke of the satisfaction of the drive. At the time of Freud's life the notion of work was almost seamless; it stood for the implementation of a quantitative magnitude of force. For Lacan, in contrast, the times of the mid-20th century called for a disturbance in an earlier seamless conception of work. Thus the notion of enjoyment mirrors the different requirements of time and opens up a path to a new formulation of psychic economy.

Surprisingly Lacan found a connection between work and enjoyment that was of major interest for psychoanalysis already in Hegel. In the lord–servant[16] chapter of *Phenomenology of Spirit*, which became famous in France especially through Alexandre Kojève, the tension between work and enjoyment is articulated in a truly impressive manner. Enjoyment falls on the side of the lord, while work remains on the side of the servant. The servant *works* on the thing, 'for the lord, on the other hand, enjoys' (Hegel 1977: 116). As Hegel writes:

> the *immediate* relation becomes through this mediation the sheer negation of the thing, or the enjoyment of it. What desire failed to achieve, he succeeds in

doing, viz. to have done with the thing altogether, and to achieve satisfaction in the enjoyment of it. Desire failed to do this because of the thing's independence.

(Ibid.)

The enjoyment of the lord arises from the lack of his engagement with the thing (the object of work) and its resistiveness. He 'has the pure enjoyment of it' (ibid.). The work and hence the mediation that the lord is spared from remains on the side of the servant. For this reason, enjoyment, as it was already mentioned, can only exist as a 'pure negation', which means that the profit of the lord is also his loss. As unmediated, without contact with the resistiveness of the thing that is enjoyed, 'this satisfaction [is] in itself only a fleeting one, for it lacks the side of objectivity and permanence' (ibid.: 118). The lord lacks the knowledge or the actual experience of physical force that went into the production of enjoyment. Hegel's definition thus states that enjoyment aims at negation. Without something interposing, enjoyment is 'only a fleeting one', *Verschwinden,* disappearance, as Hegel concludes. Enjoyment destroys or devours itself. Lacan's notion of enjoyment bears some resemblance with Hegel's view: for him, too, enjoyment is not delimited from negation and is linked to death.

'Work, on the other hand,' Hegel continues, 'is desire held in check, fleetingness staved off; in other words, work forms and shapes the thing' (ibid.). The process of work is always accompanied by resistance, which comes from the thing itself. Why is this the case? The literal meaning of the German term *Gegenstand* (object) provides an answer to this question: the thing is experienced as counter-standing. The fleetingness thereby encounters a limit and the negation turns out not to be absolute. However, on the side of the servant the fruits of work are not enjoyed, for all enjoyment falls on the side of the master. What remains for the servant is only a reduced, limited enjoyment. One could say that he obtains merely the means of enjoyment that he needs in order to stay alive. Can such bare enjoyment still be called enjoyment?

What is placed under question here is the following: on the one side is a pure enjoyment of the lord or enjoyment as pure negation, and on the other side a desire of the servant as inhibited, i.e. as work, whose gain he was deprived of because the lord took away the enjoyment. Both sides are thus lacking in enjoyment. There is a negation in both cases: on the side of pure negation, that is the enjoyment that consumes itself and is therefore always-already lost; and on the side of privation, it is the expropriation of enjoyment that is always-already withdrawn, or belonging to the other.

What is proposed next is perhaps, to some, of somewhat objectionable nature. I propose to include the lord–servant logic in Freud's theory of dreams, in particular in relation to the unconscious desire and *dream-work*. To do so, a return to Freud's comparison to the capitalist is needed. In what I suggest, the unconscious desire that Freud called the capitalist stands on the side of the lord, and the unconscious work, which is put into practice or fed by desire, is on the side of the servant. In doing so, the lord and the servant are made into the two sides of the same coin: the two sides of the subject, which is characterized by the split.

Following this new scheme one can say that the *dream-work* works as a servant of the unconscious desire. The unconscious desire dominates the process and acts as a lord. The desire of course does not dominate in a lordly way: it directs the process as something non-realized or unfulfilled, as already mentioned. The unconscious desire is 'indestructible', says Freud at the end of *The Interpretation of Dreams*, and relentless. At this point there is no positive enjoyment, only the association and expectation of an overwhelming enjoyment. There is a negation of enjoyment, or shall we say a supreme negative of enjoyment. The *dream-work* – on the side of the servant – would then be an attempt to deploy the negative in a hallucinatory way over and over again, but the images it produces necessarily go astray. What gets realized here is an insufficient enjoyment. To help us understand this situation, let us think of photography and a photographic negative. When the enjoyment goes wrong a negative (of a photo) per se cannot be developed. To translate this in Lacan's terminology of the signifiers, the issue at stake addresses the state of the master-signifier. Instead of allocating meaning to its chain of signifiers, the master-signifier is left as a signifier without the signified. Thus, similarly to a photographic negative, which, as such, promises an image but its repeated developing gives none. If the *dream-work* comes too close to this negative, it too can evoke enjoyment that is no longer recognized as pleasurable for it lies *beyond the pleasure principle*. As a consequence, the dream cannot deal with it, the dreamer awakens but does not stop working on it; it 'stays with him' and thus falls in the realm of repetition. This failure in fact protects the pleasure of the dreamer. It keeps enjoyment at a distance and ensures that the pleasure principle remains in power and that the sleep is preserved.

Again, as in Hegel, albeit for different reasons, enjoyment is lacking: beaten by negation or castration, to put it in Freudian terms, enjoyment that the *dream-work* realizes under the dictate of the unconscious desire is, for inner reasons, either traumatic or flawed. Of course, as non-realized and unredeemed, this enjoyment is not entirely lost and thus somehow remains in the picture. Precisely because of this remnant in which enjoyment appears, Lacan in 1968 introduces the term *plus-de-jouir* or surplus-enjoyment, a term he coins in analogy with Marx's concept of *surplus-value* (see Lacan 2006). Marx defines the surplus-value as a value that emerges from work: the worker works *more*, i.e. beyond work that is necessary for his subsistence. The capitalist pays the worker only for his subsistence; whereas that which is produced in a particular time and goes beyond the value of subsistence (a surplus) is on the side of the worker only perceived as a loss. The worker's loss parades as surplus-value in the hands of the capitalist: he bought worker's work yet its surplus comes gratis. Similarly to Marx, Lacan defines the *surplus-enjoyment* as a part of enjoyment that the subject of the unconscious can claim only as a loss because it belongs to the Other.

When thought from this perspective, capitalism emerges as a specific way of occupying the place of the Other. That place which is indeed structurally empty, functioning as empty place, and should remain as such empty. Capitalism has created

178 Mai Wegener

a special capitalist version of the master. That is, a master that everyone can become (this is the promise), if we know how to reinvest and accumulate surplus-enjoyment; and (this is the second promise), if everyone works well on it (and this is also what we are, at once little masters and their workers), someday nothing will be lacking. In other words, one day there will be a master, which escapes the renunciation, or said blatantly, which escapes castration. Even though the master is actually grounded in renunciation, as psychoanalysis knows, he is a master only qua *castration*.

The unconscious – 'let us say that it is the ideal worker' (Lacan 1990: 14) – is here the exploited place, which can be skimmed and stimulated. Under the imperative of enjoyment, work turns into excess. The unconscious is thereby the only thing we have against this imperative. It is not exactly much as it is an empty space, a void, or a strike.

Notes

1 For Jutta Prasse.
2 Heidegger quoted in Hamacher 2002: 166. For more on Hamacher's, text see further in this chapter.
3 See Chemama 1994: 16. On 'work today' in general, see Tyradellis and Lepp 200: 165, 179. The notion of work in psychoanalysis was discussed recently in Tuschling and Porath (2012).
4 Grimm 1984: 538ff. The differentiation between work and labour does not exist in the German language.
5 Josef Bierbichler, 'Arbeit', in the programme brochure of the Schaubühne Berlin for the piece Holzschlachten. Ein Stück Arbeit. Based on the interviews with the concentration camp doctor Hans Münch and the monologues of the writer Florian List. Premiered on 21 June 2006.
6 Ibid.
7 Lacan 2007: 168. The valuation of work goes, as Max Weber has shown, essentially back to Protestantism, namely to Luther and Calvin.
8 Freud *SE* 12: 145ff.
9 The degree to which psychology contributes to this tendency is clearly shown in the film *Work Hard Play Hard*.
10 See Goldmann 2001: 223–45.
11 Ibid.: 238 (quote Alois Höfer 1895).
12 See Wegener 2004.
13 'Energy is not a substance [...], it's a numerical constant' (Lacan 1990: 18).
14 Marx 1990: 283. Here we must recall that there is no differentiation between work and labour in the German language.
15 Friedrich Engels, *The Dialectics of Nature, IX: The Part Played by Labour in the Transition from Ape to Man*, available online at: www.marxists.org/ (accessed on 13 September 2014).
16 The English translation of Hegel brings a new term 'lord' into play, but one should keep in mind that 'lord' translates the German Herr (in French maître) that Lacan uses for coining the expressions 'master's discourse' and 'master-signifier'.

Bibliography

Chemama, Roland (1994) 'Le travail aujourd'hui. Jalons pour une réflexion psychanalytique', in *Le Discours Psychanalytique*, 12.
Du Bois-Reymond (1887) 'Über die Lebenskraft', in *Reden*, Vol. 2, Leipzig.

Freud, Sigmund (2001) *The Standard Edition of the Complete Psychological Works of Sigmund Freud*, Vols. 1–24. London: Vintage.

Goldmann, Stefan (2001) 'Simmel und Freud. Randnotizen zur Psychologie des Geldes und des Traumes', in *Traum, Logik, Geld: Freud, Husserl und Simmel zum Denken der Moderne*, ed. Ulrike Kadi. Tübingen: Brandes & Apsel.

Grimm, Jacob and Wilhelm (1984 [1854]). *Deutsches Wörterbuch*, Vol. 1. Munich.

Hamacher, Werner (2002) 'Arbeiten Durcharbeiten', in *Archäologie der Arbeit*, ed. Dirk Baecker. Berlin: Kadmos.

Hegel, Georg Wilhelm Friedrich (1977) *Phenomenology of Spirit*. Oxford: Oxford University Press.

Lacan, Jacques (1990) *Television. A Challenge to the Psychoanalytic Establishment*. New York: W.W. Norton.

Lacan, Jacques (1991) *Seminar, Book II, The Ego in Freud's Theory and in Technique of Psychoanalysis*. New York: W. W. Norton and Company.

Lacan, Jacques (1992) *Seminar, Book VII, The Ethics of Psychoanalysis*. London and New York: W. W. Norton and Company.

Lacan, Jacques (2006) *Le Séminaire, livre XVI, D'un Autre à l'autre*. Paris: Seuil.

Lacan, Jacques (2007) *Seminar, Book XVII, The Other Side of Psychoanalysis*. London and New York: W. W. Norton and Company.

Marx, Karl (1990) *Capital*, Vol. 1. London: Penguin Books.

Nietzsche, Friedrich (2001) *The Gay Science*. Cambridge: Cambridge University Press.

Tuschling, Anna and Porath, Erik (2012) *Arbeit in der Psychoanalyse*. Bielefeld: Transcript Verlag.

Tyradellis, Daniel and Lepp, Nicola (2009) *Arbeit: Sinn und Sorge*. Berlin: Diaphanes.

Wegener, Mai (2004) *Neuronen und Neurosen. Der psychische Apparat bei Freud und Lacan. Ein historischtheoretischer Versuch zu Freuds Entwurf von 1895*. München: Fink Verlag.

PART 3

Psychoanalysis and political encounters

12

A STRANGER POLITICS

Toward a theory of resistance in psychoanalytic thought and practice

Juliet Brough Rogers

UNIVERSITY OF MELBOURNE, AUSTRALIA

> Resistance is a law of being. It is internal to its object. From the moment being takes form, or a power asymmetry is established, it encounters resistances which irreversibly twist and fissure it.
>
> *(Douzinas 2014)*

In psychoanalytic thought and practice, resistance as militant political action and resistance in analysis are actions that demand intervention. While Jacques Lacan (2006: 498) saw resistance in psychoanalytic treatment as an ultimately incurable effect of the function of desire, there is another problem at work when resistance becomes an act of foreclosure, or, an act which denies the presence of another. When this happens resistance may be diagnosed as a psychotic act. And psychosis – with its symptomatic foreclosures – poses another question in analysis. Even if it cannot be cured, psychosis requires intervention and the effort toward relief, and resistance, as militant political action – particularly that which requires violence to others and the self – is the very definition of a psychotic act. Violence provokes this definition because violence imposes (or hopes to impose) an answer – in the hope that it is *the answer* – with no opportunity for revision. And the belief in a knowing of *the* answer – or a belief in an absolute possession of such knowledge – is what can be described in psychoanalysis as a state of psychosis.

The forms of resistance we have seen and are seeing in the squares of Egypt, Syria, Turkey, Greece, and at the checkpoints, shopping centres, and military zones of Israel/Palestine, and those of the United States (in Iraq, Afghanistan, and New York), and even as the actions of the African National Congress in their resistances to the former Apartheid regime in South Africa, are subject to the charge of psychosis in psychoanalytic thought. This is perhaps particularly the case if these actions promote or require the risk of injury or annihilation of one's body. Such risks are arguably the case with participation in all the forms of resistance above – they may not be actions which promote aggression or violence, but the choices to remain in Tahrir Square, in the Syntagma in Athens, and in the public spaces of protest in Syria – like the choices to resist Apartheid in former South Africa and certainly to resist the Third Reich – are choices to subject one's body to possible beatings, imprisonment, torture, or death. They are choices to potentially submit one's body to violence, and perhaps to submit another's body to violence or even death.

There are few activists who are not aware of the likelihoods of imprisonment, torture, or death as they chose to sit, stand, or speak in the face of riot police and oppressive regimes. It is in these spaces, in the light of risk to the body, that we can understand at least one emphasis of psychoanalytic thought and practice to the performance of resistances in contemporary politics. This is as an emphasis on a privileging of the integrity of the body. That is, through examining practices of resistance exercised through the body, we can understand psychoanalytic inclinations toward the problematizing of political resistance that may compromise that body. But this problematizing must be positioned against what Costas Douzinas (2014) would describe as the enactment of a 'law of being' that insists in acts of resistance. And, it must be positioned against what I will discuss here as the importance of performing resistance as a displacement of a biopolitical subjectivity that demands an integrity of the body.

Resistance, one can extrapolate in Douzinas' work, is the very enactment of natural law in a democratic polis, the very enactment of what it means to be a political subject and thus a subject at all. Resistance *is* the practice of this 'law of being' for Douzinas, and it denotes what it is to *be* at all in contemporary democratic space. Following Douzinas' earlier work we can speculate that he sees this enactment as fitting with his definitions of natural law.[1] To resist is what a political subject becomes and is always becoming in its teleological presence in the polis. It follows then that for Douzinas, to resist the enactment of resistance can be understood as an *unhealthy* resignation to *unnatural law,* and this would be echoed by psychoanalysts. Ideas of naturalness and health play a powerful part in an analysis and certainly in a diagnosis. Terms such as 'health', 'cure', and 'nature' are grossly inadequate in the terrain of the psychoanalytic and the political, however – as trite as they seem – these terms cannot be ignored, and they are mobilized to legitimate the practice (and policy) of both spaces. They are the very core of psychoanalytic work, if we are honest with ourselves.[2] In psychoanalytic thought and practice normatives apply, cures are desirable, living is good, living 'naturally' is best. As with human rights rhetorics,[3] bodily integrity is to be protected. Further, the heteronormatives in psychoanalytic theory, despite their disavowals, are testimony to such presumptions. What I am examining in this chapter is the presumptions in the discourses of, particularly Lacanian, psychoanalysis that demand a resistance to political resistance. And I ponder, in this chapter – with the help of Douzinas' work on resistance – if we might not think better if we bring inquiries into biopolitics to bear, more intensely, on the normatives of psychoanalysis, and indeed if we might not be better to think carefully about the importance, and the desirability, of a form of political psychosis, or a psychosis *of* resistance rather than psychosis *as* resistance. A diagnosis which, in psychoanalysis, has explicitly suggested the need for a cure.[4]

What is at stake in these considerations is simply whether the space to *decide against (natural) order*, and the space to then *act against (natural) order*, is desirable in psychoanalytic thought and practice, and therefore made possible when one is in analysis. To examine whether psychoanalysis can accommodate such a practice I consider practices of resistance which put the body at the fore of political action. These acts are always framed within, and largely directly against, a politico-legal order which seeks to maintain a particular biopolitical order that thrives on the integrity of the body – fuelled by human rights rhetoric – and the maintenance of 'health' qua life, as Foucault has told us well.[5] When bodies are required to perform resistance through subjecting life to the threat of death – either through risking defiance of persecution in Nazi Germany or through starvation, such as in the 'blanket' protests in Northern Ireland in the 1980s, the 'detention centre' protests in Australia over the past two decades, and the *Hepatia* protest in Greece in 2011; through risking persecution, beatings, torture, imprisonment, and death in Greece, Egypt, Syria, Turkey in the past few years, of course in South Africa before 1994, and in Israel/Palestine for the latter parts of the last century – then what has psychoanalysis to say in support or defiance of such acts? Now, as we live in what Douzinas describes as an 'age of resistance', we must ask, can psychoanalysis accommodate such resistance? Or perhaps more specifically, must the practice of psychoanalysis *always* remain antagonistic to a politics of resistance that risks life? Must cure always privilege life? And if so, what is psychoanalysis' relation to the (biopolitical) practice of that life?

To consider these questions I discuss Lacan's work on 'knowledge' in response to the student uprisings in France in 1968 that spilled into his seminars in 1969 (2007). His work at this time helps us think about the will to *the* answer that acts of resistance may pursue or claim. But it is perhaps his earlier work which gives us a frame for political resistance in an age of biopolitics. Lacan's discussions in *Seminar IV* (1994) on the *passage à l'acte* offer one scene that runs counter to Oedipal law, which can be called psychosis. I position the *acte* as not simply an enactment of a psychosis but as a method of politics; a capture of Douzinas' characterization of resistance as a 'law of being'. To understand it in this way I discuss the *passage à l'acte* as a state of being-political that, while partial, momentary – and in Freud's story that frames Lacan's thesis on *passage à l'acte* (Freud 2001) as a moment of falling to the ground – is also a moment of non-capture *by* the symbolic; a moment between heaven and earth where no law can save or imprison the subject. The *passage à l'acte,* I suggest, is a moment of falling flesh that has no determined or, what I will explain as, no psychotic destination. Without this destination it can be understood as a metaphor for acts of political resistance that go beyond what Žižek has described, as an 'acting out';[6] simply, they go beyond the knowing of the answer. The *passage à l'acte*, I suggest, is falling flesh that is split from the body of the subject locked in what Lacan (2006) describes, in another context, as its 'imaginary servitude', and, as such, it can be understood as flesh which exceeds the

186 Juliet Brough Rogers

signifying parameters of biopolitical life. Flesh which performs the *passage à l'acte*, I suggest, is precisely how Douzinas (2013: 137) describes the condition of resisting subjects, as evoking 'the stranger in ourselves'. It is falling flesh in a state of resistance.

Occupied subjects

There may be no generalizable comment on acts of political resistance but to say this: in acts of political resistance the subject attempts a refusal or an undermining of *something* or someone, whether this *thing* be an ideal or an identity. In contemporary scenes of resistance, while their goals are clearly different,[7] we could say, there is some*thing*, as an ideology enacted through policy and/or force, which is being imposed, it is being refused.[8] To paraphrase Douzinas, in current scenes of resistance we see 'an excluded part demand[ing] to be heard' and necessarily changing 'the rules of inclusion' (Douzinas 2013: 141). But the texture of that 'part' differs, and the knowledge of what that texture is, is precisely the concern of psychoanalysis. Because, of course, what the subject of psychoanalysis wants to change, and what s/he wants to have heard, unconsciously may be quite different from what the analysand believes they are attempting to change and to say. In psychoanalysis we can understand attempts to enact change as often attempts, in reality, to reinforce identity. Examples which highlight such seeming contradictions are seen in individuals who enter analysis with the stated aim of stopping the pattern of entering domineering relationships. These people may then be frustrated by the analyst who does not tell them how to change their patterns and they may find analysis intolerable because it is not instructive (read: domineering) enough. Thus the very effort toward change was in fact an effort to reinforce the same. The condition which plagues such efforts toward change is what Lacan (2006: 80) is referencing when he speaks of the 'knot' of 'imaginary servitude'[9] in which the subject's identity is at-service to the signifiers that produce and provoke its desire. Sometimes this service, no matter how much the conscious desire for it to be otherwise, may result in a repetition of the same rather than a changing of the 'rules of inclusion', both in the analysand and in the activist.

The conundrum of *change* in psychoanalysis (and beyond) highlights the first of two particular problems of, and with, resistance that appear when the subject attempts such a change of rules. First, *change* rarely (if ever) involves the creation of what Douzinas (2013: 141) calls 'a new political subject'. That is, subjects are always already subjected – let us say occupied – a priori and thus all imaginations of resistance are framed in a priori discourse. As such, the subjects' imaginations, including their imaginations of the results of revolution – or of a new mode of being – are always colonized with what is available to them. This is why – for Žižek (2007) and for Lacan (2007) – in post-revolutionary states, what the subject will get is more of the same. The second problematic that haunts acts of resistance, and of more specific concern to psychoanalytic practice, is that any employment of violence as a means to an end, and particularly as an effort toward a violent unsettling of the regime, can only be understood as the effort to capture a

A Stranger Politics   **187**

definitive answer to the insistent and formative question to the Other, expressed by Lacan (2006) as, 'che vuoi Autre?' − 'what do you want from me?' In some cases this may be a violent effort toward capture, exercised to the point of a defiance of the existence of the question. What this means is that one acts, violently, in order to produce a known future, as *the* answer. The two problematics of resistance overlap because *the answer* is always imagined in the terms/signifiers available from the past. That is, the answer appears in the frame of the categories which produce the subject, and thus recruits the first problematic: 'you are (always) already subjected'.

I'll tackle these problematics in turn. First, 'you are already subjected'. If we even partially accept Judith Butler's (1997: 6) treatise on the formation of subjectivity as a series of 'passionate attachments' to 'subjection',[10] then it is difficult to understand how the subject might be what Douzinas (2014) described as 're- or de-subjectivised' in the first site of becoming a resisting subject.[11] For the political subject of democracy, recognition is, as Claude Lefort (1989) has told us well, the condition of being a subject. This means recognition within the signifiers − let us call them biopolitical categories − allocated to the identity of the subject of democracy. The stage of political recognition is populated by signifiers which broker little dissent − by others and even by the self. In Butler's terms, we are 'passionately attached' to our gender, imaginations of health, rights, and, in Lacan's terms, the 'goods'[12] − as objects and as ideas − which offer us the imagination of recognition. We are occupied as subjects through our own occupation with a recognizable identity before democracy, with the qualities (objects) that reflect that identity. This occupation allows for little, if any, dissent as to the naturalness, goodness, and reality of the signifiers that produce the subject − as signifiers which adhere *fundamentally* to economies of desires: as desires for recognition of identity and rights, as desires for capital. That is, the subject is occupied a priori[13] with these categories and recognizes (and demands recognition) via these categories.

If we accept the premises of subjection framed above then the argument follows that the resisting subject is still a subject, but one who looks for recognition beyond the common political forms. That is, we can say that the resisting subject is still 'passionately attached' to the ideas and objects which offer recognition, but these may be recognition by an alternative political party, a Cause or, in Lacanian psychoanalysis, we would say s/he attaches to (another) Master's discourse. They may resist one Master, but they chose another Master. They do not resist *mastery*. And here we have the basic difficulty with theories and actions of resistance. These difficulties are that somehow, in some way, any acts of resistance *always* become modes of, in Lacan's terms, the desire for (another) Master (2007). Resistance, understood this way, is a state of being that is always already subjectivized within the parameters of its own claims, or within the parameters of the subject's imagination of its goals. This is the obvious reference made by Lacan in his comments to the students who participated in the 'resistances' of 1968 in France (and elsewhere). As he says, 'What you aspire to as revolutionaries is a Master. You will get one' (Lacan 2007: 207).[14] The provocative comment to the students − some of whom have come to listen to him and some who have come to (apparently) resist him − is a comment on their acting out the discourse of the Master that they imagine they can over-come, through listening (or even objecting) to another Master, namely, Lacan. In this attempt at resistance which falls prey to its own conditions of subjection, we can say that the subjectivity of the resisting subject – the student – is preoccupied with the signifiers available to resist, where the best they can hope for is to be *re*-occupied by the imagination of securing (another) truth. This hope, at least for the students in France at this time – understood through Lacan (and his discussions in 1969) – is the hope for the Other's knowledge. A knowledge which the subject presumes the Other has. A knowledge which is imagined to be able to be accessed and *had*. A knowledge which is presented as the answer to the question '*che vois Autre?*' And here appears the second psychoanalytic concern with resistance: resis-tance as a belief in an access to an answer, or, in its most extreme or crude terms, resistance as psychosis.

Resistance, understood as a desire for a Master, becomes a performance of what the subject imagines is *the* answer. The answer as a closed course of action with a fixed teleological imagination, such that the resisting subject might say: 'If I do this I will be this', or 'if I do this then the *final* result will be this', or, in its psychotic form, 'if I do this *the world* will be this'. It is important to stress, however, that this may not follow for all acts of resistance – which I will postulate later – but when Lacan says of the students in France that what they want is a Master, this form of psy-chotic achievement of an answer is precisely what he is referring to. Theirs is the desire for a discourse that holds within it the *knowledge* that the subject imagines is required (and can be acquired/obtained/had) to achieve *a perfection of the signifier*, an imagi-nation that the subject can acquire, what Lacan (2007: 14–15) describes as the 'Other's *jouissance*'. The students, in Lacan's suggestion, want to resist in order to obtain *the* answer when it is the *existence of an* answer *at all* they are supposedly resisting.

The use of violence

The desire for an answer as resistance is likely to be more aggressively problematized in psychoanalysis when the subject employs violence – to either the self or another – to secure the answer. Violence pretends to *a be definitive* access to *the* answer to the question '*che vois Autre?*', as an access to the *jouissance* of the Other, the substance Lacan (2007: 14) describes definitively in this seminar as 'knowledge'. Knowledge is one form of the *objet petit a* – the very substance that causes desire – but in all forms this *objet* is imagined as what Lacan (2006) describes as non-specular,[15] in reference to the 'mirror stage'. In its status as non-specular the *objet petit a* cannot be represented and this is precisely what renders it definitive, as knowledge per se. When it does not appear in the mirror – non-specular – then it cannot be repre-sented, and therefore cannot be contested in this representation. The *objet* defies the contestations that haunt all forms of representation – what we can understand as a haunting by what Lacan calls the Real.[16] A foreclosure on the spectre of the Real is precisely what emerges in any claims to knowledge as truth, brokering no pretenders to that status.

Lacan suggests that the very promise of the existence of such a status *as objet* [17] is what drives desire itself, but the desire to acquire such an object always employs the definitive inclinations of the death drive – and here is its connection to acts of violence. The claiming of the *objet petit a* is precisely, in Lacan's terms, an indulgence of the death drive. As Lacan interprets Freud on the death drive, it is the drive to attain the point at which 'tension is maintained at its lowest level' (Lacan 2007: 16).[18] The penultimate point of minimal tension is, of course, death.[19] Death is *the answer par excellence*. That is, when death occurs there is no more question of the reality of the subject, or, at least, there is no more question as to the reality of the subject who is dead. Knowledge, or at least imagining one has *the knowledge*, in Lacanian psychoanalysis, is the achievement of an answer in the same way that death is an achievement of an answer. Both require the enlistment of the dynamics of property – as an imagination of possession, as a having of the object – to enable the fantasy of a possession of knowledge or indeed of an answer.[20] Knowledge, as the object possessed by the Master, is, as we say, 'the final word', where no question or doubt – or indeed tension – can exist. And this state of non-tension is the end point of all life that might intervene in perfect signification. It is the end of others, that is, it is death.

We can say that in deliberate acts of violence the effort to assert a particular reality – the perpetrator's reality, whether this be linked to a cause, a war, or an interpersonal desire – as a reality for all is an effort to assert 'the final word' for the self and for others. As one of Allen Feldman's interviewees in Northern Ireland says of the infliction of violence during The Troubles – it is done because 'people forget' (Feldman 2003: 60). But forget what? For this man the memory he wishes to inflict is populated by his own significance (recruited from the rationales of his political affiliates) of what both the victim and the polis *should know*. It is an infliction of *a* reality as *the* reality, in an effort to inscribe the reality of the past and proscribe the reality of the future.

Violence – and perhaps particularly violence to the body of oneself or others[21] – recruits the death drive to the point of inserting knowledge as truth into a reality that cannot be contested. Violence produces an effect that cannot be reversed and demands uncontestable signification. Simply put, in its presentation in the flesh – of oneself or another – it cannot be erased. Thus violence is the aggressive effort to access an answer to the question, and, while violence may not be a necessary practice of all resistance – as Gandhi has proved in at least one context – violence to the self is certainly a likely effect of any form of resistance.

Strange psychosis

In acts of violence we can say that there is no uncertainty – or there is a wish for no uncertainty.[22] And it is for this reason that, in their performance, acts of violence to the self or to others bear the very definition of psychosis. For Lacan the state of psychosis is a definitive alignment with, or submission to, the pure functioning of the death drive to the point of *knowing* a singular reality. The

190   Juliet Brough Rogers

performance of the psychotic act is then an enactment of *that knowing*, as an effort to produce *that reality* as a reality for all. In some cases this means enacting the only singular reality there is (again, this would be death). A singular reality is impossible, but draws on the claim to *one's own reality,* an impossible reality derived from nothing but imaginings, and captured through symbols one perceives as one's own; a death of the paternity of the signifier, and hence a psychosis. As Lacan (2007: 18) says of the effort to act on the *knowledge* of the Master, 'Knowledge is what brings life to a halt at a certain limit on the path to *jouissance'*. Indeed the ultimate form of resistance to life under occupation is the refusal of life – as we can see in some of the acts of resistance in occupied Palestine, recently in occupied Iraq, in Northern Ireland under Margaret Thatcher's policies, and in the *Hepatia* in Athens in 2011, to name a few. And, we can say that this is the refusal of *another's life*, not as the killing of another subject, but as the refusal of the life chosen for the subject by the regime or occupying force.[23]

In one form we can say that this refusal is an effort to create a reality that exists as an exclusive reality for the subject resisting, or, in the act of death, nothing else exists (for the protester) but the protester's reality.[24] Perhaps then we can say in acts of political violence as resistance that the effect is to create an enduring answer, a change that cannot be reversed. Let us call it a political scar that cannot be healed; something the people (and perhaps The People) *will not forget*, but this enduring scar might not always be thought of as psychotic, or problematized as psychotic.

Somewhere between psychosis and an unquestioning acceptance of the imaginary knot of servitude to politico-legal subjection – somewhere between resistance as death and life as only biopolitical life – Douzinas finds another interpretation of resistance and, without departing from Butler, extracts from the usual forms of discussion of subjection, the insistent presence of a 'law of being' that cannot be reduced to either death or *life as we know it*. It may be the refusal of life as we know it while still retaining life. Perhaps we can call it a life that is strange to the politics of the time. Such a life embodies Douzinas' law of being and is the characterization of the subject as always preoccupied elsewhere, or one might say, with a *part* that is always subjectivized elsewhere. And it is this part that is strange to the polis and perhaps even strange to the subject.

The stranger *in/as* the subject is poetically illustrated in Douzinas' account of an act of political resistance performed by one man at Syntagma Square in Athens in June 2011. In Douzinas' account this man was to address the crowd in Syntagma but he 'was shaking and trembling with evident symptoms of stagefright before his address [to the 10,000 activists in the Square]' (Douzinas 2013: 137). What appeared on the stage, however, was a man who spoke beautifully, eloquently, 'presenting a complete and persuasive plan for the future of the movement' (ibid.). When Douzinas asked him 'How did you do it?', the man replied that it was the 'stranger in me' that emerged to give the address. This man's trembling and his subsequent capacity to overcome such trembling, through what Douzinas discusses as a *split,* gives us the scene which helps us understand the way a body can perform resistance while defying the ordinary, common, or claustrophobic categories of biopolitical subjection. With this example we can see the importance of the body's trembling – in light of Kierkegaard's (1985) emphasis – that allows for the biopolitical categories *and* possibly the diagnoses of psychoanalysis not to arrive on the subject of resistance, and thus allows for what I will describe as a *falling between*; a fall where the 'stranger' of Douzinas' narrative, can emerge in the polis and potentially in analysis.

The split

In the fourth of his theses on resistance Douzinas (2014) says 'Resistance is a process or experience of subjectivization. We become new subjects, the "stranger in me emerges" when we experience a split in identity'. When the 'stranger in me' emerges in the polis as an 'excluded part' this then changes the coordinates which constitute a subject. The particular reference points of subjectivity are *split* through the act of resistance, and can no longer be regarded as 'common'.[25] In this emergence we can say that the recruitment of the death drive is only partial and some form of tension in signification is allowed (even desired) to remain. In Lacanian terms, the Master no longer exists as a definitive location from which coordinates of being emanate, but the location of the Master is recognized – politically – as a space of ambivalence. If we take this space of ambivalence as the location of a new subject – which articulates conspicuously with Agamben's 'whatever being' (1993)[26] – then this has its dangers, because when there are no answers there may be only questions. While this sounds appealing to the 'openness' democracy aspires to, it is also a location of no rest, no reality, no communality, indeed, no 'common', and in any polis something must arrive sometime (or we can be assured that the binary attached to openness is a closure that resembles something of 'the terror' of late 18th-century France). Without arrival somewhere, what we are left with is a location of 'whatever', and such a location would seem to have little resonance with Douzinas' description of the politics of such places of resistance as Syntagma Square in 2011. Here, using Lacan and Freud's discussion of the *passage à l'acte*, I want to postulate how psychoanalysis can put some flesh on the 'whatever' form of being without reducing it to the point of no thought – what Alain Badiou (2012: 97) might characterize as without any 'idea' – nor reducing it to the point of the common, or a singular reality, one that can be only and always dead.

Passage à l'acte *as resistance*

Between the endless openness of the question, and the closure of a politics in which policy and policing defy acts of resistance, or where acts of resistance perform only the desire for a Master, there are moments that might offer less need for cure, or indeed, less diagnostic certainty of psychosis. In Douzinas' discussions of moments of resistance in Greece – such as the stranger in Syntagma Square – and beyond, there are what we can understand as moments where a particular and *particalized* physicality of politics, as a form of flesh relation to the polis – that articulates well with Eric Santner's (2011) description of the flesh-like polis[27] – allows for states of action, of mastery, *and* of relinquishing the Master. States, where the simple use of flesh – as the decaying form of the body of the political subject – allows for the changes and uncertainties that flesh exemplifies; states of aging, illness, deterioration, and what I will describe as a form of falling.

In this section I will discuss perhaps the quintessential a–biopolitical act in psychoanalytic thought – the *passage à l'acte* – that both entails an act of psychosis and the promise of an uncertainty to the Master's discourse – particularly in its contemporary affiliations with human rights and biomedical fundamentalisms that tolerate only an integrity (read: health) of the body. This fall might then be the metaphor for resistance as Douzinas' *split subject*. The *passage à l'acte* encompasses this because the fall – as the form of the act – is both the fall to death *and* a defying of the biopolitical categories of life. In its interpretation by Freud and then by Lacan, it employs a very particular subverting of life and law, one which, as I will explain, defies the biopolitical categories of the common through its performance of a specifically gendered nature of the impossible.

Lacan takes his framework for *passage à l'acte* from a case study of Freud's (2001) 'The psychogenesis of a case of homosexuality in a woman'.[28] In Freud's case study, a homosexual young woman has fallen in love with an older woman. The young woman's parents despair of their daughter's homosexuality, and specifically her obsession with this particular older woman (who is considered a lady of ill-repute), and they send their daughter for psychoanalytic treatment, for a cure in fact. In the critical incident that brings her to Freud: the young woman is walking with her 'lady' in the street, her father sees them together and gives the daughter an 'angry glance'; the lady (of ill-repute) asks who this man was and when the young woman informs her it is her father, the older lady demands that the 'affair' end immediately. And she insists that the young woman's attentions cease and all contact between them end. The young woman promptly throws herself off a bridge.

The fall provides us with an image of a slow performance of death that grasps, and yet does not grasp, the imminent presence of the ground (as an accelerated effort toward death). For Lacan, the fall from the bridge is not only the act as an attempt at suicide – for a suicide is not enough in itself to disturb the symbolic order – the *passage à l'acte* is the performing of an act *not in relation*. It is the killing of oneself *beyond* the parameters of the law – or in this instance, not in relation to the father's angry gaze. In Lacan's terms, it is the being – if one can call it being – not in relation to the symbol. In the case in question, the young woman does not attempt to kill herself as a subject; she attempts *not to exist as a subject,* or – in the explanation of psychoanalysis – not as a subject of the law of the father, but as the object that the law prohibits. To understand this, it is crucial to remember that she is her father's daughter, and that the fundamental tenet of the law is an Oedipal prohibition. In Lacan's description:

> It is just a matter of a counter-aggressive phenomenon, of a return onto the subject of aggression towards the father, combined with a sort of crumbling of

the whole situation on its primitive givens, which symbolically satisfies what is at stake by a precipitation, a levelling of objects that are truly at play.

(1994: 113)

In this 'precipitation' as a fall from the bridge, Lacan and Freud concur she is enacting a condition of pregnancy to her father *and* infancy – as her father's off-spring – simultaneously. This is because *neiderkommen* – 'to fall' in colloquial German – is to fall pregnant, only she is the *falling object* and the *fallen woman* – that is, she is the infantile product of an impossible Oedipal relation. As Lacan continues:

In short when the young girl falls to the bottom of the little bridge, she accomplishes a symbolic act, which is nothing other than the *neiderkommen* of a child being born. It is the term used in German to say that one is 'dropped'.

(1994: 113)

'To fall' or, literally, to drop a baby is precisely to become the object she makes of herself. Hence we can say that the young woman, in making of herself the baby who is dropped by herself, is making herself an impossible object. To make herself thus requires a dual effort (albeit an unconscious one) in which she both attempts to kill herself *and* make the father's law – in which she was moments before in relation (or in which she was the *self* instantiated by the law of the father) – not exist. This is because to not be subject to law is to not be subject at all, or, as I will explain, to not *appear* as a subject at all (in the father's angry gaze).

Passage à l'acte is the destruction of the subject as subject, in psychoanalytic terms it is the destruction of the symbolic for the subject insofar as the symbolic order consists of symbols arranged precisely *through* the acceptance of law of the father – the law which positions the subject against what one cannot have: a return to the mother, consummation with the father, a filling out of the Real with all that was cut. In politico-legal terms, we can say the *passage à l'acte* is a violence, not towards the sovereign or even to the law, but to the very symbols of law. And this violence can only occur as a disturbance to the names, or categories, to which we assign biopolitical meanings – that of gender and paternity, biopolitical meanings that are subsumed in commonsense and only appear when the whole situation crumbles in its 'primitive givens'; givens which have come to acquire a self-evidency in biopolitical discourse.

The stranger inside

I want to now read the *passage à l'acte* as the performance of an act that resonates with Douzinas' description of the acts of resistance in Syntagma Square in Athens in 2011, and Douzinas' account above of the man on the stage who was 'trembling with stagefright' and whom Douzinas thought might 'collapse': the man who articulates his capacity to express his resistance as the emergence of the 'stranger in me'. This moment comes to frame, for Douzinas, the performance of the resisting

194 Juliet Brough Rogers

subject. A performance, I suggest, which mirrors the *passage à l'acte* in several important ways. In the first sense we could say that the stranger was embodied, precisely – evoking Kierkegaard's meditations on Abraham before God[29] – in the trembling flesh that indicates a form of refusal to be fully obedient to what God commands. Second, the speaker did indeed collapse (fall), but – unlike the collapse of such figures as Yehiel Dinur testifying before the judges in the Eichmann trial[30] – the stranger remained, standing, speaking, appearing in parts, in the cracks of representation. What the speaker in Syntagma Square enabled, in this collapse, was the death of the subject who is already subjected, and what was left was the flesh of the stranger, split off, in Douzinas' idiom, with parts retaining only the impossible symbolization's associated with a new polis, where Douzinas' 'rules of inclusion' were fundamentally changed, or, for Lacan, crumbled on their primitive givens.

Beyond the aggressive forms of recognition-practice of the state, we can say that the stranger inside the subject who speaks, appears – in the flesh – in the square at the point of unity with the polis. But the key feature here – that Douzinas gestures to in his reference to Arendt – is *appearance*; an Aristotelian performance of politics (Aristotle 1994, in Arendt 1998: 198–9) that brings the *part* of the individual into the fold of the polis by turning him, literally, inside out. And is this not precisely how we can read the *passage à l'acte*? The young woman's body falls in a state that presents her as inside out, as the infant she perhaps was, as the woman she may be – pregnant – as the object that is strange in its appearance because it emerges as something which cannot appear, as *a pregnancy*. Let us not say that the young woman emerges as pregnant. This would be an all too easy form of biopolitical signification that recoups her act into the law of the common. A pregnant woman can *appear* in the polis, but a pregnancy cannot *appear*, although it can be *known to occur*, it is not able to be signified beyond its technical particles, that is, it is not *knowledge* in the form that Lacan describes. It is, in a sense, only a hypothesis made of particles of conjecture.

This impossibility of signification of Woman, *as her body,* is precisely where Lacan would arrive at later with the formidable and much contested statement that 'Woman does not exist' (Lacan 1998a: 81), but it is precisely this lack of appearance of *a pregnancy*, like the lack of appearance of the resisting stranger, that confirms the significance of the formula. A body cannot be signified from the inside. A body only appears outside, even in surgery, even in a state of dissection; what appears is that which can be recognized as the reality of the body. A pregnancy, inside out as it were, is unsignifiable, indeed it is only signifiable as a *still birth*, which is, of course, what an 'acting out' of the common categories of law amounts to: a presentation of all that already is, a body that is known (in death).[31]

The stranger in me – Douzinas' comrade on the Syntagma stage – is the body inside out, a body without integrity (as integration), but attempting to *put together* the stranger and the subject through the act of (almost) collapse on the stage. Thus his almost falling is a crucial element to the practice of resistance. One must be able to let go of the flesh, to allow it to fall, alive and with desire, into the changing polis. In other forms of protest that blatantly employ the falling away of flesh – the

Hepatia, blanket, detention centre, Tiananmen Square – hunger strikers undoubtably know this all too well. The body of the hunger striker recedes in an effort to appear, but this is more than the effort toward representation – more than an acting out of a desire for rights (although of course it often and also that), it is a representation of *neiderkommen,* of falling toward death and as such turning life inside out. Defying the categories of biopolitics – enshrined in the very discourse of human rights that cannot not demand an integrity of the body.

A strange desire

Perhaps what Lacan meant by retaining the resistance between speech and desire was retaining the 'stranger', who is also, and must remain, strange to the analyst. Perhaps an analysis incorporating Lacan's insistence on a necessary resistance is, indeed, allowing the subject to turn inside out, and to remain unrecognizable in its appearance.

Lacan believed between speech and desire resides the non-specular unrepresentational substance that can never *appear* as substance. This is to say that what (does not) appear in the necessary resistance that insists in analysis is the quality of Douzinas' 'law of being'. In the polis this subject is produced in the 'twists and fissures' of, and as, subjectivity, but the fissures can be said to also denote the location between analyst and analysand. In these fissures insist that which can never be acquired by either and must be allowed to be. Political resistance and resistance in psychoanalysis may therefore have more in common than is generally thought, at least in their symptomology. In Lacan's form of Freudian psychoanalysis, the analysand's desire must triumph *in the end*,[32] but it must be allowed to triumph and not be endlessly subjected to the *dictations* of the oppressive analyst.[33] In a simple formula we can equate this understanding of resistance-relation as similar to that employed in the rhetoric of Nelson Mandela (1994) – 'that the oppressor dictates the terms of the struggle'. This resonance indicates the demand that Lacan made clearly: that the analysis needed to be that of the analysand. In short, in order for the 'relation' to be an analysis at all the analysand must dictate the struggle. This was precisely a struggle which he claimed favoured the triumph of the analyst in ego-psychology and, in this form of practice, reduced the analysis to that of an imaginary relation between the two. In ego-psychology the suggestion is that the analysand's interpretations are an attempt to educate the ego of the analysand, rather than allow the desire of the analysand to emerge – unknown and unknowable. The quality of an unknown and unknowable desire is what is intolerable in ego-psychology and so crucial to Lacanian psychoanalysis. The desire must be the desire of the analysand, and not *known,* or presumed to be possessed as knowledge, by the analyst. This desire must also take precedence over the analyst's desire, necessarily leaving the analyst (potentially) floundering in their own desire as a *separate desire* from the analysand. This is why Douzinas finds psychoanalysis' account of the end of analysis resonant with the embrace of the stranger in ourselves.

196 Juliet Brough Rogers

In Douzinas' and Slavoj Žižek's description of the end of analysis the subject no longer regards the analyst as Master, or in Žižek's (more anxious) terms, helpfully employed by Douzinas: 'what a moment ago evokes in us a mixture of fear and respect is now experienced as a rather different mixture of ridiculous imposture and brutal, illegitimate display of force' (Žižek 1993: 234); that is, at the end of analysis (former) analysands are ambivalent about the status of knowledge as the truth-object previously imagined to be definitively located in (and violently guarded by) the (big O) Other. This release from the *brutal force* of the Other is an embrace of the 'stranger in ourselves', and hence why political resistance, for Douzinas, means a *triumph of the desire* of the political subject.

To understand this form of stranger-subjectivity we need to invert Douzinas' (2000) earlier formula of 'rights as desire'[34] – rights being the desires of the subject enshrined and articulated as available by the nation state – and suggest that his configuration, in discussions of resistance, resembles more the claim of a *right to desire*. Desire here is understood in the Lacanian sense as that which emerges in the very lack of recognition by the Other, and in this case by the state. This desire, specifically, is not a desire subsumed in the rights discourse of liberal law – it is not occupied a priori with the analyst qua state's desire. Desire here becomes the stranger because it is, in the terms of the state, unrecognizable. It is strange. And the state must change its gaze – let us call it its biopolitical categories for the reference of life – in order to produce other forms of recognition, or it can, of course, exercise a more aggressive violence to reinforce its own prior categories for recognition. Torture, imprisonment, death – legal categories which enable an assertive form of recognition of the body before the law.[35]

Conclusions

The importance of psychoanalysis allowing for the emergence of a politics of resistance and offering the space for the practice of resistance is bitterly highlighted in its own history. The story that tragically highlights psychoanalytic practice toward acts of resistance in psychoanalysis was the refusal of German psychoanalytic organizations in the 1930s to resist Nazi ideology – and then practice; the refusal, of psychoanalysts, to put their bodies on the line. Resistance was not entertained as a community.[36] The question was how much the psychoanalytic community should align with the Nazi regime, as a means to salvage psychoanalysis. In hindsight we can say that German psychoanalytic organizations were at best cowardly and at worst complicit in the death and exile of many. However, whether even Jewish analysts of the time would have encouraged the resistance of their patients – which would certainly have entailed the risk of injury, imprisonment, or death – evokes the questions of our age. The questions of how much to obey or how much to resist when law, and even Oedipal law, tells you otherwise. It is questions such as these to which psychoanalytic thought must attend. Now, in the new millennium, we have the benefit of hindsight in seeing how likely it is that obedience (to law) produces death and even genocide.

Leaving aside the obvious problems of political resistance being tied to such a Western-dominated and informed tool as psychoanalysis,[37] we can suggest that one can *remain in an analysis and resist* if, and only if, there is a space for falling in analysis. That is – and here we can reframe Gayatri Spivak's recent meditations on forms of representation as a 'fall through the fracture' (2012: 103) – if there is a space for non-representation that allows for the *power* of non-recognition. In short, one can enact resistance while in psychoanalysis if the analysand is allowed to fall through the fracture of representation, or if the analysand's desire is allowed to triumph in a manner which can allow the possibility of death, but a death that is not subsumed in the biopolitical knowledge that underpins (and arguably undermines) Western democracies. This might have been the fall which was disallowed in Nazi Germany when terror polluted the scene of politics as well as the scene of analysis. Resistance – that might mean death – could not be allowed to triumph as the desire of the analysand when the desire for the death of the Jewish people was the operation of biopolitics par excellence.

To be allowed to fall though the fracture of representation may mean not to appear before the *recognizing* faculties of the analyst. Just as the resisting subject is beyond the biopolitical categories that signify life, the patient is strange to the analyst. To allow this may be definitively what it means for a psychoanalyst to displace their own position as Master, which is no easy thing, even for an analyst, and particularly one faced with both the resistance of the patient *and* the possibility that the patient may die through her/his choice to practice resistance outside the analysis. The only relevant question for considering the possibility of political resistance in a psychoanalysis is therefore – can the analyst allow his or her patients to die or to kill? Because, before the policing practices of biopolitical life, to fall may also mean to fall to one's death.

Notes

1 Douzinas' complex and well-received discussions of natural law are extrapolated (2000).
2 For a broader discussion of these normatives, see Soler (2006).
3 I have discussed the use of human rights rhetoric and doctrine, and its privileging of flesh over politics, particularly in relation to debates on female circumcision, in Rogers (2013).
4 Even if such a cure is impossible, as Lacan (1993) suggests of psychosis. Thus what Lacan proposes is that psychosis is a structure and it cannot be cured.
5 This terrain is well laid out in Foucault's work from his three discussions of 'care' in the volumes on the *History of Sexuality* and beyond, see Foucault (1978, 1985, 1986, 2008).
6 Žižek has made the link between acting out as one from politics (perhaps a-politics) and its antonym the *passage à l'acte* in his plenary lecture at the Critical Legal Studies Conference, London (2007). I am extrapolating from here in a direction he may not have chosen.
7 As Douzinas says, even of the recent movements 'The Arab spring had different aims from the Spanish *indignados*, the Greek *aganaktismenoi* and "Occupy"' (2013: 9).
8 Alain Badiou might disagree with the mode of the 'refusal' being an act of resistance because it lacks 'an idea'. This is a consideration which remains pertinent to the issues of subjection and the role of the Master, discussed later (Badiou 2012: 97).

9 Lacan was emphatic on this point and said of the confusions of imaginary servitude that plague the subject in subjection, it is '*only* psychoanalysis that unties the knot' (2006: 80).

10 'the attachment to subjection is produced through the workings of power, and that part of the operation of power is made clear in this psychic effect ... the subject is formed by a will that turns back upon itself, assuming a reflexive form, then the subject is the modality of power that turns on itself; the subject is the effect of power in recoil' (Butler 1997: 6).

11 As Douzinas describes the 'first site of conflict...[as] de- and re-subjectification, the dis-articulation of people from the position of desiring and consuming machines and their emergence as resisting subjectivities (the "stranger in me")' (2014).

12 This version of the object appears significantly in *Seminar XVII*, but it was already well constituted as the issue of identity in his earlier seminars, particularly in *Seminar VII* when he says: 'It is a fact of experience that what I want is the good of others in the image of my own. That doesn't cost so much. What I want is the good of others pro-vided it remain in the image of my own ... provided that it depends on my efforts' (1992: 187).

13 The relation between the quality of the refusal and the quality of the imposition are certainly not mutually exclusive. When considering this similarity it is best to invoke Gayatri Chakravorty Spivak's thoughtful words on theorizing subjects in subjection when she notes the important disparity in theorizing economic modes of production – consolidated as global capitalism – as opposed to 'the machinery production and per-formance of the mental theatre' (1999: 177).

14 Zevnik summarizes Lacan's thoughts on this as the Master as sovereignm and thus revolution demands the reinstatement of a sovereign. She suggests Lacan argues 'all revolutions ... result in the re-instalment of another sovereign and the revolution con-tinues' (2009: 83–106).

15 As he says of the *objet a*, these objects have one common feature in my elaboration of them – they have no specular image, or, in other words, alterity (Lacan 1998b: 268).

16 The Real is that which insists in undermining any universal claims on 'reality'.

17 And we can reference here the previous mention of goods as objects, which he discusses in depth in *Seminar VII* (1992), and why he elaborates in both seminars on Marx's configuration of goods and capitalism's employment of the ideology of the Good.

18 Lacan also elaborates this concept further in *Seminar XI* (1998b).

19 We can speculate that this is precisely the seduction of suicide to the depressed subject. Depression lowers the tension to an encounter less and less. Suicide is the fantasy of that reduction to its zero point.

20 Hence Lacan turns to Marx to explain the dynamics of a *jouissance* of the Other. The enlistment of Marx for Lacan's argument goes beyond the parameters of this discussion, however, it is also useful to contemplate here the enlistment of ideas of capitalism and the possibilities of possession of 'private property', as they participate in the production of a symbolic order that enables a particular *form* of fantasy for even the subject revolting. See Lacan (2007: 20).

21 I am mindful of Žižek's helpful parsing of categories of violence into subjective and systematic violence. I am referencing the former. See Žižek (2008).

22 This is very different from suggesting that there may be no ambivalence or doubt about committing the act. One can be uncertain about whether one wants to perform vio-lence, while still being *certain* about *the* outcome that will result from that performance.

23 In relation to Palestine I am drawing on the work of Ghassan Hage (see Hage 2013). But Hage also makes an important intervention into ideas of life and protest in respect to stone throwing (see Hage 2003).

24 I have made some comments on this particular form of production of an exclusive reality: Rogers (2014). It is also worth adding another comment from Lacan on this, in his affiliation with Hegel – and Hegel's affiliation with death as the defining presence of the absolute – when he says 'Hegel can do no more than refer to death as the signifier

of the absolute master, is, on this occasion, a sign that nothing is resolved by this pseudo-origin' (Lacan 2007: 31).

25 This is Jacques Rancière's terms, employed by Douzinas (2014).

26 *Coming Community*, but I am affiliating with Zevnik's description of 'whatever being' (2009: 89).

27 Santner offers a complex formula for the understanding of flesh in the post-French revolution environment and in its relation to politics. I take this logic through the direction of law and literally the skin of the subject in *Law's Cut* (Rogers 2013a).

28 I have discussed this scene elsewhere in Rogers (2009). I have repeated some of the phrasing here because it seemed disingenuous to rephrase in the interests of saying something *new*.

29 It is the 'shudder of thought' (Kierkegaard 1985).

30 See Arendt (1963: 224). I have discussed this collapse in Rogers (2013b), and as also a form of refusal (to perform the required catharsis of the trial) in Rogers (2011).

31 And this is precisely the aggression of knowing that frames rights rhetoric, and particularly that of human rights. As Douzinas (2000: 12) describes 'Human rights break down the body into functions and parts and replace its unity with rights, which symbolically compensate for the denied and barred bodily wholeness. Encountering rights nihilates and dismembers the body: the right to privacy isolates the genital area and creates a "zone of privacy" around it; the mouth is severed and reappears "metonymized" as free speech which protects its communicative, but not its eating function …'. This is human rights as a politics of recognition which has already been recovered and represented in the terms/categories/names of the polis. As power, in the Foucauldian sense, that only repeats and reinforces the existing apparatus.

32 This discussion is well articulated in Lacan's 1958 paper 'The Direction of the Treatment and the Principles of its Power' (see Lacan 2006).

33 That is, for Lacan there is no other resistance to analysis than that of the analyst himself (2006: 278).

34 Douzinas captures the condition of rights claims in relation to contemporary subjectivities as 'every desire is a potential right' (2000: 8).

35 This is precisely what Elaine Scarry (1985) is referring to as the imperative for the practice of torture.

36 Any alliance was formed, of course, with the gentiles of German psychoanalysis, while they encouraged the expulsion and enabled the destruction of many of the association's numbers. Jewish analysts formed the backbone of psychoanalysis in the earlier parts of the 20th century, and needless to say, their lives were certainly and unavoidably at risk (see Goggin and Goggin 2001). Of course there were certainly some psychoanalysts who did entertain and execute such resistance, probably in Germany, and certainly in broader Europe, for one such powerful example see Dori Laub's discussion of the resistance practice of Marion Pritchard (Laub 2012: 65–6).

37 I have discussed the problems with this in Rogers (2007).

Bibliography

Agamben, G. (1993) *The Coming Community*. Minneapolis, MN: University of Minnesota Press.

Arendt, H. (1963) *Eichmann in Jerusalem: A Report on the Banality of Evil*. New York: Penguin Books.

Arendt, H. (1998) *The Human Condition*. Chicago, IL: University of Chicago Press.

Aristotle (2004) *The Nichomachean Ethics*. London: Penguin Books.

Badiou, A. (2012) *The Rebirth of History, Times of Riots and Uprisings*, trans. Gregory Eliot. London and New York: Verso.

Butler, J. (1997) *The Psychic Life of Power: Theories in Subjection*. Redwood City, CA: Stanford University Press..

Douzinas, C. (2000) *The End of Human Rights: Critical Legal Thought at the Turn of the Century*. Oxford: Hart Publishing.

Douzinas, C. (2013) *Philosophy and Resistance in the Crisis*. Cambridge: Routledge and Polity.

Douzinas, C. (2014) 'Welcome to the Age of Resistance', *openDemocracy*. 1 March 2014 (www.opendemocracy.net).

Feldman, A. (2003) 'Political Terror and the Technologies of Memory: Excuse, Sacrifice, Commodification, and Actuarial Moralities', *Radical History Review*, 85: 58–73.

Foucault, M. (1978) *The History of Sexuality: An Introduction*. London: Penguin.

Foucault, M. (1985) *History of Sexuality Vol. 2: The Use of Pleasure*. New York: Random House.

Foucault, M. (1986) *History of Sexuality Vol. 3: Care of the Self*. New York: Random House.

Foucault, M. (2008) *The Birth of Biopolitics: Lectures at the College de France 1978–79*, trans. Graham Burchell. New York: Palgrave Macmillan..

Freud, S. (2001) 'The Psychogenesis of a Case of Homosexuality in a Woman', in *Beyond the Pleasure Principle: Group Psychology and Other Works (1920–1922)*, trans. J. Strachey. London: Vintage.

Goggin, J. E. and Goggin, E. B. (2001) *Death of a 'Jewish Science': Psychoanalysis in the Third Reich*. West Lafayette, IN: Purdue University Press.

Hage, G. (2003) '"Comes a Time We Are All Enthusiasm": Understanding Palestinian Suicide Bombers in Times of Exighophobia', *Public Culture*, 15(1): 65–89.

Hage, G. (2013) '"In Unoccupied Palestine" Between Dependence and Independence: What Future for Palestine?' conference, Ibrahim Abu-Lughod Institute of International Studies, Birzeit University, Ramallah, Palestine, 9 March.

Kierkegaard, S. (1985) *Fear and Trembling: Dialectical Lyric by Johannes de silentio*, trans. Alastair Hannay. London: Penguin.

Lacan, J. (1991 [1954–1955]) *The Seminar of Jacques Lacan: Book II The Ego in Freud's Theory and in the Technique of Psychoanalysis*. ed. Jacques-Alain Miller, trans. Sylvana Tomaselli. New York: W. W. Norton and Company.

Lacan, J. (1992 [1959–1960]) *Ethics of Psychoanalysis, Book VII*, ed. Jacques–Alain Miller, trans. Dennis Porter. New York: W. W. Norton and Company.

Lacan, J. (1993 [1955–1956]) *The Seminar of Jacques Lacan, Book III: The Psychoses*, ed. Jacques-Alain Miller, trans. Russell Grigg. New York: W. W. Norton and Company.

Lacan, J. (1994 [1956–1957]) *Le séminaire, Livre IV: La relation d'objet et les structures freudiennes*, ed. Jacques-Alain Miller. Paris: Seuil (unpublished in English).

Lacan, J. (1998a [1972–1973]) *Encore, The Seminar of Jacques Lacan, Book XX: On Feminine Sexuality: The Limits of Love and Knowledge*, ed. Jacques-Alain Miller, trans. Bruce Fink. New York: W. W. Norton and Company..

Lacan, J. (1998b) *The Seminar, Book XI, The Four Fundamental Concepts of Psycho-Analysis*, ed. Jacques-Alain Miller, trans. Alan Sheridan. New York: W. W. Norton and Company.

Lacan, J. (2006) *Ecrits: The First Complete Edition in English*, trans. Bruce Fink. New York: W. W. Norton and Company.

Lacan, J. (2007 [1991]) *The Other Side of Psychoanalysis: The Seminar of Jacques Lacan, Book XVII*, trans. R. Grigg. New York and London: W. W. Norton and Company,

Laub, D. (2012) 'Testimony as Life Experience and Legacy', in *Power of Witnessing: Reflections Reverberations and Traces of the Holocaust*, ed. Nancy Goodman and Marilyn Meyers. London: Routledge.

Lefort, C. (1989) *Democracy and Political Theory*. Cambridge, MA: MIT Press.

Mandela, N. (1994) *Long Walk to Freedom*. London: Little Brown and Co.

Rogers, J. (2007) 'Who's Your Daddy? A Question of Sovereignty and the Use of Psychoanalysis', *Law Text Culture*, 11.

Rogers, J. (2009) 'Beyond the Script of Law - Dildos, Tranny Cops and Protesting Anti-Terrorism', *Griffith Law Review*, 18.

Rogers, J. (2011) 'Nostalgia for a Reconciled Future – Scenes of Catharsis and Apology in Israel and Australia', *Griffith Law Review*, 20(2): 252–270.

Rogers, J. (2013a) *Law's Cut on the Body of Human Rights: Female Circumcision, Torture and Sacred Flesh*. London: Routledge.

Rogers, J. (2013b) 'A Love for the Fallen: A Melancholic Relation to the Art of September 11, 2001' *Discipline*, 3(Winter).

Rogers, J. (2014) 'The Jouissance of the Torturer as the Enjoyment of the Unacceptable in Zero Dark Thirty', *Portal*, 11(2): 1–11.

Rozmarin, E. (2014) 'Talking About Gaza in Psychoanalysis'. *Public Seminar*. 11 August, available online at: www.publicseminar.org/2014/08/talking-about-gaza-in-psychoanalysis/#.U-ny3F5Rdg0.

Santner, E. (2011) *The Royal Remains: The People's Two Bodies and the Endgames of Sovereignty*. Chicago, IL: University of Chicago.

Scarry, E. (1985) *Body in Pain: The Making and Unmaking of the World*. New York: Oxford University Press.

Soler, C. (2006) *What Lacan Said About Women: A Psychoanalytic Study*, trans. John Hollands. New York: Other Press.

Spivak, G. C. (1999) *A Critique of Postcolonial Reason: Toward a History of the Vanishing Present*. Boston, MA: Harvard University Press.

Spivak, G. C. (2012) *An Aesthetic Education in the Era of Globalization*. London: Harvard University Press.

Zevnik, A. (2009) 'Sovereign-less Subjectand the Possibility of Resistance', *Millennium: Journal of International Studies*, 38(1): 83–106.

Žižek, S. (1993) *Tarrying with the Negative: Kant, Hegel and the Critique of Ideology*. Durham, NC: Duke University Press.

Žižek, S. (2008) *Violence*. New York: Picador.

13

THE TRUTH OF DESIRE

Lack, law, and phallus

Ari Hirvonen

UNIVERSITY OF HELSINKI, FINLAND

Introduction

From the psychoanalytic point of view one can be guilty only of one thing, Jacques Lacan (1992: 319) says, *c'est d'avoir cédé sur son désir*, 'that is of having given ground relative to one's desire'. What is this desire that is so important for psychoanalysis? What is the subject's relationship to her/his desire from which she/he ought not to back down? I will answer this fundamental question through a case study, the case of Hamlet.

In Shakespeare's *Hamlet,* Prince Hamlet's father, the late King Hamlet, has been killed by his brother Claudius. Claudius is crowned as a new king. He marries Hamlet's mother, Gertrude. Hamlet confronts the ghost of his father, who reveals the crime committed by Claudius and demands that Hamlet seek revenge. Hamlet postpones the revenge time after time despite having had opportunities to kill Claudius. Hamlet kills Polonius, whose daughter Ophelia is in love with Hamlet. Hamlet has begun to ignore her after having met the ghost. Ophelia goes mad and commits suicide.

In the end, Polonius' son Laertes and Hamlet have a duel with foils and daggers. To get rid of Hamlet, Claudius convinces Laertes to use a sharpened and poisoned foil rather than a blunt foil that is used in friendly duels. Moreover, Claudius poisons Hamlet's wine. Gertrude takes a lethal drink from Hamlet's goblet. Laertes wounds Hamlet with the poisoned foil. In a scuffle, this foil is switched from Laertes to Hamlet, who wounds Laertes with it. Gertrude collapses, declares that she has been poisoned and dies. Laertes confesses Claudius' and his conspiracy. Hamlet strikes Claudius with the foil and forces him to drink from the poisoned goblet. Laertes asks Hamlet's forgiveness and Hamlet asks Horatio to tell his story. With Gertrude, Claudius, Laertes, and Hamlet all dead, Norwegian prince Fortinbras enters.

Oedipal Hamlet

In *The Interpretation of Dreams* (1900), Freud (1958: 298) defines the main problem of *Hamlet*: 'the play is built up on Hamlet's hesitations over fulfilling the task of revenge that is assigned to him; but its text offers no reasons or motives for these hesitations'.

Even if the ghost of Hamlet's father makes an unconditional demand, 'Revenge his foul and most unnatural murder' (I.v.25), even if Hamlet, the good son, is subject to this demand, 'I'll follow thee' (I.iv.78), even if Hamlet wipes everything else from his mind, so that 'thy commandment all alone shall live / Within the book and volume of my brain, / Unmixed with baser matter' (I.v.102–4), it is impossible for him to act. He postpones the act until he is fatally wounded.

In *Hamlet and Oedipus* (1949), Ernst Jones elaborates on Freudian Hamlet. Jones (1976: 45) writes: 'We are compelled then to take the position that there is some cause for Hamlet's vacillation which has not yet been fathomed.' The central determinant of the tragedy's ultimate meaning is the question of why Hamlet hesitates to kill the king. This shortcoming is precisely *the* problem for psychoanalytic readings of *Hamlet*. In their attempt to uncover the enigma of Hamlet, both Freud and Jones turn against the romantic tradition which considered that a great deed had been imposed as a duty upon a noble soul; yet the soul was not to live up to the expectations of the imposed duty for its oversensitive or over-contemplative constitution.

For Freud and Jones, Hamlet is far from incapable of taking action. He does not hesitate to kill Polonius and send Rosencrantz and Guildenstern to their deaths. 'He was always clear enough about what he *ought* to do' (Jones 1976: 48). Since Hamlet's hesitation is neither in 'his incapacity for action in general, nor in the inordinate difficulty of the particular task in question', then it must lie 'in some special feature of the task that renders it repugnant to him' (Jones 1976: 45).

According to Freud (1958: 265), 'Hamlet is able to do anything – except to take vengeance to the man who did away his father and took that father's place with his mother.' It is exactly at this point that the answer to Hamlet's riddle lies. Claudius embodies for Hamlet his own repressed childhood's desires. The reason for the torment Hamlet suffers is 'the obscure memory that he himself had contemplated the same deed against his father out of passion for his mother' (Freud 1985: 273). Loathing of Claudius is replaced by self-reproach because the scruples of Hamlet's conscience remind Hamlet of his wishes to do what Claudius has done. Thus, he is reminded that he is no better than the sinner whom he ought to kill. His 'conscience is his unconscious sense of guilt' (Freud 1985: 273). Also for Jones (1976: 90), 'The call of duty to kill his stepfather cannot be obeyed because it links itself with the unconscious call of his nature to kill his mother's husband.' This is because the 'long "repressed" desire to take his father's place in his mother's affection is stimulated to unconscious activity by the sight of someone usurping this place exactly as he himself had once longed to do' (Jones 1976: 82). Claudius' crime and Hamlet's need for action reawakens repressed infantile impulses and wishes, which result in the necessity of still stronger repression. As Freud (1958: 265) writes, 'the loathing which should drive him on to revenge is replaced in him by self-reproaches, by scruples of conscience, which remind him that he himself is literally no better than the sinner whom he is to punish'.

Freud sees in Hamlet a figure that represents in an appropriate way the newly found Oedipus complex.[1] Freud's Hamlet is an Oedipal figure, who confronts his repressed Oedipal wishes and who cannot act because Claudius has enacted Hamlet's own murderous and incestuous wishes. Hamlet reveals to us a universal phenomenon of childhood. As for *Hamlet,* it offers a royal road to the unconscious.

For Freud, Hamlet is a case study of psychoneurosis as a failed attempt to bring the Oedipal crisis to a successful conclusion. His analysis measures Hamlet against a model of normal development in which the Oedipus complex is resolved. Hence, there is a normative and normalizing element in Freud's reading (cf. van Haute and Geyskens 2012: 18–19).

Desire and psychoanalytic cure

I will now turn to Lacan's interpretation of Hamlet that appears in *Seminar VI* (1958–59) titled 'Desire and its interpretation' (*Le désir et son interprétation*, 2013). Attention is focused not so much on the Oedipus complex, but rather on Hamlet's relationship to his desire. According to Jacques-Alain Miller, this seminar reworks Lacan's previous formalization of Oedipus: 'Oedipus is not the unique solution of desire, it is only its normalized form' (Miller 2013). Psychoanalysis is not, Lacan says at the end of the seminar, 'a reduction to the preformed norms' (Lacan 2013: 572).

As a search for the lost desire, *Hamlet,* the tragedy of desire, may be compared with the function of psychoanalysis. As Lacan (2013: 319) starts to go through *Hamlet,* he tells his audience that we are not far from clinical practice, because the question is how to 'situate the meaning of desire [*le sense du désir*], of human desire.' *Hamlet* offers, as Philippe Van Haute (2007: 555, see also 537) writes, an insight into the course and logical end of psychoanalytic cure as it, like analysis, 'sets up a framework in which a particular life can (once again) unfold'. What is staged in the play – an attempt to weave together the strings of the subject's being that have come undone – 'touches very close to the experience of being a psychoanalyst', as Simon Critchley and Jamieson Webster (2013: 95) write.

For Lacan, *Hamlet,* the play, constructs layers within which the subject and her/ his relation to desire can find their place. Due to its articulation and composition, *Hamlet* succeeds in uncovering the core of our being as it discloses the truth of desire. If for Freud, *Hamlet* puts on stage the Oedipus complex, then for Lacan, the play offers a stage for the psychoanalytic views he elaborated on in previous seminars.

The constitution of the subject

For Lacan (2013: 291), 'there is something that is not in the desire of Hamlet'. Hamlet has lost the track of his desire. This is related to Hamlet's relation, first, to the mother, more exactly to the desire of the mother, and second, to the father, more exactly to the functioning of the paternal metaphor. Before we continue with Lacan's reading of *Hamlet* we have to see what the desire of the mother and the paternal metaphor mean.

In the dyadic relationship between the mother and the infant, the mother seems to be the omnipotent Other. This relationship is broken by the absences of the mother. Every so often, the mother leaves the infant to get something she needs. The mother lacks something. She is not the omnipotent and absolutely perfect Other. Moreover, the infant realizes that she/he is not the sole object of the desire of the mother. She wants something else. Otherwise, the mother would never reject her/him. Thus, the infant begins to wonder what the mother desires so that she/he would again become the object of her desire. The mother introduces in her discourse the phallus for the infant by explaining why she has to go away from time to time: she is going to have a dinner with the father, she will go to the bedroom, she has to go to work. In this process, the exclusive relationship between the mother and the infant is transformed into a triangular one involving the infant, the mother, and the object of the desire of the mother. This object is the phallus, which does not refer to the anatomical sex, but to the image of potency and the representation of that which would fulfil the mother. Therefore, the infant identifies with the phallus which she/he imagines to be the object that the mother desires. Through this imaginary identification with the phallus, the infant assumes that it is recognized as the object of the totality of the desire of the mother. To be the phallus would guarantee the presence of the mother and constant maternal solicitude.

If the infant is not to remain the object of the desire of the mother, she/he must identify her/himself as a subject, as a being distinguishable from the mother. This takes place in the space of the symbolic order – the sphere of social and economic exchange, history, culture, language, signification, representation, and law – where the infant is freed from her/his total dependence upon the desire of the mother. 'Through the word – which is already a presence made of absence – absence itself comes to be named' (Lacan 2006, 228). This is Lacan's translation of the *fort-da* game Freud had described. The child had a wooden reel with a piece of string tied around it. He held the reel by the string and threw it over the edge of his curtained cot. When it disappeared, he uttered 'oooo' (*fort*, gone). Then he pulled the reel back and hailed the event with a joyful '*da*' (there). The reel is a metaphor for the mother and the game symbolizes the absence and presence of the mother. Now he has control over the absence of the mother (Freud 1920: 16). He masters the fact that he is not the only object of the desire of the mother, the phallus, but he is able to mobilize his desire as the subject's desire towards objects that are substitutes for the lost one (Dor 2004: 113). In other words, when the infant confronts the enigma of the desire of the mother, she/he 'tries to verbalize this desire and thus constitutes her/himself by identifying with the signifiers' in the field of the symbolic order (Verhaeghe 1998: 168).

To gain access to the symbolic circuit and networks and thus to become a desiring subject, the infant must undergo the symbolic castration of the imaginary phallus, that is, give up her/his identification with the imaginary phallus. She/he is not and cannot be the phallus, the thing that would fill the lack in the mother. She/he has to give up the idea of being the perfect object of the desire of the mother. Only in this way is the infant able to take her/his position in the symbolic order as a desiring and speaking subject.

The father plays a central role in this symbolic, subject-becoming process. If the mother lacks the phallus and I cannot be it for her, the infant considers, the father has it. The imaginary relationship established between the mother and the infant is interrupted by the father. The father is whatever separates the mother and the infant, the reason for the mother's absence and the possessor of the desired phallus. This father is not so much the actual father (even if he can incarnate it). Instead, it is to be understood as the symbolic father, who is the representative of the symbolic order beyond the imaginary relationship between the mother and the infant. Due to the intervention of this symbolic father, the imaginary identification is substituted by the symbolic identification. This intervening symbolic father, this symbolic function of paternity, is called the Name-of-the-Father, which can be compared to Freud's dead father.[2] In this initial act of symbolization and substitution, the symbolic father names the desire of the mother.

The sign consists of the signifier (words, cries, gestures, etc.) and the signified (ideas, concepts). For Lacan, the meaning of a signifier is not self-evident and unambiguous, since there is a resisting bar between the signifier and the signified. Isolated words do not immediately reveal their meaning. Actually, the true or ultimate meaning is deferred endlessly. Rather than referring to the signified, the signifier refers to other signifiers in the network of references. The meaning of a signifier is constituted due to its difference from other signifiers. Signification is a process that takes place in signifying chains. As an example, there are two identical doors at the back of a pub. On one door there is a word 'Ladies', on the other 'Gentlemen'. The only thing that discerns these doors is the difference between these two signifiers.

The desire of the mother is the signifier and the signified is the idea of phallus. What takes place in this symbolic function is a process of substitution in which the signifier of the Name-of-the-Father comes in place of the signifier of the desire of the mother. In this metaphoric substitution, the signifier of the desire of the mother, the phallic signifier, is pushed under the bar. It is repressed and becomes unconscious. The original signified – the idea of the phallus, the imaginary object that was presumed to satisfy the desire of the mother – becomes an impossible object. The phallic signifier or the signifier of the phallus then does not refer to any member or object. Its signified is lack and, thus, it is the signifier of lack, hole, and absence. The Name-of-the-Father, which is from now on associated to the phallus, metaphorically names the unconscious fundamental object of the desire of the infant (Dor 2004: 117). The Name-of-the-Father is the master signifier that structures the symbolic universe of the subject. Through it, 'the phallus is installed as the central organizing signifier of the unconscious' (Homer 2005: 56, see also 98–99). Castration is this symbolic process in and through which the infant enters the symbolic order, the arsenal of signifiers and the process of signification.

When the infant takes on a place in the symbolic order, it is positioned in language and social, cultural, political, and juridical discourses. The world of language substitutes for the world of images, immediate experiences, and imagined fullness. The subject identifies with signifiers that produce pleasure in the sphere of the Other, that is, the symbolic order. Thus, the subject is constituted within signification processes through symbolic materials, that is, signifiers. The subject is an effect of signifiers, that is, the subject of the signifier. Moreover, a signifier is that which represents the subject to another signifier. Thus, the subject of the signifier, that is, the subject who has accessed the sphere of language, is an alienated subject. The subject becomes alienated from 'being itself, the pure being, the real, the thing without a name', but only through this alienation in, through, and due to language we become human beings, that is, speaking and desiring beings: 'Man thus speaks, but it is because the symbol has made him man' (Lacan 2006: 229). Moreover, the alienation in language is primordial, since the symbolic sphere, the social structures, and language precede the birth of the infant:

> The alienated subject is a split or divided subject: on the one hand, the subject is separated from her/himself when the unconscious comes into being due to the primal repression, on the other hand, the subject disappears as she/he finds her/himself represented in the form of signifiers.
>
> *(Dor 2004: 119, 136)*

The initial act of submission launches the endless process of substitution of one signifier for another. At the same time this triggers desire that is then transferred from one signifier to another. Like the speaking and desiring subject, the desire of the subject is beguiled by language. The symbolic order is the sphere where the subject articulates her/his desire. It is the Other that consists of the desires of other subjects that flow into the subject through language and discourses. The desire of the subject is subjected to language, shaped by language. Desire becomes language and speech as it functions in the signifying chains of discourses. It emerges through the chain of signifiers, through language, through speech as it functions between signifiers. The chain of signifiers is not consistent since between signifiers there is always a gap or rupture. The metonymic movement of desire is endless because there is no signifier that would completely express and/or satisfy it. It is impossible to reach the original object of desire, the phallus, not merely because it is forever lost, but rather because the subject actually never was or possessed it.

The objects of desire are metonymic objects. Desire perpetually materializes in particular objects that present themselves as objects of desire and function as substitutes of the lost phallus. In this movement and investiture of desire in particular objects symbolized by signifiers, the desire never ceases to exist, since the subject never reaches the ultimate object that was lost. The desiring subject is barred from the lost object or the unattainable object of desire, what Lacan calls as the *objet petit a* ('a' is the first letter of the word *autre*, other). This object is no particular object but the object cause of desire, which sets in motion the movement of desire.

Therefore, there is fundamental lack not only in the subject (the loss of the phallus) but also in the symbolic order (on the one hand, there is no signifier that would fulfil the loss and, on the other hand, there is always a gap between signifiers).

Desire, symbolic order, language, and law are necessarily interconnected. The paternal metaphor (*le nom*, the name) that is also the law of the father (*le non*, the no) – which intervenes in the mother–infant dyad, negates the phantasm of the limitlessness and fullness of the infant, and marks the infant with this fundamental lack – regulates but does not prohibit desire. Instead, the law is the precondition of desire that infinitely moves from a signifier to signifier. 'The father, the Name-of-the-Father, sustains the structure of desire with the structure of the law,' Lacan (1998: 34) says, when he, in 1964, returns to *Hamlet*.

The desire of the mother

It is time for us to return to *Hamlet*. After the murder of his father and his mother's remarriage, Hamlet's position in the symbolic order as a desiring subject is thrown into crisis. The crucial point is Hamlet's encounter with the ghost, who reveals the crime committed. The tragedy, Lacan (2013: 405) says, 'begins with the denunciation of the crime' as it is revealed to 'the ear of the subject'.

Thus, as in the case of Oedipus, the prime mover is a crime. Oedipus, an innocent and unconscious figure, is able to commit patricide and incest for the very reason that he does not know what he does and who the criminal is. In contrast to Oedipus, Hamlet knows who is who. He even knows too much. The ghost of Hamlet's father knows that he is dead and how he died, killed by his brother Claudius. The ghost knows that Claudius has not only usurped his throne but also married his wife Gertrude. Thus, he knows that the royal bed of Denmark has become a couch for 'damned incest' (I.v.83), since the new king has taken his place as husband and Gertrude has devoted herself to Claudius. The ghost of Hamlet's father 'has arisen in order to reveal [all this] to the consciousness of the subject', that is, to Hamlet (Lacan 2013: 289). In 'their community of knowing', Hamlet knows both *what* the ghost knows and *that* the ghost knows these facts (Lacan 2013: 295).

Since Gertrude has substituted marriage with Claudius for mourning the death of Hamlet's father, she has betrayed the father, who was supposed to be the object of her desire. Even if the father was 'so loving to my mother' (I.ii.140), she has shown that her love was nothing but a delusion. Her tears are 'unrighteous' (I.ii.154), since her grief and mourning are belied by her demeanour. She might have even been involved in the murder of her husband.

Hamlet frantically and repeatedly wonders how she can desire the loathsome new king. In his first soliloquy Hamlet is less upset by the murder of the father than by his mother's corrupted desire, and her willingness in getting 'With such Dexterity to incestuous Sheets' (I.ii.138). For Hamlet, his mother's desire presents itself as a desire that does not choose between an eminent, idealized, and exalted object – his father – and a degraded, criminal, and adulterous object – Claudius.

Her desire has become 'an instinctual voracity', which does not differentiate objects of desire (Lacan 2013: 365). She has submitted to desire that emerges as excessive. In her sexuality, the desiring mother is for Hamlet enigmatic, excessive, rampant, intimidating, and pernicious. Hamlet pleads with his mother: 'You cannot call it love; for at your age' (III.iv.68).

Hamlet is grappling with this voracious desire that is not his desire for his mother, but rather his mother's desire. Hamlet is fixated by the dominating desire of his mother. Instead of being constituted in relation to the symbolic order as the Other, he considers his desire to be the desire of the mother. The mother as the Other does not leave any room for the true desire of the subject. Hamlet is dominated by the desire of the mother, or more precisely, he is trapped within the desire of the mother. The maternal flesh keeps deleting Hamlet's identity (Halpern 1997: 283–84). Hamlet is faced with the re-emergence of 'a polysemic, hetero-geneous, and fragmented realm of the (m)other' [which] is governed by the 'rhythms of the (m)other' (Polatinsky and Hook 2008: 369, 374).

Rotten father

Hamlet is unable to act since he has retreated from his desire and totally submitted to her mother's desire. As a consequence of this, he has lost the track of his desire and is thus unable to act. The problems surrounding Hamlet's relation to his desire determine his relation to the revenge for his father's murder that he feels obliged to seek. But why is he unable to step back from the overwhelming desire of his mother? The answer lies in the fact that there is something rotten not only in Denmark but also in the function of the paternal metaphor.

For Hamlet, the original signifier of his mother's desire, the phallus, is not fully repressed and it manages to return not as the symbolic phallus but as the imaginary phallus. There is a regression in Hamlet's shift from imaginary identification with the imaginary phallus to symbolic identification with the paternal metaphor. There is a failure in the process of substitution – the Name-of-the-Father comes in place of the desire of the mother – and so the intervention of the paternal metaphor fails and the law of the father is unsuccessfully promulgated. Since the fundamental signifier – the Name-of-the-Father – does not function properly, the signification process staggers. The true function of the symbolic father is to unite desire and law, but in the case of Hamlet this focal integration does not take place. Hamlet's participation in the social, cultural, and political chains of discourses is thwarted.

Therefore, the position Hamlet has assumed in the symbolic order as a desiring subject falters. His identity within this sphere of language, law, and culture is unstable, since the Name-of-the-Father does not situate Hamlet in the symbolic order. Instead of having the phallus symbolically – identifying with the Name-of-the-Father and taking his position as the legitimate heir of the late King Hamlet – he seeks the phallus in reality, that is, from the imaginary universe. Hamlet refuses to give up the imaginary phallus in his desperate search for the object presumed to satisfy the desire of the mother. Hamlet's desire is nothing but the desire of the mother as the Other. Instead of the metonymic process of desire, where desire moves endlessly from one signifier to another, the desire of the mother is not checked by the law and reigns in Hamlet's universe. For Lacan, van Haute (2007: 542) writes, Hamlet is a powerless plaything of the desire of the mother that does not leave any room for his desire. Thus, Hamlet is 'all along suspended within the time of the Other, and this until the very end' (Lacan 2013: 374). For example, Hamlet is unable to kill the praying Claudius because he does not consider this the proper time for revenge: he has to surprise Claudius at the moment of incestuous pleasure, that is, in the situation that is defined by his mother's desire. Only in this way, will Claudius 'suffer the eternal torture of the hell' (Lacan 2013: 294).

It would be tempting to argue that the paternal authority has fallen into crisis due to the murder of the father. However, the symbolic father is not the same as the actual father. The Name-of-the-Father can very well operate in the absence of the actual father; Freud's dead father already illustrated this. The symbolic father is a position in the symbolic order and the problem of Hamlet's relation to desire, identity, and revenge is related to this position.

There is one more thing that the ghost and Hamlet both know. They know that the father was suddenly snatched from the realm of the living: he was killed in his sleep. He could not defend himself and could not take revenge for the murder. The possibility of 'the just reward' is sealed off forever (Lacan 2013: 406). More-over, as the ghost says, he was cut off 'in the blossoms of my sin' (I.v.76). He is thus fixed forever at the moment of his sin for which he cannot atone: he had killed the King of Norway. For Hamlet, this is 'the most horrible, the most anguishing' implication of his father's revelation (Lacan 2013: 406).

But the sin of the father goes beyond the murder he had committed. The father has not paid, Lacan (2013: 293) says, for 'the crime of existing' [*le crime d'éxister*]. This means that all of us have to pay the debt that accrues from our inscription in the symbolic order as subjects of language, law, and desire, as the subject of the signifier. The debt that must be paid is the symbolic castration. The subject has to renounce the imaginary plenitude and the absolute fulfilment of enjoyment, abandon the idea of becoming the phallus incarnate and accept the fundamental lack of the phallus. The subject that has paid for the crime of existing as the speaking and desiring being is a split and alienated subject. For she/he, the thing must be lost in order to be represented.

Oedipus paid for the crime of existing by blinding himself, but Hamlet's father had not paid the debt as he was alive – and as a ghost, he is unable to pay it. In the eyes of Hamlet, his father was without flaws and a perfect husband who incarnated the object of the desire of the mother, that is, the phallus. And as an omnipotent king, he was a sovereign legislator, the origin of the law. For Hamlet, the father was an ideal father, too ideal. He had not paid the price; that is, he had not sub-mitted to the paternal metaphor and undergone the symbolic castration. Thus, he could not function as the representative of law, as the symbolic father. The ghost also commands Hamlet to remember him as an ideal father. Then again, as a ghost, the father is not sufficiently dead. He is too fleeting and illusionary to have paternal authority and he 'embodies an inefficacious version of the Law' (Polatinsky and Hook 2008: 368). The ghost is like the idea of the phallus: imaginary. He cannot, Lacan (1998: 35) says, provide Hamlet with the prohibitions of the law, which would allow his desire to survive: 'this too ideal father is constantly being doubted'. Hamlet ought to choose 'to be, or not to be' (III.i.56) the phallus. Not to be the phallus, the sole object, the desire of the mother, is the precondition of the possibility of having the phallus. Hamlet can neither pay the debt in his father's place nor leave it unpaid, although ultimately 'he must have it paid' (Lacan 2013: 294). Paying the price means that Hamlet must change over from the mode of being to the mode of having and, thus, realize his subjectivity.

Neither can Claudius function as the representative of the law. Hamlet shows nothing but contempt, rejection, and deprecation to him. However, this unconditional loathing that Hamlet casts on Claudius Lacan sees as denial, *Verneinung*. In other words, Hamlet idealizes him as he did his father, but this idealization is possible only in the form of negation. Claudius has taken the place of his idealized father as the incarnation of the object that satisfies the desire of the mother and as the sovereign legislator. The late King Hamlet did not and Claudius does not experience lack or shame. They are tyrants: absolute and shameless characters (cf. Critchley and Webster 2013: 229).

Hamlet's father was once the phallus incarnate. After he has become a transient ghost, which is nothing, the phallus remains. It is Claudius 'who is charged with incarnating it' (Lacan 2013: 416). Instead of the representative of the symbolic father – and whom the mother would legitimize in her discourse as the symbolic father – Hamlet confronts merely imaginary fathers presumed to satisfy the desire of the mother. Hamlet's world is dominated by, on the one hand, the circulation of the imaginary phallus, on the other hand, the absence of the paternal signifier, the Name-of-the-Father. In other words, Hamlet is preoccupied with this phallus that he imagines his mother has 'either in the form of Claudius or in the very flush of her sexual appetite' (Critchley and Webster 2013: 167). Hamlet attempts to be this imaginary object, the phallus, for his mother. Therefore, he drifts around the desire of the mother without establishing a more stable symbolic position.

Hamlet's inability to act is linked to the fact of the inadequacy of the signifier Name-of-the-Father. The position of the paternal authority in the symbolic order is defective. The paternal metaphor, which would instigate the law, functions inadequately. Because of this, Hamlet is not able to internalize and assimilate the paternal codification that would make his passage into the symbolic order and appropriation of a symbolic identity possible. He is confined to the imaginary universe and prevented from gaining an appropriate relationship with his desire. Hamlet has not managed to play the *fort-da* game. Instead of being a desiring *subject,* whose desire would be the desire towards objects, Hamlet is the *object* of desire.

To re-find his desire, to become a desiring subject, Hamlet must make a passage from the imaginary identification with the phallus to the symbolic identification with the Name-of-the-Father. The paternal metaphor must be constituted: the advent of Name-of-the-Father replacing the signifier of the desire of the mother brings forth Hamlet as speaking and desiring subject. Only if this symbolization process takes place, the Name-of-the-Father will become the signifier that represents Hamlet – the subject and not merely the object – in relation to other signifiers. This same process will then be repeated as signification chains constitute themselves (see Dor 2004: 139).

The precondition for this is that Hamlet pays the crime of existing, that he accepts the symbolic castration, the primary repression, and the fundamental lack in his being. He must renounce the possibility of being the phallus for the mother. Hamlet must mourn the loss of the phallus.

Mourning the phallus

The death of another person opens an absence, a hole in the world. Mourning rites are a means to stitch up this hole. A successful mourning process is accomplished through 'the totality of the signifier [...] at the level of the *logos*' (Lacan 2013: 398). In *Hamlet* these symbolic rites are either abbreviated or take place in secrecy. Polonius is buried swiftly without ceremony. Ophelia is buried more or less clandestinely in the Christian burial ground. The late King Hamlet is not properly mourned. He himself had no time to repent his crimes and appears as such 'before the final Judgement' (Lacan 2013: 403).

The death of his father and the marriage of his mother triggers Hamlet's melancholy. Moreover, the encounter with the ghost evokes for Hamlet the issue of paternity, but what Hamlet confronts in the symbolic order is a gap in the place of the Name-of-the-Father. Since the failure of the paternal metaphor, Hamlet has no signifying means to stitch up the hole the death of his father has opened. He is lost in melancholia and narcissistic self-reflectiveness. His 'libidinal investments have withdrawn from the world' and he is filled with a desire that is not his own (Shepherdson 2008: 85). He is subjected to the desire of the mother, which 'is not Hamlet's desire *for* his mother', but 'his fixation *within* his mother's desire' (Homer 2005: 78). Hamlet can only attempt to fill the hole with becoming the imaginary phallus instead of filling it symbolically with the mourning process.

Hamlet ought to mourn not merely the real father but, and more fundamentally, the loss of the ultimate object of desire, the phallus, which is the price for the existing as a speaking and desiring being. Such mourning is necessary for launching the chain of signifiers and the movement of desire in motion. Hamlet cannot act, because he is not able to desire. And he is not able to desire, because he has failed to mourn the lack of phallus, which is 'the originally mourned object whose loss is recalled in later experiences of mourning' (Muller 1980: 159).

A turning point in the tragedy is Ophelia's death or, more precisely, her funeral. Ophelia was once – 'I did love you once' (III.i.1259) – the object of Hamlet's desire. Ophelia, from the perspective of Hamlet, is not herself but merely a double of his mother. His scorn of his mother's excessive sexuality is displaced onto Ophelia. In this process of estrangement, Ophelia, 'the supreme object of exaltation' (Lacan 2013: 379), becomes 'for him completely dissolved as the object of love' (Lacan 2013: 380). Hamlet has 'an absolute horror of femininity' (Critchley and Webster 2013: 98) and Ophelia becomes the 'very symbol of the rejection of his desire' (Lacan 2013: 396).

At the graveyard scene Hamlet's position in relation to desire seems to be transformed. In his deep grief, Laertes leaps into the grave to embrace his sister. This is too much for Hamlet who secretly witnesses the funeral. He cries, 'What is he whose grief / Bears such an emphasis, whose phrase of sorrow / Conjures the wandering stars and makes them stand / Like wonder wounded hearers? This is I, / Hamlet the Dane' (V.i.248–54). Hamlet jumps into the grave to fight with Laertes.

Hamlet sees in Laertes a relation to Ophelia, the lost object. Now Hamlet manages to declare his love for Ophelia. The image of the grief-stricken other, Laertes, absorbs Hamlet. He identifies with Laertes, his double, his alter ego. Even though this rivalry identification is an 'imaginary absorption, formally articulated as a specular relationship' between Hamlet and Laertes (Lacan 2013: 390–91), it initiates a change in Hamlet's relationship to his desire. Hamlet's mourning is triggered by Laertes' expression of a passionate relationship of the subject to an object. Through identification with Laertes, Hamlet is able to find his own love, loss, and grief. Laertes 'traces out for him the path of a libidinal investment that he could not attain by himself' and this makes it possible for Hamlet to move from melancholic state to 'the act of mourning' (Shepherdson 2007: 62). Hamlet finds his grief and 'the very symbol of the rejection of his desire [...] regains all its value for him' as the object of his desire (Lacan 2013: 396).

What takes place is the reintegration of the object in the economy of Hamlet's desire – but the function of the object is only 're-conquered at the price of mourning and death' (Lacan 2013: 382). Ophelia becomes the object in Hamlet's desire only insofar she has become an impossible object. Mourning and the constitution of desire are interrelated. The mourning releases the blocked desire. No object is able to fully satisfy Hamlet's desire. This object of desire Lacan calls *objet petit a* (object little other). In his interpretation of *Hamlet*, Lacan widens the concept of *objet petit a* beyond the imaginary Other (Miller 2013).

On the one hand, the *objet petit a* does not represent any lost object that Hamlet could re-find. It is the hole and lack in the symbolic order that cannot be fulfilled. It stands for the lack itself. As such it is the object cause of desire around which desire is structured.

On the other hand, *objet petit a* is an object that momentarily comes to veil both the subject's fundamental lack and the void in the symbolic order, the gap in the signifying chain. This is what is called the formula of fantasy, $ <> a$, that is the barred subject's relationship to the *objet petit a*. At the graveyard scene, Hamlet's relationships to Laertes and Ophelia, these two objects, turn out to be 'two quintessential points of emergency of fantasy' by way of which 'desire implies a relation to the object' (Miller 2013). As said, Laertes is Hamlet's double and in this role he plays the role of *objet petit a*. Ophelia is *objet petit a* as the sublime object of Hamlet's desire. When Hamlet realizes that at the origin of his desire there is a necessary and inevitable radical loss, he is able to desire and love Ophelia, the impossible object.

Hamlet senses his own fundamental lack. He is able to mourn the phallus that no one is able to incarnate. The symbolic sacrifice of the fullness of being, the renouncement of the primordial object, and the reintegration of his desire become possible. Hamlet 'discovers for the first time his desire in its totality' (Lacan 2013: 318). He is now able to identify with the signifier 'Hamlet the Dane'. His desire in relation to lost Ophelia 'gives him back his name, Hamlet' (Critchley and Webster 2013: 137).

All this leads Hamlet 'to become the subject of his fate' (Fink 1996: 193). In the duel between Hamlet and Laertes, the phallus achieves its final embodiment as the poisoned foil. Laertes cuts Hamlet with the poisoned foil after which, in scuffling, the foil is switched from Laertes to Hamlet, who fatally wounds him back. It is in this 'encounter with the other that Hamlet will finally identify with the fatal signifier' given him by the other (Lacan 2013: 392). The signifier is fatal since word kills the thing in its immediate reality. At the same time, through this identification with this phallic signifier (and not with the idea of the phallus, the imaginary phallus), the process of signification and social differentiation are launched. And this makes it possible for Hamlet to identify with the Name-of-the-Father and assume his symbolic position in the domain of language, law, culture, and society as a subject.

Only after Gertrude, within whose desire Hamlet was fixed, has been killed by the poison and 'only when he is fatally wounded and knows it he can perform the act which gets Claudius' (Lacan 2013: 417), that is, stab Claudius with the poisoned foil and force him to drink the poisoned wine. And so, Hamlet can only strike when 'he has made the complete sacrifice [...] of all the narcissistic attachments' (Lacan 2013: 417).

Resistance and desire

However, does Hamlet manage to confront the hour of his truth? In the final act, Lacan (2013: 389) says, Hamlet is finally 'at the point of his resolution', but at this moment he hires himself out to another, to his enemy, to Claudius, for whom he pretends to fight. One could argue that Hamlet acts too late, that his time will never come, that the revenge is merely a revenge of his own death, that he performs the act only after Laertes has condemned Claudius and that, all things considered, he cannot act on his desire.

This conclusion is problematic if we see *Hamlet* providing a model for the psychoanalytic cure, which aims at a new subjective position in relation to one's being and desire (van Haute 2007: 557). Lacan's interpretation seems to assure that, once mortally wounded, Hamlet is able to separate from the desire of the mother, stop procrastination, act on his desire, and achieve his revenge. Thus, Hamlet's time has finally come as he gains a new subjective position in relation to his desire. Just before dying, Hamlet names the legitimate successor to the Danish crown: 'On Fortinbras. He has my dying voice' (V.ii.360). Hamlet has finally found his voice. That is, he has finally identified with the father – not the imaginary but the symbolic one, the king as the signifier of law and authority – and assumed his position as a speaking and desiring subject in the symbolic world. Only from that position he is able to name *his* successor.

Hamlet's narcissism inhibited both love and political action, but when he learns to mourn the phallus, he, step by step, finds his subjectivity and his desire and is finally able to act as a responsible subject. Lacan's interpretation of *Hamlet* is the interpretation of desire: Hamlet confronts his truth, that is, the truth of his desire. No more attempts he to fulfil the gap in the symbolic world or the lack in his being through identifying himself with absolutely sovereign figures presumed to be the phallus.

Perhaps Lacanian *Hamlet* is not merely a touchstone of psychoanalysis. Perhaps, it also indicates that desire – the paternal metaphor, law, signifier, lack, gap, and cut – is necessarily and intimately linked to the possibility of resisting politics based on the idea of absolute fullness of the people, community, or nation. The desiring subject that confronts its truth is a subject that stands her/his fundamental lack and nothingness, that does not seek totalitarian figures embodying the imaginary phallus (Lacan [2013: 416] draws a parallel between Claudius and Hitler).

The desiring subject is not totally subjected to either to totalitarian figures or the preformed norms. Desire is extravagant and 'elusive to anything that wants to master it' (Miller 2013). Only when Hamlet confronts his desire, his relationship to the truth of his being, he is able to act and resist.

Notes

1 Oedipus was a mythical Greek King of Thebes, who as an infant was left to die on a mountainside. He survived and was raised in the city of Corinth. Without recognizing them, Oedipus kills his biological father and marries his biological mother. When he learns that he has unwittingly committed patricide and incest, Oedipus punishes himself by blinding himself. Based on this legend, Freud introduces the concept of the Oedipus complex. The child develops a libidinal object-cathexis for his mother, that is, the child directs his sexual desire to his mother. The father is an obstacle to his desire. Thus, the child wishes to get rid of him and take his place with the mother. When this complex is successfully resolved, the child's desire for his mother is repressed and he learns to identify with his father, the rival. The child internalizes the parental function which manifests itself in conscience and guilt. The superego is formed.

2 In *Totem and Taboo* (1913) Freud tells the myth of the primal horde. In this horde, the tyrannical father kept all the females for himself and banished his sons when they grew up. One day his sons formed a coalition to kill and devour him. In this act of devouring, the sons identified with the father. After this, the sons felt remorse and guilt. The dead father became stronger than the living father had been. Two fundamental taboos were created out of the sons' sense of guilt. The laws of prohibition of incest and patricide are fundamental to civilization, culture, morality, and legal order. Thus, we can conceive 'the order of law only on the basis of something more primordial, which presents itself as a crime' (Lacan 2013: 404).

Bibliography

Critchley, Simon and Webster, Jamieson (2013) *Stay, Illusion!: The Hamlet Doctrine.* New York: Random House.

Dor, Joël (2004) *Introduction to the Reading of Lacan. The Unconscious Structured Like a Language*, trans. Susan Fairfield. New York: Other Press.

Fink, Bruce (1996) 'Reading Hamlet with Lacan', in *Lacan, Politics, Aesthetics*, ed. Willy Apollon and Richard Feldstein. Albany, NY: State University of New York Press.

Freud, Sigmund (1920) *Beyond the Pleasure Principle*. The Standard Edition, Vol. XVIII, trans. James Strachey. London: The Hogart Press.

Freud, Sigmund (1958) *The Interpretation of Dreams*. The Standard Edition, Vol. IV, trans. James Strachey. London: The Hogart Press.

Freud, Sigmund (1985) 'Letter to Fliess, 15 October 1897', *The Complete Letters of Sigmund Freud to Wilhelm Fliess, 1887–1904*, trans. Jeffrey Moussaieff Masson. Cambridge, MA: Harvard University Press.

Halpern, Richard (1997) *Shakespeare among the Moderns*. Ithaca, NY: Cornell University Press.

Homer, Sean (2005) *Jacques Lacan*. Abingdon and New York: Routledge.

Jones, Ernst (1976) *Hamlet and Oedipus. A Classical Study in Psychoanalytical Criticism*. New York and London: W. W. Norton and Company.

Lacan, Jacques (1992) *Seminar VII, The Ethics of Psychoanalysis, 1959–1960*, trans. Dennis Porter. London: Routledge.

Lacan, Jacques (1998) *Seminar XI, The Four Fundamental Concepts of Psychoanalysis, 1964*, trans. Alan Sheridan. New York: W. W. Norton and Company.

Lacan, Jacques (2006) 'The Function and Field of Speech and Language in Psychoanalysis', in *Écrits*, trans. Bruce Fink. New York: W. W. Norton and Company.

Lacan, Jacques (2013) *Le Séminaire VI, Le désir et son interprétation, 1958–1959*. Paris: Seuil.

Miller, Jacques-Alain (2013) *Presentation of Book VI of the Seminar of Jacques Lacan*, trans. A. R. Price. Available online at: www.latigolacaniano.com/assets/2-ingles-pdf-miller-presentation-of-book-vi.pdf (accessed 1 October 2014).

Muller, John P. (1980) 'Psychosis and Mourning in Lacan's Hamlet', *New Literary History*, 12(1): 147–165.

Polatinsky, Stefan and Hook, Derek (2008) 'On the Ghostly Father: Lacan on Hamlet', *Psychoanalytic Review*, 95(3): 359–385.

Shakespeare, William (2003) *Hamlet*. London: Thomson.

Shepherdson, Charles (2007) 'Emotion, Affect, Drive: For Teresa Brennan', in *Living Attention: On Teresa Brennan*, ed. Alice A. Jardine, Shannon Lundeen and Kelly Olivers. Albany, NY: State University of New York Press.

Shepherdson, Charles (2008) *Lacan and the Limits of Language*. New York: Fordham University Press.

Van Haute, Philippe (2007) 'Lacan leest Hamlet: Tussen fenomenologie en psychoanalyse?', *Tijdschrift voor Filosofie*, 69(3): 535–558.

Van Haute, Philippe and Geyskens, Thomas (2012) *A Non-Oedipal Psychoanalysis? A Clinical Anthropology of Hysteria in the Works of Freud and Lacan*. Leuven: Leuven University Press.

Verhaeghe, Paul (1998) 'Causation and Destitution of a Pre-ontological Non-entity: On the Lacanian Subject', in *Key Concepts of Lacanian Psychoanalysis*, Danny Nobus. London: Rebus Press.

14

KANT AVEC SADE

Ethics entrapped in perversions of law and politics

Andreja Zevnik

UNIVERSITY OF MANCHESTER

Everyday antagonisms experienced by an individual, an institution, and society, or even by state structures can most often be reduced to the relationship between ethics and politics. This is a relationship that is explosive, contingent, dangerous, but also one which, to follow a liberal strand, can lead and facilitate a harmonious, prosperous, and peaceful society. In practice, politics or political struggles, as it is commonly thought, strive towards the greatest good for the greatest number of people living in a community. In order to achieve such 'greatest good', politics mobilizes various means – its material and symbolic capital – while aiming to maintain an ethical face. These 'universal ethical standards' are also a backbone of the existing legal principles and notions of right and wrong, while their perceived universality is consensual and societal. However, the universality of shared ethical norms and moral standards is such only for as long as it exists on the level of the form. That is, at the level of the discourse it is possible to address, engage, and even solve injustices, inequalities, or disagreements. Yet, the problem facing the political is that life in a community is not lived on the level of the discursive form.

To take this somewhat abstract discussion into the realm of human rights, as a discourse, human rights can easily be justified and the rationale for their universality and contribution to common good can be made without too much effort. However, their universal language is rarely translated into politics in an effective manner. Human rights discourse comes to effect as a legal provision when it is mobilized to address a particular grievance, abuse, or injustice. Yet, at these moments it often transpires that as a discourse or a legal provision human rights are unfit to address the situation. They either fall short in acknowledging – in its often legal language – the actual grievance of the suffering subject or they only retroactively recognize a situation as a situation of peril. If human rights are mobilized only after a grievance has been identified, or after a particular injustice took place, then what does this tell us about the way in which society addresses grievances and injustices, and most importantly, what it says about the working of ethics in a community?

218 Andreja Zevnik

It is possible to say that such a disjunction between the universal normative ideal and its actualization is inherent to a philosophical and metaphysical problem concerning the relationship between the universal and the particular; or perhaps even between the actual and ideational. Ethics and universal norms such as human rights make sense at the level of the form (as an ideational structure), yet when uttered – when they become the subject of utterance – they crumble. This can suggest that universal discursive formation cannot be put in words and as such account for the situation of individual peril. Or as Šumič-Riha (1995: 60) argues: 'this injustice about which one cannot say much is a place where ethics is articulated as speech'.

Paradoxically, politics (and its political subjects) is constituted on the assumption that the gap between the universal rights and their representation of the subject can be overcome. In fact, it is politics with its means, practices, institutions, which must be able to abrogate and repay the suffering. The illusion that one day all suffering and injustice will be overcome appears as a driving force of the modern political and social. The constitutive antagonism of politics mentioned earlier then rests precisely on the realization, as Šumič-Riha (1995: 66) argues: 'that every attempt to absolve the society from injustice leads into abyss, not only because every solution is temporary, but mostly because every attempt to overcome this antagonism overlooks the lack of foundations constituting the social'. In other words, ethical norms and legal rules create an illusion that politics with its means can overcome injustice in a society; but actually believing that political means will bring to life a perfect society rests on the assumption that this society was once just and equal or that shared moral principles are anchored in some material or mythical source which will reveal itself once the time is right. A religious undertone of this assumption is no coincidence.

Thus, how did ethical politics become trapped in-between the universal or ideational level and its actualizations on the level of the particular? What shape or form does the subject of ethics take? These are the two central questions that this contribution aims to address. The paper opens by introducing a political deadlock in which ethics has found itself and highlights some particularities of psychoanalytic critiques of ethics. In doing so two key issues are identified: one is that what counts as ethics in modern society depends on the idea of good, and the other is that ethics moulds the good on the image of the subject who is making a decision. In turn this leads to the conclusion that ethical and moral acts are always guided by the idea of good as 'I' the subject of action consider it. As any word, ethics too has two sides, one concerns the language of morals (Kant's categorical imperative) and the other the language of law. This contribution proceeds by looking at how according to psychoanalysis, law constructs its subject, before moving onto discussing the limits of ethics (or *Kant avec Sade*), and concluding by alluding to whom is the subject of ethics.

The (dis)illusions of ethics

From this introductory discussion one can extrapolate that the discourse of morality and ethics relies on illusions: that is the illusion of objective good actually existing and the illusion of it being a factor leading to a better more ethical life. If a subject acts as a moral subject towards its 'neighbour', that is a person who is at the receiving end of 'ethical actions', a life of a community can be considered as better and more ethical. As Alenka Zupančič points out in her piece 'The Subject of the Law', the psychoanalytic intervention into the realm of ethics addresses this illusion of good as a factor of a better life.[1] Psychoanalysis, so Zupančič argues (1998) speaks of two disillusionments: the first is Freud's and the second Lacan's. However, the Lacanian one is of greater importance, as it reveals the truth about the Freud's critique, as well as of Kant's theory of ethics.[2] Thus in terms of psychoanalysis we can speak of first a Freudian and then a Lacanian blow. The Freudian blow is directed at Kant and targets the idea that moral imperative is freed of pathological origins. Zupančič (1998: 41) summarizes Freud's objection in the following way:

> What philosophy calls the moral law and, more precisely, what Kant calls the categorical imperative is in fact nothing other but the superego. [...] This judgement provokes an 'effect of disenchantment' that calls into doubt any endeavour to base ethics on foundations other than 'pathological'. [...] ethics is thus nothing more than a convenient tool for any ideology that tries to pass off its own commandments as authentic, spontaneous and honourable inclinations of the subject.

The second Lacanian blow is aimed first at Freud and secondly at Kant. Lacan in his critique does not challenge Freud's ideological or superegoical interpretations of ethics but focuses on what Freud (and Kant) considered as the cornerstone of ethical attitude.[3] 'Thy shall love your neighbour as thyself' is commonly considered an ethical axiom par excellence. Yet Lacan is of a different opinion and sets out to critique it. First, Lacan in *The Ethics of Psychoanalysis* sees the above statement as a representation of traditional ethics, which is in 'service of good' and the sharing of good, but points out that the act of 'sharing' is different from ethics. The sharing of good comes 'naturally' or rather 'it is in the nature of the good to be altruistic', as he states (Lacan 1992: 186). And further, the good that is shared or acknowledged as an asset of a good life in a community is of a particular kind. It is, as Lacan (1992: 187) continues: 'the good of others provided that it remains in the image of my own'. Thus the above statement paints a very closed picture of an ethical community. Love that is one to share with the neighbours is a type of love *one* considers as good, which in turn creates an 'ethical act' in an image of one's good. Such a community is altruistic rather than ethical, and the good guiding it is not universal but that which the subject considers it *as such*. In turn it means that the other is a recipient of one's good only for as long as it ascribes to the same value of good.

Lacan thus highlighted that traditional ethics operates with highly individualized accounts of good. This realization bears great political significance. If good is always made in the image of the subject recognizing it then the good that is shared is likewise a reflection of the subject's desires. Or to put it differently, the neighbour receives what the subject recognizes as in need. This point is very straightforward and easily translated in modern political discourse: think of human rights discourse in relation to postcolonial, 'third-world', or feminist struggles. The observations of the Western subjects (or international organizations) concerning the struggles for emancipation or human rights breaches taking place in so-called 'underdeveloped' countries follow that logic. We 'judge' others' situation according to our expectations and knowledge. What it means to live a humane life and whether others live life worthy of a human being, whether others' rights are violated, are all questions judged on our image of humanity, good life, or rights. This game between the desire and the image in which we judge what surrounds us is at the heart of the liberal conception of rights, duties, and morality. However, this play of desire reveals something else. Lacan said that one's desire is always the desire of the Other (Lacan 1998). Thus the moment of tension occurs when the two desires are met in contradiction. That is when the Other does not correspond with the image we have of it. Who then is the Other we can tolerate? Zupančič (1998) gives a modern example of the aforementioned moral imperative. Instead of asking to love your neighbour as yourself, the modern imperative, she states, calls for the recognition of the Other. No longer is there the need to 'love your neighbour as yourself', the modern age mantra is that the Other has the right to be different. 'Admittedly', as Zupančič (1998: 43) writes:

> [T]his commandment does not require that we love this other, it is enough that we tolerate him/her. [... But] what happens if this other is really the Other, if his/her difference is not only 'cultural', 'folkloric' but a fundamental difference. Are we still to respect him/her, to love him/her?

The answer to this question is rather obvious. The Other whom we should love and respect is the Other we are comfortable with, one, who is not too different and we can respect. The Other earns our respect, as Alain Badiou (2001: 24) writes, only when and if he is respecting the differences. 'Just as there can be no freedom for the enemies of freedom, so there can be no respect for those whose difference consists precisely in not respecting differences' (ibid.). This encounter with radical difference – or intolerance – is precisely the point at which ethics should be thought. That is, unlike the liberal discourse of ethics, which would have stopped when met with the impasse of intolerance, the psychoanalytic ethics advocated by Lacan begins precisely at the moment of intolerance or radical difference. Lacan would see this encounter as an encounter concerning our *jouissance*. By definition *jouissance* is in itself strange, other, and dissimilar; thus it is not the Other who makes it disruptive. But, as Zupančič (1998: 43–44) puts it: 'it is not simply the *jouissance* of the neighbour [...] that is strange to me. The kernel of the problem is that I experience my own *jouissance* as strange, dissimilar, other and hostile'. In other words, it is my experience of something within me that I find hostile and that in turn I externalize and recognize it in the image of the Other (my neighbour). Hence psychoanalysis intervenes in the field of politics and ethics at the level of *jouissance* or the level which was more traditionally ascribed to evil.

The psychoanalytic accounts thus consider ethical that which addresses the subject's repressed material, and deals with moments in which it comes to the surface.

The political and social domains grapple with the evil inside every subject mostly in two ways: they attempt to manage it through the institution of law and through the structures of ethics or moral imperatives. However, the deadlock they often encounter is how to strike a balance between pure legality (that is actions which follow the law) and a blind following of the moral imperative (or that which the subject considers to be good). If the subject blindly follows either of the two to the very end, his actions, as psychoanalysis reveals, end up being perverse rather than ethical. Slavoj Žižek gives a good example of the rule-following blindness. He writes: 'Sorry, I know it was unpleasant, but I couldn't help it, the moral law imposed that act on me as my unconditional duty!' (Žižek 1996: 170). Actions that exercise no moral judgement are no ethical acts, but acts of perversion, for they pass on the responsibility for the actions taken onto some external non-existing 'third party' which cannot be held accountable. 'The type of discourse where I use my duty as an excuse for my actions is perverse in the strictest sense of the word' as Zupančič (1998: 49) argues, 'as [this is a] case [where] the subject hides behind the law'. The ethical subject is thus someone who does not hide behind the 'duty' but takes agency and responsibility for the actions. I will revisit the issue of perversion and responsibility later on.

The split that the example of perversion introduced is one concerning the institution of a moral subject. The subject of ethics and the subject of law are thus two different yet interrelated structures; one could say that they are two embodiments of the universal form, which grapple with the duty to act ethically yet struggle with the responsibility their actions introduce. While different, both subjects are constituted on the premise of how they relate to *jouissance* and desire. For a firmer understanding of what is at stake when speaking about the subject of law and of the subject of ethics, I turn to law to explain how the subject of law comes to being and then return to ethics and consider what the subject of ethics, who is caught between the moral imperative and the limits of law, can stand for.

Psychoanalytic law and its subject

Alain Supiot (2007) points to three major elements which shape the character of legal authority in Western law: first, the existing idea of law as enigma with dogmatic or mythical origins is a typically Western idea; second, the notion that the human body is the site on which the law should be inscribed was one of the breaking points between the Jewish and the Christian tradition; and third, the Western mind has always been fascinated by the thought that the literal incarnation of the law could lead to a form of revelation (Supiot 2002: 107–24). In other words, invoking the mytho-Christian origins of Western law, it has always been hoped that law will reveal itself in something more than just a pure letter of law. The same illusion persists in ethics whereby there is hope good or ethical acts will once materialize. Such structure of ethics and law implies a mythical rather than an absent foundation. There is something external to the system which gives it legitimacy, yet it also disturbs the system from within and calls for its constant re-adjustments. The force that transcends the boundaries between the exterior and the interior is the superego. On the one hand, prohibition and a threat of punishment, on the other, the promise of gratification when overstepping the rules, and in the middle, the superego pulling the subject both ways.

Lacan, in his first seminar on Freud's technique, explains the *superego* as both:

> the law and its destruction. As such, it is the speech [word] itself, the commandment of law, insofar as nothing more but its root remains. The law is entirely reduced to something which cannot even be expressed, like the *You must*, which is speech [a word] deprived of all meaning.
>
> *(Lacan 1991: 102)*

Superego is a double-layered function of law. It shouts void commands that must be obeyed while upholding the reverse or the hidden side of law (that is the prohibition the subject internalizes). The perversion of law is complete only in the face of the superego. As the unwritten law of the society, as Žižek (2002: 30) sees it, it is in a direct opposition to the positive law. It represents the exceptional and the traumatic whereas the positive law calls for unity. However, the identification with law and universalization of legal principles, both cornerstones of the social bond between individuals living in a community, relies on a presumption that the 'law of the *superego*' exists. To put it differently, the universal ideas of rights or common good are only upheld if underpinned by the superego. Žižek (1995) explains this further with a reference to Reiner's movie *A Few Good Men*. In the movie – a court martial drama – the defence tries to dispute murder charges by claiming that the defendant was just following the 'Code Red' orders that authorize a clandestine night-time beating of any soldier whose actions are not in line with the United States Marine's ethical code. As Žižek (1995: 925) argues, the double function of 'Code Red' is extremely interesting for it condones the act of transgression yet reaffirms the cohesion of the group; it represents the community spirit, yet violates the rules of community life. On the one hand, law demands obedience, on the other hand, there is an equally strong demand to break and transgress it. With an act of transgression those who break the law do not shatter but reaffirm the identity and the unity of their distinct community. Because of the double side of law and its perverse demand to break it, the accused marines when faced with charges did not know what they did wrong, to their mind, they were simply following the orders.

The seduction of superego and transgression, however, is rooted in the constitution of the subject as a social being. Jacques Lacan in his *Seminar XX* addresses the subject of law in a provocative yet very incisive way. He writes: 'I won't leave this bed today, and I will remind the jurist that law basically talks about what I am going to talk to you about – *jouissance*' (Lacan 1999: 2–3). It might seem trivial, yet this statement is paramount to understanding psychoanalytic law. It points to an intrinsic relationship between law, desire, and the superego as an imperative to obey or enjoy. In contrast to Freud who considered law as an institution, which represses the subject's desires, Lacan's take is somewhat different. For Lacan (2006b), desire is the reverse side of law. That is, desire is a product of prohibition; that which is prohibited frames and sets limits to desire. In contrast to Freud, Lacan's law does not repress or prohibit pleasure, but produces it as 'repressed'. Thus law is grounded in prohibition rather than the other way around. Lacan (2006c: 696) writes: 'But it is not the Law itself that bars the subject's access to *jouissance* – rather it creates out of an almost natural barrier a barred subject'. The prohibition moulds the subject of law in the image of that which is prohibited. The barrier the subject experiences at the entry into the society are one of desire (what to desire?) translated into the prohibition in the form of law. But for a desiring subject, its object of desire transgresses the limits of law, and it is precisely the transgression of these limits that the subject finds enjoyable. The urge or the seduction of transgression derives from the other side of law – from the imperative to enjoy or obey – from the superego. 'Enjoyment is never a spontaneous transgression of the Law' but, as Saul Newman (2001: 144) writes: 'rather an injunction of the Law – an injunction to "Enjoy!"'. Thus the law is not devoid of *jouissance* but grounded in it; and the prohibition is an appearance – a mask – through which law strives for its legitimacy. The desiring subject is faced with the law and prohibition but for the superegoical imperative, it is driven into transgression. Whatever the subject does, it needs to mercilessly enjoy or obey. This final move into transgression is a moment when law reveals itself as perverse.[4]

The law relates to its subjects by means of *jouissance*; and it does so in two distinct ways. First, law limits desire or 'socializes desire' in ways which correspond to the limits of social norms within a particular community. That is it makes possible the subject's second birth into the institution of law. Second, law makes a 'mark' on the body at the moment of its entry into society; that mark binds the body to a particular understanding of legal norms and rituals and to distinct ways of enjoyment. In such a way, law intervenes twice. First, it determines the character and the limits of one's existence, and second, it marks the body as a sign of possession, almost like saying 'this body now belongs to me, and the body has to obey the rules I set'. To slightly paraphrase Pierre Legendre (1995, 1997), individual is born twice, first in nature as a human being, and second in the structures of society as a political subject with duties and rights. The difference between the two forms is vast: while in the first we can speak of a pathological, 'bestial', pre-political being who follows its natural instincts and craves immediate satisfaction of desires, the second form is a socialized subject with a mandate and knowledge of what, how, and when to desire. In a very plain language, one could say that the process of socialization into a community is to insure that the subjects relate to their repressed material and *jouissance* in the same way. The implications for ethics are that those living in a community experience the same discomfort when encountering *jouissance*. But equally it is *jouissance* which frames how subjects relate to legal authority.

The marking of the body is not particular to law; language, as Lacan (2006a: 197–268) reminds us, signifies its subjects in a similar way. Language makes a mark on the body by introducing and imposing linguistic structures onto it. These structures determine what can and what cannot be expressed, they form particular representations and expressions. Both language and law then make a mark on the body and determine its social context, e.g. acceptable ways of behaviour, conduct, and enjoyment into which a particular body belongs. Law and language determine a way in which the subject – as a particular form of existence characteristic to a particular structure of order – sees the social, and equally ways in which it relates to the social. In other words, law and language capture, almost imprison, being into a form of existence common to particular social norms and moral and ethical standards, making a subject a product of a particular expression of being.

The image of the subject of law that emerges through this psychoanalytic reading is one whose place in a society is guaranteed through the intervention of law onto the level of its *jouissance*. That is, *jouissance*, which is the most foreign element in the subject (that which the subject is not quite in control of), ties the subject to law, yet equally, it is that which transgresses the law and the subject. The play between the system of law on the one side and its transgression on the other side is what marks the subject. Within the system of law, the subject emerges as a rational being who is endowed with rights and duties and is taught how to behave, but on another level, the *jouissance* (or the superego) suggests that this is just a mask and that there is something more the subject law cannot know much about. Ethics works in a similar way. It uses law and legal provisions to deter the subject from doing wrong while presuming that the rule of law is always congruent with ethical demands. Yet, there are always situations which push subjects to make ethical choices and in doing so, break the law. What psychoanalysis is getting at here is a particular disjunction that can be illustrated well with the experience of Antigone. Trapped between the 'earthly laws' and 'godly laws' she chose to go against the earthly laws and bury her brother. She chose to follow her duty, but for breaking the law she, despite doing an ethical act par excellence, had to be punished. A true ethical dilemma, one which psychoanalysis aims to address, is then one which juxtaposes the ethical demands on the one end and the letter of the law on the other end; or one, which sees a disjunction between the duty and the good of the Other and where my duty can only be accomplished to the detriment of my 'fellowmen' or neighbour. Lacan explicitly addresses this disjunction in his critique of Kant.

Kant avec Sade: or who is the subject of ethics

Kant's *Critique of Practical Reason*, as Lacan states in his *Kant avec Sade* essay where he takes up the limits of ethics, is central for understanding the modern idea of ethics and moral law. With a move away from explicitly mythic or religious sources, Kant opened a new space in which the subject's own agency for action can be rethought. Lacan does not disagree with these advancements but offers a psychoanalytic critique of Kant's ethical position and introduces the so-called second moment of psychoanalytic dis-illusionment.

Kant places good in an intrinsic relationship with the law. While there is no substance or an object which could claim an instant and constant relationship to (feeling) good, Kant places good as the object of moral law (Lacan 2006b: 646). A Lacanian analysis of this statement uncovers a preposition already voiced by Freud (1990): that is, the subject is driven by a principle of pleasure and its actions pursue this principle mercilessly. For Kant (1993), however, such a merciless pursuit of pleasure was unforeseen; for as long as there is no intrinsic relation between the phenomenon and pleasure, as Kant explains, the drive for pleasure cannot become the object of the subject's will or the impetus for its actions. Instead of pleasure Kant speaks of good. 'Experience tells us that we make ourselves hear commandments inside of ourselves', as Lacan (2006b: 646) writes, 'the imperative nature of which is presented as categorical, in other words, unconditional'. Moreover the subject is able to suspend its pathological drives, suffering, or pleasure-seeking activities, and replace them with the masquerade of reason. With this suspension of pleasure, Kant set a formalized ground upon which modern ethical principles can be built. Regardless of their effect, the ultimate ethical good is one which, in a pursuit of truth, sacrifices everything. Coming in forms of law and moral imperatives, the good life begins to dictate the ethical decisions as well as expectations of the modern political man. It is no longer a reward or an experience of pleasure that drives the person to act, but a service to moral duty – or law – that completes the subject (or where the subject receives recognition of his social mandate). A move away from the pursuit of pleasure to the pursuit of moral good as an imperative translated to the subject in the form of law was deemed necessary to defend the public from the immorality of excessive pleasure and to institute a community of working, free, and equal individuals. However, Lacan, in his text *Kant avec Sade*, questions the effectiveness of swapping pleasure for law when in search for ethics.

Once the subject is met with a situation requiring a decision, which side is she/he to follow? What is at stake here is a struggle between two moral positions or two questions. Here lies a dilemma, as Lacan (1992: 189) writes, of:

> [M]ust I go toward my duty of truth insofar as it preserves the authentic place of my *jouissance*, even if it is empty? Or must I resign myself to this lie which, by making me substitute forcefully the good for the principle of my *jouissance*, commands me to blow alternatively hot and cold?

That is to sign up to someone's notion of good, but who's good it is? These two moral positions signify the case of duty on one end and the good of the neighbour on the other end. Kant and modern ethics would opt to follow one's duty (and hence the 'communal' or societal good); that is a duty to tell the truth regardless of the consequences the action might have on the neighbour. The decision to do so – if Kant's moral imperative is understood as a case of law – is somewhat common-sensical, but what happens if the obligation to follow one's duty is taken to the extreme? That is, if truth needs to be told no matter of its consequences for the subject or its neighbour? Can the subject see the pain its actions caused? This is a moment which Kant does not see as being part of ethical decision. Following one's duty to tell the truth cannot excuse the subject from doing harm. Yet, commonly it is precisely the 'deferral of responsibility' that the duty (or the law) to tell the truth institutes.

Traditional ethics aims to anticipate situations and align ethical principles with the expected responses, whereas psychoanalytic does the opposite. It hangs on to responsibility for the actions and in there seeks ethics. The rationale for such action is straightforward: for example, in a framework of politics it is precisely a deferral of responsibility that suspends the subject's own judgement and opens a space for atrocities. There are numerous political cases where responsibility has been deferred to some higher ethical instance: just think of the Holocaust, genocide, or killings of civilians in war. In these cases responsibility can often be traced to some external non-existent third person. George Bush Jr. and Tony Blair, for example, both at least implicitly invoked God in justification for the 2003 intervention in Iraq. Or similarly there are many cases of guards in Guantanamo Bay or other secret detention centres who abused the detainees, or of psychologists who helped to 'perfect' techniques of 'torture' or 'interrogation' who in hindsight cannot understand what wrong they did; nevertheless they only helped to secure the homeland. Aren't these clear cases of responsibility being deferred onto some third non-existing person? The Kantian duty thus allows the person to hide behind the law and avoid an encounter with an ethical demand.

Zupančič in her discussion of Kant and Sade highlights the key problem of ethics grounded in the moral imperative and the duty to follow it. The subject that emerges out of Kant's moral action is not an ethical but a perverse subject, as she writes. That is: 'the subject can justify his actions by saying that they were imposed upon him by unconditional duty, to hide behind the law, and present itself as a "mere instrument" of its will' (Zupančič 1998: 50–51). Just like the interrogators in the case of Guantanamo detention centre or in Pier Paolo Pasolini's *Salò* movie, these individuals, if we follow Kant, did nothing wrong; they only followed the duty that was imposed on them. At the moment when they are seen as nothing more but mere instruments in the hands of some higher good the other – superegoical – side of law is revealed. What Kant fails to recognize is the reverse side of the right to good. Sade unmasked the Kantian legal reason by recognizing the right to pleasure as the logical extension of the basic rights of man. As Lacan in his discussion of Kant and Sade states: 'I have the right to enjoy your body, anyone can say to me, and I will exercise this right without any limit to the capriciousness of the exactions I may wish to satiate with your body' (Lacan 2006b: 648). If pleasure is taken to the extreme, perversion reveals itself as the other side of law. That is precisely as a side which is governed by desire and superegoic imperative. In seeing oneself as a tool in the hand of the Other, the pleasure of the law becomes the law of the pleasure, whose limits overlap with those of the imperative to enjoy.

But if these are examples that somewhat border on the extreme or the obscene, actions whereby the subject of ethics appears as a subject of perversion can come from the everyday (as perversion of ethical position requires no real obscenities). Kant himself states it clearly when he says: 'the subject who tells the murdered the truth is not responsible for the consequences of this action; whereas the subject who tells a lie is fully responsible for the outcome of the situation' (Kant in: Zupančič 1998: 51). The statement points to the lack of freedom and responsibility of a Kantian moral subject. If the subject is to follow what has been predestined as good he will not be held responsible, yet if he is to do otherwise, he can be held accountable. Zupančič sees this Kantian position as a position of a pervert par excellence. That is, a pervert 'who hides the enjoyment that he finds in the betrayal behind the Law' (Zupančič 1998: 51).

The above of course is not meant to imply that every following of duty ends in perversion. The ethical commands can order the subject to tell the truth or give information, but the problem in Kant lies in the waving of the responsibility that comes with doing good. Thus good needs to be abandoned when assessing ethical acts. Instead, as Zupančič (1998: 51) recognizes, ethics needs to be linked with the place of the subject and its role in the constitution of an ethical act. On the level of ethics, the subject needs to hold on to responsibility if his action is to be perceived as ethical; and on a metaphysical level, an ethical act needs to incorporate the subject. That is, the subject has to remain integral to ethical action. To look at Kant again, his proposal to wave off the responsibility for the subject's good actions degrades the subject to the level of a mere object. To put it differently, ethics requires the subject to maintain its enunciating power. In the words of Lacan (2006b: 650):

> Bipolarity upon which the moral law is founded is nothing but the split [refente] in the subject brought about by any and every intervention of the signifier: the split between the enunciating subject [sujet de l'énonciation] and the subject of the enunciated [sujet de l'énoncé].[5]

That is a split between the universal ideal to which ethics is inscribed and its realization as a missed encounter in the realm of the particular.

If ethics emerges at the end of an act, after its consequences are determined and responsibility for actions taken, rather than at the very beginning, when the subject ponders on whether to follow good, then what is the image of ethics we speak about, and in what image does the subject of ethics present itself? Zupančič offers a very succinct explanation of the subject we are dealing with. She writes (Zupančič 1998: 52):

> The ethical subject is not an agent of the universal [...] but its *agens*. That does not mean that the universal is always 'subjectively mediated' [...] it does not point towards a certain definition of the universal, but rather toward a defini- tion of the subject: it means that the subject is nothing other but this moment of universalization, of the constitution or determination of the law. The ethical subject is not a subject who brings into a given (moral) situation all the sub- jective baggage and affects with it, but a subject who is strictly speaking born from this situation.

The statement highlights two crucial aspects of ethics and its subject. The subject of ethics is instituted only at the end of the act. Which means that there is a difference between the subject who entered an act of ethical concern and the subject who emerged from this act. Regardless of what subject entered the act, the subject of ethics can only be that which comes out at the other end. For having an experience of 'ethical decision', the subject can be considered as the subject of ethics; but under what conditions can this subject be called ethical? Lacan pointed out that good cannot be a category deciding upon the ethicality of actions, and neither can it be the image of the Other or law. Instead, ethics always relies on responsibility: on whether responsibility for decisions and its consequences has been taken. What such an account reveals is that the subject does not have to do only 'good' to be ethical. In fact – and to counter Kant's statement where he waves the responsibility for the consequences the subject's actions were to cause if the subject was to follow good – its decisions can still do harm, but if he assumes responsibility for those actions and is ready to accept the punishment, at least one condition of ethics is fulfilled. While such an ethical strand might not be too far from Kant's initial account, its formulation does not lose sight of the subject. Instead of turning the subject which ethical discourse enunciates as its object, the subject maintains its enunciating power. The subject of ethics is thus one which stands in place or as an image of universal idea. It is its embodiment or its action; unlike the agent who would remain separate from the universal and act in its name, *agens* is part of the universal and thus its expression. A true ethical subject is an expression of the universal idea of ethics.

The second point Zupančič's statement reveals concerns the temporality of ethics. If the subject of ethics is the subject who emerges at the other end of an ethical act, then ethics can only be constituted retroactively. That is, only after the event has taken place and a subject emerged can one locate ethics in the spectrum of the social and the political. In turn this renders ethics of the order of language and discourse. The retroactive logic of language where meaning is assigned after the master signifier or an ordering principle intervenes into the chain of signifiers (Lacan 2006a), is resembled in ethics. Only after the subject of ethics takes form can the limits and qualities of an ethical act be determined. Such a retroactive positioning of ethics also implies that one can never know in what form ethics will emerge in a particular situation (or if it at all will); all that can be said is that if the condition of responsibility is fulfilled ethical acts can be constituted. There are no norms, goods, and duties to follow the good, or law behind which the subject can hide. In a moment when ethical act is constituted, it is only the subject and its responsibility for taken decisions.

The above outline of ethics can at first imply a particular puritanism of reason – perhaps one that is similar to Kant's moral imperative. Only that in ethics of responsibility, the act can go in two ways, and nothing prevents both decisions from being equally ethical. When faced with an ethical dilemma, the action the subject is to take will depend on representation. Language, images, discourses, and social bonds are ways in which things appear to the subject and ways through which subject gains knowledge. As the only source of information, the subject is profoundly affected by the way things appear to him. Zupančič (1998: 65) further wrote: 'The subject is affected by a certain representation and this affection is the cause of his actions and, at the same time, the reason why his actions are determined pathologically'. In other words, pathology is the source for the ambiguity of action. While knowledge or reason rely on representation, the subject's actions result from the pathological side and draw on the unconscious material. This is the very same pathological that Kant aimed to bulletproof his theory from; by building a shell of reason, Kant fought against pathology in ethical thinking (for pathology leaves out all morality).

Reason and pathology emerge as two forces setting the frame for an ethical act from which the subject of ethics is to emerge. Facing an act in which an ethical decision is to be taken, the subject ponders its decision (he encounters 'moral law'). Regardless of his decision he is to face some consequences (which of course are specific to each decision). However, it is not reason which has a final say in the decision. It is the effect of the unconscious material the subject carries with it that will sway the decision in either way. The moral law, as Zupančič (1998: 63) writes, affects the subject.

Conclusion: Lacan, ethics, politics

Kant's moral imperative and ethics of good, when put to the extreme, meet what is the perversion of Sade. What Sadean reading of Kant highlights is the danger of taking away the agency of the subject and instituting law or some higher good in its place. If the subject believes itself to be endowed with greater powers (to be God) or to serve a greater good, he can place his actions at the guard of that Other. He can begin to see himself as a tool of sovereign power, national security, or even God. Nothing that the subject does is seen as an act of choice, everything becomes duty, a duty to follow the rule. The perversion of such a position has already been explicated; to avoid such a Sado-Kantian trap the ideas of ethics and the subject of ethics have to be such that they preserve the agency of the subject and maintain its responsibility for the actions taken, those being either good or bad. As a form of conclusion I shall briefly reflect as to what such propositions of ethics and the subject of ethics mean for human rights or questions of injustice with which the antagonism of the politics of ethics was initially introduced.

The human rights discourse rests on three key assumptions. First, the idea of human rights' breaches depends on the image of good or on assuming the state when rights are not breached. That brings to mind the earlier discussion whereby ethics is determined on the individual image of good that is assumed to hold universal value. Second, that human rights discourse sees its subject as a victim whose agency is taken away and who needs care. And finally, human rights rests on the notion of evil or doing evil that comes out either as the evil in men (as in *jouissance*) or as evil which creates situations where ethical actions need to be taken. The last two points are of particular importance for discussions of ethics and a move from a purely formalist traditional understanding of ethics to the one proposed here. The subject of human rights is a person who is first seen as a victim and second subjected to evil. Structurally speaking, the victim is someone who, to recall Lacan's distinction between the subject of enunciation and the subjected of the enunciated, falls solely on the second level, that is a 'subject' who is being enunciated. In the moment of enunciation the victim emerges as an object in a discursive structure; its agency is in the hands of enunciation; that is of the 'person' enunciating or dependent on the recognition of the discourse of human rights. The level of enunciation is the level where the discourse of rights operates as a universal category, whereas the level of the enunciated is that of recognition. Thus the logic of discourse – and the relationship between the universal and the particular – are already set up as such that the subject of enunciation cannot emerge as anything different but a victim. Gilles Deleuze in his brief discussion of human rights gives a good illustration of this missed encounter. When speaking of genocide in Armenia he says:

> There is this massacre [...] and, on top of all that, an earthquake. [...] We say human rights. But finally these are discourses for intellectuals, [...] these declarations of human rights are never made in conjunction with those concerned, with Armenian societies, with Armenian communities, etc.
>
> *(Deleuze 2004)*

The agency of the 'victim' is not taken away by the peril or evil they experience, but by the discourse that is, how they as individuals experiencing evil are represented in a discursive framework and the power relation that emerges from a relation between those seen as 'in need' and 'others' who are to help. The discursive structures perpetrate such a relation; and what is more, as law is nothing but an expression of the discursive ordering logic, it too secures such a relation. At the level of law, however, the idea of evil is even stronger. Recalling the earlier discussion, evil (or *jouissance*) is at the centre of political problems for which ethical norms, moral standards, and legal obligations are deemed a solution. The emergence of evil automatically mobilizes mechanisms of ethics and law. Thus it is law which ultimately bears the authority to intervene in the situation and victimize those in peril. As Alain Badiou (2001: 8–9) writes:

> Law alone authorizes a space for identification of evil [...] and provides the means of arbitration when the issue is not clear. [... W]hatever evil befalls [the subject] is universally identifiable [...], such that this subject is both, on the one hand, a passive, pathetic, or reflexive subject – he who suffers – and, on the other, the active, determining subject of judgement – he who, in identifying suffering knows that it must be stopped by all available means.

Badiou's discussion of ethics and evil demonstrates the nature of the existing subject of ethics and law. In consequence it means we first get to know the set of rights belonging to someone seen or conceived as the subject and only second are we concerned with who that 'subject with rights' actually is. Such an understanding of ethics and the subject implies the subject's identification with a universalizing principle, which enables the recognition of evil in the first and 'ethical actions' only in the second place. Evil thus works as a mirror creating and acknowledging all the breaches and victimizations. The subject recognizes the universal evil done to him on the grounds of his identification with the universalizing principle of evil (or what is thought to be a universal principle of evil) (Badiou 2001: 10). Another level of alienation is added to the scheme in the form of a third person identifying the situation as a product of evil. In this context, human rights, as Badiou (2001: 9) writes, emerge as a right 'to non-Evil: rights not to be offended or mistreated with respect to one's life (the horrors of murder and execution), one's body (the horrors of torture, cruelty and famine), or one's cultural identity (the horrors of the humiliation of women, of minorities, etc.)'.

To break such, the discourse of victimization, the notion of ethics, and ethical acts should be referred back to the particular situation. And 'rather than reduce it to an aspect of pity for victims', as Badiou (2001: 3) continues, 'it should become the enduring maxim of singular processes'. This statement captures the gist of discussions about the making of new forms of law and the idea of the subject who is not a victim, but whose subjectivity is created and re-created in the context of the situation. Such a position can address key ethical concerns: it would not break with the illusion that political antagonisms driven by *jouissance* can ever reach the ultimate solution or achieve the state of universal ethics, yet it would prevent subjects and their action from ever seeking and finding refuge for their actions in the arms of law. The displacement of law when an ethical act is sought is pertinent if responsibility instead of perversion is to become a central ethical guiding principle.

But as ethics and the subject of ethics are always constituted retroactively the subject of action is trapped. Devoid of universal guiding principles each situation appears as unique. Staring at the ethical abyss, the subject never knows what is to be done. Aware of being at the same time 'inside' and 'outside', the subject, as Zupančič writes (1998: 71), is: 'at the same time the insignificant trifle, the grain of sand that the wild forces play with, and the observer of this spectacle. The subject watches himself being subjected to the law, he watches himself being humiliated and terrified by it'. The ethical position that was proposed embraces the topological ambiguity of the subject and the situation, the subject watches himself being turned and tossed around, subjected to law, but, and this is crucial, he never gives into his desire. That is, he never let's his *jouissance* be mastered by law, and he is never afraid of it re-emerging in a question of 'che vuoi?' or 'what is it that the Other wants from me?' Ethics is thus not about overcoming the problem and neither about suppressing *jouissance*, but always about facing it.

Notes

1 See also Alenka Zupančič, *Ethics of the Real: Kant and Lacan* (London: Verso, 2000).
2 Kantian ethics is considered a model for the way ethics is conceptualized and thought about today and is a subject of Freud's and Lacan's critique.

232 Andreja Zevnik

3 The law of a *superego* has a double role: it provides unconscious orientation for the law, or the spirit of the logic in which laws should be made; as well as acting as its reverse – the other – side, for which law cannot account, and which is, in fact, outside the principles of positive law. Thus, the *superego* embodies the source of authority that the subject internalizes once it becomes part of a society.

4 I return to perversion in the following section.

5 This translation is slightly modified; instead of the subject of enunciation and the subject of the statement (Fink's translation), a more appropriate translation of Lacan's statement is the one marking out the difference between 'enunciation' and of the 'enunciated'.

Bibliography

Badiou, Alain (2001) *Ethics: An Essay of the Understanding of Evil*. London: Verso.

Deleuze, Gilles (2004) *L'Abécédaire de Gilles Deleuze, avec Claire Parnet*. Paris: DVD Editions Montparnasse.

Freud, Sigmund (1990) *Beyond the Pleasure Principle*. New York: W. W. Norton and Company.

Kant, Immanuel (1993) *Critique of Practical Reason*. New York: Macmillan.

Lacan, Jacques (1991 [1953–54]). *The Seminar, Book I, Freud's Papers on Technique*, ed. Jacques-Alain Miller. New York: W. W. Norton and Company.

Lacan, Jacques (1992 [1959–60]). *The Seminar, Book VII, The Ethics of Psychoanalysis*, ed. Jacques-Alain Miller. New York: W. W. Norton and Company.

Lacan, Jacques (1998) *The Seminar, Book XI, Four Fundamental Concepts of Psychoanalysis*. New York: W. W. Norton and Company.

Lacan, Jacques (1999) *The Seminar, Book XX, Encore: On Feminine Sexuality, the Limits of Love and Knowledge*, ed. Jacques-Alain Miller. New York: W. W. Norton and Company.

Lacan, Jacques (2006a) 'The Function and Field of Speech and Language in Psychoanalysis', in *Écrits*, ed. Bruce Fink. London and New York: W. W. Norton and Company.

Lacan, Jacques (2006b) 'Kant avec Sade', in *Écrits*, ed. Bruce Fink. London and New York: W.W. Norton and Company, 645–671.

Lacan, Jacques (2006c). 'The Subversion of the Subject and the Dialectics of Desire', in *Écrits*, ed. Bruce Fink. London and New York: W.W. Norton & Company, 671–702.

Legendre, Pierre (1995) 'The Other Dimension of Law', *Cardozo Law Review*, 16(3–4): 943–961.

Legendre, Pierre (1997) 'The Masters of Law: A Study of Dogmatic Function', in *Law and the Unconscious: A Legendre Reader*, ed. Peter Goodrich. Basingstoke and London: Macmillan Press Ltd, 98–133.

Newman, Saul (2001) *From Bakunin to Lacan: an Anti-Authoritarianism and the Dislocation of Power*. Lanham, MD: Lexington Books.

Supiot, Alain (2002) 'Ontologies of Law'. *New Left Review*, 13: 107–124.

Supiot, Alain (2007) *Homo Juridicus: On the Anthropological Function of the Law*. London: Verso.

Šumič -Riha, Jelica (1995) *Avtoriteta in Argumentacija* . Ljubljana: Analecta.

Žižek, Slavoj (1995) 'Superego by Default', *Cardozo Law Review*, 16(3–4): 925–942..

Žižek, Slavoj (1996) *The Indivisible Remainder*. London: Verso.

Žižek, Slavoj (2002) *For They Don't Know What They Do: Enjoyment as a Political Factor*. London: Verso.

Zupančič, Alenka (1998) 'The Subject of the Law', in *Cogito and the Unconscious*, Sic 2, ed. Slavoj Žižek. Durham, NC: Duke University Press, 41–73.

Zupančič, Alenka (2000) *Ethics of the Real: Kant and Lacan*. London: Verso.

15

POLITICAL ENCOUNTERS

Feminism and Lacanian psychoanalysis

Kirsten Campbell

GOLDSMITHS, UNIVERSITY OF LONDON

Feminism is having a moment

> It may be the explosion of social media, or it could be the straightened circumstances young women find themselves in thanks to the past five years of economic downturn, but feminism is, to put it mildly, having a moment.
>
> *(Halpin 2014: 15)*

From the 'feminism campaigns' of *Elle* and *Marie Claire* to Beyoncé sampling 'We Should All be Feminists', it seems that feminism has now become fashionable. This trend reflects a wider resurgence of feminist politics for a new generation engaged in online campaigns, street protests, grass-root meetings, and university groups (Cochrane 2013). The 'fourth wave of feminism' attends to the current pleasures and miseries of masculinities and femininities, and the issue of 'women and equality in society today' (Halpin 2014: 15; Candy 2014: 57). In this moment, gender has once again become a political problem. This re-emergence of 'gender trouble' opens the possibility of a new encounter between feminism and psychoanalysis.

This chapter examines the political encounters between feminist movements and Lacanian psychoanalysis. It argues that fourth wave feminism might usefully re-engage with Lacan's work in the current political conjuncture. It begins this analysis by examining the first encounter of the feminist movement and Lacanian psychoanalysis in the 1970s. This encounter takes place in the context of second wave feminist analyses of the politics of gender, and was both highly contentious and also highly productive. The second wave developed an important strategy of productive appropriations of Lacan's work. This strategy identifies the political problematic that frames these readings of Lacan, as well as engaging with the specificity and precision of psychoanalytic concepts. Building on this second wave strategy of reading Lacan, the chapter then identifies sexual difference and the new sexual contract as the problematic confronting fourth wave politics. It argues that this problematic frames the potential political encounter between this feminist generation and Lacanian psychoanalysis. This encounter can be elaborated in a feminist account of fraternal and feminist social links, which draws on the later Lacanian theory of sexuation and the social bond of discourse. This fourth wave appropriation of Lacanian psychoanalysis can offer an important strategy for understanding not only the psychic life of power that makes social change so difficult, but also for identifying transformative possibilities for fourth wave feminist politics.

Should fourth wave feminists know better than to re-read Lacan?

Encountering Lacan from the second to the third feminist wave

The first encounter between feminism and Lacan took place in an earlier period of radical social change. This was the emergence of second wave feminism in the 1970s, which insisted that women's liberation was integral to social revolution, and that the sexual was also necessarily the political. In this context of the feminist politicization of female sexuality and the rejection of Freudian accounts of femininity, Lacan returned to the question of feminine sexuality in his 1971 seminar, *Seminar XX*.

The earlier 'classical' Lacanian account of the formation of the sexed subject had appeared in his influential work, *Écrits* (2002). *Écrits* consisted of papers written from 1936 to 1966 that Lacan selected as representative of his psychoanalytic theory. In the key papers, such as the 'The Signification of the Phallus' (1958) and 'Guiding Remarks for a Congress on Feminine Sexuality' (1960), Lacan outlined his theory of sexed subjectivity.

In this account, the child becomes a subject after the intervention of the paternal interdict of the Law-of-the-Father in the Oedipus complex. Lacan adapted Lévi-Strauss' notion of culture as a symbolic system, which is structured by a foundational prohibition against intrafamilial marriage. For Lacan, this prohibition upon incestuous desire for the mother is Law-of-the-Father, which structures culture as a system of symbolic exchange. The Law-of-the-Father symbolizes the father as the bearer of cultural law. This symbolic father functions as the figure of the prohibition upon the infant's desire for the mother (2002: 229–30). This symbolic function represents the separation of child and mother. It should not be confused with the real or imaginary father that acts as an agent of the paternal law that bars the child's desire for the mother.

In the Oedipus complex, the infant desires its mother and perceives its father as a rival to its mother's love. The child 'resolves' the Oedipus complex through identification with the symbolic father, and thereby enters the Symbolic order. In the Symbolic order, subjects are sexually differentiated according to their relation to the phallus, a symbolic element (Lacan 2002: 582–83). The phallus represents the lack of the signifier in the Symbolic order. For Lacan, the phallic function is 'the function that institutes lack, that is, the alienating function of language' that all subjects suffer (Fink 1995: 103). The masculine subject has the phallus while the feminine subject lacks it. In Lacan's account, subjects have a masculine or feminine structure, which provides a signification of anatomical sexual difference. That assignation is contingent such that men can have feminine psychic structures and women can have a masculine relation to the phallus. However, it also gives meaning to the biological body, such that this process of sexualization inscribes sexual difference upon the physical body. Lacan's account, therefore, insists that masculinity and femininity do not reflect biological sexual difference. Rather, they are forms of identification that structure our lived experience of our bodies and ourselves.

Lacan's return to the problem of sexual difference in his later seminars of the 1970s built upon and moved beyond this theory. Lacan had given year-long seminars from 1953 to 1981, each of which explored different themes such as the ego, the object, the unconscious, and psychoanalytic ethics. Of these later seminars of the 1970s exploring this new theory of feminine sexuality, only *The Other Side of Psychoanalysis* (*Seminar XVII*) and *Encore* (*Seminar XX*) have been fully translated, with sections of other seminars appearing in translation (see Mitchell and Rose 1982). Of these, *Seminar XX* marks 'a turning point in Lacan's work, both at a conceptual level and in terms of its polemic. It represents Lacan's most direct attempt to take up the question of feminine sexuality' (Rose 1982: 137).

Similarly to the earlier accounts of the sexed subject, the phallus remains the pivot of the later Lacanian account of sexuality and sexual difference. Lacan's 'Graph of Sexuation' represents the sexed subject and sexual relation to the phallic function. A different relation to the phallus structures the masculine and feminine positions (1998a: 79–80). The phallic function inscribes the male subject 'man as whole' or 'as all' (*l'homme comme tout*) (1998a: 79). This inscription produces 'a universe of men', a masculine universal (Copjec 1994: 235). The masculine subject claims to be a man who is whole and all, a master of himself who '[b]y denying the trauma of primary Castration … unconsciously perpetuates the suppression of the person's own division and the belief in her or his autonomy' (Ragland-Sullivan 1987: 305). This fantasy of masculinity masks the dual function of the phallus. It signifies the *jouissance*, or bodily pleasure, that is sacrificed when entering the Symbolic order. However, it also signifies the absence of *jouissance* that this sacrifice creates within that order. For this reason, the masculine claim to be whole rests on the exception of castration – such that he defines his universality in relation to an other without the phallus.

That other position of the subject is that of ~~The Woman~~ – a fantasy that affirms that the masculine subject has the phallus. In this fantasy, ~~The Woman~~ desires the phallus, confirming that he has it (Lacan 1998a: 131). For this reason, Lacan argues that ~~The Woman~~ does not exist. She exists only as a fantasy of the masculine subject, formed in his phallic *jouissance* and in his desire. The fantasy Woman does not exist in the real, because no woman could enact the fantasy that he substitutes for her. This is why Lacan writes ~~The Woman~~ with a bar through the words. Lacan points out in his earlier work on feminine masquerade that women may attempt to fulfil that fantasy of ideal femininity (1998b: 193). However, while a woman may

236 Kirsten Campbell

attempt to play out the masculine fantasy, in doing so she does not exist as other than in (and through) fantasy.

In *Seminar XX*, the position of the female subject is not rendered as nothing, but as 'not all' of the phallus: 'I said "of woman", whereas in fact woman does not exist, woman is not whole (*pas toute*)' (Lacan 1998a: 7). Reading the 'Graph of Sexuation' from the side of the masculine subject positions the female subject as an exception to the phallic signifier, and hence as a signification of its limit. The phallus does not define her sexed subjectivity, because she comes to be a sexed subject through normative identifications with a member of the opposite sex. It does not define her body, for the phallus does not symbolize her body (Lacan 1993: 176). It does not represent her sexuality, since her *jouissance* is not phallic (Lacan 1998a: 74). This does not mean that women are excluded from language. Rather, for Lacan, '[i]t's not because she is not wholly in the phallic function that she is not there at all. She is there in full (*à plein*). But there is something more (*en plus*)' (1998a: 74). The paradox of the female subject is that she is within the phallic law of the signifier and yet 'there is something more'. Lacan argues that the position of exception to the phallic signifier is not that of negation or contradiction, but rather of indeterminacy (1998a: 103). The 'not all' of the female subject is a position which the symbolic does not capture.

Lacan's return to feminine sexuality aimed to both address the contemporary feminist critiques of Freudian phallocentrism and to develop his theory of the feminine subject (Roudinesco 1997: 369). In *Seminar XX*, Lacan situates his discussion of feminine sexuality in the context of 'that aspect of relationships between men and women that is related to current trends (*la mode*)' (1998a: 74). There are passing references to *Mouvement de libération des femmes* throughout the later seminars. However, he also asserts that 'woman' tell nothing of their sexuality. Despite the fact that 'in all the time that people having been begging them, begging them on their hands and knees – I spoke last time of women psychoanalysts – to try to tell us, not a word!' (1998a: 75). Lacan's work reveals little sustained engagement with the many words of contemporary psychoanalytic feminists about feminine sexuality and subjectivity.

In contrast, an important current within the French second wave turned to Lacanian psychoanalysis to develop an alternative politics to the prevalent ideas of women as an oppressed class, as a unitary social group, or as a stable category of embodied persons (see Duchen 1986). These feminists believed that Lacanian thought offered a crucial account of the constitution of sexed subjectivity, and hence of the psychic dimensions of sexual oppression and liberation (see Roudinesco 1990: 506ff.). In English feminist scholarship, this approach has now come to be called 'post-Lacanian feminism' (Campbell 2000: 102). This includes the influential work of Luce Irigaray and Julia Kristeva, who trained as Lacanian analysts and became members of his psychoanalytic school. Their critical engagement with Lacanian thought and practice is a crucial part of their theories of language, subjectivity, and sexual difference. For example, in *This Sex Which Is Not One* (1977), Irigaray engaged in an extended critique of the phallocentrism of Lacan's later theory of sexual difference. Kristeva focused on Lacan's theory of language in her alternative account of the materiality of the semiotic and maternal registers of signification in *Revolution in Poetic Language* (1984). Despite their different relation to the feminist movement as well as to Lacanian psychoanalysis, their feminist re-readings of Lacan would become central to an influential reformulation of sexual difference in the Anglo-American movement.

This so-called 'new French feminism' first emerged within the American movement (Marks and de Coutrivron 1981). While this inaccurate term was highly contested by French feminists of the time, nevertheless it now marks the impact of these ideas on international feminist theory and practice (see Delphy 1995 and Braidotti 2014). Through the work of these feminist thinkers, the Lacanian account of sexual difference and language became an integral part of a new second wave politics. This politics refused liberal ideas of inequality, radical ideas of sexual oppression, and Marxist ideas of class oppression as inadequate accounts of the oppression of women. Instead, this post-Lacanian feminism argues that the phallic structures of language, culture, and intellectual thought (such as philosophy) constitute the feminine only in relation to the masculine, and that a fundamental disruption of this order is necessary to create new forms of sexuality and subjectivity. By the 1980s, these post-Lacanian feminist approaches to language and subjectivity had become part of the international feminist 'canon'.

However, another second wave encounter of feminism and Lacanian psychoanalysis took place in the context of Marxist feminism of the 1970s. Marxist feminists undertook a 'powerful critique of materialist perspectives which prioritize class', and sought to develop an account of patriarchal capitalism (Brah 1996: 104). Althusserian Marxism was particularly influential in British socialist feminism, which led to the question of how to 'locate sexuality and gender identity in the specificity of historical ideological processes [and] culminated in the ... feminist appropriation of psychoanalysis' (Barrett 1984: 53). The most influential of these feminist appropriations was Juliet Mitchell's text, *Psychoanalysis and Feminism* (2000). This argued for the importance of Lacanian psychoanalysis in understanding the operation of an ideological mode of patriarchy in general, and the reproduction of the (Oedipal) subject in the family in particular (Mitchell 2000: xxx). Mitchell's later work with Jacqueline Rose developed this reading of Lacanian psychoanalysis, returning to the Lacan's later work on feminine sexuality, and providing key translations of *Seminar XX* and the later seminars (Mitchell and Rose 1982). In this influential reading of Lacan, Mitchell and Rose argued that his work offered feminist thought 'an account of how the status of the phallus in sexuality enjoins on woman a definition in which she is simultaneously a symptom and a myth' of the phallic organization of sexual identity (Mitchell 1982: 57).

These readings of Lacan informed a wide range of feminist cultural analyses, particularly those influenced by British Cultural Studies. The political context for these readings was two key challenges for the British left in the 1980s. The first was an increasing focus upon identity, which was thought to reflect the rise of the 'new social movements' such as second wave feminism. The second was an increasing interest in ideology, which was thought to explain the failure of social revolution in the

238 Kirsten Campbell

1970s and resurgent conservatism in the 1980s (see Hall 1989 and Brah 2012). These concerns gave rise to 'post-Althusserian Lacanian' feminism, which argued that sexed subjects are produced by ideological interpellation (the process by which individuals recognize themselves as subjects) (Clough 2007: 343). This approach focused upon the production of the 'feminine' in the field of culture, and the development of alternative cultural politics. The influence of this approach was particularly notable in feminist film, art, and literary theory (Penley 1988: 4). By the 1980s, this approach became central to feminist post-structuralist theory, and so moved into international feminist thought (Weedon 1997). With this theoretical shift came a reorientation of political struggle from the state and the economic to the subject and the cultural.

The feminist second wave predominantly read Lacanian theory as (and for) an account of the constitution of 'femininity', subjectivity, and sexuality. This sympathetic interpretation of Lacanian theory argued that it provided a compelling description of the difficulty of the phallic organization of 'femininity'. However, the pivotal role of the phallus in Lacanian theory has also given rise to highly contentious feminist debates concerning the appropriation of his work. The first objection is that Lacan ties his concept of the phallus to the biological organ of the penis, and that by doing so Lacan privileges masculinity and the male body as his model of sexual difference. The second objection concerns the 'monolithic, all-pervasive, and all determining symbolic order', which appears to prevent any possibility of changing the phallic ordering of sexuality (Fraser 2013: 10). These debates have continually returned to the unresolved problem of sexual difference that constructs femininity as either phallic or as other to the phallus, thereby defining femininity in relation to the phallus. It is unsurprising, then, that '[a]s we turn to the twenty-first century, amidst the ebb and flow of waves of feminism, a few spectral questions return: does feminism finally come to the end of its "analysis terminable interminable" with sexual differences? Is feminism done with the phallus? with psychoanalysis?' (Hsieh 2012: 102).

The third wave that emerged at the end of the 20th century did not engage with Lacanian psychoanalysis, even as its ideas continued to have spectral existence in this movement (Lueptniz 2003). In the feminist politics of the 1990s, it seemed that the third wave had come to the end of its encounter with psychoanalysis (Mitchell et al. 2010). This reflected the wider disengagement from psychoanalysis in the British and American societies from which this feminist wave emerged. However, it was also due to the political sensibilities of the third wave. Lacanian psychoanalysis, with its emphasis upon theoretical analysis, sexual difference, the emptiness of identity, and the costs of sexuality and consumption did not sit well with the third wave emphasis upon personal politics, flexible sexualities, multiple identities, and the pleasures of sexuality and consumption.

Re-reading Lacanian psychoanalysis in the field of fourth wave feminisms

The fourth wave of feminism is now typically described as the building of a critical and transnational movement of young feminists from 2008 onwards, most visibly in the US and the UK. It is characterized by the deployment of social media, an immersion in late commodity capitalism, the acceptance of sexual diversity, and a politics of gender equality (Baumgardner 2011; Halberstam 2012). In this, the fourth wave has similar political sensibilities to the third wave of the 1990s. Unlike the third wave, the fourth wave does not reject second wave critiques of sexual inequality, capitalist exploitation, and patriarchal sexism. Instead, for the fourth wave desire and sexuality have become an evident element of new globalizing neoliberal circuits of exchange (see, for example, Penny 2014). In this context, the fourth wave has returned to the second wave problems of gender equality and the costliness of femininities (Banyard 2010). However, this return is rearticulated through the neoliberal market, which is seen restructuring as gender and femininity in new ways. Against Oedipal and generational understandings of feminist waves, the fourth feminist wave can be understood as an ongoing problematic within feminist movements (see Snyder 2008). In this approach, feminist waves do not reflect chronological generations as such. Rather, they mark the emergence of new articulations of 'gender' as a political problem and as a renewed category of political analysis.

These are the contemporary conditions of the possible encounter between fourth wave feminism and Lacanian psychoanalysis. However, it is necessary to displace the ideas of the union or rejection of feminism/psychoanalysis that dominated the second and third wave. Instead, the fourth wave should look to another form of this encounter that also emerged in earlier feminist movements, exemplified by a range of thinkers from the cultural theorist Parveen Adams (1996) to the postcolonial theorist Kalpana Seshadri-Crooks (2000). This approach acknowledges both the particularity of the feminist problematic that framed this encounter, as well as the specificity of Lacanian theory and practice. This important strategy for feminist readings of Lacan can be described as 'productive appropriation' (Campbell 2004: 26).

This strategy of productive appropriation has two elements. First, it identifies the specific feminist problematics that frame this engagement with Lacanian psychoanalysis. It asks what Lacanian theory and practice can do, or fail to do, for specific theoretical and practical problems in the feminist field. However, it also recognizes the psychoanalytic specificity of Lacanian theory and practice. This acknowledges the 'peculiarity of the psychoanalytic object with which feminism engages' (Rose 1986: 84). That 'peculiarity' derives from the clinical dimensions of Lacanian work, and its concomitant commitment to the unconscious. This acknowledgement marks the limits of 'applied' psychoanalysis, insofar as it is necessary to acknowledge the distinction between clinical and feminist problems of theory and practice, together with the difficulty of shifting these from one field to another. It also acknowledges that such a re-reading reconfigures Lacanian psychoanalysis in the feminist field. This reconfiguration takes place because feminist practice differs from psychoanalytic practice; and feminist politics implies a commitment to social, rather than individual, change. However, it also marks the productivity of feminist engagement with Lacanian work, how it unsettles the underlying terms of feminist politics, and opens up other ways of understanding the political.

Fourth wave gender troubles

The feminist problematics of the fourth wave emerge in a new conjunction of desire, sexuality, and 'femininity' in the differentiated forms of late capitalist consumption and neoliberal politics currently evolving from London to Beijing (Gill and Scharff 2010; Hsing and Lee 2010). In this neoliberal phase of late capitalism, this 'new sexual contract appears to displace traditional modes of patriarchal authority and attribute to young women all manner of social, political, and economic freedoms' (Adkins 2008: 191). Under the terms of this contract, women agree to use their freedoms to enjoy this new world of globalizing capitalism (Oksala 2011). However, the physical and psychic pain of normative sexuality is the cost of entering the new sexual contract for young women (McRobbie 2009: 54). The emergence of a self-named fourth wave feminist generation in Britain and America is symptomatic of these contemporary forms of gender trouble emerging in the post-industrial Europe and in the industrializing Asian and Latin American economies (see Mohanty 2003 and Fraser 2009).

The 2014 *Marie Claire* list of 'key drivers to gaining true equality' typifies the rearticulation of these gender troubles as a feminist politics. Three related sets of problems circulate in this field of fourth wave feminism. The first are problems of femininities, which concern issues of sexuality, embodiment, and power, such as the sexualization of young women or the experience of sexual violence. The second set of problems concerns economic and political empowerment. These arise from the new sexual contract, and include issues such as unequal pay for men and women or the inequitable division of domestic labour. The third concerns how to achieve 'true equality', which is seen as 'the most basic definition of feminism' (Halpin 2014: 15). However, there is little collective agreement as to what equality is, or how best to achieve it.

How can fourth wave feminists re-read Lacan to engage with this problematic? And which Lacan? Instead of following the second and third wave in focusing upon whether it is possible for psychoanalytic feminism to have 'sex without the phallus', the fourth wave should instead develop another strategy for re-reading Lacanian psychoanalysis. This productive appropriation of Lacan focuses upon his later work, and develops the Lacanian accounts of sexuation and the social bond. To undertake a productive appropriation of this later Lacanian theory involves re-reading it as a feminist account of the sexuation of the subject in the new forms of post-patriarchal social ties. Recognizing the differences between feminist and analytic practice requires reinscribing the social and the sexual into this reading of Lacan. This is because Lacan's concern is to develop a psychoanalytic theory, and not a theory of the social and the political. However, to develop a Lacanian account of contemporary forms of subjectivity and sexuality does not involve reading Lacan against himself. Rather, it involves a feminist re-reading Lacan's theory of discourse together with his contemporaneous account of sexuation and his idea of the emergence of the modern socio-symbolic form.

The social bond of discourse

In *L'envers* (*Seminar XVII*) and *Encore* (*Seminar XX*), Lacan presents his formulae of the discourses of the master, the hysteric, the university, and the psychoanalyst. Each formula represents four different positions of the subject – the master, the hysteric, the academic, and the psychoanalyst – and four different forms of the discursive social link – mastering, hysterical, academic, and psychoanalytic (see Chapters I and II, *Seminar XVII*). These social bonds produce different relations to the subject and the unconscious, such that the lack in the Symbolic order and the veil of fantasy that covers it have different functions in these discursive structures. These formulae represent possible subject positions and social bonds within the psychoanalytic field.

This theory of the four discourses identifies different and foundational types of social bonds of speaking subjects. For Lacan, '[d]iscourse is a fundamental apparatus which is prior to and which determines the whole relation of subjects to subjects and subjects to objects' (Adams 1996: 72). In these later seminars, Lacan develops this conception of discourse as the minimal social bond, in which the subject always comes into being in relation to other subjects (for further discussion, see Dolar 2006). The social bond of subjects is discursive because language anchors the relation between them (Lacan 1998a: 54). For Lacan, language produces a 'speaking being' and the relation between such subjects (1998a: 54). For this reason, 'the notion of discourse should be taken as a social link (*lien social*), founded on language' (Lacan 1998a: 17). Discourse thus produces the social link between subjects, because discursive chains of signifiers structure stable relations of subjects. The Lacanian concept of discourse links the structure of signification and the relationship between subjects because it describes signifying chains that produce those subjects in relation to each other.

For Lacan, the fundamental social tie is the Discourse of the Master. This discourse produces all speaking subjects, such that '[i]n the final analysis, the "person" always has to do with the master's discourse' (Lacan 1998a: 69). As such, it is a position that all persons – both men and women – take up in becoming subjects. The fantasy that this person is a man or woman, with their imagined idealized masculine or feminine qualities, veils the fundamental lack that all subjects suffer in entering the socio-symbolic order.

The modern Discourse of the Master and the fraternal bond

The four discourses do not stand outside history, but instead are inscribed 'in the historicity of modern European development' (Žižek 2006: 109). For Lacan, the social tie of the Discourse of the Master is the horizon of the Modern. The advent of the social order of modern capitalism stabilizes the Discourse of the Master (Lacan 2007: 177). It is the discourse of capitalism and its other face, imperialism (2007: 92). For Lacan, this is a contemporary social discourse of mastery, control, and domination. In *L'envers*, Lacan argues that the Discourse of the Master has

242 Kirsten Campbell

expanded in the society in which we now live, which is dominated by fakery, advertising, and commodification (2007: 126). He describes the allure and deception of this society, and thereby emphasizes its participation in the Imaginary order. As a register of signification, the imaginary fills the signifier with egoistic content, fixing its meaning in phantasmic constructions, and thereby making it appear real to the subject (for further discussion of real, imaginary, and symbolic, see Campbell 2004). This is the society of the spectacle, a world of 'fascinated looking and desiring', which McRobbie describes as central to contemporary consumer culture (2009: 98). What, then, is the gender order that emerges in this modern Discourse of the Master? And how does it produce the gender troubles of the fourth wave of femininity, inequality, and the new sexual contract?

The social bonds of 'neoliberal neopatriarchy'

The new gender order of the Discourse of the Master produces the gender troubles identified by the fourth wave. This gender order is the masculine social bond of the new sexual contract. This social tie takes the form of a fraternal relationship, in which a relationship between brothers founds the social order. Lacan argues that an analysis of the Oedipal myth reveals the fantasy of the brothers of the primal horde that supports the fraternal relation. He suggests that this symbolic murder of the father is the symbolic foundation of the modern fraternal form (2007: 114–15). For Lacan, the Oedipus complex is contingent on the murder of the father, because it establishes the interdict against the *jouissance* of the mother. In this Oedipal myth, the brothers are the murderous sons who, after killing their father, enter into the contract between them that will constitute the new social order. Lacan suggests that the fraternal relation is a social tie between brothers. This tie forms the modern social bond with its founding discourse of equality, liberty, and brotherhood (2007: 114–15). The sons of the primal father inaugurate a new political form – that of fraternity. They are no longer the sons of the father, but brothers. This pact is not the neutral agreement of social existence presented in the myth of the social contract. Rather, it represents a particular ordering of the polity – a fraternal form. This gender order is founded in a phallic representational economy that differentiates 'masculine' and 'feminine' subjects. The symbolic father – the symbolic function that represents the murdered father – is the pivot of this order. Despite the murder of the father, the fraternal form does not indicate the end of patriarchy, because it is not a post-patriarchal order. Rather, it represents a different form of phallic social bonds.

This new sexual contract produces the hegemonic masculine subject, and establishes the social bonds of hegemonic masculinity. In this gender order, the hegemonic masculine subject functions as the universal subject. This masculine subject claims presence and universality, such that it posits its identity as a whole and complete self who is the universal representative of all being. However, the universality of the masculine subject defines itself in relationship to a non-universal, the 'feminine' position of a being without the phallus. The masculine subject displaces his lack-in-being to a castrated other, which enables the construction of his fantasy of being a unified, omnipotent, and universal subject, which masters itself and its others.

The fraternal order is not a relation between siblings. It is not a relation between brothers and sisters or between sisters, but only a relation between brothers as the male children of the father. Accordingly, the Discourse of the Master is a social contract between masculine subjects. It is a social link between those who recognize themselves (and each other) as masculine subjects. The fraternal subject is a masculine subject, constituted by the paternal identification that founds his relation to other subjects. In Juliet Flower MacCannell's important elaboration of the Lacanian theme of the fraternal tie, she argues that '[w]hat we have in the place of patriarchy is the Regime of the Brother' (1991: 3). For Flower MacCannell, a relationship to fraternal members of the social group forms the subject. These '"fraternal objects" are eroticized' in a sublimating identification between brothers (1991: 52). It is not a contract between men and women, since women function in its symbolic economy as objects of exchange rather than as political subjects who enter the social contract as equal citizens of a polity.

This Lacanian description of the masculine side of the new sexual contract draws out the reconstitution of patriarchal culture in modern fraternal form. In her analysis of social contract theory, Carole Pateman rightly argues that 'in the modern world women are subordinated to men as men, or to men as a fraternity. The original contract takes place after the political defeat of the father and creates modern fraternal patriarchy' (1988: 3). This description of a shift from the feudal patriarchal to modern sexist gender order traces the continuing operation of the paternal function and its signifier, the phallus, in the production of the new sexual contract. While there is a 'shift from a genuinely patriarchal feudal society to a sexist capitalist one', modern social forms are born of, and precipitated in, patriarchy (Brennan 1993: 167). The Lacanian account reveals the crisis of traditional patriarchy and the reconstitution of a phallic order in the modern form of the fraternal social bond and the political order of citizen subjects that is based upon it. This delegitimation of traditional patriarchy centres on the 'loss of the paternal fiction, the West's heritage and guarantee' (Jardine 1985: 67). The figure of the traditional patriarch no longer functions as the guarantee of the social order, with his guarantees of violence, coercion, and repression (Pateman 1988: 88). However, the modern paternal figure of social power and prestige serves in his place. The fourth wave has identified the continuation of social, economic, and political inequalities between men and women into the contemporary gender order. The social order remains a masculine order in its forms of domination and power. Through this account of the fraternal form, it is possible to perceive how the differential and disadvantageous terms of older patriarchal orders re-emerge in the new sexual contract.

These neoliberal and neopatriarchal social bonds form the 'guyland' of a new form of hegemonic masculinity characterized by fraternal bonding, sexual aggressivity, and social dominance (Kimmel 2008). This fraternal masculinity has been extensively described by the fourth wave: 'As for young men, they were told they lived in a brave new world of economic and sexual opportunity, and if they felt angry or afraid, if they felt constrained or bewildered by contradictory expectations, by the pressure to act masculine, make money, demonstrate dominance and fuck a lot of pretty women while remaining a decent human being, then their distress was the fault of women and minorities' (Penny 2014: 7). These fraternal forms of masculinity range from aggressive online 'everyday sexism', to male bonding through the exchange of sexual images of women, to the assertion of social dominance when challenged (see, for example, Bates 2014). While the fourth wave has described these fraternal masculinities they encounter in detail, they conceptually remain under-explored in this literature. This feminist Lacanian account shows how this new form of hegenomonic masculinity produces a subject that imagines itself as omnipotent and masterful. It relies on the fantasy of the (castrated) feminine to refuse its own lack, and aggressively fears any challenge to this subjective and social position.

The feminist Lacanian account of fraternal masculinity also reveals how the sexual exchange of women is crucial to the social bonds of the neoliberal neopatriarchy. This fraternal bond includes women as objects of sexual and economic exchange, but excludes feminine subjects as such from this post-patriarchal sexual contract. In *This Sex Which Is Not One* (1977), Irigaray describes a 'hom(m)o-sexual' order, in which the masculine subject only recognizes other masculine subjects (1977: 172). She argues that this order is founded upon systems of material and symbolic exchange between men, and specifically upon the material and symbolic exchange of 'wives, daughters, and sisters' (1977: 172).[1] Irigaray's work fundamentally concerns 'a single problem, in its multiple aspects: the absence of and exclusion of woman/women from the symbolic/social order' (Whitford 1991: 170). Her description of 'the between-men culture' provides a feminist description of the fraternal social bond of the new sexual contract. That agreement forms a fraternal social bond, which produces feminine subjects as objects of exchange, rather than as equal subjects of a new political order. They exist in this social bond only in terms of their absence and exclusion.

So how, then, do women enter this new sexual contract? This post-Lacanian feminist account of the modern Discourse of the Master as a fraternal social bond explains the formation of the masculine side of the new sexual contract. However, it does not explain the feminine position of the other sexed subject, and the production of modern hegemonic femininities in this neoliberal and neopatriarchal social bond.

The new sexual contract and post-patriarchal femininities

> There is a new sexual contract issued to young women which encourages activity concentrated in education and employment so as to ensure participation in the production of successful femininity, sexuality and eventually maternity.
>
> *(McRobbie 2009: 64)*

The first position of women in the new sexual contract is that of an equal party. As the fourth wave identifies, this position depends upon the promise of economic and political empowerment, particularly in the public spheres of education and employment. This promise rests upon the discourse of equality which the modern fraternal tie between masculine subjects produces. The sexual and racial others excluded from this modern political settlement fought long and hard to achieve this promise of equality between persons. So, for example, in the 20th century, first and second wave feminist movements fought for (and largely won) formal rights marking equality of citizenship in the polity, such as the right to vote or to education. These civil and political rights claim the right to equal participation in political and economic spheres without discrimination.

While ideas of 'true equality' are fundamental to fourth politics, nevertheless the fourth wave also recognizes the 'equality illusion' that underwrites this promise (Banyard 2010). This promise of equality is illusory because it offers no more than the right to be the same as masculine subjects. This formulation of equality does not disrupt modern fraternal discourses because it requires women to enter the social contract as either masculine subjects, or as their other. In this new sexual contract, women cannot be sexually different (or will face the difficulties of sexually 'neutral' treatment, such as those of working mothers), or alternatively they can only be sexually different (and so will face the difficulties of being sexed, such as workplace discrimination and sexual harassment). In reality, women continue to suffer substantive inequality across all sectors of society, despite increasing participation rates in education and employment (see, for example, Fawcett Society 2013). The problems of economic and political empowerment identified by the fourth wave, such as the lower pay and political under-representation of women, reflect this discrimination. The terms of the fraternal sexual contract between masculine subjects remain intact.

The terms of the new sexual contract may promise that women can (and should) enjoy the political, social, and economic freedoms of late consumer capitalism. Nevertheless they do so as *sexuated subjects* such that the *sexual terms* of the new sexual contract remain unchanged. The new sexual contract offers two different forms of 'feminine' exchange, both of which are structured through different hegemonic femininities. The first position is that of the young woman enjoying sexual and economic freedom. However, this also requires that the young woman attempt to make herself over into a fantasy ideal of youthful sexuality, beauty, and glamour (see McRobbie 2007 and Harris 2004). This is a composite image, made up of different signifiers of feminine heterosexuality. These signifiers range from the (lower class) hyper-sexualized femininities of 'raunch culture' (Levy 2006) to the (bourgeois) femininities of the 'fashion-beauty complex' (McRobbie 2007). The complex process of the globalization of these femininities can be seen in the most recent 'multicultural' campaigns of Estee Lauder to the all 'non-white' models of the Givenchy couture collection, which rearticulate these white European norms into global femininities. If the young woman can perform this ideal, then she can effectively enter the sexual competition of 'women on the market' (Irigaray 1977) that has intensified in this globalizing consumer capitalism (Harris 2012: 214). The fourth wave has identified the costs of undertaking this path.

These are the problems of femininities, such as 'the sexualisation of young women' or 'body-image issues' (Halpin 2014: 15).

The second is the conventional position of wife and mother. However, this position is also being remade through the new figure of 'affluent, feminine maternity' (McRobbie 2013; see also Stivens 2007). As McRobbie describes, '[t]his idea of active (i.e. en route to the gym), sexually confident motherhood marks an extension of its pre-maternal equivalent, the ambitious and aspirational young working woman' (McRobbie 2013: 120). This bourgeois ideal requires that the mother – who cannot be too young (lower class) or too old (outside the sexual economy) – attempt to make herself into the fantasy of the 'yummy mummy', a sexually desirable and high-consuming maternal figure, or the 'mumtrepreneur', the woman who has it all – satisfying work and maternal fulfilment (Littler 2013). The rearticulation of these maternal fantasies in global consumer culture can be seen in the emergence of this figure of the upwardly mobile and professional mother in Asian cultures, exemplified by the highly influential editor of *Vogue* China, and self-described 'working mother', Angelica Cheung (see Stivens 2007 and Donner 2008). However, the fourth wavers look to their imagined maternal futures and already see the costs of this position. These problems concern economic disempowerment, in which their working mothers struggle to find employment, receive lower salaries for the paid labour they obtain, undertake higher hours of unpaid labour in the home, and pay for private childcare (Banyard, 2010).

Following Judith Butler and the psychoanalyst Joan Riviere, McRobbie argues that contemporary forms of femininity emerge as a new cultural dominant because of the current challenges to the older patriarchal forms of the socio-symbolic order. She suggests that 'the Symbolic is faced with the problem of how to retain the dominance of phallocentrism when the logic of global capitalism is to loosen women from their prescribed roles and grant them degrees of economic independence' (2009: 61). From this gender trouble emerges the 'post-feminist masquerade as a mode of feminine inscription, across the whole surface of the body' (McRobbie 2009: 64). The post-feminist masquerade conceals that patriarchy is still in place by insisting that women choose to take up these positions to empower themselves in the (sexual and work) marketplace, while at the same time ensuring their regulation according to rigid and punitive cultural norms (2009: 68–69).

However, the feminist Lacanian account shows how fraternal social bonds produce these norms of femininity (and their masculine counterpart), and illuminates the psychic life of these subjective forms in this new gender order (see Campbell 2004). It traces how the modern fraternal discourses of the new sexual contract emerge from the collapse of the older paternal law of force and authority. Older patriarchal forms are not left in place, but are superseded by the fraternal social tie. As McRobbie suggests, this is still a phallocentric socio-symbolic order. However, it is no longer a patriarchal order, but a fraternal order in which the social power and dominance of the brother replaces the repression and violence of the patriarch. For this reason, it creates a new gender order, with new hegemonic gender identities and their attached gender troubles.

These neoliberal neopatriarchal discourses produce the imaginary identities of hegemonic masculinities and femininities. These identities collapse fantasies of self and the 'idealizing capital I of identification' (Lacan 1998b: 272). They give flesh to these norms by filling signifiers of masculine and feminine (the ideal) with the imaginary content of the fantasies of self. Central to this Lacanian approach is the proposition that there is no 'true' feminine behind the masquerade, for the masquerade of femininity is itself a fantasy that we identify with. While McRobbie emphasizes masquerade as performance or practice, a Lacanian feminist account explores the deep attachment or 'unconscious wish' that ties us to these performances, and the psychic costs and pleasures that come with this feminine fantasy. The performative account assumes that the practices of feminine masquerade make us into 'feminine' subjects, whereas Lacanian psychoanalysis assumes that it is our attachment to ideas of 'femininity' that give these practices meaning as markers of sexual difference.

In this account, the psychic attachment to these ideas is not reducible to practices of self-governance, but instead involves the 'forced choice' to become sexed subjects. However, since the unconscious reveals the failure of all identity, sexual identity is also necessarily unstable and incomplete. It is a process that never quite maps onto our bodies or selves (Rose 1986: 90). While both masculinity and femininity are never fully achieved or stable, 'femininity' and the position of the female subject are particularly problematic. This is because the socio-symbolic order that appears to create sexual difference is in actuality structured around the 'masculine' term. It is not possible to achieve a position of 'successful femininity' precisely because it is an impossible fantasy. The fourth wave has clearly described the costs of these fantasies of ~~The Woman~~ in its different forms. This feminist Lacanian perspective helps to explain the operation of this psychic life of power, and how this phantasmic operation supports the new (fraternal) sexual contract.

This approach opens another way for fourth wave feminisms to consider the relationship between the femininities and commodities of the new sexual contract. In the act of consumption, the subject composes this normative feminine 'self' from and through each purchase. In this scene of commodity seduction, what lures the subject is a material object. This real object glimmers with 'something more', and it is this 'something more' that captures the subject's gaze. It has become a psychic object, an object that does not fulfil 'real' or material needs but rather psychic desires. The material object becomes a psychic object through the co-ordinates of the subject's desire, that is, through her wish to be her image of herself as feminine. These imaginary objects fill these representations of femininity with phantasmic content (the imaginary *a*). In this way, this object supports the subject's deepest attachments to the signifiers of 'femininity' that circulate in her world of late capitalist consumption. In the psychic life of this material economy, the infant itself becomes an object of exchange in the maternal masquerade. Nina Power (2009: 30) sharply observes of such images of contemporary womanhood that: '[t]o Freud's infamous question "*what do women want?*" it seems, then, that we have all-too-ready an answer. Why! They want shoes and chocolate and handbags and babies and curling tongs washed down with a large glass of white wine'.

248 Kirsten Campbell

However, it is also important to understand that the imaginary self 'stands simultaneously for the imaginary phantasmic lure/screen *and* for that which this lure is obfuscating, for the void behind the lure' (Žižek 1998: 80). The lure of these hegemonic femininities obfuscates the gender troubles of the feminine in the new gender order. Laurie Penny offers her own fourth wave reply to the question of what women want: '[w]e can have everything we want as long as what we want is a life spent searching for exhausting work that doesn't pay enough, shopping for things we don't need and sticking to a set of social and sexual rules that turn out, once you plough through the layers of trash and adverts, to be as rigid as ever' (2014: 7). This 'void behind the lure' is the gap in the socio-symbolic order. These hegemonic femininities veil the excluded term of fraternal discourse, the gap in (or void of) its symbolic structure. They mark a place of structural impossibility: namely, that point at which the socio-symbolic order is incomplete and lacking. The recognition of this structural impossibility of the position of women in the new sexual contract offers another kind of feminist politics for the fourth wave, for which Lacan's later idea of the *not all* of the female subject provides a useful direction.

The *not all* of the female subject is a position which the socio-symbolic order does not capture. In Lacan's later model of sexuation, the phallus only guarantees a masculine subject and Symbolic order. The subjective and symbolic structures that it supports are therefore incomplete – there is always 'something more', such that the phallic order always produces an excess to itself. The phallus fails to effect closure of what otherwise appears to be a transcendental Symbolic order. For this reason, the *not all* provides a means to re-conceive the female subject. Lacan argues that the position of exception to the phallic signifier is not that of negation or contradiction, but of indeterminacy (1998a: 103). As a position which the law of the signifier does not determine, the *not all* is a limit to its claim to represent an infinite set of all. It marks both the limit of the phallic signifier (as its exception) and the failure of that limit (as its infinite excess). The *not all* is an objection to the universal claim of the masculine (1998a: 103). The *not all* of a female subject is a position of a non-universal subject, and so is a position of specificity and particularity. In the position of *not all*, the female subject is a specific and particular subject: women 'do not lend themselves to generalization. Not even, I say this parenthetically, to phallocentric generalization' (Lacan 1975: 18).

The position of the *not all* is a political description of the position of female subjectivity in the new sexual contract, rather than an ontological description of women. The *not all* is a position that is neither 'inside' nor 'outside' the new gender order. Instead, it is in excess of its phallic fraternal imaginary. It represents the failure of phallic identity, which opens the possibility of moving beyond its limits. This strategy recognizes that ~~The Woman~~ is a masculine fantasy that does not represent women. As such, ~~The Woman~~ does not describe 'women', but is rather a site of feminist contestation. This contestation is contingent upon building new feminist discourses. These new feminist discourses posit women as speaking subjects, who bring into representation the reality – not fantasy – of the pleasures and miseries of femininities.

Fourth wave feminisms are currently doing just this in acts of 'shouting back' (Bates 2014). These acts range from campaigns against misogyny in the online and traditional public sphere, and for the inclusion of women in public life, to building new feminist counter-publics in meetings and protests. In each act, fourth wave feminisms resist the lure of the normative fantasies of contemporary femininity. Instead, they insist on revealing the gap or lack in the new sexual contract. This opens the possibility of making the hegemonic fantasies of femininity a site of feminist contestation. With this disruption of the Discourse of the Master, it then becomes possible for feminist discourse to 'bring about new forms of representation and definition of the female subject' in order to produce new social bonds and political forms (Braidotti 1992: 182).

An important part of this challenge is to build new feminist social bonds, which articulate emancipatory ways to become speaking beings, and to exist in social bonds. These social bonds provide the foundation for inventing new ways to be female subjects. However, this process inevitably involves building collective political practices, which can remake our social ties in less oppressive and more emancipatory forms. In developing these collective practices, the fourth wave can challenge the psychic life of power that makes social change so difficult, and so to build a transformative fourth wave feminist politics.

Note

1 It should be noted that Irigaray takes this neologism from Lacan's discussion of 'male-sexual' (and not homosexual) desire in *Seminar XX*. My thanks to the editors for this clarification.

Bibliography

Adams, P. (1996) *The Emptiness of the Image: Psychoanalysis and Sexual Differences*. London and New York: Routledge.

Adkins, L. (2008) 'From Retroactivisation to Futurity: The End of the Sexual Contract', *NORA – Nordic Journal of Feminist and Gender Research*. 16(3): 182–201.

Banyard, K. (2010) *The Equality Illusion: The Truth About Women and Men Today*. London: Faber.

Barrett, M. (1984) *Women's Oppression Today*. London: Verso.

Bates, L. (2014) *Everyday Sexism*. London: Simon and Schuster.

Baumgardner, J. (2011) *F'em: Goo Goo, Gaga and Some Thoughts on Balls*. Berkeley, CA: Seal.

Brah . A. (1996) *Cartographies of Diaspora*. London and New York: Routledge.

Brah, A. (2012) 'Some Fragments By Way Of An Afterword'. *Feminist Review*, 100: 172–180.

Braidotti, R. (1992) 'On the Female Feminist Subject, or: from "she-self" to "she-other"', in *Beyond Equality and Difference: Citizenship, Feminist Politics and Female Subjectivity*, ed. Gisela Bock and Susan James. London: Routledge.

Braidotti, R. (2014) 'Thinking with an Accent: Françoise Collin, Les cahiers du Grif and French Feminism', *Signs*. 39(3): 597–626.

Brennan, T. (1993) *History After Lacan*. London and New York: Routledge.

Campbell, B. (2014) *End of Equality*. London: Seagull Books.

Campbell, J. (2000) 'Arguing With The Phallus', in *Feminist, Queer and Postcolonial Theory: A Psychoanalytic Contribution*. London: Zed.

Campbell, K. (2004) *Jacques Lacan and Feminist Epistemology*. London: Routledge.

Candy, L. (2014) 'Editor's Letter', *Elle*. London: Hearst Magazines.

Clough, P. T. (2007) 'Judith Butler', in *The Blackwell Companion to Major Contemporary Social Theorists*, ed. G. Ritzer. Malden, MA: Blackwell.

Cochrane, K. (2013) 'The Fourth Wave of Feminism', *The Guardian*. 10 December, available online at: www.theguardian.com/world/2013/dec/10/fourth-wave-feminism-rebel-women (accessed 11 April 2014).

Copjec, J. (1994) *Read My Desire: Lacan Against the Historicists*. Cambridge, MA and London: MIT Press.

Delphy, C. (1995) 'The Invention of French Feminism: An Essential Move', *Yale French Studies*, 87: 190–221.

Dolar, M. (2006) *A Voice and Nothing More*. Cambridge, MA: The MIT Press.

Donner, H. (2008) *Domestic Goddesses: Maternity, Globalization and Middle-Class Identity in Contemporary India*. Farnham: Ashgate.

Duchen, C. (1986) *Feminism in France: From May '68 to Mitterrand*. Boston, MA London and Henley: Routledge and Kegan Paul.

Fawcett Society (2013) *Women's Equality in the UK*. London: Fawcett Society.

Fink, B. (1995) *The Lacanian Subject: Between Language and Jouissance*. Princeton, NJ: Princeton University Press.

Flower MacCannell, J. (1991) *The Regime of the Brother: After the Patriarchy*. New York and London: Routledge.

Fraser, N. (2009) 'Feminism, Capitalism and the Cunning of History', *New Left Review*, 56: 97–117.

Fraser, N. (2013) *Fortunes of Feminism*. London: Verso.

Gill, R. and Scharff, C. (eds) (2010) *New Femininities: Postfeminism, Neoliberalism and Subjectivity*. London and New York: Palgrave.

Halberstam, J. (2012) *Gaga Feminism: Sex, Gender, and the End of Normal*. Boston, MA: Beacon.

Hall, Stuart (1989) *Out of Apathy. Voices of the New Left Thirty Years on. Oxford University Socialist Discussion Group*. London: Verso.

Halpin, T. (2014) 'Editor's Letter', *Marie Claire*. London: European Magazines.

Harris, A. L. (2004) *Future Girl*. New York: Routledge.

Harris, A., (2012) 'Online Cultures and Future Girl Citizens', in *Feminist Media: Participatory Spaces, Networks and Cultural Citizenship*, ed. E. Zobl and R. Drueke. Bielefeld: Transcript Verlag.

Hsieh, L. (2102) 'A Queer Sex, Or, Can Feminism and Psychoanalysis Have Sex Without the Phallus', *Feminist Review*, 102: 97–115.

Hsing, Y. and Lee, C. K. (eds) (2010) *Reclaiming Chinese Society: The New Social Activism*. New York and London: Routledge.

Irigaray, L. (1977) *This Sex Which Is Not One*. trans. Catherine Porter. Ithaca, NY: Cornell University Press.

Jardine, A. (1985) *Gynesis: Configurations of Woman and Modernity*. Ithaca, NY and London: Cornell University Press.

Kimmel, M. (2008) *Guyland: The Perilous World Where Boys Become Men*. New York: HarperCollins.

Kristeva, J. (1984) *Revolution in Poetic Language*, trans. Leon S. Roudiez. New York: Columbia University Press.

Lacan, J. (1989 [1975]) 'Geneva Lectures on the Symptom', *Analysis*, trans. Russell Grigg, 1: 7–26.

Lacan, Jacques (1993 [1955–1956]) *The Seminar of Jacques Lacan. Book III. The Psychoses*, trans. Russell Grigg, ed. Jacques-Alain Miller. London: Routledge.

Lacan, J. (1998a [1972–1973]) *The Seminar of Jacques Lacan. Book XX. Encore: On Feminine Sexuality, The Limits of Love and Knowledge*, ed. Jacques-Alain Miller, trans. B. Fink. New York and London: W. W. Norton and Company.

Lacan, J. (1998b) *The Four Fundamental Concepts of Psycho-Analysis*, trans. A. Sheridan. New York: W. W. Norton and Company.

Lacan, J. (2002) *Écrits*, trans. B. Fink. London and New York: W. W. Norton and Company.

Lacan, J. (2007 [1969–1970]) *The Seminar of Jacques Lacan. Book XVII. The Other Side of Psychoanalysis*, ed. Jacques-Alain Miller, trans. R. Grigg. New York and London: W. W. Norton and Company.

Levy, A. (2006) *Female Chauvinist Pigs*. New York: Simon and Schuster.

Littler, J. (2013) 'The Rise of the "Yummy Mummy": Popular Conservatism and the Neoliberal Maternal in Contemporary British Culture', *Communication, Culture & Critique*, 6: 227–243.

Luepnitz, D. (2003) 'Beyond the Phallus: Lacan and Feminism', in *The Cambridge Companion to Lacan*. Cambridge: Cambridge University Press, 221–237.

McRobbie, A. (2007) 'Top Girls? Young Women and the Post-feminist Sexual Contract', *Cultural Studies*, 21(4): 718 –37.

McRobbie, A. (2009) *The Aftermath of Feminism*. London: Sage.

McRobbie, A. (2013) 'Feminism, the Family and the New "Mediated" Maternalism', *New Formations*, 80–1: 119–137.

Marks, E. and de Coutrivron, I. (eds) (1981) *New French Feminisms: An Anthology*. New York: Schocken.

Mitchell, J. (1982) 'Introduction – I', in *Feminine Sexuality: Jacques Lacan and the école freudienne*, J. Mitchell and J. Rose. London and New York: W. W. Norton and Company.

Mitchell, J. (2000) 'Introduction', in *Psychoanalysis and Feminism: A Radical Reassessment of Freudian Psychoanalysis*. New York: Basic Books.

Mitchell, J. and Rose, J. (eds) (1982) *Feminine Sexuality: Jacques Lacan and the* école freudienne.London and New York: W. W. Norton and Company.

Mitchell, J., Rose, J. and Radford, J. (2010) 'Psychoanalysis, Politics and the Future of Feminism: A Conversation', *Women: A Cultural Review*, 21(1): 75–103.

Mohanty. C . (2003) *Feminism Without Borders: Decolonizing Theory, Practicing Solidarity*. Durham, NC and London: Duke University Press.

Oksala, J. (2011) 'Sexual Experience: Foucault, Phenomenology and Feminist Theory', *Hypatia*, 26(1): 207–223.

Pateman, C. (1988) *The Sexual Contract*. Stanford, CA: Stanford University Press.

Penley . C. (ed.) (1988) *Feminism and Film Theory*. London and New York: Routledge/BFI.

Penny, L. (2014) *Unspeakable Things*. London: Bloomsbury.

Power, N. (2009) *One-Dimensional Woman*. London: Zero Books.

Ragland-Sullivan, E. (1987) *Jacques Lacan and the Philosophy of Psychoanalysis*. Urbana and Chicago: University of Illinois Press.

Rose, J. (1982) 'Chapter Six', in *Feminine Sexuality: Jacques Lacan and the école freudienne*, ed. J. Mitchell and J. Rose. London and New York: W. W. Norton and Company.

Rose, J. (1986) *Sexuality in the Field of Vision*. London: Verso.

Roudinesco, É. (1990) *Jacques Lacan and Co.: History of Psychoanalysis in France, 1925–1985*, trans. J. Mehlman. London: Free Association.

Roudinesco, É. (1997) *Jacques Lacan*, trans. B. Bray. Cambridge: Polity.

Seshardi-Crooks, K. (2000) *Desiring Whiteness: A Lacanian Analysis of Race*. London: Routledge.

Snyder, R. C. (2008) 'What is Third-wave Feminism? A New Directions Essay', *Signs: Journal of Women in Culture and Society*, 34(1): 175–196.

Stivens, M. (2007) 'Post-Modern Motherhoods and Cultural Contest in Malaysia and Singapore', in *Working and Mothering in Asia: Images, Ideologies and Identities*, ed. Theresa W. Devasahayam and Brenda S. A. Yeoh. Singapore: National University of Singapore Press; Copenhagen: Nordic Institute of Asian Studies.

Weedon, C. (1997) *Feminist Practice and Post-Structuralist Theory*. Oxford: Blackwell.

Whitford, M. (1991) *Luce Irigaray: Philosophy in the Feminine*. London and New York: Routledge.

Žižek, S. (1998) 'Four Discourses, Four Subjects', in *Cogito and the Unconscious*, ed. S. Žižek. Durham, NC: Duke University Press.

Žižek, S. (2006) 'Objet a in Social Links', in *Jacques Lacan and the Other Side of Psychoanalysis*, ed. J. Clemens and R. Grigg. Durham, NC and London: Duke University Press.

16

DIVINE EX-SISTENCE

Theology between politics and psychoanalysis

Slavoj Žižek

UNIVERSITY OF LJUBLJANA, SLOVENIA

At the beginning of Ridley Scott's *Prometheus*, the sequel to the *Alien* trilogy, a hovering spacecraft departs our Earth deep in prehistoric times, while a humanoid alien who remained on the Earth drinks a dark bubbling liquid and then disintegrates – when his remains cascade into a waterfall, his DNA triggers a biogenetic reaction which led to the rise of humans. The story then jumps to 2089, when archaeologists Elizabeth Shaw and Charlie Holloway discover a star map in Scotland that matches others from several unconnected ancient cultures. They interpret this as an invitation from humanity's forerunners, the 'Engineers'. Peter Weyland, the elderly CEO of Weyland Corporation, funds an expedition to follow the map to the distant moon LV-223 aboard the scientific vessel *Prometheus*. The ship's crew travels in stasis while the android David monitors their voyage. Arriving in 2093, they are informed of their mission to find the Engineers. After long battles with the Engineers, the last of them forces open the lifeboat's airlock and attacks Shaw, who releases her alien offspring onto the Engineer. It thrusts a tentacle down the Engineer's throat, subduing him. Shaw recovers David's remains, and with his help, launches another Engineer spacecraft – she intends to reach the Engineers' home-world in an attempt to understand why they wanted to destroy humanity. In the film's last scene, Shaw (played by Noomi Rapace) desperately shouts at the homicidal alien: 'I need to know why! What did we do wrong? Why do you hate us?' Is not such a cry for meaning or purpose an exemplary case of the Lacanian *Che vuoi?*, of the impenetrability of gods of the Real? (Ehrenreich 2012: 132–37).

Gods of the Real

So where do we find these living gods? In the pagan Thing: God dies in itself in Judaism and for itself in Christianity. The destructive aspect of the divine, the brutal explosion of rage mixed with ecstatic bliss, which marks a living God, is

254 Slavoj Žižek

what Lacan aims at with his statement that gods belong to the Real. An exemplary literary case of such an encounter of the divine Real is Euripides' last play *Bacchae*, which examines religious ecstasy and resistance to it. Disguised as a young holy man, the god Bacchus arrives from Asia in Thebes where he proclaims his godhood and preaches his orgiastic religion. Pentheus, the young Theban king, is horrified at the explosion of sacred orgies and prohibits his people from worshipping Bacchus. The enraged Bacchus leads Pentheus to a nearby mountain, the site of sacred orgies, where Agave, Pentheus' own mother, and the women of Thebes tear him to pieces in a Bacchic sacred destructive frenzy. The play outlines four existential positions towards the sacred orgiastic ritual. First, there is Pentheus himself, an enlightened rationalist and a sceptic in religious matters. He rejects the Bacchic sacred orgies as a mere cover for sensual indulgence and is determined to suppress them by force:

> It so happens I've been away from Thebes,
> but I hear about disgusting things going on,
> here in the city – women leaving home
> to go to silly Bacchic rituals,
> cavorting there in mountain shadows,
> with dances honoring some upstart god,
> this Dionysus, whoever he may be. Mixing bowls
> in the middle of their meetings are filled with wine.
> They creep off one by one to lonely spots
> to have sex with men, claiming they're Maenads
> busy worshipping. But they rank Aphrodite,
> goddess of sexual desire, ahead of Bacchus.[1]

Then, there are the two positions of wisdom. Tiresias, a blind man of pious and reverent soul, preaches fidelity to traditions as our sacred and imperishable inheritance:

> To the gods we mortals are all ignorant.
> Those old traditions from our ancestors,
> the ones we've had as long as time itself,
> no argument will ever overthrow,
> in spite of subtleties sharp minds invent.

However, his advice is nonetheless sustained by a Marxist-sounding notion of religion as opium for the people, Bacchus:

> brought with him liquor from the grape,
> something to match the bread from Demeter.
> He introduced it among mortal men.
> When they can drink up what streams off the vine,
> unhappy mortals are released from pain.

It grants them sleep, allows them to forget
their daily troubles. Apart from wine,
there is no cure for human hardship.

This line of thought is radicalized by Cadmus, the wise old counsellor to the king, who advises caution and submission:

You should live among us,
not outside traditions. At this point,
you're flying around – thinking, but not clearly.
For if, as you claim, this man is not a god,
why not call him one? Why not tell a lie,
a really good one?

In short, the position of Cadmus is that of Plato in his *Republic*: ordinary people need beautiful lies, so we should pretend to believe to keep them in check. And, finally, beneath these three positions, there is the wild (feminine) mob itself. While the debate between the three is going on, we hear from time to time the passionate cries and wild ecstatic prayers of the Bacchantes who proclaim their scorn for 'the wisdom of deep thinkers', and their devotion to the 'customs and beliefs of the multitude'. Bacchantes are anti-Platonic to the extreme: against abstract rationalism, they assert fidelity to the customs which form a particular life-world, so that, from their view, the true act of madness is to exclude madness, it is the madness of pure rationality – the true madman is Pentheus, not the orgiastic Bacchantes. Tiresias draws the same conclusion:

You've got a quick tongue and seem intelligent,
but your words don't make any sense at all.
/.../ You unhappy man, you've no idea
just what it is you're saying. You've gone mad!
Even before now you weren't in your right mind.

In other words, the true point of 'madness' is not the excess of the ecstatic Night of the World, but the madness of the passage to the Symbolic itself, of imposing a symbolic order onto the chaos of the Real.[2] *Every* system of meaning is thus minimally paranoiac, 'mad', as Lacan will repeatedly claim throughout his teaching. Recall Brecht's slogan: 'What is the robbing of a bank compared to the founding of a new bank?' Therein resides the lesson of David Lynch's *The Straight Story*: what is the ridiculously pathetic perversity of figures like Bobby Peru in *Wild at Heart* or Frank in *Blue Velvet* compared to deciding to traverse the US central plain in a tractor to visit a dying relative? Measured with this act, Frank's and Bobby's outbreaks of rage are the impotent theatrics of old and sedate conservatives. In the same way, we should say: what is the mere madness caused by the loss of reason, like the crazy dancing of Bacchantes, compared to the madness of reason itself?

The Event of encountering the Real Thing is brought to extreme when the Thing is no longer an inner-worldly entity but the abyss itself, the void in which inner-worldly things disappear. This abyss exerts a strange mixture of horror and attraction, it pulls us towards itself – in what direction? The famous lines of the *chorus mysticus*, which conclude Faust, are Goethe's 'wisdom' at its worst: 'Everything transient is just a simile; the deficient here really happens; the indescribable is here done; the eternal-feminine pulls us upwards.' If nothing else, this pseudo-deep bubbling gets the direction wrong: it pulls us DOWN, not up – down in the sense of Maelström from Edgar Allan Poe's story *A Descent into the Maelström* (incidentally, if there ever was a political regime where the eternal-feminine claims to draw its subjects upwards, it is today's North Korea). Poe's story is told by a narrator who reports on what an old Norwegian fisherman told him while standing at the edge of a huge cliff overlooking the stormy sea. From time to time, a furious current shapes the smaller whirlpools of the water into a huge mile-long funnel, the 'great whirlpool of the Maelström', as the narrator explains. Whenever a ship comes within a mile of the full force, it is carried to the bottom and slammed against the rocks until the Maelström ceases. Since nature's sublime strength seems to defy rational explanation, the narrator is drawn to more fantastic explanations that call the centre the entrance to the abyss opening to the middle of the Earth. However, years ago, one day in July, as the narrator continues, a terrible hurricane arrives without warning and tears away the masts of the ship of the old man and his brother who are returning home. When, after being submerged in the water, the boat recovers and floats back to the surface, the two men with horror discover that they are caught by the Maelström. They sense their doom. When the waves subside into foam, the old man becomes calm in his despair, thinking of how magnificent his death will be and awaits his exploration of the Maelström's depths (even at the cost of his life). Yet when the man opens his eyes, he sees his boat hanging on the black walls of the Maelström, and the force of the boat's whirling pins him to it. He sees a rainbow in the abyss, caused by the movement of the water, and as they slowly spiral downward, the man observes the wreckage that swirls around him and notices how small shapes and cylinders seem to descend most slowly into the abyss. He lashes himself to the water cask and cuts himself loose from the boat while his brother refuses to move from the boat and is lost. The cask sinks much more slowly than the boat, and, by the time it sinks half of the distance to the centre of the abyss, the funnel of the Maelström calms. The man finds himself on the surface where a boat picks him up. He has been saved, but, as he tells the narrator, his black hair turned white and his face rapidly aged.

The old man's ability to overcome fear and to realize that small cylinders provide the greatest safety in the Maelström makes him similar to Auguste Dupin, Poe's arch-model private detective who is a master in the art of logic and deduction. Although *A Descent into the Maelström* is an adventure horror story, it can also be read as one of Poe's mystery stories in which, at the story's end, the detective reveals the path of his reasoning, from the start to the solution of the enigma. The old man already resolved the enigma (a fact proven by him being still alive) and is now re-telling his thinking process to a rapt listener whose role is analogous to that of Dupin's commonsensical narrator friend (and a forerunner of Sherlock Holmes's Watson or Poirot's Captain Hastings). He is honest but lacks the spark that makes Dupin or the old man that survived the descent into the Maelström the hero of their stories. The victory of reason alludes that effectively the subtitle of the story should have been something like 'The spirit of the deadly vortex as the birth of rational thinking', for in the story, cold rational thinking and death drive overlap. The death drive (in its strict Freudian sense) is not the subject's willing surrender to the abyss, his acceptance of being swallowed by the deadly vortex, but the very repetitive circulation on the edge of the abyss. In other words, death drive is on the side of reason, not on the side of irrationality as often thought. And this brings us back to Hegel's notion of the abyssal *Night of the World* as the very core of sub-jectivity: is the abyss of subjectivity pierced with Lacan's 'Che vuoi?' not the ulti-mate Maelstrom? And is rational thinking not an art of circulating on the very edge of the abyss?

'When the man comes around ...'

So what happens when the living gods withdraw, when they no longer operate in collective libidinal economy? It was already Hegel who said that word is the murder of a thing, which means that the death of gods, far from liberating us from the symbolic link, enforces the power of the Word to its very limit. But how do we pass from the living gods of the Real to the dead God of the Word? The only consequent move is a step further from describing historical changes on how we think about God to historicize God himself. This idea was introduced by Schelling in his *Ages of the World,* but soon turned out too challenging and was abandoned in subsequent development of his philosophy. The key shift from the *Ages of the World* to the late Schelling's philosophy of mythology and revelation is that the *Ages of the World* thoroughly historicizes God: the process of creation and revelation is a process into which God himself is caught, the becoming of the world is the becoming of God himself, his self-creation and self-revelation, so that the human awareness of God is the self-awareness of God himself. However, the late Schelling renounces this radical historicization of God. In a return to traditional theology, God is not affected by the process of creation, He remains in himself what He is from all eternity, creation is an entirely free and contingent divine decision/act. God as Trinity exists in eternity, as the unity of the three potencies (contraction, expansion, their reconciliation) in their atemporal/virtual state; with the process of creation which opens up temporality, the three potencies acquire autonomy and are actualized as Past, Present, and Future (the dark Ground of dense matter, the light of *logos*, the reconciliation of the two in a living personality which is the Self as a point of contraction subordinated to the light of reason). The starting point, the premise, of the late Schelling's philosophy of mythology and revelation remains the self-division or self-alienation of divinity:

It is absolutely necessary for the understanding of Christianity – the *conditio sine qua non* of perceiving its true meaning – that we comprehend this cutting-off [*Abgeschnittenheit*] of the Son from the Father, this being in his own form and hence in complete freedom and independence of the Father.

(Schelling 1856–61: 39)

However, God in himself is not caught in this division – how can this be? Schelling sees creation as a process of alienation of God from himself which proceeds in three steps, where the separation of the Son from the Father is only the last step in this process. First, God sets free his lowest potency, the egotist principle of contraction. What in God is not God, thereby creating matter as something actually existing outside Himself. The goal of creation is for God to reveal/manifest itself in his creation. However, creation takes a wrong turn not intended by God, the created world becomes the fallen world of decay and sorrow, where nature is impregnated by melancholy. God's first attempt to reconcile the created world and himself by way of another creation – the creation of Adam – also fails because of Adam's fall into sin. His free choice of sin. At that moment, the higher second potency of God, the principle of love, concretizes itself as the demiurge, the 'lord of being'. What Schelling saw clearly is that this God as demiurge of the fallen world (recall the Gnostic notion that our material world was created by the evil demiurge) is a Janus-like two-faced God. He is simultaneously the demiurge, the Lord–Creator of the world, the transcendent Master elevated above the world, and a homeless god, exiled from eternity and condemned to wander anonymously in his creation. Like Wotan/Odin becoming Wanderer in Wagner's *Ring*. In this ultimate theological coincidence of the opposites, the Master of the world has to appear within the world in its 'oppositional determination [*gegensaetzliche Bestimmung*]', as its lowest element with no proper place in it, as a wanderer excluded from all social groups.[3] We thus arrive at the first opposition in – or, rather, splitting of – the divine: the 'pure' God prior to the creation of the world, the anonymous 'Godhead', set against the God-demiurge, the Master of creation, who is the God outside of God, the God of the fallen world. Schelling's achievement is to show how the Christian Incarnation can be understood only against the background of this splitting.

The God-demiurge who appears in different guises in pagan religion is the 'pre-existing Christ', the mythological God, the God of pagan phantasmagorias, not the actually existing God but its shadowy double, 'God outside himself': 'Mythology is nothing less than the hidden history of the Christ before his historical birth, the peregrinations of the God outside God' (McGrath 2012: 162). And it is crucial for Schelling that *the God who in Incarnation becomes man is not God himself or in itself, but this 'God outside God', the pagan demiurge*: 'Christ must possess an independent ground of divinity, an extra-divine divinity, a claim to sovereignty which he renounces. [...] as the God outside of God, Christ has his own proper claim to being the God of the fallen world, a claim which he renounces' (McGrath 2012: 166). With the Christian Revelation, with Incarnation proper in which Christ 'enters into the being of the fallen world to the point of becoming himself a fallen being' (ibid.), myth becomes fact, an actually existing fully human individual, which is why, as Schelling says, pointing forward towards Kierkegaard, 'Christ is not the teacher, as the saying goes, he is not the founder (of Christianity), he is the content of Christianity' (Schelling 1856–61: 35). In Incarnation, in becoming man, God doesn't empty himself of his deity, but of the *morphe theou*, of the form of God as a sovereign demiurge: 'he who was in the form of God willed to empty himself of this' (Schelling 1995: 273). "God becomes man" means: the divine became man, yet not the divine [in itself], but rather the extra-divine of the divine became man' (Schelling 1995: 275).

Here we can see where Schelling deviates from Christian Orthodoxy. Not so much with regards to the fact that, for Schelling, pagan religions are not simply wrong but an organic part of a divine history (a process which culminates in Incarnation proper), but in how he complicates the process of Incarnation. For Schelling, Incarnation is preceded by the self-splitting of God-in-itself (Godhead), by God's contraction in a God outside the divine, the Lord of the fallen world, so that Christ as mediator does not mediate primarily between the God and the creation (the fallen world), but between the pure God and the God of the fallen world. The God outside the divine. This means that the God who incarnates himself in Christ is not the pure Godhead but the God of the fallen world (the God-demiurge, the God outside the divine). It is *this* God who empties himself of his divinity, who renounces the 'form of God', becomes purely human and then dies on the cross. In short, what dies on the cross is the God-demiurge, the God who is outside the divine, and this is why Crucifixion is simultaneously reconciliation of the divine with itself.

This reference to Schelling allows us to complicate further the figure of Incarnation. Two splittings precede Incarnation: first the self-division of God into the pure Godhead and the Lord of creation; second the splitting of this God of the fallen world himself, the god of pagan mythology, into transcendent demiurge and the anonymous Wanderer. The first figure of the God in its oppositional determination, God outside himself, is thus already (the standard notion of) God as the transcendent Creator and Master of the universe. The fact that this God-demiurge again redoubles himself one into himself, and second, himself in its oppositional determination (Wanderer), signals the 'abstract' character of the God-demiurge, it signals that this God is already hampered by an imperfection. The nature of this imperfection was indicated in the most radical reading of the 'Book of Job' proposed in 1930s by the Norwegian theologian Peter Wessel Zapffe who accentuated Job's 'boundless perplexity' when God himself finally appears to him: expecting a sacred and pure God whose intellect is infinitely superior to ours:

> [Job] finds himself confronted with a world ruler of grotesque primitiveness, a cosmic cave-dweller, a braggart and blusterer, almost agreeable in his total ignorance of spiritual culture. [...] What is new for Job is *not* God's greatness in quantifiable terms; that he knew fully in advance [...]; what is new is the qualitative baseness.
>
> *(Zapffe 2004: 147)*

In other words, God – the God of the Real – is like the lady in courtly love, it is *das Ding*, a capricious cruel master who simply has no sense of universal justice. God-the-Father thus quite literally does not know what he is doing, whereas the Christ is the one who does know it, but is reduced to an impotent compassionate observer, addressing his father with 'Father, can't you see I'm burning?' (burning together with all the victims of the father's rage). Only by falling into his own creation and wandering around in it as an impassive observer can God perceive the horror of his creation and the fact that He, the highest Lawgiver, is himself the supreme Criminal. Since God-the-demiurge is not so much evil as a stupid brute lacking moral sensitivity, we should forgive him, because he does not know what he is doing. In the standard onto-theological vision, only the demiurge elevated above particular reality sees the entire picture, while particular agents caught in struggles get only partial misleading insights. In the core of Christianity we find a different vision – the demiurge elevated above reality is a brute unaware of the horror he is creating, and only when he enters his own creation and experiences it from within, as its inhabitant, can he see the nightmare he fathered. (It is easy to discern in this vision the old literary motif of a king who occasionally dresses up as an ordinary man and mingles with the poor to get the taste of how they live and feel.)

It is here that the God of the Real returns with a vengeance in the very heart of Christianity. Postmodern philosophers from Nietzsche onwards, as a rule prefer Catholicism over Protestantism. Catholicism is a culture of external playful rituals in contrast to the inner sense of guilt and the pressure of authenticity that characterize Protestantism. We are allowed to simply follow the ritual and ignore the authenticity of our inner belief. However, this playfulness should not deceive us. Catholicism is resorting to such subterfuges to save the divine big Other in his goodness, while the capriciously 'irrational' predestination in Protestantism confronts us with a God who is ultimately not good and all-powerful but stained by the indelible suspicion of being stupid, arbitrary, or even outright evil. The dark implicit lesson of Protestantism is: if you want God, you have to renounce (part of the divine) goodness. One can discern the traces of this full acceptance of God's unconditional and capricious authority in the last song Johnny Cash recorded just before his death, 'The Man Comes Around', an exemplary articulation of the anxieties contained in the Southern Baptist Christianity:

> There's a man going around taking names and he decides
> Who to free and who to blame every body won't be treated
> Quite the same there will be a golden ladder reaching down
> When the man comes around
>
> The hairs on your arm will stand up at the terror in each
> Sip and each sup will you partake of that last offered cup
> Or disappear into the potter's ground
> When the man comes around
>
> Hear the trumpets hear the pipers one hundred million angels singing
> Multitudes are marching to a big kettledrum

Voices calling and voices crying
Some are born and some are dying
Its alpha and omegas kingdom come
And the whirlwind is in the thorn trees
The virgins are all trimming their wicks
The whirlwind is in the thorn trees
It's hard for thee to kick against the pricks
Till Armageddon no shalam no sholom

Then the father hen will call his chickens home
The wise man will bow down before the thorn and at his feet
They will cast the golden crowns
When the man comes around

Whoever is unjust let him be unjust still
Whoever is righteous let him be righteous still
Whoever is filthy let him be filthy still.

The song is about Armageddon, the end of days when God will appear and perform the Last Judgement. The event is presented as pure and arbitrary terror: God almost appears as Evil personified, as a kind of political informer, a man who 'comes around' and provokes consternation by 'taking names', by deciding who is to be saved and who lost. If anything, Cash's description evokes the well-known scene of people lined up for a brutal interrogation, and the informer pointing out those selected for torture: there is no mercy, no pardon of sins, no jubilation, we are all fixed in our roles, the just remain just and the filthy remain filthy. Even worse, in this divine proclamation, we are not simply judged in a just way; we are informed from outside, as if learning about an arbitrary decision, that we were righteous or sinners, that we are saved or condemned (the arbitrary decision that has nothing to do with our inner qualities).[4] And, again, this dark excess of the ruthless divine sadism – excess over the image of a severe, but nonetheless just, God – is a necessary negative, as it stands for the underside or the excess of Christian love over the Jewish Law. For as love which suspends the law is necessarily accompanied by the arbitrary cruelty which suspends the law as well.

Recall the strange fact, regularly evoked by Primo Levi and other Holocaust survivors, on how their intimate reaction to their survival was marked by a deep split. Consciously, they were fully aware that their survival was a matter of meaningless accident, that they are not in any way guilty of it, that the only guilty perpetrators are their Nazi torturers; yet, they were (more than merely) haunted by the 'irrational' feeling of guilt, as if they survived at the expense of others who died there and are thus somehow responsible for their death (as is well-known, this unbearable guilt-feeling drove many of them to suicide). This feeling of guilt displays the agency of the superego at its purest: the obscene agency which manipulates us into a spiralling movement of self-destruction. For this very reason, there is something irreducibly comical about the superego. Let us turn again to Primo

Levi – this is how, in *If This Is a Man*, he describes the dreadful 'selekcja', the survival examination in the camp:

> The *Blockaeltester* [the elder of the hut] has closed the connecting-door and has opened the other two which lead from the dormitory and the *Tagesraum* [daily room] outside. Here, in front of the two doors, stands the arbiter of our fate, an SS subaltern. On his right is the *Blockaeltester*, on his left, the quartermaster of the hut. Each one of us, as he comes naked out of the *Tagesraum* into the cold October air, has to run the few steps between the two doors, give the card to the SS man and enter the dormitory door. The SS man, in the fraction of a second between two successive crossings, with a glance at one's back and front, judges everyone's fate, and in turn gives the card to the man on his right or his left, and this is the life or death of each of us. In three or four minutes a hut of two hundred man is 'done', as is the whole camp of twelve thousand men in the course of the afternoon.
>
> *(Levi 1987: 133–34)*

The right stands for survival, the left for gas chamber. Is there not something properly COMIC in this? The ridiculous spectacle to appear strong and healthy, to attract for a brief moment the indifferent gaze of the Nazi administrator who presides over life and death? Here, comedy and horror coincide. Imagine the prisoners practising their appearance, trying to hold head high and chest forward, walking with a brisk step, pinching their lips to appear less pale, exchanging advices on how to impress the SS man; imagine how a simple momentary confusion of cards or a lack of attention of the SS man can decide their fate. Does not this take us close to the arbitary procedure of predestination? Is the scene staged around 'the man who comes around' from Cash's song not the ultimate *selekcja* with regard to which even the Auschwitz *selekcja* is a relief? The Final Judgement is in Cash's song not 'deconstructed', it is not transformed into an endlessly postponed horizon, an event that is always-to-come: the Final Judgement takes place here and now, but as an obscene travesty of divine justice, an act performed by a crazy god who resembles the Nazi selector in Auschwitz.

The deposed God

But is this God the last word of Christianity? It is the ultimate version of the transcendent God-in-itself, and one has to go through it to reach the core of the Christian atheism. Jean-Luc Marion developed this point in detail: I only exist through being loved by the Other (God, ultimately). This, however, is not enough – God himself only exists through *ex-sistence*,[5] as the effect of men's referring to him (in the blockbuster *The Clash of Titans*, Zeus is right to complain that, if men stop praying to gods and celebrating them in their rituals, gods will cease to exist). Such a properly comical notion of God who depends on human approbation is, as one would expect it, evoked by Kierkegaard who, in his *Concept of*

Anxiety, in a mockingly antihegelian way describes how Stephen of Tournai (the 13th-century scholastic theologist from Paris):

> thought that God must be obliged to him for having furnished a proof of the Trinity [...] This story has numerous analogies, and in our time speculation has assumed such authority that it has practically tried to make God feel uncertain of himself, like a monarch who is anxiously waiting to learn whether the general assembly will make him an absolute or a limited monarch.
>
> *(Kierkegaard 1980: 151)*

We should also bear in mind that we are dealing here with a properly dialectical mediation of knowing and being in which being itself hinges on (not-)knowing. As Lacan put it, God does not know He is dead (that is why he lives) – in this case, existence hinges on not-knowing, while in Christianity God learns that He is dead. However, already the logical 'god of philosophers' is a dead God, although in a different way, so maybe Tournai was wrong or at least he should be read in a more ambiguous way: if a philosopher proves the existence of God, is the God who comes to exist in this way not a dead God? So, maybe, what God really dreads is the very success of the proof of his existence. The situation here is the same as in the well-known anecdote about the Hearst editor: God fears that the proof of his existence will fail, but he fears even more that it will *not* fail. In short, God's impasse is that He is either alive (but as such caught in a terrifying suspension about His existence) or existing but dead.

Kierkegaard of course dismisses the attempts to logically demonstrate the existence of God as absurd and pointless logical exercises (his model of such professorial blindness for the authentic religious experience was Hegel's dialectical machinery). However, his sense of humour cannot withstand the wonderful image of a God in anxiety, dreading for his own status as if it depends on the logical exercises of a philosopher, as if the philosopher's reasoning has consequences in the Real, so that, if the proof fails, God's existence itself is threatened. And one can go even further in this line of Kierkegaardian reasoning: what undoubtedly attracted him to the remark of Tornacensis was the blasphemous idea of a god himself in anxiety.

The divine impasse thus resides in the fact that the God whose existence is proven is like a monarch whom the assembly makes an absolute One: the very form of confirming his absolute power (it depends on the whim of the assembly) undermines it. The political parallel is crucial here since Kierkegaard himself resorts to the comparison of God and King. God exposed to the philosopher's whimsy wit is like a king exposed to the whimsy wit of a popular assembly. But what is Kierkegaard's point here? Is it simply that, in both cases, we should reject liberal decadence and opt for absolute monarchy? What complicates such a simple and apparently obvious solution is that, for Kierkegaard, the (properly comical) point of the Incarnation is that that Kod–King becomes a beggar, a low ordinary human. Thus would it not be more correct to conceive Christianity as the paradox of God's abdication – God steps down to be replaced by the assembly of believers called the Holy Spirit?

264 Slavoj Žižek

This is why authentic religion is incompatible with direct knowledge or unconditional certainty. A radical doubt is its innermost component, and the believer him/herself is again and again surprised at unexpected signs of divine presence or intervention ('miracles'). This is how one should read Kierkegaard's point that a miracle is merely a sign that has to be interpreted and therefore an ambiguous indication. Already the Jansenists made this point when they insisted that miracles are not 'objective' miraculous facts which demonstrate the truth of a religion to everyone. They appear as such only to the eyes of believers. To non-believers, they are mere fortuitous natural coincidences. This theological legacy survives in radical emancipatory thought, from Marxism to psychoanalysis. In his *Seminar XVIII* on a *Discourse, Which Would Not Be That of a Semblance*, Lacan provided a succinct definition of the truth of interpretation in psychoanalysis: 'Interpretation is not tested by a truth that would decide by yes or no, it unleashes truth as such. It is only true inasmuch as it is truly followed' (Lacan 2007: 13). There is nothing 'theological' in this precise formulation, only the insight into the properly dialectical unity of theory and practice in (not only) psychoanalytic interpretation. The 'test' of the analyst's interpretation is in the true effect it unleashes in the patient. This is how we should also re-read Marx's eleventh thesis on Feuerbach: the 'test' of Marxist theory is the truth-effect it unleashes in its addressee (the proletarians), in transforming them into emancipatory revolutionary subjects. The *locus communis* 'You have to see it to believe it!' should always be read together with its inversion: 'You have to believe [in] it to see it!' Although one may be tempted to oppose them as the dogmatism of blind faith versus openness toward the unexpected, one should insist also on the truth of the second version: truth, as opposed to knowledge, is something that only an engaged gaze, the gaze of a subject who 'believes in it', can see. Think of love: in love, only the lover sees in the object of love that X which causes love, so the structure of love is the same as that of the Badiouian Event which also exists only for those who recognize themselves in it: there is no Event for a non-engaged objective observer.

In his *Seminar XX: Encore*, Lacan warns against a too simplistic atheism: he says that while God does not exist (in the sense of an absolute Entity dwelling somewhere out there independently of us, humans), he nonetheless ex-sists. This ex-sistence, of course, can be understood in different ways, which can relate to the three fundamental dimensions of human experience as theorized by Lacan. In relation to the Imaginary, ex-sistence means that God does not exist in himself, but only outside himself, as humanity's imaginary projection. In relation to the Symbolic, it implies that God ex-sists in human practices and rituals which refer to him, as a symbolic Cause kept alive through human activity. And finally in relation to the Real – the meaning emphasized by Lacan – God is the impossible/real point, purely virtual point of reference, which resists symbolization, like the unbearable intensity of the *jouissance féminine*. But we can cut short the looming debate and simply posit that God ex-sists outside himself in our practice of love – not in our love for him, but our love for our neighbours (as Christ put it to his disciples, 'when there is love among you, I am there'). What this means is that man and

God are caught in a circle: a religious man perceives God as the presupposition of his entire life, but this presupposition is posited by him serving God and has no meaning outside this relationship. This is why Kierkegaard has to insist on God's thorough 'desubstantialization'. God is 'beyond the order of Being'. He is nothing but the mode of how we relate to Him, i.e. we do not relate to Him, He IS this relating:

> God himself is this: *how* one involves himself with Him. As far as physical and external objects are concerned, the object is something else than the mode: there are many modes. In respect to God, the *how* is the what. He who does not involve himself with God in the mode of absolute devotion does not become involved with God.
>
> *(Kierkegaard 1970: entry 1405)*

The Christian passage to Holy Spirit as Love is to be taken literally: God as the divine *individual* (Christ) passes into the purely *non-substantial link* between the individuals. This is why if aliens were to land on Earth, we can be certain that they would not know about Christ, Christ is exclusively a part of human history (but this is not an argument that Christ is just a human creation/projection or, even worse, that there is one divine Absolute which appears in multiple ways to different groups of people or other rational beings). And this is also why the genuine dimension of Christian doubt does not concern the existence of God, i.e. its logic is not 'I feel such a need to believe in God, but I cannot be sure that He really exists, that He is not just a chimera of my imagination' (to which a humanist atheist can easily respond: 'then drop God and simply assume the ideals God stands for as your own'), which is why a Christian subject is indifferent towards the infamous proofs of God's existence. Recall Brecht's famous Herr Keuner anecdote about the existence of God:

> Someone asked Herr Keuner if there is a God. Herr Keuner said: I advise you to think about how your behavior would change with regard to the answer to this question. If it would not change, then we can drop the question. If it would change, then I can help you at least insofar as I can tell you: You already decided: You need a God.
>
> *(Brecht 1995: 18)*

Brecht is right here: we are never in a position to directly choose between theism and atheism, since the choice as such is already located within the field of belief (in the sense of our practical engagement). What an authentic believer should do here is shift the accent of Brecht's anecdote from God to God's ex-sistence that is fully compatible with materialism. This is why doubt is immanent to an authentic religion. That is not abstract intellectual doubt about God's existence, but doubt about our practical engagement, which makes God himself ex-sist. This doubt is brought to extreme in Christianity where (as G. K. Chesterton pointed out) not only do believers doubt God, God himself gets caught in doubt (In his 'Father, why have you abandoned me?', Christ himself commits what is for a Christian the ultimate sin: he wavers in his Faith) – and Chesterton is fully aware that we are thereby approaching:

> a matter more dark and awful than it is easy to discuss […] a matter which the greatest saints and thinkers have justly feared to approach. But in that terrific tale of the Passion there is a distinct emotional suggestion that the author of all things (in some unthinkable way) went not only through agony, but through doubt.
>
> *(Chesterton 1995: 145)*

Thus what God doubts about is that the bond of human engagement, which makes him ex-sist, will be broken.

Notes

1 All *Bacchae* quotes are from https://records.viu.ca/~johnstoi/euripides/euripides.htm.
2 In his analysis of the paranoiac judge Schreber, Freud points out how the paranoiac 'system' is not madness, but a desperate attempt to *escape* madness – the disintegration of the symbolic universe – through an ersatz universe of meaning.
3 Note how, in a strictly homologous way, a will that actively wills nothing is the oppositional determination of the will which wills nothing in particular, which is a mere possibility of willing.
4 Incidentally, there is a traumatic occurrence in *Exodus* 4:24–26 in which precisely 'the man comes around': God himself comes to Moses' tent in the guise of a dark stranger and attacks him ('the Lord met him, and sought to kill him'); Moses is then saved by his wife Ziporrah who appeases God by offering him the foreskin of their son.
5 See, for instance, the following well-pointed passage, where Lacan associates the God-hypothesis with enunciation/saying (fr. *dire*): 'The Other, the Other as the locus of truth, is the only place, albeit an irreducible place, that we can give to the term "divine being", God, to call him by his name. God (*Dieu*) is the locus where, if you will allow me this wordplay, the *dieu* – the *dieur* – the *dire*, is produced. With a trifling change, the *dire* constitutes *dieu*. And as long as things are said, the God hypothesis will persist. That is why, in the end, only theologians can be truly atheistic, namely, those who speak of God' (Lacan 1998: 45). The conclusion is that God insists as a foreign existence – precisely ex-sistence – but within language and the act of saying. For the link between God and ex-sistence, see also Lacan 1975: 103.

Bibliography

Brecht, Bertolt (1995) *Prosa 3*. Frankfurt: Suhrkamp.
Chesterton, Gilbert Keith (1995) *Orthodoxy*. San Francisco, CA: Ignatius Press.
Ehrenreich, Barbara (2012) 'The Missionary Position', *The Baffler*, 21: 132–137.
Kierkegaard, Søren (1970) *Journals and Papers*. Bloomington: Indiana University Press.
Kierkegaard, Søren (1980) *The Concept of Anxiety*. Princeton, NJ: Princeton University Press.
Lacan, Jacques (1975) *Le Séminaire. Livre XXII. RSI*. in *Ornicar?*. 2. Paris: Le Graphe.
Lacan, Jacques (1998) *Seminar, Book XX, Encore*. New York: W. W. Norton and Company.

Lacan, Jacques (2007) *Le Séminaire, livre XVIII, D'un discours qui ne serait pas du semblant*. Paris: Éditions du Seuil.

Levi, Primo (1987) *If This Is a Man. The Truce*. London: Abacus 1987.

McGrath, Sean J. (2012) *The Dark Ground of Spirit*. London: Routledge.

Schelling, Friedrich Wilhelm Joseph (1856–61) *Sämtliche Werke*, Vol. 14. Stuttgart and Augsburg: J. G. Cotta.

Schelling, Friedrich Wilhelm Joseph (1995) *Philosophy of Mythology and Revelation*. Armidale: Australian Association for the Study of Religion.

Zapffe, Peter Wessel (2004) *Om det tragiske*. Oslo: De norske bokklubbene.

17

METAPSYCHOLOGY ON THE BATTLEFIELD

Political praxis as critique of the psychological essence of ideology

David Pavón-Cuéllar

STATE UNIVERSITY OF MICHOACÁN, MEXICO

This chapter adopts Marxist theory and Lacanian psychoanalysis as the frameworks for a discussion of three articulated conceptual redefinitions: first, psychology as the essence of ideology; second, metapsychology as a reflection on psychology from beyond the psychological realm; and, third, praxis as a metapsychological action with potential for the reflective critique of the psychological essence of ideology. It will be shown that these redefinitions may be useful for the development of current critical approaches in psychology, not only by justifying the expansion of their scope towards political praxis, radical metatheory, and a general analysis of ideology, but also by questioning – and crossing – the restrictive frontiers between theory and practice, knowledge and power, speculative critique and social struggle, and individual mental states and the cultural material environments. We will see here that culture and society are front lines for a metapsychological praxis that may successfully oppose ideological power by merging action and speculation. Finally, it will be argued that such political praxis, as a mere continuation of theory by other means, demands that theoreticians free themselves from their confinement to the academic sphere.

Psychology as ideology

It seems that ideologies have existed since long before the advent of what is presently known as 'psychology'. Western civilization did not need to wait for the birth of the modern psychological discipline to encounter powerful ideological constructions, including religious ones, which often facilitated political oppression by inculcating feelings of gratitude, submissiveness, obedience, inferiority, weakness, and fear among the oppressed. It was in these terms that, early on, the Greek sophist Critias (c. 480–403 BC) conceived gods as 'means of frightening' by 'introducing the pleasantest of teachings' and 'covering up the truth with a false theory'

(Freeman and Diels 1948: 157–58). Critias thus offered a pioneering critique of something that corresponds to what Žižek now designates 'ideology "in-itself"; that is, the immanent notion of ideology as a doctrine, a composite of ideas, beliefs, concepts, and so on, destined to convince us of its "truth", yet actually serving some unavowed particular power interest' (2012 [1994]:10).

Ideas that serve power interests have long enriched Western civilization. And, as Critias evidences, what we currently call 'ideology' has not only existed since the very beginning, but has been conceived and criticized for at least the past 25 centuries. In contrast, what we call 'psychology' is a rather young discipline, one less than three centuries old. Its birth has been explained by epistemological factors circumscribed to the 18th and 19th centuries, such as the victory of empiricism over rationalism under the influence of the Enlightenment, the resulting crisis of dogmatic and speculative thought, and the transition from all-embracing philoso-phical systems to the encyclopaedic fragmentation of knowledge. But we need not be Marxists to recognize that these epistemological factors involve ideological pat-terns closely intertwined with socio-economic structures. The encyclopaedic frag-mentation of knowledge is not unrelated to the capitalist division of labour, while the crisis of dogmatic–speculative thought confirms the weakening of pre-capitalist modes of production, and the victory of empiricism over rationalism is closely connected to the bourgeoisie's triumph over the aristocracy.

We know, for instance, that Western bourgeois individualism is present in many of the theoretical and methodological assumptions of psychology (Pérez Soto 2009). The reduction of human beings to individuals is presupposed by their individual representativeness of humanity, their secluded inner world, their exclu-sively inter-individual relationships, the conception of their subjectivity as their own private property, their constitutive individual membership in a nuclear family, their need to express themselves individually, their capacity for self-discipline, their basically hedonist attitude, their deeply engrained selfishness, and their self-centred strategic rationality.

When we take a Marxist critical perspective, all things in psychological knowl-edge seem to be ideological. We may then conceive psychology, not as a science, but as a modern ideological product, one among various others. We may even say that psychological ideology reigns over us today just as religious ideology sub-jugated us yesterday ... All these ideas have been common among successive gen-erations of critics of psychology (Deleule 1969; Braunstein et al. 1975; Sampson 1981; Prilleltensky 1989; Schwartz 1997). They are still common (e.g. Parker 2007). And they are fully justified! There are indeed good reasons to think that psychology constitutes a modern ideology, and if this is true, then it is obvious that ideology is older and broader than just its psychological manifestation.

These thoughts suggest that psychology is a specific historical manifestation of ideology, such that ideology would come first, and psychology would arise from it later. But, if we assume that psychology is nothing more than a modern manifes-tation of ideology, how can we then argue, as I do, that psychology is the essence of ideology? Would it not be absurd to claim that the general essence of ideology

The question of ideological power

lies in one specific ideological formation? If this were the case, then how would old religious ideologies have existed before their modern psychological essence came into being?

I will try to explain myself briefly. When I redefine psychology as the essence of ideology, my conviction is that psychology has become the current name of something that has been functioning in Western civilization for several centuries; indeed, long before the beginnings of the modern psychological discipline. What is more, I am convinced that once psychology appeared, it offered a specific revelation of the very essence of the ideological. This revelation is neither total nor general, of course, as it can only be partial and limited by its historical specificity. However, despite the limits and partiality of this revelation, I think it reveals something that pertains to the very essence of ideology.

As usually viewed, the essence of ideology consists in an operation that makes us believe in the apparent truth of certain ideas for the purpose of exercising an economic or political power that constitutes the real truth behind those ideas. This operation enables the exercise of power by disguising it through a knowledge that is misleading by its very nature. The concealed exercise of power seems to require the essential ideological operation of concealing itself. This operation is thus exerting and manifesting power, economic or political power, for the mere fact of disguising and mystifying it.

The contradictory knowledge of ideology confesses the truth of its deceiving power (Therborn 1980). It proves to be deceitfully true for its effects. Lacan would say that it 'verifies itself' and becomes 'true' by 'creating a reality' through its 'fiction structure' (1971: 133–34). Thus, besides being fictitious, ideology entails a 'pragmatic or instrumental' truth (Eagleton 1991: 44, 188). It comes to be a true knowledge thanks to its power to create a reality and then explain and govern it. Here, as in 'antique science', we must admit that 'imperia and emporiums are the same thing', since 'knowledge and power are the same thing' (Lacan 2006 [1969]: 296).

We know the aphorisms: *scientia potentia est; Wissen ist Macht*; knowledge is power; 'the sciences, are small power' (Hobbes 1651: 151). The small power increases when Lenin says that 'the Marxist doctrine is omnipotent because it is true' (1977 [1913]: 21). And it is also Lenin who recognizes the truth and the power of bourgeois ideology, of 'bourgeois sciences and philosophies', which are 'taught by official professors in order to befuddle the rising generation of the propertied classes and to *coach* it against internal and foreign enemies' (1973 [1908]: 29). Bourgeois ideology is so true and powerful, in the eyes of Lenin, that it is capable of 'producing servants needed by the capitalists' (1970 [1920]: 130). But ideology can only have this power because it is confused with the 'wealth of knowledge amassed by mankind' (ibid.: 127). Despite Foucault's attempts to differentiate his positive conception of knowledge from the Marxist negative notion of ideology, we can certainly understand this notion as a 'power-knowledge' in the

Foucaultian sense of the term: a true knowledge 'produced' by power and 'implied' by it (Foucault 1977 [1975]: 26–27).

The truth of ideology lies in its power to make the truth. This is why Marx, who discovered the ideological 'truth' in the 'fairy tales' of tabloids (1987 [1843]: 297), also insisted on the fact that 'man must prove the truth – i.e. the reality and power, the this-sidedness of his thinking in practice' (1969 [1845]: 13). The practical question of the truth is not only a question of reality, but also a question of power. It is the question of the ideological power of a thinking that creates its own reality. This power permeates all spheres of economy and politics, namely, management and government, publicity and propaganda, financial trading and lobbying, and so on.

Economic and political power is also ideological. This is especially true for the power of the state. We know well the irresistible influence of laws and constitutions, of crowns, flags, swastikas, Orwellian telescreens, military uniforms, demagogic discourses, national anthems, and cults of personality. Engels does not hesitate to say that 'the state presents itself to us as the first ideological power over man' (1990 [1886]: 392). The earliest remembered forms of power-knowledge might then be associated with lawgivers such as Hammurabi, Moses, Lycurgus, and Solon in the Western world. These 'wise and clever' personifications of the state were actually those who 'invented fear of the gods' in Critias (Freeman and Diels 1948: 158). Should we see this fear as the first effect of the ideological power on the subject?

The state may indeed be described as an ideological power for at least two reasons. The first one, the Hegelian reason discovered by the young Marx, is that the state constitutes nothing but an 'idea' of society: an 'abstract predicate' that pretentiously becomes a 'real subject' and reduces people to be its 'object' (1992 [1843]: 73). The second reason, the Pascalian one highlighted by Žižek (2008 [1989]), is that all the power of the state lies in 'custom' and in its appearance that arouses 'respect and terror' (Pascal 1670: 139).

The ideological deceptive power of the state underlies its political oppressive power that in turn presupposes an economic exploitative power. It is always the same power, which is actually indistinguishable from ideology, as its economic and political nature is also ideological. Its deceiving function is inherent in politics and economy.

Psychology as the essence of ideology

In a sense, both political power and economic power are ideological, so that ideology relates to itself when it conceals itself by concealing its own economic and political power. This leads us from Žižek's notion of 'ideology in-itself' to his conceptions of 'ideology for-itself' and 'ideology reflected into-itself'. We need all these notions of ideology in order to conceive an ideological power determined by different ideological structures, which may be economic or political, for example. But who exactly exercises this multidimensional power? We may say that power is exercised here by a kind of subject, but only as long as we do not see this subject as an individual person or human being with certain psychological attributes and tendencies, for this would mean already doing ideology when trying to understand ideology. We only know that there are subjects who exercise the power of ideological structures, and that these subjects and structures are concealed by the very operation that conceals the exercise of power.

Thus, the essential ideological operation conceals not only the exercise of structural power, but also the power structures and their executors: living, speaking, and behaving subjects. All this is obscured in an ideology that presents itself as a transparent knowledge of truth, an obvious or scientific knowledge purified from the exercise of power, from power structures and from the power executors, who are indeed the very subjects of knowledge. We may think here of the deceitfully diaphanous technocratic decisions and other neoliberal expressions of the 'transparency society' (Han 2013). These are just examples of how an ideological knowledge may pretend to be scientific by presenting itself as if it implied no subject, as a non-subjective knowledge, which really is the definition of science (Lacan 2007 [1970]).

Real science excludes the subject, while ideology simulates science by proceeding *as if* it excluded the subject. The essential operation of ideology consists in pretending not to be ideology. Is is an affectation of science, of scientifically excluding the subjects, together with their ideological power, the power they execute, and the power structures to which they are subjected. We may even say that *ideology always does that*. And it cannot do that without doing psychology. Ideology needs to deal with an idea of the psyche in order to conceal itself behind this idea. Therefore ideological power needs psychological resources. It requires them in order to separate the subject from the object, the psyche from the world, and reduce any perceptible residue of the subject into a supposed object of reliable knowledge, that is, at present, scientific inquiry.

It is not by chance that the first aim of modern scientific psychology has been the supposed decontamination of science from subjective interferences (Canguilhem 1958). Nevertheless, despite these interferences, science is science and concerns objects, while psychology has to deal with subjects. The psychological discipline may only aspire to 'scientism', which is not science, but the religious adoration of science (Lacan 1936: 64). And the best way of adoring science is the ritual of concealing ideology, of playing science and thus pretending to exclude subjects, power, and structures: an ideological ritual that corresponds precisely to what we currently call 'psychology' (ibid.: 59–64).

My point is that we cannot conceive the essential ideological operation without pondering precisely what it is that psychology does today, all that which is assimilated into the modern psychological discipline, namely, the fictitious abstraction of subjects from their knowledge, the concealment of the exercise of the power and power structures involved in the subject's facts and realities, words and ideas, perceptions and behaviours, and the resulting dissimulation of ideology by ideology. All this is achieved through a series of psychological procedures that are also essential to ideology: the individualization of subjects, the objectification and reification of their being and actions, the universalization of their singularity, the depoliticization of their mutual relations, the naturalization of their cultural environment, and the eternalization of their historical moment. The sum of these processes may be called de-subjectification, but also psychologization and ideologization. The final product is a knowledge that evidences its truth, the truth of its ideological power, by obscuring its subject, its structure, its political perspective, and its cultural and historical situation.

Christian psychology

Let us take the case of religious ideology in the Middle Ages. According to my view, its essential operation – prefiguring modern psychology – was to conceal the oppressive feudal structure with its specific social classes of lords and servants, oppressors and oppressed, while placing its focus on individualized Christians with their objectified, universalized individual psychological profile, including moral consciousness and conflicts of conscience, temptations, sins such as anger and envy, and virtues like humility, submissiveness, peacefulness, and gratitude. This psychological individualization, universalization, and objectification meant not only the concealment of such collective subjects as the social classes of lords and servants, but also a depoliticization of their mutual relations through a reduction to interindividual relationships. It was also a naturalization of their feudal cultural environment, an eternalization of the historical moment of the Middle Ages, and an occultation of the power involved in the oppression of servants by lords.

In medieval Christian ideology, the concealment of the oppressive power of lords enabled the exercise of this power through the ideological procedures of promoting submissiveness and peacefulness, while condemning and denigrating anger and envy. Thus power – ideological power – was only concealed, never neutralized or deactivated. Something similar occurred with the subjects – social classes – that were reproduced and disguised, but never really excluded. This is why the medieval religious prefiguration of modern psychology is not scientific in nature, but rather ideological, just as ideological as modern psychology, which also reproduces power structures and class relations by concealing them, fostering adaptation, and stigmatizing different forms of dissidence.

It is difficult not to perceive the procedures of modern psychology in old Christianity. For example, in the Final Judgement, just as in psychological diagnosis, it is the individual who is sinful or sick, who must go to Hell or the psychiatric hospital, and who must do penance or attend psychotherapy. The subject of Christianity, like that of psychology, can only be considered when individualized, isolated, and abstracted from its class, from culture, and from society. Modern individualism has its roots in Christian individualization (Dumont 1982, 1986).

Marx knew well that 'only under the rule of Christianity' could civil society 'dissolve the human world into a world of atomistic individuals confronting each another in enmity' (1992 [1844]: 240). This is how Christian psychological individualization paved the way for the development of modern bourgeois individualism with its individual rights, individual property, individual liberties, individual workers and consumers, individual citizens and voters, individual personalities and

274 David Pavón-Cuéllar

profiles, individual symptoms and illnesses. Christian psychological individualization produces objectified, universalized individual souls, flocks of individual souls that may then be disciplined or lumped together and controlled as populations through the secularized power devices of the anatomo-politics and bio-politics studied by Foucault (1976a, 1976b). They are the same herds of individual souls whose votes are counted in Western liberal democracies, and whose mental illnesses are calculated in national and international statistics.

The flocks of individual souls produced by Christianity are also those that may be counted, calculated, compared, and described through quantitative methods in modern psychology, those currently classified according to their illnesses and their respective remedies, as in the second section of the medieval *Malleus Malleficarum*, a work much more inspiring than our *Diagnostic and Statistical Manual of Mental Disorders*. We must also recognize that the Christian behaviourist psychology of discipline and self-discipline through rewards and punishments, penitence and recompenses, Heaven and Hell, is much more stimulating than its modern versions found in Pavlov, Watson, and Skinner. In fact, modern psychology operates upon the essence of older ideologies, though adapted and improved for the present. Perhaps this is why we needed to wait until now to see in the crude, unrefined, and blatant form of modern psychology, all those elements that already functioned in a more subtle and sophisticated way in the essence of all ideologies.

Metapsychology as a reflection on psychology from beyond the psychological realm

If we can uncover the vices of modern psychology in the essence of all ideologies, then the longstanding critique of ideology may be significantly enriched and radically deepened by the relatively recent critical approaches to the psychological discipline. This critique of psychology will be especially useful in helping us avoid falling into the trap of using psychological forms of the critique of ideology. But how can we overcome those vicious circles in which ideology is deconstructed through its psychological reconstruction on a deeper level? I think that one effective way to get around them is through a metapsychological reflection on psychology from beyond the psychological realm.

Here I take up the Lacanian understanding of metapsychological reflection as a questioning and surpassing of 'psychological prejudices' that allows us to adopt a critical stance 'beyond psychology' (Lacan 1988 [1954]: 108, 166). Lacan sought to go beyond psychology in order to explain its ideological truisms from the psycho-analytical perspective (Parker 2003). I can but embrace this Lacanian aspiration of translating descriptive psychological ideology into the explicative metapsychological terms of psychoanalysis. I also embrace the equivalent Freudian aspiration of translating religious ideology into psychoanalytical terms by 'transforming metaphysics into metapsychology' (Freud 1955 [1901]: 258). How could I not espouse this aspiration that is one of the deepest aims of any radical critique of the psychological essence of ideology?

Freud conceives metaphysics not only as a religious ideology that must be criticized, but also as a psychological projection that must be reverted. Hence we may say that psychology, the psychological essence of ideology, underlies the ideological religious metaphysics criticized in Freudian metapsychological reflection. As Freud himself puts it, the 'metaphysics' of 'the myths of Paradise and the fall of man, of God, of good and evil, of immortality, and so on', are 'nothing but psychology projected into the outer world ... destined to be changed again by science' into 'metapsychology' or 'psychology of the unconscious' (1955 [1901]: 258). But we must not become confused here. When Freud speaks of the *psychology of the unconscious*, he is referring to something completely different from what we understand as *psychology*. This is why he prefers to use the term *metapsychology* in lieu of *psychology*. Metapsychology is no longer psychology.

One thing is what Freud describes as *psychology projected into the outer world*, or what I conceive as the psychological essence of ideology, while something quite different is what he refers to as *metapsychology* or *that into which psychological projection is destined to be changed again by science*. When Freud speaks of science, he has in mind psychoanalysis, which changes psychology into a metapsychological reflection on psychology. We may say that he seeks a transformation of the psychological projection, the psychological essence of ideology, into a metapsychological reflection on this projective psychological essence.

Freudian psychoanalysis may be conceived as a metapsychological reflection on the psychological projective essence of ideology. What we learn from Lacan here is that this reflection must be situated beyond psychology. Only thus can we become capable of offering critical metapsychological explanations of ideological psychological descriptions (Orozco-Guzmán and Pavón-Cuéllar 2014).

When dealing with the descriptive religious ideology of the Middle Ages, for instance, we may explain Christian denigration of the deadly sin of envy not only as an element in the general solution of the Oedipus Complex that allows subjects to enter culture by forbidding them from envying everything that may represent the exclusive possession of the mother by the father. To be really critical, this explanation must offer a cultural and historical specification that goes beyond the reminiscences of psychological universalization, objectification, and individualization found in the Western androcentric bourgeois conception of the nuclear family that underlies the Freudian Oedipus Complex. We can explain how the moral denigration of envy may help ensure what is specified in the Middle Ages, not precisely through the exclusive possession of the mother by the father in the Victorian nuclear family, but through a feudal power structure in which the lord presents himself as a 'father' of his servants and enjoys exclusive possession of their lands and names, of their surplus wealth and production, of some of their social and political rights, and even, apparently in certain cases, of the sexual enjoyment of the virginity of their wives and daughters.

According to a certain Christian medieval psychology, feudal injustice should not provoke any kind of resentment, anger, or revolt in those good servants who must not fall into the deadly sin of envy thanks to the solution of what we may call

276 David Pavón-Cuéllar

the Complex of *jus primae noctis* or *Droit du Seigneur*. This adaptive solution of the Complex is of the kind promoted by Ego-psychology in the 20th century (Hartmann 1958). It is the same kind of adaptation still endorsed by psychoanalysts, psychologists, and psychotherapists the world over, who are there to help suffering subjects overcome any trace of envy, resentment, indignation, anger, or revolt against the globalized capitalist system that enjoys exclusive possession of their wealth (e.g. Kahneman et al. 1999; Aspinwall 2005; Matthews 2008).

Praxis as a metapsychological action with potential for the reflective critique of psychology and ideology

If we are psychologists engaged in the struggle against the capitalist system, how can we oppose adaptation to this system? How can we face the psychological essence of the bourgeois ideology that enables the good functioning of that system? Is it enough to undertake a metapsychological reflection on this essence? Is it possible to resist the system's ideological power by simply becoming aware of its functioning, its political aims, and its psychological essence? The response seems to be negative, especially nowadays, when we are dealing with current ideology, whose cynicism has been underlined by Sloterdijk (1987), Žižek (2008 [1989]), Bewes (1997), and many others.

We certainly do not discourage ourselves from assisting the reproduction of the capitalist system by becoming aware of what we are doing when we adapt, seek, or promote adaptation. Perhaps this reflexive metapsychological awareness will be effective in traditional, provincial, marginal, or peripheral zones of the capitalist system where people do not know what they do, but are doing it. However, inside the system, people usually 'know very well what they are doing, but still, they are doing it' (Žižek 2008 [1989]: 24–27). If this is the case, how can our critique of the psychological essence of ideology become effective? For instance, how can we ensure the effectiveness of the longstanding critique of adaptation in critical psychology?

Perhaps we should think of a thoughtful, deliberate, and systematic strategy of maladaptation and of promoting maladaptation as the best ways of questioning adaptation and the promotion of adaptation. What I have in mind is an intervention, critical praxis or performance, or, to be more precise, *metapsychological action*, as the most radical form of a reflexive critique of the psychological essence of ideology. Actually the implementation of this concrete political action, as an effective way to counteract the concrete ideological power, should be just another practical form of the critique of ideology like those performed by the cynical philosophers Diogenes and Crates, by some anarchists and Marxists, by surrealists and situationists, and many others.

There is an 'order of truth that our praxis engenders' (Lacan 1998 [1964]: 263). We need this order as an alternative for the powerful true knowledge of ideology. How can we oppose the ideological power without the force of our praxis?

But the practical forms of the critique of ideology are not only defensible on the basis of the recognition of the ideological power. They are also justified by the fact that praxis may be a continuation and reflective metatheoretical deepening of theory; some ideas can only be criticized and even conceived through action; to act is the only way of thinking and questioning many things. All this was understood by the Hellenistic philosophers, Stoics, Epicureans, Sceptics, and Cynics, who knew very well that the only way of carrying on and deepening the Greek philosophical project of Plato and Aristotle was through a practice conceived, not as an application of theory, but as a theoretical method, as a fundamental condition of thought and a higher level of theory. Such a perspective permits an identification of the young Marx with Epicurus, at a moment when the only way to advance and develop the critical-rationalist and romantic-idealist philosophical projects of Kant, of Fichte, and of Schelling and Hegel, was through the material practice of social struggle, the critical transformation of the world as the deepest way of critically reflecting upon it (Marx 2000 [1842]).

Conclusion: towards a continuation of theory by other means

Marx understood that the only way to deepen his knowledge of the world was to sink into it for the purpose of 'transforming it' (1969 [1845]: 15). This understanding, which Marx shared with other young Hegelians, was highly influenced by the Polish philosopher August von Cieszkowski who distinguished three successive periods in history, namely, the pre-reflective moment of the artistic 'spirit in itself', the reflective moment of the religious and philosophical 'spirit for itself' that culminated with Hegel, and finally – after Hegel – the practical moment of 'spirit out of itself', in which the dualisms spirit–matter, and action–thought, were resolved critically and superseded reflectively through practical activity (2002 [1838]: 145–49).

Without falling into an evolutionist conception, we may see the final practical stage of reflective critique as the one attained in the 19th century, first by Marx, and then by Freud. Both the Freudian and Marxian perspectives reach the deepest level of their reflective critique of ideology through practical activities: in the former, on the couch, through individual psychoanalysis; in the latter, in the streets, through social struggle. In both cases, we find a metapsychological action with potential for the struggle against the ideological power by means of the reflective critique of psychology and the psychological essence of ideology (Pavón-Cuéllar 2011, 2014).

The third materialist step of a practical critique of ideology *out-of-itself*, after the *in-itself* and *for-itself* steps, is what we cannot find in the famous Hegelian account of ideology proposed by Žižek (2012 [1994]), who prefers to restrict its analysis to a third idealist reflection *into-itself* after the *in-itself* and *for-itself* stages. We can say that here – at least here – in his analysis of ideology, Žižek is pre-Marxist and pre-Freudian. In a sense, despite his freshness and inventiveness, he is still a classical philosopher. His only political praxis is a 'theoretical practice' (Althusser 1965: 170–72). He stays in the speculative description of the world and dare not cross the threshold of its active transformation.

Žižekian dense and thick descriptive speculations leave no room for transformative interventions, precisely the practical actions we need for a deep, metapsychological explanation of, and critical reflection on, psychology and the psychological essence of ideology. But we need to go down to the battlefield! After all, it is a question of power. And, again, how can we deal with the ideological power without the strength of practical actions?

Only metapsychological praxis may successfully oppose ideological power by integrating action and speculation. And where are we to find this integration? Certainly not in the hermetically closed academic sphere. We should rather free ourselves from our confinement to this sphere and look beyond it for a practical or metatheoretical reflection on what is happening inside. But where may we look for this? In the front lines of culture and society, in social movements, in what Subcomandante Marcos refers to when he explains that 'theoretical reflection on theory is metatheory, and the metatheory of the *Zapatistas* is their practice' (2003: para. 22).

Bibliography

Althusser, L. (1965) *For Marx*. London: Verso (2005).

Aspinwall, L. G. (2005) 'The Psychology of Future-oriented Thinking: From Achievement to Proactive Coping, Adaptation, and Aging', *Motivation and Emotion*, 29(4): 203–235.

Bewes, T. (1997) *Cynicism and Postmodernity*. London: Verso.

Braunstein, N., Pasternac, M., Benedito, G., and Saal, F. (1975) *Psicología: ideología y ciencia*. Mexico: Siglo Veintiuno.

Canguilhem, G. (1958) 'Qu'est-ce que la psychologie?', *Revue de Métaphysique et de Morale*, 1: 12–25.

Cieszkowski, A. von (2002 [1838]) *Prolegómenos a la historiosofía*. Salamanca: Universidad de Salamanca.

Deleule, D. (1969) *La Psychologie mythe scientifique: pour introduire à la psychologie moderne*. Paris: Laffont.

Dumont, L. (1982) 'A Modified View of our Origins: The Christian Beginnings of Modern Individualism', *Religion*, 12(1): 1–27.

Dumont, L. (1986) *Essays on Individualism: Modern Ideology in Anthropological Perspective*. Chicago, IL: University of Chicago Press.

Eagleton, T. (1991) *Ideology. An Introduction*. London: Verso.

Engels, F. (1990 [1886]) 'Ludwig Feuerbach and the End of Classical German Philosophy', in *Marx and Engels Collected Works, Volume 26*. Moscow: Progress Publishers: 353–398.

Foucault, M. (1976a). *Society Must Be Defended: Lectures at the Collège de France, 1975–1976*. New York: Picador.

Foucault, M. (1976b). *The History of Sexuality, Vol. 1: An Iintroduction*. New York: Vintage.

Foucault, M. (1977 [1975]) *Discipline and Punish: the Birth of the Prison*. New York: Random House.

Freeman, K. and Diels, H. (1948) *Ancilla to the Pre-Socratic Philosophers: A Complete Translation of the Fragment in Diels, Fragmente der Vorsokratiker*. Cambridge, MA: Harvard University Press.

Freud, S. (1955 [1901]) *The Psychopathology of Everyday Life. Standard Edition of the Complete Psychological Works of Sigmund Freud, Volume 6*. London: Hogarth Press.

Han, Byung-Chul (2013) *La sociedad de la transparencia*. Barcelona: Herder.

Hartmann, H. (1958) *Ego Psychology and the Problem of Adaptation*. Madison, CT: International Universities Press.

Hobbes, T. (1651) *Leviathan*. Harmondsworth: Penguin (1980).

Kahneman, D., Diener, E., and Schwarz, N. (eds). (1999) *Well-being: Foundations of Hedonic Psychology*. New York: Russell Sage Foundation.

Lacan, J. (1936) 'Beyond the Reality Principle', in *Écrits I*. New York and London: W. W. Norton and Company, 58–74.

Lacan, J. (1971) *Le séminaire. Livre XVIII. D'un discours qui ne serait pas du semblant*. Paris: Seuil.

Lacan, J. (1988 [1954]) *Freud's Technical Papers*. New York: Cambridge University Press and W. W. Norton and Company.

Lacan, J. (1998 [1964]) *The Four Fundamental Concepts of Psychoanalysis*. New York and London: W. W. Norton and Company.

Lacan, J. (2006 [1969]) *Le séminaire. Livre XVI. D'un Autre à l'autre*. Paris: Seuil.

Lacan, J. (2007 [1970]) *The Other Side of Psychoanalysis*. New York and London: W. W. Norton and Company.

Lenin, V. I. (1970 [1920]) 'The Tasks of the Youth Leagues', in *On Culture and Cultural Revolution*. Moscow: Progress, 123–146.

Lenin, V. I. (1973 [1908]) 'Marxism and Revisionism', in *Lenin Collected Works, Volume 15*. Moscow: Progress, 29–39.

Lenin, V. I. (1977 [1913]) 'The Three Sources and Three Component Parts of Marxism', in *Lenin Collected Works, Volume 19*. Moscow: Progress, 21–28.

Marx, K. (1969 [1845]) 'Theses on Feuerbach', in *Marx and Engels Selected Works, Volume One*. Moscow: Progress, 13–15.

Marx, K. (1987 [1843]) 'La prohibición de la Gaceta General de Leipzig dentro del Estado Prusiano', in *Escritos de juventud*. México: Fondo de Cultura Económica, 296–298.

Marx, K. (1992 [1843]) 'Critique of Hegel's Doctrine of the State', in *Early Writings*. London: Penguin Classics, 57–198.

Marx, K. (1992 [1844]) 'On the Jewish Question', in *Early Writings*. London: Penguin Classics, 211–242.

Marx, K. (2000 [1842]) 'Doctoral Thesis', in *Selected Writings*. Oxford: Oxford University Press, 15–21.

Matthews, M. D. (2008) 'Positive Psychology: Adaptation, Leadership, and Performance in Exceptional Circumstances', in *Performance Under Stress*, ed. P. A. Hancock and J. L.Szalma . Hampshire: Ashgate, 163–180.

Orozco-Guzmán, M. and Pavón-Cuéllar, D. (2014) 'Metapsychology', in *Encyclopedia of Critical Psychology*, ed. T. Teo. New York: Springer, 1173–1176.

Parker, I. (2003) 'Jacques Lacan, Barred Psychologist', *Theory & Psychology*, 13(1): 95–115.

Parker, I. (2007) *Revolution in Psychology: Alienation to Emancipation*. London: Pluto.

Pascal (1670) *Pensées*. Paris: Garnier-Flammarion.

Pavón-Cuéllar, D. (2011) 'Marx in Lacan: Proletarian Truth in Opposition to Capitalist Psychology', *Annual Review of Critical Psychology*, 9: 70–77.

Pavón-Cuéllar, D. (2014) *Elementos políticos de marxismo lacaniano*. Mexico City: Paradiso.

Pérez Soto, C. (2009) *Sobre la condición social de la psicología*. Santiago: LOM.

Prilleltensky, I. (1989) 'Psychology and the Status Quo', *American Psychologist*, 44(5): 795–802.

Sampson, E. E. (1981) 'Cognitive Psychology as Ideology', *American Psychologist*, 36(7): 730.

Schwartz, B. (1997) 'Psychology, Idea Technology, and Ideology', *Psychological Science*, 8(1): 21–27.

Sloterdijk, P. (1987) *Critique of Cynical Reason*. Minneapolis: University of Minnesota Press.

Subcomandante Marcos (2003) 'El mundo: Siete pensamientos en mayo de 2003', *Rebeldía*. 7 May, available online at: http://palabra.ezln.org.mx/comunicados/2003/2003_05_b. htm.

Therborn, G, (1980) *The Ideology of Power and the Power of Ideology*. London: New Left.

Žižek, S. (2008 [1989]) *The Sublime Object of Ideology*. London: Verso.

Žižek, S. (2012 [1994]) 'The Spectre of Ideology', in *Mapping Ideology*, ed. S. Žižek. London: Verso, 1–33.

18

LACAN AVEC BATAILLE AVEC NIETZSCHE

A politics of the impossible?

Panu Minkkinen

UNIVERSITY OF HELSINKI, FINLAND

Introduction: the two claims

This essay has two overlapping starting points.

In 1989, the *Collège International de la Philosophie* in Paris organized an international colloquium called '*Lacan avec les philosophes*', 'Lacan with the philosophers' (see Deguy 1991). The reference to philosophers in the name of the colloquium had a twofold function. On the one hand, it provided an opportunity for scholars who considered themselves philosophers rather than, say, psychoanalysts to publicly work out their own relationship, academic or otherwise, with Lacan. Perhaps the best known of these personal philosophical accounts is Jacques Derrida's equivocal praise of friendship and love (Derrida 1998: 39–69). On the other hand, the colloquium also offered a platform for discussing Lacan's own relationship with philosophy as in the case of, for instance, Martin Heidegger, a philosopher that Lacan both admired and knew personally.[1]

But what is rather astounding in relation to this second set of presentations is that despite the close personal ties, the colloquium did not deal in any significant way with the relationship between Lacan and Georges Bataille. Indeed, as Bataille's biographer Michel Surya points out, during the years before the war, Lacan followed the activities of Bataille's *Acéphale* collective closely (on the *Acéphale*, see e.g. Bataille 1985).[2] And yet there is very little work done on this aspect of Lacan's work:

> The close intellectual and emotional relationship uniting Bataille and Lacan should one day be investigated, and it is a relationship whose effects can more than once be sensed in Lacan's works.
>
> *(Surya 2002: 534, note 34)*

The few that have attempted have not always been successful. Bernard Sichère, to take one such example, seems to reduce much of Lacan to Bataille even in the lack of any explicit evidence (see Sichère 1983; 2006: 139–64). Perhaps the best account of the intellectual environment to which both Lacan and Bataille belonged and of the possible common sources of inspiration is Mikkel Borch-Jacobsen's *The Absolute Master* (Borch-Jacobsen 1991: 1–20 in particular; see also Dean 1992; Botting 1994). But even he seems to avoid dealing with Lacan and Bataille on their own. And when he does, in the lack of evidence he must often rely on hypothesizing, as well.

The second starting point, perhaps closer to the theme of this volume, is the claim, rather persistently made by Elisabeth Roudinesco, that Lacan himself was not a particularly political person. Roudinesco for example claims that although leftist politics played an important role in Lacan's private life through Sylvia and Laurent Bataille, he openly committed himself on only two occasions in the late 1960s: first, in 1967, by signing a petition in support of Régis Debray who had been sentenced to 30 years in prison in Bolivia for aiding Che Guevara and the guerrilla movement, and second, the following year, by participating in a petition supporting the student movement (Roudinesco 1997: 334).[3] 'Lacanian' psycho-analysis has, of course, been both used and abused to further many worthy political causes (see e.g. Apollon and Feldstein 1996; for general accounts, see Stavrakakis 1999; 2007), and, on the other hand, Roudinesco should not really be taken at face value as an authority on what Lacan might or might not have been (see e.g. Jaudel 2011).[4] But the claim is plausible enough taking into account the absence of clear indications to the contrary.

A plausible claim, regardless of whether it is authenticated from verifiable sources, would nonetheless require further investigations. The aim of this essay is, however, more modest than the rigorous response that such plausibility would call for. I am merely suggesting that one possible avenue for opening a more comprehensive discussion about Lacan's own politics – rather than any 'Lacanian politics' – would be through his relationship with Bataille. Both the Bataillean connection and the politics that it may suggest seem to have received surprisingly little attention.[5]

This essay, then, partakes in a tradition of texts that hopes to clarify an issue relating to Lacan – in this case politics – by reading him together 'with' someone else (e.g. Lacan 'with' Althusser, Lacan 'with' Deleuze, more recently Lacan 'with' Žižek or Badiou). It is an admittedly dubious tradition because such pairings may be impossible couplings to begin with. In this case, the problem of the interpreter is not so much to fit together the (possibly) incompatible but, rather, to try to fill in the empty spaces that the silence leaves behind. In that sense, reading Lacan 'with' Bataille will require hypothesizing here just as it does in the already mentioned attempts.

I will first go through the few scattered mentions of Bataille that we can find in Lacan's published work and in the *Seminars*. These scattered mentions have received some attention, and I will also attempt to assess the claims made in some of the available interpretations. I will then focus on one Bataillean theme, namely 'nonknowledge', and I will try to elaborate its political dimension through the work of Jean-Michel Bernier. I am suggesting that, in so far as his politics was concerned, Lacan may have also been a 'complicit' in what Besnier calls Bataille's 'politics of the impossible'. Lastly, although the intellectual soil from which both Lacan and Bataille set onto their respective paths is Kojèvien – and by implication Hegelian – I am suggesting that with respect to politics, one common denominator of this 'politics of the impossible' may have been Nietzsche. Or at least his ghost.

Lacan and Bataille

Roudinesco certainly has reasons to call Lacan's friendship with Bataille 'rather puzzling' (Roudinesco 1997: 136). The details are well documented, and the biographies written by Roudinesco and Surya provide ample evidence of consensus. Bataille and Lacan met in the early 1930s when both were attending Alexandre Kojève's lectures on Hegel (Kojève 1980).[6] A friendship developed between the recently habilitated psychiatrist[7] and the librarian and author a few years his senior. During the course of the decade, Lacan participated in a number of activities in which Bataille was one of the instigators. In 1933, Bataille founded the surrealist journal *Minotaure* together with artist André Masson. Lacan, close to the surrealists as well (on Lacan and the surrealists, see e.g. Greely 2001), published two short articles in the journal (available in English as Lacan 1988a; 1988b), but these bear no evidence of Bataille's influence. In addition, Lacan reportedly played an active role in the early days of the secret society *Acéphale*. In 1941, Lacan married Bataille's former wife, the actress Sylvia Bataille (*née* Maklès) (for a recent biography, see David 2013), and later adopted their daughter Laurence Bataille who became a psychoanalyst in her own right (see Bataille 1987). No animosity or tension has ever been reported about these family relations (see e.g. Roudinesco 1990: 147).

And yet, there is very little to go by in terms of evidence of any 'intellectual relationship'. Lacan barely mentions Bataille. If Lacan's friendship with Bataille is 'puzzling', the same can also be said vice versa. Although Bataille must certainly have read his Freud, not a single mention of Lacan can be found in his published texts (on Bataille and psychoanalysis, see e.g. Roudinesco 1995).

But what does the little evidence there is tell us?

In the nearly 900 pages of *Écrits*, Lacan mentions Bataille once. In the essay 'On a Question Prior to Any Possible Treatment of Psychosis' from the late 1950s, Lacan identifies Schreber's psychotic episodes with an 'inner experience' and continues in an accompanying note:

> The inner experience I am speaking of here is a reference to Georges Bataille's work. In *Madame Edwarda*, he describes the odd extremity of this experience.
> *(Lacan 2006b: 488, note 36; Bataille 1989a: 135–59)*[8]

Even this one unique footnote, almost hidden and yet conspicuous in the surrounding absence of any further acknowledgements, seems to be going wrong. At least for Andrew Ryder, Bataille has very little in common with Schreber:

> Schreber's consideration of otherness is a hollow one that relies on an identification of himself with a sun that sheds light on everything and cannot contemplate darkness; his language is an eternal linking of self with other. ... Conversely, Bataille's understanding of language insists on the reliance of life on death, knowledge on nonknowledge, identity on difference, and not through a monistic uniting of these opposites but rather an awareness of the gap between them and an openness to the outside.
>
> *(Ryder 2010: 99)*

The nearly equally voluminous posthumous collection *Autres écrits* (Lacan 2001a) lacks even a single mention.

Nor is there much to go by in the *Seminars*. In the few explicit instances we can find, Lacan seems to be merely illuminating his own point with a passing note. For example, in the closing session of *Seminar IX* ('Identification', Lacan 1961–1962: session 27 June 1962), Lacan embarks on a lengthy reading of Maurice Blanchot's novel *Thomas the Obscure* (Blanchot 1988) and makes a quick mention of Bataille's experimental essay *The Impossible* (Bataille 1991b). The contrast is even more poignant because the reclusive Blanchot who Lacan here hails as 'quite simply the bard of French literature' (*'le chantre de nos Lettres'*) was a close friend and great admirer of Bataille (Blanchot 1997; see also ffrench 2007).

Similarly, towards the end of *Seminar XIII* (' The sinthome', Lacan 1965–1966: session 1 June 1966; on the seemingly 'neological' spelling of the word 'symptom', see e.g. Russell 1998), Lacan talks about the 'object (a)' and the scopic field and suggests the possibility of going through a 'whole history of the eye'. Without mentioning Bataille by name, Lacan then proceeds to clarify that he is alluding to *Story of the Eye* (Bataille 1982), a book written by an author typically representative of a 'certain uneasiness essential in our time', a book which could 'pass for' an erotic novel. But it is, Lacan notes, a novel rich in detail that will serve as a reminder of how the equivalent 'objects (a)' fit together and connect with each other, and of their central relationship with the sexual organ. So Lacan reduces Bataille's work to a mere illustration of his own argument.

Finally, in *Seminar XVI* ('From an other to the Other'), Lacan discusses the particularities of what he calls 'modern morality'. Capitalist enterprise, he further explains, does not place the means of production at the service of pleasure. Rather, something that becomes manifest at the margins, a 'timid effort' that entertains no illusions about being successful, simply casts a shadow of a doubt on what could be called a 'life style'. Lacan calls this timid gesture an 'effort to rehabilitate expenditure':

> Someone named Georges Bataille, a thinker at the margins in what concerns our affairs, has thought through and produced on this point some totally readable works that, nevertheless, are not dedicated to efficiency.
>
> *(Lacan 2006a: 109–10, translation mine)*

Bataille's 'totally readable' main work on expenditure is *The Accursed Share* (Bataille 1988a). For Bataille, the 'accursed share' is an excess residue, a leftover value present in any economical calculus or system, which must be consumed either as pure luxury or through destruction. Crudely put, Bataille's argument is that the consumption of such an excess defies the logic of capitalism and, as such, is also a threat to the existence of the system itself. With this in mind, another possible departure for further investigations may be the first sessions of the same *Seminar*, in which Lacan draws on an analogy between Marx's notion of surplus-value and what Lacan calls '*plus-de-jouir*' or 'surplus *jouissance*', a discussion that Lacan then continues the following year (Lacan 2007).[9]

Notwithstanding these passing mentions, there is especially one point in the *Seminars* at which Lacan, perhaps inadvertently, betrays his intellectual debt to Bataille. The point comes towards the end of the well-known *Seminar VII* (*The Ethics of Psychoanalysis*) as Lacan is explaining the inevitable limits of the 'transgressive enjoyment' of the Sadean libertine. Praising Blanchot's reading of Sade (Blanchot 2004), Lacan seems to once again be setting Bataille up against his friend. Bataille, albeit a 'subtler mind' than usual, allegedly finds that the social and political commentary that surrounds Sade's graphic descriptions of cruelty may contribute to a 'loss of suggestive tension' (Lacan 1992: 201). The accuracy of this seemingly dismissive comment aside, the intellectual environment in which *Seminar VII* was written included, as De Kesel notes (2009: 132), a whole tradition of prominent contemporary Sade critics such as Blanchot, Pierre Klossowski, Max Horkheimer, and including, of course, Bataille himself.

I will return to the nature of this 'intellectual debt' later.

Dylan Evans claims that while Lacan's earlier attempts at trying to define enjoyment as *jouissance* were still at heart Hegelian, the move to more openly sexual connotations in *Seminar VII* can, perhaps, be attributed to the influence of Bataille. I emphasize 'perhaps' because even Evans notes the conspicuous absence of open acknowledgements. And yet, there are hints:

> Not only is the deadly character of *jouissance* strongly reminiscent of Bataille's view of the erotic as a realm of violence which borders on death itself, but Bataille also characterises erotic joy (*joie*) as necessarily excessive in character, and compares it to an incommunicable mystical experience (as does Lacan).
>
> (*Evans 1998: 4–5*)

Lacan develops his notion of ethics by setting the Kantian categorical imperative against Sade and by then resolving the antinomy with his reading of Antigone. Lacan is inevitably closest to both Bataille and to politics here. Slavoj Žižek equates Antigone's decision to defy her father's rightful command as the radical act of politics:

> Therein consists the Lacanian definition of the authentic ethical act: an act which reaches the utter limit of the primordial forced choice and repeats it in

the reverse sense. Such an act presents the only moment when we are effectively 'free': Antigone is 'free' after she has been excommunicated from the community.

(Žižek 2008a: 77)

Later Žižek suggests that in trying to elaborate this 'pure desire' that is attributed to Antigone, Lacan's reading of Sade as the 'truth of Kant' and the accompanying ethical maxim to not compromise one's desire come alarmingly close to Bataille and, accordingly, fail to move beyond the dialectic of transgression and the law (Žižek 2006: 94–95). Žižek's claim here seems to be that at this point Lacan still fails in his attempts to work out the idea of a desire that would not be derivative of a prohibition, that would not, in other words, be dependent on a law that denies it. Similarly Lorenzo Chiesa agrees that, in the end, *Seminar VII* fails to discern adequately between Lacan's ethics of 'pure desire', that is, of a desire that is not conditioned by the law, and the 'Sado-Kantian anti-ethics' of *jouissance* that pursues fulfilment regardless. The distinction is here only in a germinal form, Chiesa claims, and will be further elaborated in subsequent *Seminars* (Chiesa 2007: 177). So although the solution to the deadlock will come in later years – especially in *Seminars XX* ('Encore') and *XXIII* ('The sinthome') – the implication here is that Lacan's possible albeit unacknowledged debt to Bataille is holding him back. Moreover, as to the politics of *Seminar VII*, Lacan himself is cautious, remarking that:

The morality of power, of the service of goods, is as follows: 'As far as desires are concerned, come back later. Make them wait'.

(Lacan 1992: 315)

Knowledge and nonknowledge

At the beginning of the 1971 *Seminars* at Sainte-Anne ('The Knowledge of the Psychoanalyst'), Lacan enters into what he rather ironically calls a 'little parenthesis' in which he tries to clarify a misunderstanding. The issue seems to concern a confusion regarding the possible link between psychoanalysis and Georges Bataille's notion of 'nonknowledge'. Lacan claims that because he has taught that truth is not knowledge, some have jumped to the hasty conclusion that truth must accordingly be nonknowledge. After a short detour Lacan concludes: 'Is there any need to demonstrate that there is in psychoanalysis firstly and fundamentally knowledge?' (Lacan 1971–72: session 4 November 1971)

One of the possible points of tension between Bataille and Lacan would, then, be the relationship between knowledge and nonknowledge.

For Bataille, the knowledge of a conscious subject must always address human being in its totality. It must, in other words, include everything that is usually excluded from it. Bataille develops this idea with the help of a number of inter-related notions such as 'inner experience', 'the sacred', 'the miraculous', 'sovereignty', and, of course, 'nonknowledge'. For the most part, this aspect of Bataille's work is a confrontation with or a 'contestation' of the traditions of scientific knowledge. And this may provide an opportunity for reading Bataille together with Lacan even in the absence of explicit references.

The political bent of Bataille's 'contestation' can, perhaps, be put in the following way: he namely argues that traditional scientific discourse subjects the pursuit of knowledge to a projected or an anticipated result. By doing so, scientific discourse renders something which is not known, that is, the 'unknown' of what has not yet been revealed, subservient to the anticipated result that is already known. Knowledge is, in other words, immediately servile because it serves a predefined purpose. This servility results from the inability to think of a 'sovereign end', an end that is not subordinated to something else. An enlightened consciousness will relegate anything that is beyond utility to the obscurity of the unconscious. By contrast, a sovereign end can never include within itself the anticipated result of a calculated effort. It can only come from the arbitrary, from chance (Bataille 1991a: 226).

The negative analogue of the 'miraculous' unexpectedness of this sovereign moment is death. Death represents the radical thrust that transforms the anticipation of a given result into the presence of the moment. The negative miracle of death is, as Bataille's well-known expression puts it, the 'NOTHING' into which anticipation then dissolves and disappears in the sovereign moment: 'that thought, subordinated to some anticipated result, completely enslaved, ceases to be in being *sovereign*, that only unknowing is *sovereign*' (Bataille 1991a: 208).

Human agency is dependent on projection. Projection is not only inherent in action in the sense that all agency is directed at a projected result, but as a mode of being, it is also caught in a temporal paradox. Projection namely defers being to a later time. In a similar way, the demand for impassive consistency and harmony that the systematic architectonics of scientific knowledge implies, rejects time, expelling it from the thought process. Its principle is repetition, the tranquil investment of time with an ever-recurring theme that eternalizes what is possible (Bataille 1988b: 56). For Bataille, the seemingly permanent architecture of knowledge provides a structure of hierarchy and domination that denies the possibility of the sovereign moment. So not only is such the scientific mentality servile, it is crippled:

> At its origin, often enough, a desire for sovereign knowledge, to go as far as one can go, a desire so quickly born, nullifies itself by accepting subordinate tasks. The disinterested type – independent of application – and the persistent use of empty words make the exchange. Science is practised by men in whom the desire to know is dead.
>
> *(Bataille 2001: 82)*

Denis Hollier sees Bataille's critique of systematized knowledge as 'architecture' as a reference to Hegel's aesthetics. One cannot describe a system without resorting to the vocabulary of architecture, Hollier explains. Because structure provides the general form of legibility, nothing is legible unless it is submitted to the architectural grid. And so architecture becomes 'archistructure', the 'system of systems'. Because it is the keystone of all general systematicity, it is also the guarantor of a general legibility. As such it dominates and totalizes the production of all signification, forcing it to confirm its neological system (Hollier 1989: 33).

What Bataille must accordingly propose is a critique that rejects the servility that is implied in projection and architecture and that pursues the limits of what is possible. Understood in such a way, critique must also address an inevitable lack, something that cannot be mastered through discourse, a deficiency in the foundation of both human being and knowledge. This lack also defines the unthinkable limits of thinking that knowledge must first exclude from its discourse and then proceed to repudiate any evidence of the exclusion. Only such an exclusion would make science and knowledge as homogeneous discourses possible. But Bataille insists that by pursuing these limits, one can grasp for a fleeting sovereign moment the horrifying truth that no ultimate answer exists. During this fleeting moment, the anticipation of any future projection dissolves into nothing:

> Our sovereign moments, when nothing matters except what is there, what is sensible and captivating in the present, are antithetical to the attention to the future and to the calculations without which there would be no labour.
>
> *(Bataille 1991a: 283)*

Sovereign moments take place as inner experiences that are subjective states of sensitivity concerning the unknown. As such, they are also at odds with the idea of architectonic systematicity that scientific knowledge represents. The principle of inner experience cannot be presented as a moral principle or as a science that strives for knowledge. Its only end is inner experience itself:

> Opening myself to inner experience, I have placed in it all value and authority. Henceforth, I can have no other value, no other authority. Value and authority imply the discipline of a method, the existence of a community.
>
> *(Bataille 1988b: 7)*

Bataille's inner experience cannot lead to knowledge, but only to nonknowledge that takes thinking to its limits. Nonknowledge, on the other hand, has no object in itself. Nor is it the experience of a conscious subject. It is the momentary fusion of subject and object that Bataille elsewhere addresses as both 'communication' and 'community' (on these aspects of Bataille's work, see e.g. Mitchell and Winfree 2009). Knowledge, by way of contrast, prioritizes the future. Because it anticipates a result, knowledge also represents a servitude and can, therefore, never be sovereign. The knowledge of an object is its apprehension beyond the moment. Only nonknowledge where anticipation dissolves into 'NOTHING' can be sovereign (Bataille 1991a: 202–04).

Bataille associates the nonknowledge of inner experience with a critical confrontation that he calls 'contestation'. In pursuing the limits of knowledge,

Lacan avec Bataille avec Nietzsche **289**

contestation does not engage with the order of things, for to do so would subject thinking to the ends of the order it contests. And these ends are external in relation to thinking itself. Michel Foucault explains that contestation does not deny existence or values. It is, rather, a way of redirecting them to their limits and, ultimately, to the final limit where the ontological decision is made: 'to contest is to proceed until one reaches the empty core where being achieves its limit and where the limit defines being' (Foucault 1977: 36; on contestation, see also Holland 2004).

Bataille's understanding of contestation has, then, nothing to do with utility and the world of consequences. It demands never to be the means of an end that is allegedly worthier; to revolt is to be there, sovereign and without limits:

> Every man is still, potentially, a sovereign being, but on the condition of loving death more than slavery. I can, from this moment on, want nothing more than my caprices and, in accordance with my luck, I will make it, or I will die.
>
> *(Bataille 2001: 188)*

The politics of the impossible?

But how should one understand the political dimension of this nonknowledge?

In the 1930s, Bataille and Lacan both participated in Kojève's legendary lectures on Hegel. These lectures provided, no doubt, the most significant melting pot of French intelligentsia before the war. But in his encounter with Hegel, Bataille was also forced to come to terms with a fatalistic 'end of history', the battle of Jena[10] that Kojève's reading of Hegel rearticulates. At the end of history, nothing remains to be done.

At this point, Bataille invokes Nietzsche in the hope of revitalizing the revolt. But as Jean-Michel Besnier has pointed out, this is no longer the revolutionary Nietzsche that Bataille had already discussed in his previous texts and that had had a huge influence on his thinking earlier, but, rather, a Nietzsche of retreat, a Nietzschean figure at the 'end of history' somehow accommodated to the political *cul-de-sac* that Bataille now found himself in (Besnier 1995).

This 'double philosophical reference' to both Hegel and Nietzsche at the same time explains, Besnier argues, Bataille's particular idea of politics before the war:

> Bataille let himself be convinced by Hegel at the very same time that he discovered, in Nietzsche, the expression of an absolute refusal of subjugation to any thought whatsoever. The 'paradoxical philosophy' to which he subscribed, and which he described succinctly as 'the sense of the impossible', goes together with a politics no less impossible: the unwillingness to submit to any recuperative dialectic.
>
> *(Besnier 1990: 175; see also Besnier 1988)*

So if after the 1930s Nietzsche became Bataille's decisive philosophical and political influence, how would one assess his influence on Lacan? Would we be able to claim, for example, that in trying to define Lacan's politics through his affiliation with Bataille, Nietzsche is a common denominator? Could we even talk of Lacan's 'politics of the impossible'? And would that 'impossibility' explain Lacan's apparent unwillingness to engage publicly in political matters?

On the outside, Lacan's dealings with Nietzsche curiously resemble his 'puzzling friendship' with Bataille. He does not engage with Nietzsche in any substantive way. In terms of explicit references, Nietzsche is almost as invisible as Bataille: two references in *Écrits*, none in *Autres écrits*, and a dozen or so in the *Seminars*. And these are once again all either passing remarks scattered here and there or explicitly dismissive – for example Nietzsche, 'a nova as dazzling as it is short-lived' (Lacan 2006b: 339; see however Babich 1996). Žižek also notes that Lacan's references to Nietzsche are almost non-existent and that the truth of psychoanalysis in Lacan's sense has nothing to do with the reduction of truth to a supposedly Nietzschean textual 'effect' (Žižek 2008b: 172).[11]

But perhaps there is another way to look at this. Roudinesco writes about *Seminar XX* ('Encore', Lacan 1998):

> The seminar is stupefying. It reveals the final return to the French scene of the great baroque Lacan of his Roman maturity and failed visit to the pope. But it is also an act of homage to the Bataille of *Madame Edwarda*, to the absolute figure of the hatred and love of God.
>
> *(Roudinesco 1990: 524)[12]*

In a short essay, Roland Léthier takes Roudinesco's claim of homage at face value and proceeds to assess the triangular linkages between Lacan, Bataille, and Nietzsche that the homage possibly implies (Léthier 1994). Léthier first tests the claim against both the *Seminar* and *Madame Edwarda*. He can, for example, verify that in the first session, Lacan will play around with the French adjective '*étrange*' ('strange') which may or may not be a reference to Bataille,[13] and that, correspondingly, the adverb '*encore*' ('again') appears a few times in Bataille's novel.[14] These hardly being evidence capable of verifying Roudinesco's claim, Léthier then recounts two narratives.

The first is about how Lacan, at the very beginning of *Seminar XX*, matches 'nonknowledge', the final '*ne pas savoir*' of the protagonist of Bataille's *récit* at the brink of madness,[15] with an admission, almost a confession. Lacan comments on why he had postponed the publication of *Seminar VII*[16]:

> With the passage of time, I learned that I could say a little more about it. And then I realized that what constituted my course was a sort of 'I don't want to know anything about it.'
>
> *(Lacan 1998: 1)*

So not an homage but, rather, an admission of a blind spot.

Léthier's second narrative is from the correspondence between Freud and his friend, the German author Arnold Zweig (see e.g. Freud and Zweig 1970: 23 and the subsequent correspondence; the whole episode is recounted in more detail in Lehrer 1995: 237–44). In 1934, Zweig had requested Freud as an expert for information concerning Nietzsche's psychotic illness, material that he would use in a literary project on the philosopher. Freud was hesitant. But Zweig insisted, and so Freud reluctantly forwarded the request to his fellow-analyst and friend Lou Andreas-Salomé who had also been a close acquaintance of Nietzsche. Andreas-Salomé responded that she found Zweig's project more than distasteful (Freud and Andreas-Salomé 1985: 202–03), and so Freud found a justification for abstaining from any further assistance. Gradually Freud diverted his correspondence with Zweig to his own 'historical novel' on Moses (Freud 1985).

Léthier claims that despite Freud's acknowledged success in the Schreber case already mentioned above, Zweig's persistent requests presented a challenge to his ability to explain psychoses in a more comprehensive way. In the correspondence that followed, Freud then gradually displaced Nietzsche; Nietzsche only to return as the figure of Moses. Moses is, then, the displaced substitution of Freud's 'nonknowledge', of his '*ne pas savoir*', that is, of Nietzsche.

Léthier illustrates the position of nonknowledge in these two narratives with the help of two equilateral triangles where the top corners represent Nietzsche and Freud, and Bataille and Lacan respectively (redrawn from Léthier 1994: 77; Figures 18.1 and 18.2).

But while the first triangle is fixed, the second rotates so that the three vertices form a circle.[17] Léthier then concludes that with his engagements with Nietzsche, Bataille unknowingly addressed something that Freud had earlier evaded in the displacement and that Lacan, in his own way, later reproduces.[18] A Nietzschean ghost, then.

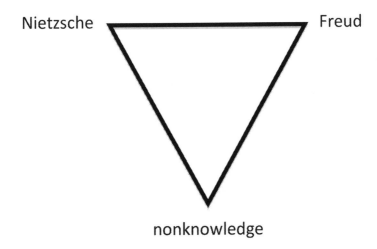

FIGURE 18.1 Léthier I

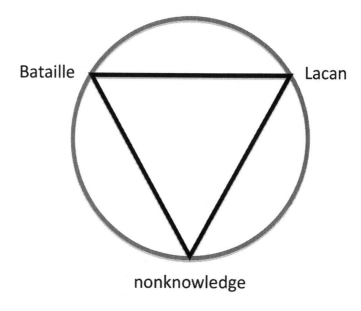

FIGURE 18.2 Léthier II

Conclusions: the ghost

This short essay has, first, made a distinction between 'Lacan's politics', a position that his texts may or may not explicitly represent, and a 'Lacanian politics', that is, the plethora of usually left-leaning political positions that take their theoretical inspiration from psychoanalysis as it has developed since Lacan. The least we can say is that there is a discrepancy between the two, that the latter cannot unequivocally be determined from the former. Lacan's own politics remain a bit of a mystery.

Second, this essay has suggested that while Lacan's reluctance to engage may be depicted as a 'relatively apolitical' position as Roudinesco insists, his personal and intellectual affiliation with Bataille may give cause for another possible explanation. During the 1930s, both Lacan and Bataille participated actively in and were deeply influenced by Kojève's lectures on Hegel. In that sense, the intellectual soil in which both grew was Hegelian, albeit interpreted in a very particular way. Both Lacan and Bataille eventually rebelled against their Hegelian 'Master', but in quite different ways. While Lacan later engaged with Heidegger, Bataille moved on to Nietzsche.

As I have tried to indicate, much like Bataille himself, Nietzsche remains a ghostlike figure or, less dramatically put, a 'silent partner' (see Ons 2006) in Lacan's background. He is rarely mentioned, and the few existing mentions are of no real value in working out the intellectual ties between the two. Moreover, this ghost is a 'double-phantom', a hazy blur, no more, that occupies the position from which Bataille himself had been displaced. So a Bataille-Nietzsche. For the Bataille of the 1930s – the friendship between the two is reported to have been at its closest during the interwar years – Nietzsche was a way of resolving the political impasse into which Hegel's 'end of history' had cornered him. Perhaps the Bataille-Nietzsche ghost is the engine of Lacan's own 'politics of the impossible', a response to the impasse that he had led himself into in *Seminar VII*: 'I don't want to know anything about it.'

But this ghost certainly makes Lacan's own politics – if there is such a thing – appear as something quite different than the fairly common perception of a left-of-centre 'Lacanian politics'. Lacan's politics would certainly be radical, but its radicalness is, I would suggest, 'conservative' by nature rather than liberal. Perhaps Lacan, just like Bataille, could best be depicted as a radical conservative, that is, as an anti-liberal thinker in the same vein as German Conservative Revolutionaries, such as the political historian Ernst Kantorowicz or the constitutional theorist Carl Schmitt (on radical conservatism in general, see e.g. Muller 1997: 27–30). Such a depiction would tie Lacan's own Heideggerian interests in well with Bataille and Nietzsche as well as with his 1974 activities in Vincennes that clearly displayed an 'ethics of responsibility' rather than a 'conviction' committed to a liberal political morality (on the ethics of responsibility, see Weber 1991; Starr 1999).

If this is the case, it would make Lacan's politics potentially much more radical than any 'Lacanian politics' fathomed so far.

But in *Less than Nothing*, Žižek differentiates between three optional interpretations of Lacan's politics. A conservative position, that is, the radical variant of which is suggested here in relation to Bataille and Nietzsche, would in Žižek's view emphasize the symbolic authority as a *sine qua non* of the social order. This would be the standard starting point that calls for the 'sovereign rule' of a statesman-like authority figure. Conversely, a leftist position – perhaps a 'Lacanian politics' – will use Lacan for the critique of the patriarchal ideology that upholds such a notion of authority. Finally, there is a 'cynically permissive liberal' position, a 'pragmatic politics without risk' that rejects radical leftist politics as 'metaphysical' and considers all radical measures, regardless of how necessary, as somehow doomed to end in totalitarian terror.

True to form, Žižek will, of course, conclude that none of these will do, as no 'correct' position is even available – the question was wrongly put in the first place – and so Lacan's politics, at least towards the end, is a fourth option, a non-heroic stance that rejects the false presuppositions of the other three:

> For the earlier Lacan, both the ethics of symbolic realization and the ethics of confronting the Real Thing call for the heroic stance of pushing things to the limit in order to leave behind our everyday *Verfallenheit*, our fallen existence. ... Renouncing this radicalism, the later Lacan re-conceives psychoanalytic treatment in a much more modest way: 'one does not need to learn all of the truth. A little bit is sufficient'. Here the very idea of psychoanalysis as a radical 'limit experience' is rejected: 'One should not push an analysis too far. When the patient thinks he is happy to live, it is enough.'
>
> (*Žižek 2012: 967, references deleted*)

Notes

1 Lacan's admiration for the German philosopher was obvious enough, and the often reproduced photograph documenting their 1955 encounter at Lacan's summer residence in Guitrancourt is apt evidence of the awkwardness involved. Lacan's high regard was hardly reciprocated by Heidegger who famously dismissed his French fan and the author of the 'obviously baroque text' called *Écrits* as a 'psychiatrist in need of a psychiatrist' (see Heidegger 2001: 279, 280–81).

2 Georges Bataille (1897–1962) was an influential French theorist and author. Despite his prominent position within French intelligentsia, he was never employed by an academic institution but, rather, chose to work through journals (e.g. *Documents, Critique*) and informal research collectives (e.g. *Contre-Attaque, Collège de Sociologie, Acéphale*) that he either founded or co-founded. *Acéphale* was a secret society that Bataille called together in the late 1930s. Its meetings are said to have included sessions dedicated to the reading of texts by Marcel Mauss, Sigmund Freud, and Friedrich Nietzsche, among others, and, more infamously, to the planning of a human sacrifice that, however, was never carried out. For a few years the society published a journal of the same name.

3 It is, of course, a matter of taste as to whether one regards Lacan's own authoritarian participation in the reorganization of the department of psychoanalysis at Vincennes in 1974 as a 'political position', as his critics clearly did (see e.g. Lyotard and Deleuze 1993).

4 Another indication is the 'trigger happy' lawsuit against Roudinesco concerning Lacan's alleged Catholicism that followed the publication of the book *Lacan. In Spite of Everything* (Roudinesco 2014).

5 E.g. Stavrakakis' book on Lacan and the political mentions Bataille twice, and both mentions are biographical and descriptive in nature rather than related to politics (Stavrakakis 1999: 10, 11).

6 The other 'Hegelian' that figured heavily in the lives of both was Alexandre Koyré, another Russian emigrant philosopher, who taught Hegel at the *École pratique* before Kojève (see Koyré 1934).

7 Lacan's 1932 doctoral thesis has later been published (Lacan 1975). A small part of it – a case analysis – is available in English (Lacan 1987; see also Benvenuto and Kennedy 1986: 31–46).

8 In the French original, Lacan describes Bataille's novel as an '*ouvrage central*' (Lacan 1966: 583, note 1). Daniel Paul Schreber (1842–1911) was a German jurist and appeals court judge from Dresden who suffered from a psychotic disorder and famously depicted his symptoms in astonishing detail in a book (Schreber 2000). Freud never treated Schreber personally but wrote an equally famous case analysis of his book (Freud 2002; see also Lacan 1993: 57–157 in particular).

9 Roudinesco interprets Lacan here as a 'pragmatic' revisionist who urges his followers to abandon the 'extremist and ridiculous' politics of Maoism and to 'return to psychoanalysis' (Roudinesco 2014: 39).

10 Hegel famously claimed that Prussia's defeat to the Napoleonic army at Jena in 1806 also marked the 'end of history' in the evolution of human societies (equally famously discussed in Fukuyama 2006).

11 Admittedly this riposte is more a criticism of Habermas' poor understanding of contemporary philosophy than it is about Lacan and Nietzsche, but at least it restates the lack of engagement (on Nietzsche and Lacan, see however Zupančič 2003; Themi 2014).

12 I have myself elsewhere sought to excavate these concealed linkages (see Minkkinen 2009: 147–49).

13 '*Étrange*' ('strange'), '*être-ange*' ('to be an angel') (see Lacan 1998: 8). The implication being that this angelic wordplay is a reference to Pierre Angélique, the pseudonym that Bataille used to write the novel.

14 'In my anguish, I yielded over and over again to the desire to be the object of my horror' (Bataille 1989a: 50). Cf. 'Jouissance – jouissance of the Other's body – remains a question, because the answer it may constitute is not necessary. We can take this further

still: it is not a sufficient answer either, because love demands love. It never stops (*ne cesse pas*) demanding it. It demands it … *encore*. "*Encore*" is the proper name of the gap (*faille*) in the Other from which the demand for love stems' (Lacan 1998: 4).

15 '… the immensity, the night engulfs it and, all on purpose, that living self is there just in order … "not to know"' (Bataille 1989a: 159).

16 The seminar was first published posthumously in 1986.

17 Léthier seems to suggest that the three vertices of his second rotating triangle (Figure 18.2) also correspond with the outer intersection points of the Borromean triquetra as Lacan theorizes it in *Seminar XXIII* ('The sinthome', see the Schema RSI in Lacan 2005: 48).

18 Léthier calls Lacan's friendship with Bataille 'cruel' rather than 'puzzling', and for evidently good reasons. He notes how Lacan, before discussing Jacopo Zucchi's 16th-century painting *Psyche surprises Amor*, claims that he has 'never heard anyone ever speak about it' (Lacan 2001b: 261). This is highly unlikely because Bataille included a discussion and a reproduction of the painting in his book *The Tears of Eros* which was published the same year after two years of preparation (see Bataille 1989b: 101).

Bibliography

Apollon, Willy and Feldstein, Richard (eds) (1996) *Lacan, Politics, Aesthetics*. Albany, NY: SUNY Press.

Babich, Babette (1996) 'The Order of the Real: Nietzsche and Lacan', in *Disseminating Lacan*, ed. David Pettigrew and François Raffoul. Albany, NY: SUNY Press, 43–68.

Bataille, Georges (1982) *Story of the Eye*, trans. Joachim Neugroschel. Harmondsworth: Penguin.

Bataille, Georges (1985) 'The Sacred Conspiracy', in *Visions of Excess. Selected Writings, 1927–1939*, Georges Bataille, trans. Allan Stoekl. Minneapolis, MN: University of Minnesota Press, 178–181.

Bataille, Georges (1988a) *The Accursed Share. An Essay on General Economy. Volume I. Consumption*, trans. Robert Hurley. New York: Zone Books.

Bataille, Georges (1988b) *Inner Experience*, trans. Leslie Anne Boldt. Albany, NY: SUNY Press.

Bataille, Georges (1989a) *My Mother / Madame Edwarda / The Dead Man*, trans. Austryn Wainhouse. London: Marion Boyars.

Bataille, Georges (1989b) *The Tears of Eros*, trans. Peter Connor. San Francisco, CA: City Lights Books.

Bataille, Georges (1991a) *The Accursed Share. An Essay on General Economy. Volumes II and III. The History of Eroticism & Sovereignty*, trans. Robert Hurley. New York: Zone Books.

Bataille, Georges (1991b) *The Impossible. A Story of Rats followed by Dianus and by The Oresteia*, trans. Robert Hurley. San Francisco, CA: City Lights Books.

Bataille, Georges (2001) *The Unfinished System of Nonknowledge*, trans. Michelle Kendall and Stuart Kendall. Minneapolis, MN: University of Minnesota Press.

Bataille, Laurence (1987) *L'ombilic du rêve. D'une pratique de la psychanalyse*. Paris: Seuil.

Benvenuto, Bice and Kennedy, Roger (1986) *The Works of Jacques Lacan. An Introduction*. London: Free Association.

Besnier, Jean-Michel (1988) *La politique de l'impossible. L'intellectuel entre révolte et engagement*. Paris: Éditions la Découverte.

Besnier, Jean-Michel (1990) 'Georges Bataille in the 1930s: A Politics of the Impossible', *Yale French Studies*. 78: 169–180.

Besnier, Jean-Michel (1995) 'Bataille, the Emotive Intellectual', in *Bataille. Writing the Sacred*, ed. Carolyn Bailey Gill. London and New York: Routledge, 13–26.

Blanchot, Maurice (1988) *Thomas the Obscure*, trans. Robert Lamberton. Barrytown, NY: Station Hill Press.

Blanchot, Maurice (1997) *Friendship*, trans. Elizabeth Rottenberg. Stanford, CA: Stanford University Press.

Blanchot, Maurice (2004) *Lautréamont and Sade*, trans. Stuart Kendall and Michelle Kendall. Stanford, CA: Stanford University Press.

Borch-Jacobsen, Mikkel (1991) *Lacan. The Absolute Master*, trans. Douglas Brick. Stanford, CA: Stanford University Press.

Botting, Fred (1994) 'Relations of the Real in Lacan, Bataille and Blanchot', *SubStance*, 23(1) (Issue 73): 24–40.

Chiesa, Lorenzo (2007) *Subjectivity and Otherness. A Philosophical Reading of Lacan*. Cambridge, MA: MIT Press.

David, Angie (2013) *Sylvia Bataille*. Paris: Léo Scheer.

De Kesel, Marc (2009) *Eros and Ethics. Reading Jacques Lacan's Seminar VII*, trans. Sigi Jottkandt. Albany, NY: SUNY Press.

Dean, Carolyn J. (1992) *The Self and Its Pleasures. Bataille, Lacan, and the History of the Decentered Subject*. Ithaca, NY: Cornell University Press.

Deguy, Michel (ed.) (1991) *Lacan avec les philosophes*. Paris: Albin Michel.

Derrida, Jacques (1998) *Resistances of Psychoanalysis*, trans. Peggy Kamuf, Pascale-Anne Brault and Michael Naas. Stanford, CA: Stanford University Press.

Evans, Dylan (1998) 'From Kantian Ethics to Mystical Experience: An Exploration of Jouissance', in *Key Concepts of Lacanian Psychoanalysis*, ed. Dany Nobus. New York: Other Press, 1–28.

French, Patrick (2007) 'Friendship, Assymmetry, Sacrifice: Bataille and Blanchot', *Parrheisia*, 3: 32–42.

Foucault, Michel (1977) 'A Preface to Transgression', in *Language, Counter-Memory, Practice: Selected Essays and Interviews*, Michel Foucault, trans. Donald F. Bouchard and Sherry Simon. Oxford: Blackwell, 29–52.

Freud, Sigmund (1985) 'Moses and Monotheism: Three Essays', in *The Origins of Religion. Totem and Taboo, Moses and Monotheism and Other Works*, trans. James Strachey. Harmondsworth: Penguin, 237–386.

Freud, Sigmund (2002) *The Schreber Case*, trans. Andrew Webber. London: Penguin.

Freud, Sigmund and Andreas-Salomé, Lou (1985) *Sigmund Freud and Lou Andreas-Salomé, Letters*, trans. Elaine Robson-Scott and William Robson-Scott. New York: W. W. Norton and Company.

Freud, Sigmund and Zweig, Arnold (1970) *The Letters of Sigmund Freud and Arnold Zweig*, trans. Elaine Robson-Scott and William Robson-Scott. London: Hogarth Press.

Fukuyama, Francis (2006) *The End of History and the Last Man*, new edn. New York and London: Free Press.

Greely, Robert Adèle (2001) 'Dalí's Fascism; Lacan's Paranoia', *Art History*, 24(4): 465–492.

Grigg, Russell (1998) 'From the Mechanism of Psychosis to the Universal Condition of the Symptom: On Foreclosure', in *Key Concepts of Lacanian Psychoanalysis*, ed. Dany Nobus. New York: Other Press, 48–74.

Heidegger, Martin (2001) *Zollikon Seminars. Protocols, Conversations, Letters*, trans. Franz Mayr and Richard Askay. Evanston, IL: Northwestern University Press.

Holland, Michael (2004) 'An Event without Witness: Contestation between Blanchot and Bataille', in *The Power of Contestation. Perspectives on Maurice Blanchot*, ed. Kevin Hart and Geoffrey H. Hartman. Baltimore, MD and London: Johns Hopkins University Press, 27–45.

Hollier, Denis (1989) *Against Architecture. The Writings of Georges Bataille*, trans. Betsy Wing. Cambridge, MA: MIT Press.

Jaudel, Nathalie (2011) *Roudinesco, plagiaire de soi-même, suivi de Lacan, Maurras et les Juifs*. Paris: Navarin.

Kojève, Alexandre (1980) *Introduction to the Reading of Hegel. Lectures on the Phenomenology of Spirit*, trans. James H. Nichols Jr. Ithaca, NY and London: Cornell University Press.

Koyré, Alexandre (1934) 'Hegel à Iéna (à propos de publications récentes)', *Revue Philosophique de la France et de l'Étranger*, 59: 274–283.

Lacan, Jacques (1961–62) *Le Séminare, livre IX: L'identification* [unpublished].

Lacan, Jacques (1965–66) *Le Séminare, livre XIII: L'objet de la psychanalyse* [unpublished].

Lacan, Jacques (1966) *Écrits*. Paris: Seuil.

Lacan, Jacques (1971–72) *Le Séminaire, livre XIX bis: Le savoir du psychanalyste* [unpublished].

Lacan, Jacques (1975) *De la psychose paranoïaque dans ses rapports avec la personnalité, suivi de Premiers écrits sur la paranoïa*. Paris: Seuil.

Lacan, Jacques (1987) 'The Case of Aimée, or Self-punitive Paranoia', in *The Clinical Roots of the Schizophrenia Concept. Translations of Seminal European Contributions on Schizophrenia*, ed. John Cutting and Michael Shepherd. Cambridge: Cambridge University Press, 213–226.

Lacan, Jacques (1988a) 'Motives of Paranoiac Crime: The Crime of the Papin Sisters', *Critical Texts*, 5(3): 7–11.

Lacan, Jacques (1988b) 'The Problem of Style and the Psychiatric Conception of Paranoiac Forms of Experience', *Critical Texts*, 5(3): 4–6.

Lacan, Jacques (1992) *The Ethics of Psychoanalysis, The Seminar of Jacques Lacan. Book VII*, trans. Dennis Porter. New York and London: W. W. Norton and Company.

Lacan, Jacques (1993) *The Psychoses, The Seminar of Jacques Lacan. Book III*, trans. Russell Grigg. New York and London: W. W. Norton and Company.

Lacan, Jacques (1998) *On Feminine Sexuality. The Limits of Love and Knowledge, The Seminar of Jacques Lacan. Book XX*, trans. Bruce Fink. New York and London: W. W. Norton and Company.

Lacan, Jacques (2001a) *Autres écrits*. Paris: Seuil.

Lacan, Jacques (2001b) *Le Séminaire, livre VIIIL: Le transfert*. Paris: Seuil.

Lacan, Jacques (2005) *Le Séminaire, livre XXIII: Le sinthome*. Paris: Seuil.

Lacan, Jacques (2006a) *Le Séminaire, livre XVI: D'un Autre à l'autre*. Paris: Seuil.

Lacan, Jacques (2006b) *Écrits. The First Complete Edition in English*, trans. Bruce Fink. New York and London: W. W. Norton and Company.

Lacan, Jacques (2007) *The Other Side of Psychoanalysis, The Seminar of Jacques Lacan. Book XVII*, trans. Russell Grigg. New York and London: W. W. Norton and Company.

Lehrer, Ronald (1995) *Nietzsche's Presence in Freud's Life and Thought. On the Origins of a Psychology of Dynamic Unconscious Mental Functioning*. Albany, NY: SUNY Press.

Léthier, Roland (1994) 'Bataille avec Lacan', *La part de l'Œil*, 10 (Dossier: Bataille et les arts plastiques): 67–80.

Lyotard, Jean-François and Deleuze, Gilles (1993) 'Concerning the Vincennes Psychoanalysis Department', in *Political Writings*, Jean-François Lyotard, trans. Bill Readings and Kevin Paul Geiman. London: UCL Press, 68–69.

Minkkinen, Panu (2009) *Sovereignty, Knowledge, Law*. Abingdon: Routledge.

Mitchell, Andrew J. and Kemp Winfree, Jason (eds) (2009) *The Obsessions of Georges Bataille. Community and Communication*. Albany, NY: SUNY Press.

Muller, Jerry Z. (1997) 'Introduction: What Is Conservative Social and Political Thought?', in *Conservatism. An Anthology of Social and Political Thought from David Hume to the Present*, ed. Jerry Z. Muller. Princeton, NJ: Princeton University Press, 3–31.

Ons, Silvia (2006) 'Nietzsche, Freud, Lacan', in *Lacan. The Silent Partners*, ed. Slavoj Žižek. London: Verso, 79–89.

Roudinesco, Elisabeth (1990) *Jacques Lacan & Co. A History of Psychoanalysis in France, 1925–1985*, trans. Jeffrey Mehlman. Chicago, IL: University of Chicago Press.

Roudinesco, Elisabeth (1995) 'Bataille entre Freud et Lacan: Une expérience cachée', in *Georges Bataille après tout*, ed. Denis Hollier. Paris: Belin, 191–212.

Roudinesco, Elisabeth (1997) *Jacques Lacan. An Outline of a Life and a History of a System of Thought*, trans. Barbara Bray. New York: Columbia University Press.

Roudinesco, Elisabeth (2014) *Lacan. In Spite of Everything*, trans. Gregory Elliott. London: Verso.

Ryder, Andrew (2010) 'Inner Experience Is Not Psychosis: Bataille's Ethics and Lacanian Subjectivity', *Parrheisa*, 9: 94–108.

Schreber, Daniel Paul (2000) *Memoirs of My Nervous Illness*, trans. Ida Macalpine and Richard A. Hunter. New York: New York Review Books.

Sichère, Bernard (1983) *Le moment lacanien*. Paris: Grosset.

Sichère, Bernard (2006) *Pour Bataille. Être, chance, souveraineté*. Paris: Gallimard.

Starr, Bradley E. (1999) 'The Structure of Max Weber's Ethic of Responsibility', *The Journal of Religious Ethics*, 27(3): 407–434.

Stavrakakis, Yannis (1999) *Lacan and the Political*. London: Routledge.

Stavrakakis, Yannis (2007) *The Lacanian Left. Psychoanalysis, Theory, Politics*. Edinburgh: Edinburgh University Press.

Surya, Michel (2002) *Georges Bataille. An Intellectual Biography*, trans. Krzysztof Fijalkowski and Michael Richardson. London: Verso.

Themi, Tim (2014) *Lacan's Ethics and Nietzsche's Critique of Platonism*. New York: SUNY Press.

Weber, Max (1991) 'Politics as a Vocation', in *From Max Weber: Essays in Sociology*, new edn, Max Weber, trans. Hans Heinrich Gerth and C Wrigth Mills. Abingdon: Routledge, 77–128,.

Žižek, Slavoj (2006) *The Parallax View*. Cambridge, MA: MIT Press.

Žižek, Slavoj (2008a) *Enjoy Your Symptom! Jacques Lacan in Hollywood and Out*. London: Routledge.

Žižek, Slavoj (2008b) *The Sublime Object of Ideology*. New edn. London: Verso.

Žižek, Slavoj (2012) *Less than Nothing. Hegel and the Shadow of Dialectical Materialism*. London: Verso.

Zupančič, Alenka (2003) *The Shortest Shadow. Nietzsche's Philosophy of the Two*. Cambridge, MA: MIT Press.

INDEX OF NAMES

Adam 258
Adams, Perveen 239
Adorno, Theodor W. 3, 74, 75, 82, 138
Agamben, Giorgio 30, 191
St. Agatha 93
Alexander the Great 126, 166
Anna O. 168
Arendt, Hannah 193
Aron, Raymond 15, 18, 25
Artaud, Antonin 26
Althusser, Louis 4, 8, 20, 22, 24, 130, 132,
    133, 137, 283
Antigone: 62, 224, 285, 286
Anzieu, Didier 21
Aristotle 5, 6, 80, 106, 109n, 123, 193, 277
Aulagnier, Piera 18

Bacchus 254
Badiou, Alain 115, 191, 220, 230, 231, 264,
    282
Balibar, Étienne 64
Barthes, Roland 22
Bataille, Georges 281 – 294
Bataille, Sylvia 282
Bentham, Jeremy: 149, 153
Besnier, Jean-Michel 283
Beyonce 233
Bierbichler, Josef 165, 167, 178n
Blair, Tony 77, 226
Blanchot, Maurice 284, 285
Borch-Jakobsen, Mikkel 282
Brecht, Bertold 94, 255, 264
Bruni, Carla 16

Bush, George Jr 226
Butler, Judith 8, 186, 189, 246

Campbell, Kirsten 10
Cash, Johnny 261, 262
Ceausescu, Nikolae 122
de Certeau, Michel 20, 21, 22
Chasselet-Smirguel, Janine 21
Chiesa, Lorenzo 286
Christ: 94, 258, 259, 260, 261, 264, 265
Cieszkowski, August von 277
Claudius 102, 104, 202, 203, 208, 210, 211,
    214, 215
Cohn-Bendit, Daniel 15, 16, 17
Copernicus, Nikolai 6, 115
Copjec, Jean 109
Critchley, Simon 204

Darwin, Charles 6
Debord, Guy 75, 84n
Deleuze, Gilles 75, 138, 150, 230, 282
Democritus 71n
Derrida, Jacques 35, 132, 281
Dinur, Yehiel 194
Dion, Céline 26
Dolar, Mladen 9
Dora 47, 48, 54, 55, 56, 59n
Douzinas, Costas 183, 184, 185, 186, 189,
    190, 191, 193, 194, 195
Dupin 256, 257

Engels, Friedrich 271, 274
Escher, Maurits Cornelis 95, 97

300 Index of names

Evans, Dylan 17, 285

Felman, Shoshana 63
Finkelkraut, Alain 16
Fliess, Wilhelm 48, 62
Fortinbras 202, 214
Foucault, Michel 22, 23, 24, 126n, 129,
  130, 131, 132, 133, 136, 140,141, 145,
  150, 185, 197n, 270, 274, 275, 289, 290.
Freud, Sigmund: 1, 2, 4, 6, 7, 10, 24, 29,
  33, 34, 35, 36, 41n., 45–51, 53, 54, 55,
  56, 62, 67, 68, 71, 73, 75, 77, 78, 82, 83,
  85, 100, 101, 108, 131, 133, 134, 135,
  138, 139, 141, 142, 143, 144, 146, 147,
  149, 150, 152, 156, 163, 164, 167–175,
  177, 185, 189, 191, 193, 201, 202, 203,
  204, 205, 206, 215n, 219, 222, 223, 225,
  231n, 236, 257, 266n, 275, 277, 283, 291
Freud, Anna 74

Gainsbourg, Serge 25, 26
Gandhi, Mahatma 91, 189
de Gaulle, Charles 15, 18, 19, 23
Gertrude 202, 208, 214
Geyskens, Thomas 9
Glawogger, Michael 165
Goldmann, Jean-Jacques 26
Goldmann, Lucien 22, 26, 126n
Goldmann, Pierre 26
Gödel, Kurt 138
Graeber, David 162n.
Gramsci, Antonio 125, 132, 133
Grigg, Russell 138
Grunberger, Bela 21
Guattari, Félix 75, 138, 150

Hage, Ghassan 198n
Hall, Stuart 131
Halliday, Johnny 26
Hamacher, Werner 167
Hamlet 10, 100, 101, 102, 104, 106, 202–
  204, 208 – 215
Hammurabi 271
Hartmann, Heinz 25
Haute, Philippe van 9, 202, 208
Hegel, Georg Wilhelm Friedrich 2, 64, 66,
  81, 97, 118, 124, 125, 154, 175, 176,
  178n, 197n, 257, 263, 277, 283, 287,
  289, 292, 293, 294n
Heidegger, Martin 69, 164, 167, 281, 292,
  293, 294n
Helmholtz, Hermann von 170
Hirvonen, Ari 10,
Hitler, Adolf 126, 166, 167, 215
Hobbes, Thomas 36, 138

Hoens, Dominiek 9
Hollier, Denis 287, 288
Horatio: 202
Horkheimer, Max 3, 285
Huston, John 85
Huxley, Aldous 144

Irigaray, Luce 236, 244, 249n
Ivens, Joris 174

Jakobson, Roman 3, 117
Jokasta 49, 53, 62
Jones, Ernst 203
Joyce, James 151
Judt, Tony 15
Jünger, Ernst 167

Kaas, Patricia 27
Kafka, Franz 65
Kant, Immanuel 2, 218, 224, 225, 226, 227,
  228, 229, 277, 286
Kantorowicz, Ernst 293
Khaled 26
Kierkegaard, Sören 190, 193, 258, 262, 263,
  264, 265
Klepec, Peter 9, 162n.
Kojève, Alexandre 108, 175, 283, 289, 292
Koyre, Alexandre 6, 107, 264n
Kristeva, Julia 8, 236

Laclau, Ernesto 134, 135
Laertes 103, 105, 202, 213, 214
Lagroye, Jacques 22
Laub, Dori 199n
Lavoine, Marc 26
Lefort, Claude 187
Legendre, Pierre 223
Lenin, Vladimir Illic 17, 162, 270
Léthier, Roland 290, 291, 295n
Levi, Primo 261 – 262
Levi – Strauss, Claude 22, 57, 59n, 118,
  135, 136, 137, 234
Liu, Catherine 26n.
Losmann, Carmen 164
Lubitch, Ernst 69
St Lucy 95
Lukács, Georg 22
Lynch, David 255
Lyotard, Jean-François 162n, 294n

MacCannell, Juliet Flower 9, 243
Mandela, Nelson 195
Marcuse, Herbert 3, 75, 79, 138
Marx, Karl 2, 4, 17, 20, 21, 24, 91, 98, 99,
  105, 138, 139, 148, 149, 150, 151, 152–

157, 159, 160, 162, 165, 174, 177, 197n, 263, 271, 277, 285
Mattoni, Frédérique 22
Miller, Jacques-Alain 16, 22, 24, 204, 215
Milner, Jean-Claude 33
Minkkinen, Panu 10
Mitchell, Juliet 8, 237
Moses 266n, 271, 291
Mouffe, Chantal 133, 134
Mounin, George 23
Mulvey, Laura132

Nassif, Jacques: 16
Negri, Antonio 75, 79
Newman, Saul 223
Nietzsche, Friedrich 11, 164, 165, 260, 283, 289, 290, 291, 293, 294n

Oedipus 9, 46, 47, 48, 51, 53, 54, 62, 63–66, 69, 73, 74, 75, 80, 102, 173, 206, 214n
Ophelia 103, 105, 108, 202, 213, 214

Pascal, Blaise 68, 105, 110
Pasolini, Pier Paolo 227
St. Paul 24
Pavón-Cuéllar, David 10
Penny, Laurie 248
Pentheus 254, 255
Perrier, François 18
Plato 88, 255, 277
Platonov, Andrei 88, 90, 91, 92, 97
Poe, Edgar Allan 256
Polonius 202, 204, 212
Pritchard, Marion 197n

Rabaté, Jean-Michel 9
Rancière, Jacques 132
Reich, Wilhelm 4, 18, 137
Rogers, Carl 21
Rogers, Juliet 10
Rose, Jacqueline 8, 237
Roudinesco, Elizabeth 11n, 18, 282, 283, 290, 292, 294n
Russell, Bertrand 139

Sade, Marquis de 35,128n, 138, 225, 226, 229, 285, 286
Santner, Eric 191, 198n
Sarkozy, Nicholas 16, 76, 85n
Sartre, Jean-Paul 21
Saussure, Ferdinand de 3, 80, 131, 135, 136, 150, 151, 156
Scarry, Elaine 198n
Schelling, Friedrich Wilhelm Joseph 257, 258, 259, 277
Schmitt, Carl 36, 37, 39, 41n, 293
Schuster, Aaron 67, 69, 71n, 89, 90, 91, 98
Scott, Ridley 253
Sharpe, Ella 111n
Sloterdijk, Peter 276
Smith, Adam 96, 97, 153
Socrates 139
Solon 271
Soler, Colette 162n
Sophocles 9, 46–48, 65, 67
Spivak, Gayatri 196, 197n
Stalin, Joseph 108
Stéphane, André 21
Stothard, Peter 76
Šumič, Jelica 9, 129n, 162n, 218

Tomšič, Samo 19, 127n, 128n

Valabrega, Jean-Paul 18

Webster, Jamieson 203
Wegener, Mai 10
Wessel Zapffe, Peter 260
Wismann, Heinz 71n
Wright, Colin 9

Zedong, Mao 23, 24
Zevnik, Andreja 10, 197, 198
Žižek, Slavoj 8. 10. 75, 99n, 127n, 133, 149, 163n, 184, 185, 195, 196n, 197n, 221, 222, 241, 269, 271, 276, 277, 282, 285, 286, 290, 293
Zupančič, Alenka 9, 69, 70n, 127n, 162n, 219, 220, 221, 226, 227, 228, 229
Zweig, Arnold 291

INDEX OF NOTIONS

Act: 23, 53, 64, 67, 98, 101, 103, 117, 123, 152–3, 170, 182, 189, 191, 193, 201, 204–5, 209–14, 219, 221, 222, 227, 244, 247, 249, 255, 257, 262, 277, 286, 290
  a. of resistance 191
  Antigone's a., 64
  ethical a., 217, 221, 224, 226–31, 284
  psychoanalytical a., 16, 20, 23
  psychotic a., 183, 188, 190
  sexual a., 17, 23
  speech a., 121, 135
  symbolic a., 192
Action: 19, 25, 26, 76, 117, 182,184, 187, 191, 203, 215, 219, 224–6, 228–31, 268, 276, 277, 286
Affect: 5, 36, 101, 117, 138, 141, 203, 227
Agency: 29, 121, 130, 131, 139, 141, 221, 224, 229–30, 261, 287
Agens: 227, 228
Alienation: 5, 25, 84, 106, 138, 152, 207, 231, 258
Analysis: 30, 35, 36, 39, 57, 75, 102, 116, 126, 132, 151, 158, 165, 168, 174, 182–4, 190, 194–5, 203, 225
  self-analysis, 50, 60, 115, 241
Analyst: 17, 39, 40, 110, 116, 122, 125–6, 136, 139, 144, 147, 159, 185, 193–6, 290
  Analyst discourse, 81, 82–4, 116–8
Anarchism: 19
Anatomy: 6,7, 9, 148

Antagonism: 79, 86, 89, 90, 91, 96, 218, 228
Anti-Sexus: 88, 90–92, 94, 97
Anxiety: 105, 109, 110, 144, 150, 173, 263
Apparatus: 33, 103, 117, 171, 241
  psychic a., 1, 147, 171, 172
  linguistic a., 2, 119, 138
  mental a., 2, 148, 150, 172–4
Appearance: 9, 22, 104, 108, 140, 146, 150, 156, 159, 161, 162, 173, 193–4, 223, 262, 272
Authority: 6, 9, 10, 16, 75, 126, 140, 154, 167, 209–11, 214, 221, 223, 230, 240, 246, 260, 263, 286, 289, 293
Autonomy: 5, 6, 150, 151, 154–6, 161–3, 235, 257
Axiom: 5, 41, 219

Being: 3, 5, 6, 15, 18, 21, 33–4, 56, 69–70, 72, 78, 83, 87–91, 104, 110, 150, 160, 162, 182–7, 188–91, 194, 204, 206, 208–11, 212–4, 220, 222, 223–3, 241, 243, 258–9, 263, 265, 272–3, 286–9
  non-being, 69–71, 104, 106–8, 137
  speaking b., 2, 117–9, 124, 133
Biology: 6, 132, 147
Biopolitics: 10, 117, 140–43, 183–4, 194, 196
Body: 2, 15, 72–3, 120, 133, 139–40, 151, 168, 170, 172, 174, 183–3,

187–9, 191, 193–5, 221, 223–4, 226, 231, 235, 238, 246, 260
b. without organs, 73, 80, 94, 108
women's b., 193, 236
Bond: 33, 95, 241, 266
fraternal b., 241, 243
social b., 29–30, 32–34, 36–7, 94, 110, 115, 125, 136–7, 222, 224, 234, 241–4,
Bourgeois: 138, 245–7, 169–70, 273, 275–6
Bureaucracy: 127

Capital: 35, 97–9, 149, 152, 153–62, 165, 169–70, 173, 186, 247
disocurse of c., 24
fictitious c., 154, 156, 158, 160–62
Capitalism: 4, 10, 20, 23–4, 31–3, 75–7, 96–9, 132, 138, 143–5, 148–61, 167, 171, 177, 237, 239–41, 245–6, 285
Castration: 17, 23, 45–6, 49, 52–3, 56, 104, 106–7, 108–9, 143, 147, 149, 160, 171–3, 178, 235
symbolic c., 124, 150–2, 204–5, 209, 211
Catholicism: 260, 294
Cause: 33, 39–40, 88, 105–6, 121, 123–4, 126, 140, 172, 186, 188, 207, 213, 265
Change: 28, 30, 79, 81–3, 109, 115–6, 118, 123, 134, 137, 149, 153, 156, 158, 170, 185, 189, 195, 210, 212, 234, 239, 249, 265
Che vuoi?: 186, 231, 253, 257
Child: 49, 72, 74, 192, 204, 234
Christ: 94, 258–60, 264–6
Christianity: 9–5, 109–11, 154, 255, 258–60, 262–3, 265, 273–4
Civilisation: 34, 36
Clinic: 1, 9, 131, 138
Cogito: 3
Command: 75–6, 84, 285
Commandment: 35, 74, 109, 202, 220, 222
Commodification: 7, 150–2, 158–9, 242, 248, 252
Commodity: 98, 138, 149–156, 161, 171, 239, 247
c. fetishism, 149, 155
Communication: 5, 25, 115, 118, 120–21, 135, 288
Community: 4, 18, 32, 35–9, 53, 56, 136, 194, 207, 214, 218, 220, 222
Compulsion: 61, 172–3
Conflict: 6, 32, 62, 64, 66, 74, 76, 79, 92, 102

Consciousness: 3, 6, 22, 70, 116, 148, 154, 156, 170, 208, 273, 287
Conservatism: 10, 238, 293
Conservativism: 87
Contract: 77, 243
sexual c., 234, 240, 242–9
social c., 79–80, 138, 242–3, 245
Contradiction: 136, 150, 159, 220, 236, 248
Critique: 3, 4, 6, 9 -10, 31, 46, 53, 56, 80, 87, 130–33, 136–41, 146, 148, 150–57, 162, 219, 224–5, 236–7, 268–9, 274, 276–7, 287–8, 293
Culture: 2, 6, 16, 20, 24, 62, 73, 84, 88, 107, 110, 120, 133, 140, 144, 148–50, 165, 174, 204, 208, 213, 234, 237 -8, 242–6, 259–60, 268, 273, 275, 278

Das Ding: 105, 260
Deadlock: 1, 10, 40, 103, 150, 218, 221, 285
Death (see also death drive): 22, 46–7, 52, 62–3, 67, 69, 74, 79, 125, 165, 167, 175, 183–4, 188–9, 191, 193–6, 207, 211–3, 256–7, 260–62, 284–5, 287, 288
father's d., 50
Debt: 155, 160, 164, 209–10, 285–6
Democracy: 33, 35, 91, 104–7, 134, 186, 190
Desire: 4, 10, 33–4, 39, 48, 50, 51, 54–6, 62–4, 66, 72–4, 79–81, 84, 100, 102–9, 117, 120, 125–7, 133, 137–8, 140, 142, 143, 149, 152, 164, 166, 168, 172–3, 175–7, 185–8, 190, 193–6, 202–15, 220, 223, 226, 231, 234–5, 239–40, 254, 286–7
child's d.,49, 234
dialectics of d., 24
mother's/female d., 50, 204–6, 207–11, 213
object of d., 206, 210, 212
Oedipal d., 73, 75, 173
Other's d., 51, 55, 102, 108, 118, 126, 208
subject's d., 33, 103, 107, 206, 247
unconscious d., 53, 65, 80, 168–70, 172–3, 175–7
Difference: 80–2, 95, 104, 110, 151–2, 154, 158, 161, 172, 213, 284
absolute d., 134
radical d., 220
sexual d., 56, 90, 233, 235–8, 247
Discourse: 1, 3, 5, 10, 16, 19, 22- 5, 29, 74, 76, 80–2, 83, 84, 115–28, 130–44,

304 Index of notions

166, 185, 187, 192, 194–5, 204, 210,
217–8, 220–21, 228–31, 234, 241–4,
248, 264, 288
Analyst/analytic d., 110, 116, 118, 120,
123, 135, 137–40, 144, 152
Fifth discourse/capital(ist) d., 24, 30–4,
126, 143–5, 150, 152, 160–71, 241
Hysteric d., 118, 123, 126–7, 135
Master d., 29, 49, 75, 116–7, 123–5,
135, 137, 139–40, 144, 152, 158–9,
161, 165, 186–7, 191, 241–5, 249
Scientific d., 22, 127, 287
D. Theory, 132–35, 240–41
University d., 75, 118–9, 123, 127, 131,
135, 138, 140, 142, 144, 159, 166
Discovery: 2, 4, 6, 15, 46, 82, 97
Domination: 9, 10, 90, 96, 127, 157–8,
241, 243, 287
Dream: 61, 77, 82–3, 109, 139, 165,
168–72
dream-work, 170–73
Freud's d., 45–9, 54–5
Drive: 4, 7, 80, 93, 94, 152, 154–5, 171,
175, 190, 203, 225
death d., 65, 70, 81–3, 173, 175, 188,
257
sexual d., 93
Economy: 20, 54, 74–5, 96, 154, 160,
165, 174, 211, 241–2, 245–6, 270
libidinal e., 4–5, 145–51, 256
political e., 4, 9, 21, 130, 145–60
Ego: 5, 6, 25, 36, 72–6, 78–80, 82–4,
101–103, 106, 117, 133, 137, 154,
169–71, 174, 194, 212, 235, 276
Emancipation: 32, 38, 90, 93, 96, 99, 220
Enemy: 36–7, 80, 138, 214
Energy: 90, 172–4
Enjoyment: 5, 9, 30, 32–5, 48, 70, 74,
80, 82, 89, 92–5, 97, 105–6, 108–10,
114, 118–9, 125, 133, 135, 138,
149–52, 157, 158–9, 166, 175–8, 209,
223–4, 227, 276, 285
surplus e., 20, 23–4, 33, 87, 91, 93,
122, 152, 178
Epistemology: 154
Equality: 23, 78, 95, 150, 154, 234,
239–40, 242, 245
Ethics: 10, 34, 75–6, 107, 117, 135, 166,
218–32, 235, 285–6, 293
Evil: 34–5, 52, 67, 74, 220–21, 229–31,
258, 260–61, 275
Exception: 2, 16, 28, 30, 37–40, 64, 66,
72, 102, 117, 148, 153, 160, 235–6, 248
Exclusion: 4, 30, 37–8, 40, 90, 108, 153,
174, 245, 288

Existence: 10, 29, 36, 39 47, 51, 67–8,
81, 90, 95, 105, 141, 148, 157, 168,
171, 173, 186–8, 223–4, 238, 242,
263, 265, 285, 288–9, 294
Ex-sistence: 106, 148, 253, 262, 264–5

Father (see also murder oft he father): 6,
21, 46–54, 57, 62–4, 65, 67, 73,
102–3, 105–6, 108, 139, 191–2,
201–2, 204–7, 209–12, 212, 234,
242–3, 258, 260–61, 266, 275
name-of-the-father, 207–12, 214 , 234
Feminism: 10, 131, 233–50
Fetishism (see also commodity fetishism):
153–7, 160–71
Financialization: 148, 155, 158
Force: 4, 26, 31, 42, 63, 69, 72, 74, 77,
90, 96, 151, 161, 169–72, 174–6, 185,
190, 193, 213, 218, 222, 246, 254,
256, 276
Formalization: 24, 121, 142, 157, 204
Fort-da: 204, 210
Fraternity: 242–3

Gender: 9, 131, 187, 192, 233, 237,
239–40, 242–3, 246, 248
Genesis: 2, 24, 101, 155
Genocide: 195, 226, 230
Ghost: 201–2, 207, 209–11, 283, 292–3
Globalization: 18, 34, 37, 115, 140, 245
God: 22, 24, 65, 106, 108–10, 155,
193, 226, 229, 253–5, 257–66, 275,
290
Good: 25, 37, 40, 57, 68, 90, 92, 97, 140,
164–5, 184, 202, 217, 219–222,
224–30, 255, 259, 269, 275–6
Guilt: 49, 64, 66, 75, 202, 260–61

Hegemony: 125, 127, 134
History: 6, 21–2, 25, 48, 64, 81, 84, 88,
90, 119, 125, 132, 158, 167, 168, 171,
195, 204, 241, 258–9, 265, 277, 284,
289, 293
Holy Spirit: 263, 265
Homology: 3, 7, 21, 153, 157–8
Homo oeconomicus: 4, 154, 157
Hysteria: 46–7, 53–6

Identification: 19, 36, 39–40, 77–8, 82–4,
102, 123, 211, 213–4, 222, 230–31,
234–5, 243, 247, 277, 284
imaginary i., 204–5, 208, 210
Identity: 36–7, 39, 57, 76, 82, 104, 125,
133–5, 186–7, 190, 210–11, 222, 231,
237–8, 242, 247–8, 284

Ideology: 25, 77, 87, 90, 109, 115, 132–3, 153, 168, 186, 196, 219, 238, 268–78, 293
  Marx's critique of i., 3, 10, 153
Illusion: 33, 84, 110, 112, 152, 219–20, 222, 232, 242
Image: 76–8, 80, 82–3, 90, 96, 149–51, 178, 192, 204, 212, 218–20, 223–4, 227–9, 245–7, 261, 263
  body's i., 30
  mirror i., 72
Imaginary: 9–10, 30, 72–84, 95, 101, 103–6, 109, 121, 133–6, 140, 142–3, 185–6, 190, 194, 204–5, 209–15, 234, 242, 247–8, 264
Imperative: 10, 76, 83, 120, 124, 149–51, 155–6, 163, 178, 218–21, 223, 225–6, 228–9, 285
Impossibility: 6, 30, 37–40, 46, 48–51, 54, 57, 63 -5, 70, 87, 104, 116, 121, 136–7, 139, 143–5, 193, 248, 290
Incest: 62, 65, 80, 136, 174, 208
Inexistence: 34, 89, 148, 150
  I. Other, 9, 28, 34
Interpretation: 2, 35, 46–7, 49, 55–6, 63, 66, 68, 103, 105, 121, 135, 169, 178, 190, 192, 203–4, 212–3, 238, 264
Invention: 2, 9, 91, 134

Jewish Law: 261
Jouissance: 20–1, 23–4, 32–5, 49, 55–7, 73–5, 79–81, 94, 109, 118–20, 123–5, 137–9, 142–3, 167, 175, 187, 189, 220–25, 229–31, 235–6, 242, 264, 285–6
Justice: 16, 65, 96–7, 99, 260, 262

Knowledge: 8, 18, 20–3, 52–6, 75, 81–83, 102, 115, 120–3, 125, 127, 131, 133–7, 139–40, 142–4, 147, 154–5, 159, 161–3, 169, 177, 183, 185–6, 188–9, 220, 223, 229, 264, 268–70, 272–3, 276–7, 284, 287–9
  desire for k., 55–6
  nonknowledge, 286–9
  psychoanalytic k., 9, 137, 141, 269
  truth and knowledge, 20–2, 46, 53, 188, 195
Labour: 8, 24, 97–8, 126, 139, 144, 150, 152–6, 158, 160–2, 173, 175, 241, 246, 269, 288
  labour-power, 98, 153–5, 157–8, 160–2
Lack: 17, 23, 30, 33–4, 52–3, 56–7, 73, 75, 79–81, 82–3, 101, 103–5, 107, 109–10, 133–5, 139–40, 144, 152,

155, 160, 173, 177, 194, 196, 206, 208, 210–14, 218, 227, 234, 241, 243–4, 249, 262, 282, 288
Language: 2–3, 5–6, 29, 45, 53, 73–5, 79, 81, 83, 106, 108, 115–22, 124, 133, 138–9, 142, 149, 151–53, 156, 158, 205, 207–9, 214, 218–20, 224–6, 229, 235, 237–8, 242, 285
  meta-language (also metalanguage), 24, 118, 122, 139
Law: 4, 10, 17, 46, 48–9, 65, 73, 76, 183–5, 190, 192, 193–5, 202, 207, 209–10, 213–4, 218–9, 221– 31, 236, 248, 260–1, 286
  l. on the body, 223
  moral l., 219, 221, 224–7, 229
  natural l., 184, 196
  Oedipal l., 185, 196
  paternal l., 66, 107, 133, 138, 171, 192, 234, 246
  subject of l. (see also subject), 221–4, 228, 232
Law-of-the-Father: 48, 191–2, 207–8, 234
Liberal: 85, 135, 147, 149, 162, 196, 218, 221, 238, 240, 263, 274, 293
Liberalism: 85–7, 150, 154
Libido: 4, 137–8, 173
Life: 1–2, 6–8, 24–5, 49, 66–7, 69–70, 72, 74, 79–81, 88, 102–3, 105, 109, 138, 140, 148, 150, 166, 168, 170, 175, 184–5, 188–9, 191, 194–6, 203, 217–20, 222, 225, 231, 234, 246–9, 255–6, 262, 265, 282, 284
Linguistics: 3, 22–3, 117, 131–3, 135–7, 152, 157
Logic: 3, 5–6, 9, 16–7, 23–5, 29, 36, 73, 82, 89, 96–7, 122, 142, 144, 157, 159, 165, 171, 173, 177, 220, 228, 230, 246, 256, 265, 285
Loss: 49, 55, 81, 105–6, 120–2, 125, 138–9, 155, 173, 177–8, 208, 212–4, 243, 255, 285
Love: 16–7, 25, 34–8, 55, 62, 76, 79, 88, 94–7, 103–4, 108–10, 124, 133, 152, 192, 201, 207–8, 211–4, 219–20, 234, 258, 260–1, 264–5, 281, 290

Market: 20, 33, 91, 96–9, 142–4, 150, 153–4, 156, 162, 167, 240, 246
Marxism: 19, 131–2, 237, 264
  Freudo-Marxism, 4, 24,
Masquerade: 225, 235, 246–7
Master: 6, 45–6, 53–7, 82, 118, 120, 122–8, 134, 137–9, 144, 149, 160,

306 Index of notions

168, 170–1, 177–9, 187–92, 196–7, 205, 214, 228, 235, 241, 244, 256, 258–60, 282, 292

Master Disocurse (see Discourse)

Master-Signifier, 122, 124–7, 160, 178

Mastery: 28, 31, 75, 78, 80, 115, 121, 123, 124–7

M. in four discourses, 115–27

Mathematics: 6, 135

Mechanism: 92, 102, 138, 173

Melancholy: 211, 258

Metaphor: 2, 78, 162, 169, 185, 192, 205
paternal m., 205, 209–10, 210–11, 214

Metapsychology: 274–5

Materiality: 108, 134, 155–6, 237

Metonymy: 2, 30, 151, 169

Money: 77, 98, 141, 154–7, 160–2, 170, 173, 244

Morality: 76, 126, 218, 220, 229, 284, 286, 293

Mother 16–7, 46–9, 54–5, 62–3, 67, 80, 102–3, 174, 192, 201–2, 204–14, 234, 242, 246, 254, 275

Mourning: 103, 106, 166, 168, 207, 211–2

Murder (of the father): 46, 49–53, 80, 1002, 202, 207–9, 242, 257

Myth: 45, 48–9, 54, 62, 97, 117, 135–6, 237, 242, 259
Oedipus m., 45–7, 53–4, 174, 242

Name-of-the-Father: 205, 208–211, 213

Narcissism: 6, 72, 148, 150, 214

National Socialism: 3, 166, 168

Naturalism: 16, 17

Negation: 22, 70, 102, 173, 176–8, 236, 248

Negativity: 87, 89, 91, 96, 98, 99, 100n, 148, 150, 151, 157, 160–2, 172

Neoliberalism: 109, 131, 150, 154, 166

Neurosis: 3, 6

Neurotic: 46, 51, 103, 135, 140, 142, 148

Non-Being: 69, 70, 104

Non-Relation: 87–91, 94, 95, 96–9, 100n

Not-All: 29, 30, 38–40, 106

Object: 51, 53, 55, 66, 78, 80, 82, 83, 98, 103, 142, 143, 152, 155, 156, 157, 160, 177, 187, 189, 191, 192, 197n., 204, 206, 207, 210, 211, 223, 225, 228, 230, 235, 243, 244, 247, 265, 271, 272, 288
impossible o., 95, 205, 212; lost o., 126, 212; partial o., 94, 95; o. of psychoanalysis, 31, 149
real o., 21

Object a: 9, 17, 20, 33, 57, 73, 74, 89, 101, 104–108, 110, 118, 123, 124, 127, 144, 158, 284

Oedipus complex: 9, 45, 46, 48, 49, 52, 53, 56, 57, 174, 203, 234, 242, 275

Ontology: 89, 91, 124

Order: 123, 150, 160, 185, 224, 228, 276, 289
discursive o., 96
gender o., 242, 243, 246, 248
political o., 86, 108, 243
social o., 9, 29, 40, 73, 75, 76, 78, 79, 80, 83, 90, 91, 96, 97, 98, 99, 147, 241, 293
symbolic o., 50, 56, 73, 94, 96, 108, 110, 118, 125, 191, 192, 204, 205–211, 234, 235, 238, 241, 244, 246, 247, 255

Origin: 57n., 94, 141, 174, 287
o. of the law, 47, 209
mythical o., 221
o. of society, 48

Other: 9, 19, 21, 24, 29, 30, 32, 34–37, 39, 46, 51, 53, 56, 81, 83, 87, 92–4, 97, 99, 101, 102, 103, 104, 105–7, 110, 118, 122, 126, 133, 135, 136, 139, 140, 142, 143, 154, 163, 178, 187, 188, 196, 205, 206, 208, 209, 220, 231, 238, 260, 262

Paradox: 17, 40, 68, 78, 92, 95, 105, 236, 263, 287

Pathology: 229

Patriarchy: 237, 240, 243, 246
neoliberal neopatriarchy 242, 244, 247

People: 52, 106, 167, 190, 214, 254

Perversion: 110, 158, 214, 222, 226, 227, 229, 231
p. of law, 10, 222

Phallocentrism: 10, 51, 57, 59n., 236, 246, 248

Phallus: 50, 56, 59n., 103, 107, 204, 205, 207–11, 213, 214, 234–6, 238, 240, 242, 243, 248

Phantasm: 75, 104, 105, 107, 108, 207

Philosophy: 1, 28, 117, 220, 238, 257, 281, 289
political p., 6, 8, 138

Pleasure: 5, 48, 50, 66, 70, 73, 75, 79, 91, 92, 93, 104, 105, 119, 153, 176, 178, 206, 209, 225, 226, 235, 238, 247, 284

Politics: 2, 3, 5–7, 10, 16, 18, 28–33, 35–39, 86, 87, 107, 110, 116, 119, 124, 139, 149, 154, 162, 167, 173,

185, 190, 181, 194, 196, 214, 217, 220, 229, 236, 237, 271, 282, 283, 289, 290
emancipatory p., 40, 89, 99, 153
feminist p., 233, 234, 238, 239, 240, 248, 249
identity p., 76, 133, 135
international p., 8
Lacanian p., 110, 292, 293
psychoanalytic p., 109
Poverty: 109, 155
Power: 21, 25, 47, 48, 73, 75, 96, 125, 126, 127, 131, 132, 135, 140, 155, 167, 177, 197n., 228, 229, 240, 257, 263, 269, 271
emancipatory p., 31
ideological p., 260–273, 276, 277
labour-power, 98, 153, 154, 155, 157, 158, 160, 161, 162
political p., 6, 19, 107
power-relation, 5, 115, 230
social p., 96, 243, 246
sovereign p., 167
Practice: 1, 21, 30, 38, 127, 140, 166, 168, 177, 184, 185, 189, 195, 197, 218, 237, 239, 247, 264, 277, 278
clinical p., 131, 134, 135, 137, 203
political p., 144, 249
psychoanalytic p., 7, 186, 196
sexual p., 87
theoretical p., 8, 277
Principle: 20, 33, 102, 107, 171, 231, 258, 288
ethical p., 225, 226
legal p., 222
moral p., 218
Nirvana p., 79
pleasure p., 66, 119, 174, 176, 178
political p., 106
reality p., 66
Production: 30, 80, 96, 105, 109, 121, 138, 141, 143, 151, 153, 154, 156, 159, 160, 162, 171, 197n., 243, 244, 275
capitalist p., 33
discursive p., 4, 152, 153, 158
dream p., 170, 173
knowledge-production, 134
means of p., 284
mode of p. 5, 9, 98, 110, 157
social p., 155
Prohibition: 5, 34, 62, 63, 74, 90, 119, 174, 192, 210, 215, 222, 223, 234, 286
Protest: 4, 67, 185, 194, 249
student p., 9

subjective p., 152, 214
Psychoanalysis: 1, 4, 6–8, 10, 17, 19, 28, 30–32, 38, 40, 63, 69, 70, 80, 84, 90, 94, 96, 102, 106, 117, 123, 127, 135, 137, 139, 140, 148, 152, 153, 163, 166, 167, 169, 171, 173, 176, 184, 195, 196, 203, 214, 219, 220, 286
ethics of p., 105, 117
Freudian p., 132
Lacanian p., 2, 3, 9, 86, 107, 108, 109, 110, 144, 147, 189, 195, 233, 234, 238–41, 247, 268, 282
politics of p., 34, 35
traditional p., 21
Psychology: 10, 47, 171, 268–70, 272–5, 278
ego p., 72, 73, 117, 137, 194, 276
group p., 75, 84
individual p., 75
Psychosis: 183, 185, 188–90, 192, 283, 291
political p., 184
Psychotic: 85n., 118

Real: 6, 30, 32, 39, 40, 51, 72, 74, 83, 84, 87, 88, 89, 105, 134, 136, 137, 139, 188, 193, 206, 235, 242, 254–6, 260, 263
Reality: 25, 50, 54, 62, 66, 77, 79, 88, 118, 119, 137, 187, 189–91, 249, 261, 271, 272
human r., 95
social r., 2, 3, 4, 5, 9, 29, 46, 57, 80, 99, 148, 149, 151, 152, 163
subjective r., 157, 159
transindividual r., 84
Rejection: 2, 4, 21, 25, 55, 153, 160, 210, 212, 234, 239
r. of castration, 150, 152, 160
r. of negativity, 151, 162
Relation: 1, 2, 3, 4, 5, 31, 32, 35, 55, 57, 87, 89, 92, 95, 96, 118, 134, 136, 149, 151, 155, 157, 159, 160, 162, 192, 193, 195, 241, 242, 243, 273
causal r., 5
economic r., 154
intersubjective r., 83, 116, 124
non-relation, 88, 89, 90, 91, 94, 95, 97, 98, 99, 100n.
power-relation, 5,6, 115, 230
sexual r., 7, 88, 90, 95, 148, 235
symbolic r., 6
social r., 5, 33, 90, 92, 93, 96, 150, 153, 154
Religion: 2, 10, 79, 95, 154, 255, 258, 259, 264, 265

308 Index of notions

Repetition: 120, 137, 176, 178, 185, 287
Representation: 6, 30, 102, 106, 121,
  134, 154, 159, 162, 188, 194, 195,
  197, 204, 218, 219, 224, 228, 228,
  242, 245, 247, 248, 249
  political r., 107
  subject of r., 158, 160
Repression: 7,70, 84, 102, 138, 147, 148,
  150, 203, 243
  primary r., 206, 211
  social r., 90, 134
Resistance: 10, 29, 83, 86, 147, 148, 149,
  152, 177, 182–191, 193–197, 213,
  214, 254
Responsibility: 106, 108, 109, 221, 226,
  227, 228, 229, 231, 293
Revolution: 10, 19, 75, 80, 90, 117, 127,
  137, 149, 186, 234, 237;
  1848 r., 21
  cultural r., 23
  French Revolution, 20, 30
  industrial r., 97
  information r., 136
  scientific r., 7, 149
  sexual r., 150
Rights: 26, 39, 76, 187 195, 196, 222,
  223, 224, 226, 244, 275
  human r., 183, 184, 191, 198n., 217,
  218, 220, 229, 230, 231
Rule: 23, 46, 64, 66, 73, 107, 135, 136,
  221, 222, 223, 229
  r. of inclusion, 186, 194
  r. of law, 224
  legal r., 218
  sovereign r., 293
Satisfaction: 66, 74, 78, 79, 117, 144, 152,
  177
  s. of desire, 4, 105, 223
  s. of the drive, 80, 95, 176
  organic s., 73
School: Frankfurt School, 3, 75, 138;
  Lacan's s., 18, 20, 21, 22, 39, 40, 127,
  149; psychoanalytic s., 9, 140, 240
Science: 1, 2, 7, 19, 127, 134, 140, 143,
  160, 171, 172, 270, 272, 275, 287, 288
  antique s., 270
  progress of s., 6
Seduction: 222, 223, 247
Self-Love: 76, 97
Sex: 9, 10, 16, 17, 47, 55, 57, 86, 88, 89,
  92, 93, 94, 95, 150, 151, 205, 240
Sexuality: 6, 7, 17, 54, 55, 73, 87, 88, 89,
  90, 94, 95, 148, 149, 150, 151, 152,
  176, 208, 211, 237

female (feminine) s., 234, 235, 236,
  237, 238, 240
heterosexuality, 148, 245
homosexuality, 192
infantile s., 86, 147
theory of s., 9, 86, 163n.
Sexuation: 10, 16, 57, 234, 235, 236,
  240, 248
Sign: 2, 37, 81, 125, 151, 152, 206, 223,
  264
Signified: 63, 81, 116, 133, 153, 156,
  178, 206
Signifier: 3, 7, 54, 63, 73, 75, 81, 82, 91,
  94, 102, 104, 105, 106, 107, 117, 118,
  119, 120, 124, 134, 137, 140, 151,
  156, 158, 162, 174, 186, 187, 188,
  190, 205, 206, 207, 208, 211, 234,
  243, 245, 246
  autonomy of the s., 153
  chain of s., 53, 178
  s. of lack, 52, 57
  logic of the s., 9, 29, 159
  master-signifier, 34, 123, 124, 124,
  127, 134, 144, 160, 228
  missing s., 33
  phallic s., 54, 214, 236, 248
Singularity: 31, 35, 37, 40, 78, 135, 272
Slave: 98, 125, 126, 166, 172
Socialism: 127
Society: 7, 10, 18, 25, 46, 48, 53, 63, 72,
  73, 74, 75, 76, 78, 79, 97, 110, 119,
  149, 155, 165, 166, 213, 214, 217,
  218, 222, 223, 224, 232n., 242, 271,
  273, 279
  capitalist s., 133
  contemporary s., 34
  feudal s., 243
  French s., 15
  imaginary s., 79, 80, 82, 83, 84
Solipsism: s. of enjoyment, 32, 34
Soul: 5, 22, 65, 89, 92, 203, 254, 274
Sovereign (sovereignty): 138, 193, 197n.,
  258, 286, 287, 288
Space: 29, 84, 102, 103, 153, 184, 190,
  196, 224, 226
  chaotic s., 6
  discursive s., 89, 91
  empty s., 39, 178
  political s., 2, 5, 6, 148
  public s., 184
  social s., 3, 134
Speech: 5, 73, 74, 75, 81, 82, 117, 118,
  122, 124, 133, 135, 136, 137, 142,
  143, 144, 149, 169, 194, 206, 218, 222

Split: 18, 53, 110, 151, 153, 160, 178, 190, 221, 227, 261
Structuralism: 2, 3, 4, 9, 22, 24, 117, 118, 132, 158
Structure: 6, 7, 21, 22, 33, 46, 69, 70n., 73, 89, 94, 116, 118, 120, 121, 133, 136, 137, 140, 142, 149, 152, 157, 158, 159, 218, 221, 223, 224, 235, 248, 269, 273, 275, 287
  capitalist s., 162
  discursive s., 230, 241
  family s., 64
  formal s., 83
  ideological s., 272
  social s., 3, 4, 149, 207
Subject: 1, 5, 6, 9, 19, 22, 23, 24, 30, 32, 33, 34, 35, 37, 49, 51, 57, 63, 65, 69, 73, 74, 75, 78, 79, 82, 83, 84, 85n., 94, 101, 103, 104, 107, 108, 109, 117, 118, 121, 123, 124, 126, 127, 131, 133, 135, 142, 143, 144, 149, 150, 151, 152, 153, 155–162, 164n., 171, 178, 183, 184, 185, 187, 189, 190, 191, 193, 194, 195, 197n., 202, 203, 204, 206, 207, 208, 210, 212–214, 219, 219, 222, 225, 226, 229, 240, 241, 271, 272
  s. of cognition, 4, 154
  conscious s., 287
  s. of desire, 103, 110
  ethical s., 221, 228
  female (feminine) s., 236, 242, 244, 247, 248, 249
  headless s., 169
  hysterical s., 52, 56
  indebted s., 155
  Lacanian s., 3, 5, 133
  s. of law, 221, 223, 224, 230
  masculine s., 235, 236, 242, 243, 244, 245, 248
  moral s., 227
  occupied s., 185
  political s., 183, 185, 191, 195, 218, 223
  s. of psychoanalysis, 2, 185
  resisting s., 185, 186, 187, 196
  revolutionary s., 264
  sexed s., 235, 236, 238
  s. of the signifier, 104, 106, 118, 133, 206, 209
  speaking s., 73, 206, 241
  split s., 125, 126, 154, 191
  s. supposed to know, 140, 161
  s. of the unconscious, 2, 3, 4, 5, 106, 108, 134, 178

universal s., 242, 243
Subjection: 73, 187, 188, 190, 191, 197n.
Subjectivation: 3, 5, 10, 33, 152
Subjectivity: 2, 4, 5, 6, 19, 34, 63, 83, 102, 106, 107, 108, 110, 135, 151, 152, 153, 154, 155, 158, 160, 186, 187, 190, 194, 210, 214, 231, 234, 236, 237, 240, 248, 257, 269
  biopolitical s., 184
  capitalist s., 155
Superego: 72, 75, 85n., 120, 149, 150, 219, 222, 223, 224, 226, 232n., 261
Surplus-Enjoyment: 20, 23, 24, 33, 87, 91, 94, 122, 153, 178, 179
Symbolic: 21, 30, 48, 52, 57, 72, 73, 74, 75, 77, 79–83, 94, 101, 102, 104, 105, 106, 107, 108, 119, 138, 150, 169, 185, 193, 237, 244, 246, 255, 264
Symptom: 2, 20, 24, 25, 30, 32, 33, 81, 82, 102, 144, 157, 190, 237, 274, 284
  s. of capitalism, 20
  social s., 3, 34, 152
Theology: 10, 253, 257
Theory: 8, 9, 56, 108, 135, 150, 152, 235, 264, 277, 278
  critical t., 3
  cultural t., 8, 140
  discourse t., 134
  t. of discourse, 4, 24, 46, 57, 87, 115, 118, 121, 131, 132, 149, 158, 240, 241
  feminist t., 237, 238
  Foucauldian t., 10
  Freud's t., 1, 6, 7, 47, 171, 174, 177
  t. of hysteria, 53
  information t., 135, 136
  Kant's theory, 219, 229
  labour theory, 153, 154, 161
  Lacan's (Lacanian) t., 1, 7, 10, 29, 55, 57, 83, 101, 104, 159, 163, 234, 236, 238, 239, 240
  linguistic t., 2, 81
  Marx's t., 17
  Marxist t., 22, 264, 268
  t. of the Oedipus complex, 48
  political t., 11, 131, 134, 144
  psychoanalytic t., 10, 46, 57, 64, 89, 103, 138, 167, 184, 235, 241
  queer t., 31
  Schmitt's t., 36
  t. of sexuality, 9, 86, 152
  t. of the subject, 35, 153, 236
Thinking: 1, 2, 5, 8, 87, 89, 148, 149, 172, 271, 288, 289
  ethical t., 229

310 Index of notions

political t., 8
rational t., 257
Topology: 2, 5, 135, 139, 149
Totality: 76, 78, 90, 92, 93, 123, 204,
  211, 213, 287
  imaginary t., 83
  knowledge-totality, 82
  social t., 77
Tradition: 11, 254, 255, 282, 287
  Christian t., 221
  critical t., 1, 2, 151
  Freudo-Marxist t., 138
  intellectual t., 28
  philosophical t., 110n., 138
  romantic t., 202
Tragedy: 54, 66, 70, 202, 203, 207, 211
  modern t., 108
  Sophocles' t., 9, 47, 48
Transference: 39, 101, 140
  institutional t., 149
Transgression: 15, 38, 74, 120, 138, 222,
  223, 224, 286
Trauma: 173, 235
Truth: 17, 18, 20, 22, 23, 45, 46, 48, 49,
  51, 53, 54, 55, 84, 88, 107, 119, 121,
  122, 126, 142, 166, 187, 188, 202,
  213, 214, 219, 225, 226, 227, 264,
  269, 270, 271, 273, 276, 286, 290, 294
  censored t., 155
  hidden t., 122
  position (place) of t., 127, 144
  repressed t., 4, 153
  truth-regime, 133
  ultimate t., 50
Unconscious: 1–6, 28, 29, 47, 70, 73, 74,
  75, 81, 101, 102, 103, 106, 117, 118,
  119, 127n., 134, 135, 136, 137, 140,
  147, 149, 153, 167, 169, 170, 171,
  172, 173, 178, 202, 204, 206, 207,
  235, 237, 241, 247, 275, 287
United States: 183, 222
Universal: 1, 30, 31, 33, 37, 38, 40, 102,
  140, 217, 218, 219, 227, 228, 230,
  235, 242
University: 24, 82, 118, 127, 132, 158,
  159, 164
  discourse of the u. (university
    discourse), 75, 118, 119, 123, 126,
    127, 131, 135, 138, 140, 142, 144,
    158, 241

Verneinug: 210
Value: 20, 62, 77, 78, 92, 98, 109, 150,
  151, 153–157, 160, 161n., 165, 170,
  172, 177, 212, 219, 285, 288, 293
  autonomy of v., 152
  critical v., 8
  exchange-value, 152, 153, 162n., 17q
  revolutionary v., 137
  social v., 10
  surplus-value, 17, 24, 33, 120, 138,
    153, 154, 157, 158, 159, 160, 161,
    162, 162n., 178, 286
  theory of v., 153, 155
  universal v., 229
  use-value, 20, 98, 153, 156, 157,
    162n., 172
Violence: 23, 37, 132, 167, 182, 183,
  185, 187, 188, 192, 195, 197n., 243,
  246, 285
  sexual violence, 240
War: 3, 19, 48, 73, 79, 189, 226, 281,
  289
  civil w., 37
  "Make love not war", 16
  post-war, 25
  science w., 132
  WW I, 2
  WW II, 79, 141
Wealth: 75, 76, 77, 79, 95, 96, 98, 109,
  154, 155, 174, 270, 275, 276
Woman: 16, 17, 50, 53, 55, 56, 57n.,
  58n., 90, 105, 191, 192, 193, 236, 237,
  241, 244, 245, 246
  hysterical woman, 53–55
  The Woman, 10, 90, 193, 235, 247,
    248
Work: 10, 23, 39, 40, 87, 97, 98, 119,
  120, 125, 126, 138, 142, 144,
  164–167, 170, 171, 172, 174–178, 246
  cultural w., 173
  dream-work, 168–169, 170, 171,
    172–177
  psychical w., 168
  psychoanalytic w., 183
  unconscious w., 168, 172, 173, 176
Worker: 15, 39, 40, 92, 98, 99, 154, 166,
  168, 170, 174, 177, 178

Zapatistas: 278